ONLY BY PUBLIC CONSENT

ONLY
BY
PUBLIC CONSENT

American Corporations Search for
Favorable Opinion

by
L. L. L. Golden

Hawthorn Books, Inc.   Publishers   New York

ONLY BY PUBLIC CONSENT

First Edition: 1968

Design: Gene Gordon
2190

To
Mary

ACKNOWLEDGMENTS

Wherever feasible, acknowledgment has been made within the text of this book. But in gathering material for a work such as this a great deal depends, of necessity, on interviews with those who have been involved, and who have special knowledge gained at first hand as participants in the events described. Many of the interviewees are still employees of the corporations which are the heart of the book. They talked with the author on the understanding that their identity not be revealed. Others are former employees or officers of the companies and for their own reasons desire to remain anonymous. But there were scores of additional individuals not mentioned in the text who directed the writer to the sources of information or were themselves such sources.

Records were not always available for study, but a good deal is a matter of public record in publications of the periods, in annual reports, in articles, in company statements, and in the files of the companies discussed. Of those who have been credited, one of the most valuable for his intimate knowledge and to whom special thanks are due is the late Alfred P. Sloan, Jr. The tape-recorded interview with him was a vital source of information and direction.

The librarians of the American Telephone and Telegraph Company, General Motors Corporation, Standard Oil Company (New Jersey), and E. I. du Pont de Nemours and Company were helpful indeed. So were Miss Dorothy Arthur, George Buckingham, Mrs. Brown-Mayers, L. J. Coffin, Robert Carlson, John Driscoll, James

Freeman, W. P. Headden, Charles Hackett, Parker Lusk, George Lawrence, Arthur Lamb, Paul Morgan, Walter H. Page, Arthur H. Page, Edward Roberts, Paul Svoboda, and C. E. Wampler.

To the innumerable others who are not mentioned above or in other places in this volume go the author's warmest thanks as well. Other sources of information to whom a debt is owed are: The New York Public Library and *The New York Times*, whose issues on microfilm and whose Index helped make this book possible.

CONTENTS

ONLY BY PUBLIC CONSENT

NOT BY DIVINE RIGHT

It was early afternoon on Tuesday, April 10, 1962. Nine members of the executive committee of the United States Steel Corporation had made their decision. Steel prices would be increased by three and a half per cent; Roger M. Blough, the board chairman, would fly to Washington to tell President Kennedy; Leslie B. Worthington, the president, would announce the price action—the first in four years—for release in the next morning's papers.

At 5:45 p.m. Blough sat in the President's office and handed him a copy of the three and a half page price-increase press release, forty-five minutes before it was given to the newspapers. Exactly seventy-two hours and three minutes later the Associated Press teletype machines clacked out this bulletin: United States Steel Corporation had rescinded the increase.

In that short time the crushing might of the Federal Government was unleashed in continuous assault. The President himself, at a televised press conference carried live, in undiluted anger, finger stabbing said: "In this serious hour in our nation's history, when we are confronted with grave crises in Berlin and Southeast Asia . . . at a time when restraint and sacrifice are being asked of every citizen, the American people will find it hard, as I do, to accept a situation in which a tiny handful of steel executives whose pursuit of private power and profit exceeds their sense of public responsibility can show such utter contempt for the interests of 185,000,000 Americans. . . . Some time ago I asked each American to consider what he would do for his country and I asked the steel companies. In the last twenty-four hours we have had their answer."

The President's brother, Attorney General Robert Kennedy, announced that the Justice Department had ordered a grand jury investigation into steel prices; FBI agents served subpoenas at headquarters offices of United States Steel, Bethlehem, Republic, Jones & Laughlin, and other steel companies for documents which might provide evidence of collusive price fixing, a criminal offense.

Senator Estes Kefauver, chairman of the Senate Antitrust and Monopoly subcommittee, proclaimed that he would begin an investigation into the steel industry. So did Congressman Emanuel Celler, chairman of the House Antitrust and Monopoly subcommittee.

Defense Secretary Robert S. McNamara held a press conference to tell of his department's new policy: defense contractors had been ordered to buy only from those steel companies that did not follow U. S. Steel's lead in raising prices. In addition, to show he was serious he announced that a small steel company had been granted a $5 million contract that U. S. Steel might otherwise have received.

The Federal Trade Commission chairman, Paul Rand Dixon, announced that he had started an investigation that could lead to penalties of $5,000 a day for violation of the Commission's consent decree of June 15, 1951. Commerce Secretary Luther Hodges, one of whose basic jobs was to act as a liaison with industry, held a press conference at which he hit hard at "a handful of men who said in effect that the United States Steel comes first, the United States of America second." The Treasury joined in the pressure to roll back the increase and Labor Secretary Arthur Goldberg contacted steel industry leaders that he knew to persuade them not to follow U. S. Steel or to withdraw their increase.

Solicitor General Archibald Cox started to draft legislation dealing with steel prices. He had been chairman of the Wage Stabilization Board during the Korean conflict and it had given him extensive experience in wage-price problems.

Yet, despite this pressure, Bethelehem Steel, next in size to U. S. Steel, announced a price increase. So did Republic, Jones & Laughlin, Youngstown, Wheeling and two others—eight in all. But there was no word from Inland Steel of Chicago, seventh largest in terms of steel production.

At three o'clock one morning during the crisis, the FBI woke Lee Linder, a reporter who worked in the Philadelphia Bureau of the Associated Press, to question him about a report he had written following the Bethlehem Steel stockholders' meeting. He had reported that Edmund F. Martin, the president of Bethlehem Steel, had told him and two other reporters that a price increase was unwise at that time. The report was later denied but the FBI was anxious to find out from the reporters what had actually happened. And at 6:30 A.M. two FBI agents were waiting for James L. Parks, Jr., one of the other reporters, when he arrived at his office at the Wilmington *Evening Journal*. Later the same morning the FBI interrogated a *Wall Street Journal* reporter, John Lawrence, the third newsman who had seen Martin.

The Senate Majority Leader, Mike Mansfield, called the price increase "unjustified"; the Speaker of the House of Representatives, John McCormack, said it was "shocking, arrogant, irresponsible"; to Senator Hubert H. Humphrey, the Democratic Whip, it was "an affront to the President."

The Republicans said little, but Congressman William Scranton, his party's candidate for Governor of Pennsylvania, wired Blough: "The increase at this time is wrong—wrong for Pennsylvania, wrong for America, wrong for the free world. The increase will surely set off another round of inflation. It will hurt the people who can least afford to be hurt."

Since Inland Steel had not yet announced it would follow Big Steel's lead, phone calls went out to its senior managers. In addition to the Labor Secretary's, calls were made by the Undersecretary of the Treasury and the Undersecretary of Commerce. Calls were also made by leading cabinet and subcabinet officers to directors of other steel companies who were asked, pressured, cajoled, and pleaded with to rescind the increases, or not to go along with those who had raised prices.

Finally Inland Steel announced it would not increase its prices. Then Bethlehem backed down. Others followed. U. S. Steel capitulated.

Blough didn't have a chance, his voice totally lost in the uproar. He was no match for the President. Nor would any other private citizen have done better against the full might of the Federal Government led by an aroused, articulate President who knew how to mobilize public opinion and who did not in the least mind using muscle to win his point.

But this was more far-reaching than the victory of President Kennedy over Roger Blough after a brutal power struggle. It showed that fact had caught up with theory: that in any direct confrontation between the national government and big business, business, no matter how powerful, would surely lose. It proved that public opinion is king: presidential resources to rouse it are almost limitless, and it is public opinion which decides who shall govern.

The lessons for corporations are clear and unmistakable. They cannot function without public consent. To obtain that consent they must act in the public interest as the public interprets it at any given time. On the day that management forgets that an institution cannot continue to exist if the general public feels that it is not useful, or that it is anti-social in the public concept of what is anti-social, the institution will begin to die.

Public opinion is not easy to understand, even under the best of circumstances. It is subjective. It has wild moods, and extraordinary events can bring sweeping changes. Its gusts can topple governments and destroy reputations of eminent politicians and titans of industry. Not even the best opinion pollsters know what the public is thinking at certain times, and pollsters are the first to admit that many people polled do not reveal their innermost thoughts. In addition, what the public thinks in a hypothetical case will not always be the same as in a real situation.

Public consent does not stem from gimmicks or tricks. It exists because of performance in the public interest—plus an imbedded policy of explaining to the public what an organization is doing and why. This holds especially strongly for the big organizations, for they are highly visible. Obtaining public consent is difficult. It takes hard work, harder thinking, an understanding of public moods, and specialists who know something of public attitudes and the many different means of reaching the public.

No hokus-pokus can alter public opinion. Those who promise this are the sharp operators who feed off innocent management, and to whom putting whipped cream on the manure pile is easier than clearing away the mess. True, the public interest is not easy to define. And what the public interprets as being in its interest may change a week from next Wednesday morning. That is why understanding public opinion is highly complex, not something to be learned or understood while standing on one foot. Certainly it needs training, and an understanding of what moves people. It demands an appreciation of the public needs, inner and obvious, and an objectivity that makes it a field in which the sycophant is useless and the glad-hander with the big hello, worthless.

In a free society the public elects its servants to office, and the politicians must serve its will or be replaced at the next election. Whether any individual may like this or not is beside the point. That is the way it is, and that is the way it will continue to be. Of course this does not mean that an unpopular cause today will always remain one. It means instead that if the cause is good it must be explained to the public and must be shown to be truly in the national interest. To do that demands not alone an appreciation of the public's desires, but an understanding of those who are leaders in public thinking.

It is not flattering the intellectual community to say that what its leaders think today, the general public will often think tomorrow. It is a hard fact of our society that the opinion formers in the press, in television, in magazines, in films, in publishing, and in scholarship lead the general public. The politician, having only a short run, generally takes the public as he finds it. He, because of his profession, has long known that a public which does not understand what he is saying or doing is a public which will vote for his opponent.

As government continues to grow more dominant, as its actions affect more individuals more intimately—whether they be college presidents, business executives, or trade union organizers—so the opinions of those who vote become more important. This natural development in our society has escaped many of the country's leaders, particularly in business. In the midst of violent upheavals in the world there has been a silent revolution with power—real power—shifting from some of its old haunts to the general public. This is so not only in the United States but in many other areas throughout the world. The people are the ones who are deciding what is "good for them." With improved education and improved communication has come a greater awareness by the general public that the control over governments is in its hands. The politicians—or at least the better ones— learn this early. The fact has caught up with the theory that in a democratic society the voter is in ultimate control.

In this context it is worth taking a look at some salient points in the struggle between U. S. Steel and President Kennedy. Four days before the announced price increase, United States Steel and the United Steelworkers of America signed a two-year contract. The President called the contract "non-inflationary" and asked both sides to use restraint in wages and prices so that the U.S. economy would remain stable and competitive with foreign industry.

There are, of course, no price and wage controls in the United States in normal times. And, under normal circumstances, the operation of our economic system demands that there be as little government regulation of wages and prices as possible. There are very few who favor price controls, and fewer still who support wage controls. Certainly President Kennedy was opposed to both. The American Federation of Labor-Congress of Industrial Organizations has long been opposed to price and wage controls. Its policy was repeated on May 19, 1964, when the executive council of the AFL-CIO issued its statement on a National Wage Formula. One of its main points was this: "Neither wage nor price restraints are tolerable in a free society except in the gravest national emergency and then only when coupled with stringent restraints upon excess profits."

Obviously Blough and the executive committee of U. S. Steel felt they needed a price increase. Since business cannot survive, let alone invest in new plants and equipment, without an adequate profit, and since the steel people felt that the profit squeeze impelled an increase in steel prices, they decided to go ahead and announce it. It was that simple. What the corporation did not fully understand, however, was that it had to be certain that the public knew about the increase and thought it both necessary and fair.

Why then did President Kennedy fight Blough?

Because under the circumstances of the time, the action of U. S. Steel looked like a slap in the face of the President, and no business, no matter how big, no matter how pure at heart, can get away with that. Then, in this confrontation, the decision between a price increase and no price increase became the decision of the people of the United States of America—every last one of them. The President, winner with public opinion, forced the rescinding of the increase. An angry and determined President, if he should use, or even threaten to use, the almost unlimited power of the Government, can destroy an opponent.

Blough is a quiet, exceptionally able lawyer. Before he joined the corporation he was in general practice with the law firm of White & Case in New York City. A graduate of Yale Law School, where he was editor of the *Yale Law Journal*, he has worked with U. S. Steel since 1939, succeeding Benjamin F. Fairless as chairman and chief executive officer on May 3, 1955. His peers in other corporations respect him highly, and he has the kind of resilience that brought him through the struggle over steel prices. He also can change position when the needs, and the interests of the corporation, demand. But how could he be an effective opponent for a politician as able and aggressive as President Kennedy?

Blough struck doggedly to his point that the corporation had made no commitment to keep prices at their old level, and argued his case before the public as if he were appearing before an appeal court judge in the stillness of the court room. And like some other lawyers, he seemed to assume that the fine print in a contract should be studied and understood by the man who reads as he runs.

On May 7, 1962, at the annual meeting of his stockholders in Hoboken, New Jersey, Blough stated his case in these terms:

On September 6, you may recall that President Kennedy sent to the heads of eleven steel companies a letter in which he said, among other things: "I recognize, too, that the steel industry, by absorbing increases in employment costs since 1958, has demonstrated a will to halt the price-wage spiral in steel. If the industry were now to forego a price increase, it would enter collective bargaining negotiations next spring with a record of three and a half years of price stability. It would clearly then be the turn of the labor representatives to limit wage demands to a level consistent with continued price stability. The moral position of the steel industry next spring—and its claim to the support of public opinion—will be strengthened by the exercise of price restraint now."

In response to the President's letter, I replied on September 13—and here I would like to repeat my exact words. I said: "We in the United States Steel cannot forecast the future trend of prices in any segment of the steel industry and have no definite conclusions regarding our own course during the foreseeable future. . . ."

My letter went on to say that the causes of inflation in the United States— past, present and future—are not to be found in the levels of steel prices or steel profits. It reviewed, factually and thoroughly, the cost increases we had experienced, and the severity of the profit squeeze that had resulted. It discussed the competitive forces which inevitably govern price actions. It stated our firm belief that the national interest itself required the maintenance of strong, healthy industrial units in America—as a source of new jobs, as a source of research and new products, as a source of purchasing power, as a source of Federal tax revenues, and—above all—as a source of national strength and growth.

Then it concluded with a frank statement of the responsibility that we believe we share with all other industrial units in America—the responsibility to maintain the economic freedom of the country—and it pledged that we would continue to discharge that responsibility in the future as we had endeavored always to do in the past. Shortly after that letter had reached the President's desk, copies of it were widely distributed in pamphlet form.

I do not see how anyone who reads those letters could fail to understand clearly three things: first, that we had declined to enter into any commitment—express or implied—regarding future price actions; second that we believed a substantial improvement in our cost-price relationship to be necessary not only in the interests of the company, its owners and its employees, but in the interest of the entire nation; and third that any price decision we might make would be—as it inevitably must be—controlled by competitive forces that govern the market place.

It is obvious that Blough thought that because he himself believed that no commitment to keep prices at their old level had been made, everyone else did. This kind of thinking, which surely lacks understanding of the public, could not help but bring U. S. Steel into a position from which it had to back down. But the responsibility for a lack of understanding of the society in which U. S. Steel operates is not Blough's alone.

On March 31, the labor agreement between U. S. Steel and the Steelworkers' Union was reached and initialled. The official contracts were then prepared in proper legal form and formally signed six days later, on April 6. The following day, Saturday, April 7, a week after the agreement was reached and one day after its formal signing, the ten-man operations policy committee of U. S. Steel met in Pittsburgh and decided to recommend the price increase to the executive committee of the board. Then, on Tuesday, April 10, the executive committee said yes to the operations policy committee's proposal.

The final decisions on the timing and the price rise were those of the executive committee of the corporation, which, in addition to the chairman, was made up of Enders M. Voorhees, Cleo F. Craig, Clifford F. Hood, Arthur A. Houghton, Jr., Joseph P. Spang, Jr., Leslie B. Worthington, Henry T. Heald, C. J. Ingersoll, John M. Meyer, Jr., Alexander C. Nagle, and Robert C. Tyson.

Three of the twelve members of the executive committee were absent from the meeting which decided to raise prices. They were Meyer, a senior vice-president of the Morgan Guaranty Trust Company of New York; Ingersoll, chairman of the board of the Muskogee Company (a railroad holding company); and Houghton, president of Steuben Glass.

Of those who took part in the decision, five were "inside" directors, officials, or former officials of the company, and four were "outside" directors. The inside directors were: Worthington, who in addition to being president of the corporation, is chairman of its executive committee; Blough; Tyson, chairman of the corporation's finance committee; Hood, a former president of the corporation; and Voorhees, a former chairman of the corporation's finance committee.

The outside directors at the April 10 meeting were: Craig, a former president of the American Telephone and Telegraph Company; Heald, president of the Ford Foundation; Nagle, a former chairman of the executive committee of the First National City Bank of New York; and Spang, a former chairman of the Gillette Company. There is no public record of how these men voted.

The fact that U. S. Steel has annual sales of some $3.75 billion, some 180,000 employees, and some 370,000 stockholders should make it much more alert to public opinion than if it were a mite of a corporation. Yet how many members of the operations policy committee and the executive committee took public attitudes and the attitude of the President into serious consideration? It will probably never be known unless they write their memoirs and include the story—all of it—of the day the price of steel was increased.

For many years, some of the biggest problems of large corporations have been political. It is incomprehensible that mature businessmen, responsible for one of the great industrial concentrations in the country, knew so little about the facts of life of the world in which they had been so successful. Surely it was obvious how little information the public had of the need for a price increase. How then did the executive committee fail to give that factor decisive weight? Did its members never realize that President Kennedy would be strongly antagonistic? Yet all the evidence points to the fact that they failed to consider what the President might think of a price increase, and what his response would probably be. In the only press conference Blough held during the seventy-two hour crisis he was asked by a reporter if he was "surprised" at President Kennedy's violent "reaction" to his company's price increase. His reply was: "I think the answer to that should be that I was." And in the same conference he told another reporter that he "knew nothing about politics," one of the oddest confessions of a chief executive whose corporation of necessity must be continuously aware of politics, and of the gusts of opinion that affect so many political decisions, which in turn can have violent impacts on the corporation itself.

Just how intense was the depth of the President's feeling of outrage at U. S. Steel's action? His certainty that an understanding was violated, that he was being affronted as the President, as well as an individual, are clearly shown in Theodore C. Sorensen's *Kennedy*, published in 1965 (New York: Harper & Row). No one, with the exception of Kennedy's brother Robert, was closer to the President than his special counsel. No one is better able to interpret what the President thought, said, and did than Sorensen, for he was in the confidence of Kennedy and his colleagues during the entire steel crisis.

To Sorensen, once Kennedy made the commitment not to back away from the struggle with Big Steel, he simply had to win. He quotes the President as having said, "There is no sense in raising hell and then not being successful. There is no sense in putting the office of the Presidency on the line and then being defeated." To Sorensen, the steel confrontation has to be put within the context of the fight against inflation, not as an isolated incident, and he does so in his book.

No one misunderstood, writes Sorensen, the President's desire that the 1962 settlement neither necessitate nor lead to a price increase, and he cites several occasions when leaders in the industry and the steel union were made to understand this by Kennedy. In all the private talks Kennedy and Goldberg had with Blough and David Mc-Donald, president of the United Steelworkers Union, it was clearly emphasized, according to Sorensen, that it had to be a settlement which would make a price rise unnecessary. "No formal pledge to hold prices steady," writes Sorensen, "was requested, and none was forthcoming. For the government to have asked for such a commitment, the President said, would have been "passing over the line of propriety." But while Blough and other industry spokesmen in what was assumed to be the usual "poor-mouthing" that opens labor negotiations, grumbled on each occasion about rising costs and the profit squeeze, the industry accepted the administration's help without any illusion as to the President's only purpose and without any indication that it intended to raise prices no matter what settlement was reached.

> While Roger Blough would later claim that all kinds of public hints about a pending price rise had been made—hints which no one else in either industry or the press seem to have grasped— he and other industry officials in direct contact with the administration made no use of those opportunities to inform the President of such an action. On the contrary, the industry voluntarily made itself a party to what was in effect a tripartite transaction clearly based on the President's premise that steel price increases were undesirable and, unless necessitated by a wage increase exceeding productivity increases, not to be attempted.

Of Blough's visit to Kennedy in which he handed the President the press release announcing the price increase, Sorensen writes that the President was "stunned." He felt that his whole fight against inflation was in tatters, that if the steel industry

> could make a mockery of his plea for self-restraint in the national interest, then every industry and every union in the country would thereafter feel free to defy him. Above all he felt duped. . . . The prestige and powers of the Presidency had been used to help persuade the Steelworkers to accept less from the companies in the interest of price stability, and now the contract had no sooner been signed than the industry was announcing a large, across-the-board price increase for all products. "The question of good faith was involved," as the President said later. "The unions could have rightfully felt that they had been misled"—and no other union would ever listen to his plea for self-discipline again.

It was at this time, reports Sorensen, that Kennedy said that his father had told him "that steel men were sons-of-bitches, but I never realized until now how right he was." It is Sorensen's own view that Blough "seemed genuinely surprised and concerned by the President's response." As for Kennedy's ability "to mobilize and concentrate every talent and tool he possessed and could borrow to prevent a serious blow to his program, his prestige and his office," the "victory was less a victory against Big Steel than a victory for the American Presidency."

Arthur Schlesinger, Jr., who, Sorensen records, "had nothing to do with the steel case or other economic decisions," also deals with the Kennedy-Blough confrontation in *A Thousand Days* (Boston: Houghton Mifflin Co., 1965), published shortly after Sorensen's book. The former Harvard professor and special assistant to President Kennedy says that "Blough's whole demeanor suggested a genuine belief that an increase in steel prices was no more the business of government than an increase in the price of the lemonade a child might sell in the front of his house." Schlesinger also says that Kennedy regarded the action of U. S. Steel as "premeditated deceit," and adds that Kennedy "remarked to Adlai Stevenson and me," on the subject of steel men, " 'They *are* a bunch of bastards—and I am saying this on my own now, not just because my father told it to me.' "

It is instructive to go back to take a look at some of the comments by a variety of publications following the attempt to raise prices.

In its May, 1962, issue, the First National City Bank *Monthly Letter on Business and Economic Conditions* told the story this way:

> The April 10 price announcement came as a surprise and not

only to President Kennedy but to industry and the public at large. The recent steel wage settlement, described by the President as "noninflationary," had encouraged the assumption that prices would not be increased.

It has since been disclosed that neither the President nor the nation had any understandings with the steel companies on the matter of prices. Yet the public announcement of a three-and-one-half per cent general price advance seemed at the time a personal affront to the President, an effort to take unfair advantage of the two-and-one-half per cent wage settlement negotiated with the help of Labor Secretary Arthur J. Goldberg. Few people stopped to examine the cumulative effect of successive wage and fringe benefits granted workers since the last price advance in 1958.

The New York Times "News of the Week in Review" of April 15 reported:

> Although no formal commitment was sought from the companies not to raise prices, the Administration made plain to them that its efforts to restrain the union demands were based on the assumption . . . that if it were successful, there would be no price increase. As Mr. Kennedy put it last week: "That was the thread that ran through every discussion which I had or Secretary Goldberg had."
>
> Mr. Blough said on that point last week: "No assurances were asked and none were given regarding price action."

And further in the "News of the Week in Review" summary the *Times* commented: "Apart from the question of economic consequences, it was evident that the President felt the steel companies had been guilty of bad faith. He clearly regarded their tactics as a deliberate mouse-trapping of the steel union and a slap in the face of his Administration."

Time magazine, in its issue dated April 20, wrote: "The Administration's massive attack brought a countereffort by U. S. Steel. But it was too late, and too little. Kennedy had already corralled public opinion; even among businessmen, there was an overwhelming sense that U. S. Steel, in its timing and tactlessness, had been fantastically stupid in its public relations."

James Reston, the acute Washington man for *The New York Times*, wrote on April 15, "The President has proved what almost everybody but Roger Blough knew: that the United States is bigger than United States Steel."

In the same issue, Arthur Krock, in his column headed "Steel Mousetrap," wrote:

If bitter experience has taught them [Blough and his associates] what should have been foreseen they now know some important things for sure. It is one thing to base a decision solely on cost-and-earnings statistics. And this kind of decision can be ventured in circumstances which mousetrap an unwilling competitor (Bethlehem in this case), and, for a period even a big union. But no mousetrap will hold the President—especially this President—of the United States. Then the trapper will surely be the one to end up in the trap.

The *Times'* leading editorial on the same day had this to say: "The forces of our democracy scored a dramatic triumph last week when the major steel companies bowed to the storm of both governmental and public protest and rescinded the price increases they had decreed."

Reporter magazine ended its editorial, "The Steelman's Gamble," in the issue of April 26, with these words: "Considering the still very great importance of steel, it is imperative that new men acquire positions of authority in U. S. Steel who are endowed with a thorough knowledge of production, of public relations and of politics."

More than a year later, in the July, 1963, *Commentary*, A. H. Raskin, probably the best-informed labor reporter in the country, wrote: "Last year, after considerable pressure from the administration to hold the line, the union agreed to a modest package of job-security benefits three months before the strike deadline. When the industry followed with higher prices, the President and the union both considered themselves to have been double-crossed; and the violence of Kennedy's reaction brought a quick reversal on the part of Big Steel."

Nor has the passage of even more time made U. S. Steel's decision sound any wiser. Hobart Rowen, a *Newsweek* Washington editor, and the author of the book *Free Enterprisers: Kennedy, Johnson and the Business Establishment* (New York: G. P. Putnam's Sons, 1964), wrote in the *Progressive* of March, 1965: "Three years ago, the major steel companies had led President Kennedy to believe they would hold the price line if he helped them squeeze a non-inflationary wage package out of David McDonald, president of the United Steelworkers Union. That he did, only to be stunned by the industry's response—a six dollar per ton increase across the board."

And on January 21, 1966, *Time* said: "Kennedy simply felt that he had been double-crossed by U. S. Steel chairman Roger Blough and he lost his Irish temper."

In one of the books written on the steel crisis, *Steel and the Presidency, 1962* (New York: W. W. Norton & Co., 1963), Grant McConnell of the University of Chicago says in his summation,

> Whatever the intentions of Mr. Blough and his associates in United States Steel, the announcement of the price increase amounted to a direct challenge of the presidency. If the action by Big Steel had been successful, the power of the presidency could only have been diminished. The ultimate results of such success are unfathomable, but it is not unthinkable that they would have been felt in Europe and the Caribbean. If United States Steel should not have placed the President in such a situation, perhaps the President should not have made himself open to such a challenge. The danger implicit in such a bargain as was attempted, an exchange of support in achieving a labor settlement in return for price stability, was that its terms would not be kept and that the government would be left without recourse. In the event, the danger became the reality.

If any underlining were needed of the public mood at U. S. Steel's price increase at the time it was announced, one need only recall a few of the epithets hurled at the corporation: "personal affront to the President"; "guilty of bad faith"; "mouse trapper"; "slap in the face to the President"; "tactlessness"; "fantastically stupid"; "double crossed." These are only a scattering from publications which are not antagonistic to big business. The terms used by the liberal magazines, by some columnists, and by newspapermen covering politics were far more violent. Big Steel had fallen in public esteem to a low mark in recent history. It totally misjudged not only the temper of the President, but the public temper as well.

Since U. S. Steel did not get its price increase and got a black eye to boot, where did the corporation's judgment go wrong? How could its managers have so grossly misjudged the public reaction and as a result received so little support from the press and the public at the time of its dispute with the President?

It is not that U. S. Steel has no public relations department. It has a well-organized and rather good-sized one. In an industry where some companies and, accordingly, their public relations departments are almost medieval in their approach to their environment, U. S. Steel's public relations people are highly enlightened. They have been in the forefront with modern techniques in their approach to the various segments of society with which the corporation has to live. It was Myron C. Taylor, chairman of the board of the corporation and later President Truman's ambassador to the Vatican, who in 1936 brought in J. Carlisle MacDonald to set up a public relations department. MacDonald had been public relations counsel to Guggenheim Brothers, and had headquarters in Paris and London. He had been on the foreign staff of the Associated Press and in the Paris office of *The New York Times*. He had had sixteen years' experience in public relations before Taylor hired him.

MacDonald started with one assistant, John H. Osmers, whose entire career had been with the corporation. He had joined it on graduation from business college as a stenographer to Judge Elbert H. Gary, who was chairman of the board. In those days it was fashionable for corporate heads to have male secretaries and when Taylor became chairman Osmers served as his secretary and handled special assignments for him. He knew the corporation in a way MacDonald could not know it. MacDonald and Osmers, with two secretaries, set out to build a department.

Today U. S. Steel's public relations department has eighty-two executive personnel and ninety-seven in the secretarial and clerical category. It works on an annual budget of $4 million.

According to the by-laws of the corporation, the responsibility for public relations rests with the chairman of the board. The administrative vice-president in charge of public relations keeps a day-to-day liaison with the chairman on planning and public relations action. If plans are approved they then go to the vice-president in charge of public relations. He in turn acts through the staff sections of the department in New York, the thirteen public relations district offices and the six field offices covering the entire country, including Hawaii and Alaska.

The extent of the operation, and its coverage of the country, can be gauged by the locations of the district offices and the field offices. The public relations district offices are located in Boston, Philadelphia, Washington, Pittsburgh, Cleveland, Chicago, Duluth, St. Paul, Salt Lake City, Birmingham, Houston, San Francisco, and Los Angeles. The public relations field offices are at the Fairless works, near Morrisville, Pa.; Youngstown, Ohio; Detroit; Gary; South Chicago; and Hibbing, Minnesota. All are linked with New York by teletype and leased telephone lines. The system works pretty much as do the national press wire services.

The staff function, carried on in New York, is divided into six sections.

The press relations section's job is to channel news of the corporation to the national press, news services, and radio and television networks and stations. It also services magazines, trade journals, and business periodicals.

The educational service section plans, and keeps an eye on, the programs of service to educators and students. This includes the preparation and distribution of teaching aids used in the classrooms of schools and colleges. This section also has the responsibility of creating and producing classroom study aids, including booklets, film strips, raw material sample kits, and scientific classroom experiments. In addition, it distributes technical papers on the manufacture of iron and steel.

The television and visual media section used to direct the production and promotion of the national television program, *The United States Steel Hour*, until the summer of 1963, when it was cancelled. This section still plans and supervises the making of public relations films. *Rhapsody in Steel*, full length and in color, which cost $400,-000, was made by the Commercial Department in Pittsburgh and served a public relations purpose.

The speeches and special assignments section does the research and writes the drafts of speeches for many of the executives for major occasions; drafts articles asked for by magazines and other publications, and edits *The United States Steel Quarterly* for stockholders of the corporation.

The research section helps evaluate the public relations department's performance and anticipates future problems and needs, suggesting changes in organization and activity to meet them. It also keeps a close watch on what other corporations are doing in public relations, as well as suggesting, planning, and designing the public opinion surveys which the corporation undertakes.

The product information section handles product and marketing news to specialized media which are interested in the corporation's current and developing products.

In addition to all this there are two public relations directors outside of the United States, working for two subsidiaries of the corporation. One is in Caracas, Venezuela, handling the Orinoco Mining Company. The other, in Port Cartier, Quebec, handles the Quebec Cartier Mining Company. In addition to all this, there are public relations representatives in New York working for United States Steel International and the Universal Cement Division.

The professional who headed the public relations department for the corporation at the time of the Kennedy-Blough struggle was an old-timer in his field. Phelps Adams, fifty-nine years old at the time of the blowup, had been a member of the staff since February 21, 1950.

He had come to U. S. Steel from the *New York Sun* when it folded.

Political problems were not new to Adams, for he had been chief Washington correspondent for his paper for almost twenty years. He had travelled with Presidents Coolidge, Hoover, Roosevelt, and Truman, and had covered ten national conventions, five of each party. If any man should not have been a tyro in politically colored thinking it was Phelps Adams.

Nor had he been new in important work at U. S. Steel. He had the major hand in the build-up of Benjamin Fairless, Blough's predecessor. Adams had written Fairless' speeches, and through that route was promoted steadily until Blough appointed him vice-president in charge of public relations in 1957. What is more, he was highly rated in his field by fellow professionals.

The question that arose at the time of the shambles that followed the price increase was: Did Adams have a voice in the decision; was he consulted by Blough and the executive committee of the corporation?

In an interview with the author shortly after the rescinding of the price increase, Adams insisted that he had been consulted. But was he consulted on the timing of the announcement, or simply consulted on the form of the press release?

Some public relations men who know Adams well say that he was out in the cold when the decision was made by the operations policy committee and by the executive committee; that he had as much to say about the timing of the price rise as had the public relations director of the steelworkers' union. Despite this view, other friends of Adams insist that he was consulted, and that, several days before the operations policy committee met on April 7, a press release on a possible increase was drafted by Adams for use in case an actual announcement were made. They also insist that it was reviewed at the April 17 meeting.

However, on July 27, 1966, after a further request for clarification of Adams' part in the decision to raise prices, he said:

> I do want to say for the record—and to correct numerous published reports to the contrary—that as head of the public relations department, I was fully consulted during the discussions leading up to the price action and that I counselled in favor of the action.
>
> In doing so, I fully realized—as did the other executives of the company—that a price increase would be highly unpopular and would create some problems both in Washington and with

the public generally; but in the light of the economic circumstances, which were also fully discussed, it seemed to me that
the price action was the proper course to take, not only in the
interests of the company, its stockholders and its employees, but
also in the long-range national interest since—as the release later
pointed out—it would facilitate the modernization of our steel-
making facilities, increase efficiency, improve the quality of our
product, enhance our competitive position—both domestically
and internationally—and thus, in the long run, would help to
improve, rather than injure, the balance of payments position
of the nation. Believing this to be true (and I still do)—and
believing that sound public relations consists of doing what you
believe to be right rather than what may be momentarily popular—I fully concurred in the proposed price action.

I might add that despite my experience with the ways of
government and politics, gained through more than twenty years
of service as the Washington correspondent of the old *New
York Sun*, I failed to anticipate the fury of the resulting attack
and the massive mobilization of governmental power that was
directed against United States Steel and other steel companies
in the days that followed. And the only excuse I have to offer
is that nothing quite like that has ever happened to the course
of American history, so far as I know.

It may have happened that Adams had gone the way of so many
corporate public relations men. Had he become so company-minded
that his work became a one-way street, that of interpreting the company to the public? Yet every public relations director, to be worth
his salt, must also interpret the various parts of society to management.

On January 3, 1964, Adams was promoted to administrative vice-
president, public relations. It was a promotion not only in rank in the
corporation but in salary as well.

In only one publication was Adams' position as a public relations
practitioner defended. That was in *Public Relations News*, the four-
page public relations newsletter that is the most widely circulated of
its kind. In the issue of April 23, 1962, Mrs. Denny Griswold, its
editor-owner, wrote:

Was the United States Steel Corporation's unsuccessful attempt to raise the price of steel by a relatively small amount
(3-½%) a public relations blunder—one which compares with
Commodore Vanderbilt's "The public be damned!"? The nation's

press almost unanimously has condemned the company as have practically all the PR professionals with whom we have discussed the subject. Unfortunately many of these criticisms were made, we feel, on the basis of inadequate information or without sufficient consideration.

It was a defense Adams liked, for it was distributed by his public relations department to any who asked for an explanation of the public relations aspect of the price increase decision.

Some questions then naturally arise: What is the use of a public relations department to a corporation if management can rush headlong into a major catastrophe? What good is a $400,000 film? What good is a multi-million-dollar budget for public relations? What good is a network of public relations offices? What good are widely distributed speeches, institutional advertising, corporate gifts, film strips, brochures by the ton, or highly trained public relations personnel?

The answer is simple: precious little.

The basis of the public's acceptance of an institution is its performance. It is not its public relations department, not any facade it may have built, not a Niagara Falls of press releases, but the acts of the institution as a whole. The job of gaining acceptance and acting in what the public believes to be the public interest, is one for the entire corporation, especially its top management. And here the failure is obvious, for U. S. Steel suffered twice: it was scolded by the President of the country and by an almost unanimous press, and still failed to get its price increase. On the face of it, despite the later attacks on President Kennedy for his over-reaction to Blough's move, the attempt to bull through the increase was a disaster for the corporation, a ghastly and expensive error, and one harmful to all business.

To Blough's credit, he set out on a tough course; not of fighting the unbeatable, but of seeking closer cooperation with the Federal Government. This came as a relief of the businessmen who were chilled by the prospect of a war between big business and big government.

On July 3, 1962, only fifty-two days after his bruising defeat by President Kennedy, U. S. Steel's chairman spoke to the Edison Electric Institute in Atlantic City. He posed this question: "Are we doing everything we can to increase the government's confidence in business?"

Then he went on to give his answer:

Solutions to questions like these are never easy, but to repeat, in my view action by both in a cooperative spirit is the only

feasible answer. Business cannot afford to think of those in government as Machiavellian overlords whose prime purpose in life
is to push business around. I do not think this is the case, nor
do I think we can let ourselves fall into the critical state of mind
that that kind of thinking generates. . . . If the concept of underlying and inevitable antagonism between business and government can be laid to rest by mutual understanding and mutual
action in our time, then the generations which follow will have
reason to accord us all their undying gratitude. It is the only way
that the great industrial complex and the great movement of
this great nation can live and rise together in a demanding
future.

Nor was that an isolated action. Blough tried to heal the breach
between himself and the President, and spoke on several more
occasions of the need for government-business cooperation. On September 25, 1964, he was reported by the Scripps-Howard chain of
newspapers as saying: "Business and government just cannot be
antagonistic if we are to have a successful country, a successful
economy. You might say, 'Never the twain shall meet.' I say the
opposite. The twain have to meet continuously if government and
business are to perform their functions properly. That has been my
attitude, and that will continue to be my attitude regardless of any
momentary problems which arise." On October 7, 1964, speaking in
Chicago before two trade associations, he said, "No one expects the
millennium to arrive tomorrow; and until it does, business will certainly
continue to have its problems, some of which, to be sure, will result
from its own mistakes. But on balance, it seems to me there is a
new and developing attitude of cooperation between government and
business—a new understanding of each other's problems and a new
willingness on both sides to work out realistic solutions that are
truly in the long-range public interest."

On August 1, 1966, Blough outlined for the author his views on
the relations between government and business:

Business and government are not—and should not be cast in
the role of—contending parties. Each is as interested as the other
in the economic and social progress of the people. This does not
mean that there may not be—or should not be—an exchange
between them with hearty competition between viewpoints. For
example, it is in the nature of government to evidence a constantly expanding involvement in areas previously within the
private sector. For the common good, business needs to debate
the wisdom of such tendencies in particular instances.

A difference of viewpoint need not cause mutual distrust—particularly if leaders of both business and government approach touchy situations with a sincere desire for understanding, and with reliance on fact rather than preconceived attitude. Considerable progress has been made in recent years toward a helpful kind of dialogue. But this is only a beginning.

Not so long ago managers of large corporations had a relatively simple life. They had to turn out goods, keep the few large stockholders happy, and make certain that the corporation's profit position was good. There was little cause to worry about the environment in which the chief executive conducted his business. Trade unions were not a major headache, for few large industrial corporations had them. Employees could be fired at will, and when new men were needed there was always a big pool of new people coming on the labor market, whether it was the immigrant or others glad of a chance to work long hours for low pay. Legislators were not much of a problem, for the wish of many large corporations was the will of the elected officials.

Of all these factors the only one that is unchanged is the urgency for the corporation head to so run his shop that it makes a reasonable profit: without it no business enterprise can ever survive. But all other factors have changed: trade unions are powerful; legislators heed the desires of the voters more than they ever did; stockholders are now small as well as large; the feelings of the communities in which the plants are located are important; customers must consider the firm a good and fair supplier; and, above all, the general public insists on looking over the shoulders of the corporation chiefs as they do their jobs.

The pressures on the business manager are more onerous than they have ever been. The competition for promotion within the company is so strong and the competition between industrial mammoths so keen, that the manager has far too little time to look about him. He is not able to study the social environment of his company; to gauge what the groups with whom the company does business think of it; or find out how the politicians assess its contribution to the common good.

Most businessmen have risen to the top because of their single-minded devotion to the job. They have not had the time, or, in many cases, the inclination, to worry about public attitudes. They have been specialists. Had they not been, their chances of climbing to greater responsibility, and still greater salaries, and stock options would have been pretty thin. When they do reach to the highest levels they

suddenly have to become generalists. A man who rises from production, from finance, or from law to be chief executive of his corporation
now runs into all kinds of problems with which he never had to be
concerned before. And the one that seems least important to him is
the hazy one of what the public thinks of his company. Concern about
a corporation's relations to the public or to the government is a
concept foreign to many of these men. To them, the talk about public
opinion is so much piffle.

Luckily for the survival of American business—and our economic
system—there are business leaders who understand that public respect, public acceptance, and often even public approval are essential
to the profitable operation of business, particularly large businesses.
The insistence by some corporate heads that no major decisions be
made without taking into consideration public opinion is not just a
"do-gooder" act. It is directly related to the corporation's ability to
make a profit and, in some cases, even to survive.

The American Telephone and Telegraph Company is eminently
successful. The world's largest corporation is profitable for many
reasons, and one of them is that it has a full understanding and
appreciation of the importance of public opinion; not only by those
whose job is in the public relations department, but by management
at all levels. Every manager at AT&T has throughout his career
been impressed with the importance of the views of the public. A
plain, but often overlooked, fact of American business life is drummed
into him: the company cannot function properly without a continuous
consciousness of the importance of favorable publc attitudes.

Frederick R. Kappel, chairman of AT&T's board for ten years,
in his book *Business Purpose and Performance* (Des Moines, Iowa:
Duell, Sloan and Pearce, 1964) had this to say on the connection
between business actions and public attitudes:

> Some may think that the judgments people make in a drug
> store or a used-car lot, or in a telephone booth, are unrelated
> to the judgments they arrive at in the voting booth. I don't think
> they are unrelated. Economic experience and political choice
> are mixed like Tom and Jerry. In our society the relations be-
> tween industry and government do not begin in Washington.
> They begin in millions of minds that are influenced every day
> by the kind of job that we in business do: the goods we sell,
> the wages we pay, our behaviour in the community, how we
> sound when we speak, and whether we show ourselves as people
> that other people can trust. And the mistakes we make, the
> shortcomings we exhibit, do not merely send customers into a

competitor's arms. They also make people think as citizens, and influence their political decisions.

Quality performance, therefore, solid accomplishment, good citizenship—these are the necessary foundations for business progress in a political world. Perhaps this seems self-evident. I stress it however because I think we in business need to be sure of the ground we stand on before we raise our voices.

E. I. du Pont de Nemours & Company is a major enterprise which has had its problems with public opinion and with governments. It is also a highly profitable company, and it is so for many solid reasons. One of them is that it, too, like AT&T, fully appreciates that the views of the voter and the rank and file politician cannot be shrugged off. Lammot du Pont Copeland, president of Du Pont, outlined his company's policy before the Public Relations Society of America at Miami Beach on November 5, 1959. Here is part of what he said:

> The general public is alert, well educated and interested. The people will increase their scrutiny of business and other institutions to see if what they regard as the common good is fully served. People won't be fooled by verbal smoke screens or moral pretensions behind which institutions can operate as they choose. Public understanding can't be achieved with mirrors, and no public relations program can make black white or brown blue. What we must have is good solid business accomplishment and business conduct that is in concert with and not opposed to the public good. . . . Back in the third decade of this century, businessmen learned the hard way that they could not be indifferent to what the public thought of them and their deeds. They found that the public had an agency through which it could speak and act, an agency larger and more powerful than any company, or even than all companies as a group. They learned that the government of the United States could, under public pressure, compel obedience to the public will. It was a hard lesson, and the scars are still with us. But I believe it was thoroughly learned by most businessmen.

On October 31, 1962, a little more than six months after the Blough-Kennedy confrontation, M. J. Rathbone, chief executive for five years until he retired early in 1965 and chairman of the board of Standard Oil Company (New Jersey), which, too, has had its trouble with public opinion and politicians, told the Wharton School Alumni Society: "We know perfectly well that business does not function by divine right, but, like any other part of our society, exists with the sanction of the community as a whole." He went on further to say: "A wise firm makes public relations a function not simply of a staff department but of top management, so that every business decision is considered from the standpoint of its public impact."

And what of General Motors Corporation, the largest industrial corporation in the world with annual sales greater than the budgets of many of the highly developed nations of Europe? Frederic G. Donner, GM's chairman, put it this way for the author:

> The goals of General Motors are to serve society and in so doing to benefit its owners. This is accomplished first of all, by producing and merchandising products that are attractive, dependable and of high quality. A second requirement is that the company be alert to the development of new products and new processes. It must also be a good place in which to work, a good neighbor in its plant communities, a good firm to do business with, and a good corporate citizen in the sense of maintaining high ethical principles, participating in the processes of social change, and accepting without reservation what has been decided to be public policy.

Sad to say, companies like AT&T, Du Pont, Jersey Standard, and General Motors are closer to being the exception than the rule. Other corporations are concerned about the social environment in which they operate, but far too many think that public opinion is something that can be bamboozled; that the function of public relations is to build a false front behind which they can do as they wish. To still other firms, often of middle size, public relations and the establishment of a public relations department, is like panelling the board room: something pleasant, to give the appearance of having arrived, but not really basic to the company's effectiveness.

It is not easy for management to follow the AT&T-Du Pont-Jersey Standard-GM line. It takes time, effort, and alertness by top management. But there is no other way if private corporate enterprise is to survive. These four companies reached their present posture of active concern for public opinion from four different starting points. Often they had their feet put to the fire before they were fully convinced they were living in a new society. None of them is riding high on cloud nine in the unreality of never-never land. All four companies are highly successful where it counts: in profits. Why they all decided, at different times and under different circumstances, that public opinion is sovereign, is worth a look.

THE GRANDDADDY OF THEM ALL

EVERY MONDAY MORNING AT TEN O'CLOCK, TWENTY-TWO OFFI-
cers of the world's biggest private business pull red leather chairs up
to a long oval mahogany table to begin their deliberations. In the
high-ceilinged twenty-by-forty-foot room, on the twenty-sixth floor of
a white granite copy of the Parthenon at 195 Broadway in New York
City, decisions are made which will govern the careers of 800,000
employees and the telephone service of the United States.

As H. I. Romnes, American Telephone and Telegraph Company
chairman and chief executive, opens the cabinet meeting he looks
around the mahogany-panelled board room at his top staff. To his
right, in the vast central wall panel, hangs a portrait in oil on linen-
canvas. Set in a four-inch-wide gold frame is the three-quarter length
figure of a man in black frock coat, grey vest, wide-open wing collar,
and black cravat. In the figure's right hand, which is crossed over his
paunch, is a pince-nez. The face is florid, the nose large, the grey
hair bushy, and the moustache flowing and white, as are the side-
burns. The eyes are clear blue. The smile adds softness to a face
marked with the habit of command.

The portrait, painted in 1898 by the skillful realist, Paris-born
Ferdinand Humbert, with the dark background typical of the 1890's,
is of Theodore Newton Vail, the first president of the corporation,
at the age of fifty-three. That the painting should dominate the cabinet
meeting is not a surprise. Had it not been for this one man, Romnes
and all the others in the room would probably be working for the

government as high-class bureaucrats if they had chosen the telephone business as a career.

The telephone as a natural monopoly is an easy subject for government take-over. From government control to government ownership is a short step. In all of Europe, the telephone company in San Marino with its 1,115 phones for a population of 14,000, is the only one privately owned. Three of Canada's provinces—Manitoba, Saskatchewan and Alberta—have government-owned systems. In Japan the telephone system, while privately operated, is government owned.

How was it then that the telephone system in the United States was able to continue under private ownership and operation? How has the vast AT&T avoided government ownership? Why is it that the public accepts, and the men running for public office do not attack, the private ownership of the telephone when it is so easy for government to move in?

A large part of the answer lies in the wisdom of Theodore Vail. He understood the importance of public opinion. He realized that the then-young telephone business had to put public interest above private concern. He knew public opinion was dominant in our society, and that in the long run the politicians do carry out the public will. These concepts are not revolutionary. Yet they were repugnant to many businessmen in the pioneer days of the telephone and are still strange to many business leaders today.

Vail was not a philosopher. He did not attend college. The son of a Quaker farmer and iron worker, he was born in Ohio, the third of ten children. He went to work in a drug store when he was seventeen years old.

At that time, in 1862, businessmen were on the threshold of the phase that gave birth to the term "robber barons"; to them, the public interest was almost meaningless. Government in this era was something for businessmen to ignore, manipulate, or corrupt. The concept that dominates the better-run corporations today—that public acceptance is essential to survival of business—was virtually unknown when Vail was maturing.

Working in the drug store was important to Vail, for it was also a telegraph office and he learned to operate the instrument. Within two years Vail was working in New York as an operator for the Western Union Telegraphy Company. He went to work for the Post Office in 1869 and rose in it until, in 1876, when he was thirty-one, he became superintendent of the railway mail service. He stayed until 1878. Theodore Vail's nine years in the Postal Department taught him a great deal about government, politicians, voters, and the elective process. It taught him above all the importance of public opinion, and what he learned at Washington he never forgot.

When the organizers of the infant telephone business in Boston found that they needed a skilled and creative administrator they picked Vail, and made him general manager of the American Bell Telephone Company, the forerunner of American Telephone and Telegraph Company. The salary was $3,500 for the first year and $5,000 for the second. He took the chance, moving from the safety of government into a business in which he had faith. He was anxious to prove that an amazing invention could result in the building of an important business.

To many business managers, even today, public opinion is something beyond their interest. Yet there is an amazing letter in the files of AT&T which shows how far Vail was ahead of his time. It is this letter, and what followed from it, that developed into the philosophy of the telephone company, now a keystone of its policy in its relations with the public. The letter is typewritten under the letterhead of The American Bell Telephone Co., No. 95 Milk Street, Boston. It is dated December 28, 1883. It was addressed to W. A. Leary, Esq., Iowa Union Tel. & Tel. Co., Davenport, Iowa. It is signed by Theo. N. Vail, general manager.

The letter reads:

Dear Sir:-

Now that the Telephone business has passed its experimental stage, I would like to get your opinion upon points given below. This opinion to be based upon our existing relations, and upon your own and your associates' observations and experience in your particular field:-

Is the Telephone service as it is now being furnished, satisfactory to the public.

Are the prices satisfactory to the public, considering the facilities and service that is given.

Would it be advantageous to furnish the same service now being furnished at any lower rate provided it could be done.

Is it possible in view of the contingencies of storm, under ground legislation &c., to make any lower rate to the public for some classes of service.

Is it desirable, and what would be the most practicable way, to provide a service at a rate which would be within the reach of families, etc.

Is it practicable to give different classes of service within the same Exchange.

What has been the tendency of the relationship between the public and the local Co.'s, for the past year, i.e., are the relations between the public and the Co.'s improving.

Where there has been any conflict between the local Exchange and the public, what has been the cause of the difficulties, and what has been the result.

A full and detailed reply from you by the 8th, of January, would be of great service to me. Trusting that I am not asking too much,

I am,

Very respectfully, &c.

If opinion pollsters are looking for a businessman who might be the father of their craft it could be Vail. And if public relations men are looking for a pioneer in corporate concern with public attitudes, it might also be Vail. In this one letter the general manager of the company asked for opinions on service, rates, types of service, special rates for families, the relations between the public and the local telephone companies, and the causes for customer complaints and how they were handled.

The problems of customer relations, the importance of service, and how to satisfy the telephone user have all changed, as has the way of finding out what Vail wanted to know. But the basic principles on which AT&T operates in its relations with its subscribers have not changed. They are still the foundation upon which public acceptance is attained, even though the span between 1883 and today is long and the public problems vaster both in size and complexity.

Despite Vail's usefulness to the telephone company and his contributions to its advancement, conflict rose between him and the company's directors. The details of the divisions which led to Vail's resignation are not clear, but he did oppose the directors' decision to pay out more in dividends than he thought fit, and put too little back into the business. In 1889 he left the presidency of AT&T. He was forty-four years old.

For the next eighteen years Vail worked in all sorts of enterprises, mostly in Latin America. Meanwhile, through friends, he kept in touch with what was going on in the company that he had done so much to build. There is very little source material available of the period during which Vail was away from the company but it is clear that some of his basic principles concerning the relations between the company and the public were violated time and again.

Albert Bigelow Paine, Vail's biographer, describes the regime of John E. Hudson, president of AT&T during most of Vail's absence, in these words:

> For about eleven years President Hudson administered telephone affairs in a manner that accorded with his traditions. He was an able lawyer, a cultured, conservative man, who regarded the telephone business as a patent-owning concern—a monopoly with rights to be protected—an aristocrat like himself, whose service it was a privilege of the public to use and pay for without much voice as to its quality. His was not exactly "the public be damned" policy, but it partook of that nature.

Hudson's successors were little better when it came to paying heed to what the public demanded. The Bell system became a thoroughly disliked corporation. What was worse, and perhaps as a result, there were stories about the financial difficulties of the company; stock prices were going steadily down. The directors again turned to Vail. They persuaded him to return, and on May 1, 1907, he was chosen president of AT&T and this time he put his imprint on the company so solidly that his fundamental policies are still in force. He saved the company from financial troubles, but above all he saved it from being taken over by the government and he did it by showing, as no other businessman did before him, how private profit without public acceptance is impossible.

The following thirteen years—Vail died on April 16, 1920—were his most fruitful for the company. They were years of social upheaval, of labor violence, of stiff-necked anti-unionism, of a whole literature of protest, of muckraking, of demands for government ownership of public utilities, of mass immigration, of trade union organization, of armed company opposition—of accumulation of vast wealth by relatively few, and deprivation, despair, and the bitterness of abject poverty for millions.

These were the days of President Theodore Roosevelt, his cries against the "malefactors of great wealth," and his trust-busting. These were the days of William Howard Taft and the accusations of betrayal from other Republicans—Senators LaFollette of Wisconsin and Norris of Nebraska. These were the days of Woodrow Wilson and his New Freedom, and when more than 900,000 Americans voted for Eugene Debs, running for President on the Socialist ticket—a vote equivalent to better than two million in terms of current population. These were the days of entry into World War I, victory, and the beginning of the hiatus of peace.

It was during this period that the Standard Oil Company empire was broken up; that the railroads fought bitterly against any kind of regulation; that private monopolies grew and the cries for their nationalization were widely repeated. It was in this period that *McClure's, Everybody's, Cosmopolitan, Collier's* and the *American* magazines, all of them with national audiences, carried the hammer-blows of expose of big business. It was the period of Henry George's *Progress and Poverty* which sold more than two million copies; when Thorstein Veblen's *Theory of Business Enterprise*, with its thesis that business' concern for profit was against the public good, was the textbook of intellectuals; when Ida Tarbell's *History of the Standard Oil Company* had great influence; when Charles Edward Russell attacked the beef industry in *The Greatest Trust in the World;* when Thomas Lawson's *Frenzied Finance* told the story of Amalgamated Copper; when Burton J. Hendrick's *Story of Life Insurance* helped force the demand for strict regulation of the life insurance business; when the details of the filth in the Chicago stockyards, published in Upton Sinclair's *The Jungle*, broke the back of the meat packing industry's bitter fight against federal meat inspection laws; when the *Ladies' Home Journal* campaigned against poisonous medicines and misleading advertising, and the American Medical Association fought the patent medicine lobby and helped get a Pure Food and Drug Act passed by Congress.

These were also times of mass immigration. From 1901 to 1910, 8,795,386 immigrants came to the United States: 21.7 per cent from northern and western Europe; 70.8 per cent from southern and eastern Europe. From 1911 to 1920, 5,735,811 new immigrants came: 17.4 per cent from northern and western Europe and 58.9 per cent from southern and eastern Europe. Irish, Poles, Austrians, Russians, Jews, and Italians—all the immigrants, in fact—preferred to settle in the cities; in 1900, 39.7 per cent of the population lived in urban areas; in 1910 the figure was 44.7 per cent; in 1920 the concentration was 51.2 per cent of the total population in urban centers.

It was during Vail's second period with the telephone company that the radical labor movement grew in strength. From 1904, when they were formed after the cracked heads, the bloody violence, the ruthless struggle of the strike in the coal mines of Cripple Creek, Colorado, until 1918, the International Workers of the World—

or Wobblies—were the leaders in some 150 strikes. The Wobblies were not reformers. They were industrial unionists, thorough-going socialists to whom the goal was the destruction of capitalism, not co-existence with it. From the coal mines in Colorado, through pitched battles at Ludlow, the violence of West Virginia, the organization of the textile mills of Paterson, New Jersey, and Lawrence, Massachusetts, the terrorists of the union and the hired guns of management clashed. The IWW was as aggressively *for* union organization as plant owners were unalterably *against* it. This, too, was the time of the American Federation of Labor's growth from little more than 500,000 members to better than 4,000,000, and when its economic platform demanded government ownership of all public utilities.

This then was the mood of the nation, the climate of public opinion, in which Vail had to build American Telephone and Telegraph, unify the telephone industry, bolster the company's financial reputation, extend its service, satisfy the stockholders, improve the feeling between the company and its subscribers, encourage the employees, satisfy the general public that the operation was in the public interest, and convince legislators that this monopoly was one which should, for the common good, remain privately owned and privately managed.

The problems were multiplied by the expiration of Bell's telephone patents in 1893 and 1894. Entrepreneurs set up independent telephone companies by the hundreds, selling a combination of service and stock in the companies to subscribers while attacking Bell as an octopus whose tentacles they would lop off. In many communities the shopkeepers would have to have two separate telephones, and the subscribers of one system could not talk to the subscribers of another. It finally got through to the butcher, the baker, the candlestick maker, who all had to have two distinct services, that perhaps the telephone was in reality a natural monopoly; that one telephone company would have to be the answer to their grief.

In addition, AT&T needed money for expansion even as the price of its stock had been falling. Vail moved quickly and announced, almost immediately on his taking over, a stock issue of 220,000 shares to go to the present stockholders, allocating one new share at par to each owner of six old shares. This one stroke of timing put more than $20 million in cash into the treasury. The decision was as sound as it was bold, for within some four months, the nation's financial structure seemed to bust loose in one of the worst panics in history. Banks, trust companies, and major industries closed their doors. But the telephone company's credit remained solid.

At the same time, Vail began to push his plan of "One Policy, One System, Universal Service." He set out to get to know all the heads of the Bell companies throughout the country as a first step and to get cooperation with the independent telephone companies. He bought out those which would sell. The others he did not try to drive to the wall. Instead, if they insisted on remaining independent, he made arrangements for them to be connected with the Bell system, via the closest Bell company, so that the independents could use the national or regional services of Bell. These Bell-connected companies could then offer their subscribers, who were often stockholder-subscribers, service beyond their own immediate locality, the advantage the Bell companies had by being part of one national system.

To do all this, to develop good morale within his own company, to make certain that his efforts would not be frustrated by misunderstanding of what he was doing, he needed public support. He set out to get it, using two basic tools: good policies and full information about them.

Vail always made good use of the annual report. Instead of dull-as-ditch-water reports, Vail made them readable. Even read today they are pleasant and informative. The language of his annual reports was simple, clear, and easily understood. The reports were like interesting stories, and lacked the stilted language of the unimaginative lawyer.

Vail believed in full disclosure in his financial reports. His first report, made December 31, 1907, was so straightforward that some of his directors thought that it might be wiser if some items be excluded for they might not be understood and might hurt the credit of the company.

Vail's answer was, "No. We will lay our cards on the table. There is never anything to be gained by concealment."

Instead of the report harming the company's financial position, it enhanced it. Vail's clear statement of the weaknesses of the company, together with the actions taken to remedy them, brought additional confidence from the financial community.

In Vail's annual report dated March, 1908, he dealt bluntly with the problems posed by the independent companies, the inefficiency of two telephone systems within one community, fair rates, the proper return on capital, the difficulties of maintenance and the future of the company if it moved toward "universality" of service. And throughout the report there are statements like these:

> With a full knowledge of all surrounding circumstances and conditions, it is believed that this [fair rates] would be fully

acquiesced in by the public. . . . If these questions are answered satisfactorily, there can be no basis for conflict between the company and the public, and the less the working conditions are made inflexible by legislative prescription, the better will be the solution of the constantly changing problems incident to a growing business.

And in Vail's annual report dated March, 1911, this is said:

In all times, in all lands, public opinion has had control at the last word—public opinion is but the concert of individual opinion, and is as much subject to change or to education.

It is based on information and belief. If it is wrong it is wrong because of wrong information, and consequent erroneous belief.

It is not only the right but the obligation of all individuals, or aggregations of individuals, who come before the public, to see that the public have full and correct information.

Or further in the same report:

The excuse for setting forth at great length the policy, facts, beliefs and desires of the Bell System and those administering it, even to the extent of repeating much that has already been said and explaining some things familiar to many, is to inform the new public, the new subscribers and the new shareholders.

Every fact that is stated is correct.

Every argument or reason is believed to be well founded and based on facts and is intended to be impartial.

Again and again in annual reports, in speeches, in magazine articles, and in talks to his managers and to all who would listen, Vail repeated his basic theme—that the public interest was the over-riding concern, that nothing would or could take the place of good policies clearly explained to the public.

As one more example—in his annual report of March, 1917— Vail repeated his views that, "It is not inappropriate to restate clearly the attitude of the Bell System toward the public. Repetition of facts prevents misunderstanding, as misunderstanding is based on either misleading, mistaken or meagre information."

When it is considered that so many businessmen today do not yet understand the fact of our society that the public, inarticulate as it often is, prejudiced as it may be, uninformed as it too frequently is, is still the master of the country, Vail's soundness is even more remarkable. There is no chief executive of a corporation, no matter how large and powerful, who can long act in a manner the public considers to be against the common good; that is, if he wants to stay in business.

Vail was not a prisoner of his prejudices. Of course he believed in the essential good of private ownership of public utilities. But he did not fool himself into thinking that all the corporations had acted wisely. He thought, rather, that they had been doing a pretty good job of digging their own graves. At the opening of the annual conference of the Bell Telephone System in New York, in October, 1913, Vail said:

> The immediate future is bound to be a very critical period, in that the public mind is in an unsettled condition towards all utilities. The present attitude towards all utility corporations has been largely created by the past attitude of corporations toward the public by assuming to be acting as if they were masters of the situation. The public are awakening to the fact that they, the public, are the masters of the situation, that the utilities have their plant "in situ," fixed and immovable, dependent upon public consent to operate, and, without that consent, of small liquidating value relative to its value as a going concern or its cost of creation.

Dependent on public consent to operate. This unusual clarity of thinking and expression by Vail showed that he was not only a pioneering businessman and the builder of a large telephone system, but that he knew that all his skills, or those of others who headed other public utilities, would be of little meaning unless the public was not opposed. They had the right to mark a ballot at election time as they willed. And that power was bigger than the power of any arrogant businessman, no matter how well schooled, of what intellectual capacity, or old family, or connections in Congress, or expensive lobbyists he might hire, or newspaper publishers he might have in his hip pocket.

Vail not only understood the facts of life; he was able to act on his understanding. Good policies, efficient and courteous service, sound practices, adequate pensions and satisfactory working conditions for employees of AT&T, or careful attention to stockholders and the community were in themselves insufficient without direct communication through the media that the general public read.

Vail, in line with his belief that the story of the corporation had to be widely told, acted to set up a system within the company so that the telling would be consistent, accurate, and well-thought out. The company had, in 1903, hired a Boston firm of press agents, the Publicity Bureau. But this was not what Vail wanted. He wanted

someone with him, solely on AT&T's payroll and responsible directly
to the chief executive. In 1908, a year after Vail returned to run
the company, he chose one of the partners in the Publicity Bureau,
a former *Boston Herald* reporter, James D. Ellsworth, to handle both
the publicity and the advertising.

Although it was not until 1910 that Ellsworth was given the title
of director of the Information Department, both the publicity and the
advertising began almost immediately on his hiring. This was not
only the beginning of the use of professional help in releasing copy
for press use, it was also the start of a consistent advertising campaign to explain the policies and activities of the corporation, both
in newspapers and magazines.

The first year of Ellsworth's job was a national election year. Taft
was running against William Jennings Bryan. The new publicity
man had prepared an advertisement, the first of its institutional campaigns, which outlined how close the relationship was between AT&T
and the Bell companies associated with it, telling of the benefits of
"One Policy, One System, Universal Service." It was slated to run
in magazines in November. Some of the corporation's executives questioned the timing of the advertisement. Their objection was that it
might be used by politicians as evidence that the Bell system was a
trust—at a time when trust-busting was a theme that roused the
voters.

Ellsworth took the objections to Vail, detailed the dangers in
running the ads at this time and the possibility of their becoming a
campaign issue, and asked for a decision. Vail asked Ellsworth only
one question: "Are the statements in the advertisements true?"

Ellsworth said, "Yes."

"Very well, then. Let's print it and beat them to it," was the
Vail order.

Vail never used Ellsworth as a buffer between him and inquiring
reporters. He wanted to see newsmen. It helped him learn what was
on the minds of readers, for the newspaper was a lot closer to the
public than a corporate executive could be. Not only did Vail become
a good source of news for the men on the telephone company beat,
but he developed a rapport with them and never gave them a bum
steer. The result was that he often discussed, not only telephone
business, but all kinds of public issues, and when he had some worthwhile comment he found no difficulty in getting his views across
through the press.

A story is told of how Vail took great care not to mislead reporters.
On one occasion he found that, by an oversight, he had given an

incorrect fact to a newspaperman. He immediately ordered Ellsworth to look up the reporter for him and explain how the mistake had been made. The result, of course, was that the reporter to whom Vail had given his corrected version trusted the corporation; his colleagues did as well. It is not very hard to get a bad press, as politicians have always known, and Vail worked as willingly with the press as any successful politician does.

The policy of frankness paid off, not only with the press and in his reports to stockholders, but also in the plethora of investigations into public utilities. It was the habit of businessmen then, as it is too often today, to scream murder every time a Congressional committee or government agency investigates, or even suggests investigation of, a public utility, industry, or corporation. Vail took quite a different tack. He always appeared willingly, and what is more, he never withheld on his testimony. He knew his company better than any investigator ever could, and, since he was the kind of man who always did his homework, nothing that could be asked by the investigating body's counsel would put him in a position where he would have to say, "I don't know." For the same reason he could not be misled into damaging statements, another awkward situation businessmen have often found themselves in when under examination.

"What is it you want to know? We will show you anything you will want to see, and do anything you ask. Just tell us what you want," was Vail's reply to one investigative body, and it was his firm policy all the way through. Of course, this meant that the business had to be run so that there was never anything to hide. Clean hands are always the basic answer, and Vail insisted on good practices, based on good policies, for his corporation.

Shortly after Vail returned to the company there was an announcement of an investigation in Missouri. It dealt with the relationship between AT&T and the independent lines that it had absorbed. The president of the Missouri and Kansas Company was instructed to tell the Missouri attorney general this: "Mr. Vail will welcome this investigation. He is particularly anxious to show just what is our position. You can put him on the witness stand, or prepare a list of questions and he will answer them."

Vail did not oppose regulation of the telephone business. In this he was different from other businessmen, who were usually opposed to any regulation of a corporation or public utility. To Vail, the telephone could only be an effective instrument if it did not have competition within its own area. Two telephone companies in one town had proved an impractical, expensive failure and could not give the public decent service. But Vail knew that a natural monopoly had to be regulated by the government. The type of regulation was of basic importance. To him, regulation by government had to be carried out through the appointment of men who had the respect of the government, the industry, and the general public, and who would act under a set of principles acceptable to all involved.

In his March, 1912, annual report Vail put his case this way: "All regulation and control of corporations serving the public should be by permanent bodies, judicial in their attitude, equitable in their purposes and actions, governed by a few simple laws based on the rights of the individual, the corporation and the community, and applied after the fullest examination and consideration."

But as for government control—he was in full, complete opposition. His experiences in the Post Office Department and his knowledge of the patronage system made him realistic as to what might happen to the telephone if it ever came under government control. To him, government administration was more or less a game of politics, and while with government operation it was sometimes possible to have efficiency, it would always be impossible to have economy.

Yet when Vail was seventy-three years old the dread moment arrived. The United States had entered World War I on April 6, 1917. Less than three weeks earlier he had offered his services to the government to bring together the telephone and telegraph interests to better help in time of crisis. Rumors had begun almost immediately after the declaration of war that the government would take over the wires for the duration of the war and that there was a possibility of government ownership.

There was no government action until July 24, when President Wilson proclaimed that the government was taking control of all telephone and telegraph systems. They were to become part of the postal department under the supervision of Postmaster General Albert S. Burleson.

Then came the telegram summoning Vail to Washington for Monday, July 29. Vail was depressed. All he had worked for seemed to be slipping away. On the morning of his appointment with the Postmaster General, on his way up the steps of the Post Office, he stopped, turned to one of his colleagues and said, "Well, I never in my life felt so helpless. These people have got us entirely in their hands—they have taken over our property and probably intend to keep it. They can do what they please with us, and we cannot help ourselves. For once in my life I am completely at sea."

But the principles of his devotion to the public interest were Vail's strength with the Postmaster General. Burleson had explained that he was acting as a trustee to preserve the property and return it in good condition, if it were returned; that he had had no experience in running a telephone company; that though he had been a strong advocate of government ownership, he did not intend to run the service toward this end; and that he would like Vail's cooperation.

Again Vail showed how different he was from some other business-men of his period. He told the Postmaster General that he wished to help in every possible way; that all the officers of the company would do everything in their power to make the government's work a success; that every employee would give his best service; that any of his own views on government ownership would be put aside and the government would get the same support as if the subject of take-over had never been discussed; that as far as the preservation of the property was concerned, the interest of both the government and the company was the same, for if the business were nationalized then the government would need it to be at top efficiency and if it were returned then it had to be just as efficient for the public service under private ownership.

Even when it came to discussing the terms of payment by the government, Vail did not hedge or wheel and deal. He left it to the Post-master General. The contrast between Vail and other business leaders, particularly the railroad presidents, was so marked that it left an immense impression on the Postmaster General. Vail was asked to continue, with his own organization, to run the telephone system for the duration of the war.

Vail did not back down on his promise to the Postmaster General. He went further: In a message to all AT&T employees he not only told them of the change of the company's status, but asked them to give, because "it is not too much to ask of you, the same loyalty, fidelity and devotion to service under the new order of things." This was not a gimmick or trick on the part of Vail. He meant all he said. He knew that, as he and his company performed, so would the chances of government or private ownership fare.

So wholehearted was Vail's cooperation, so clear was his position made to the public, that the press gave wide approval to his stand and _The New York Times_ had this to say: "Mr. Vail has never been a believer in the right of big business to go its way unhindered. No big businessman ever submitted to control more loyally, and regulation and control of private operation was his idea of what public interest required."

Neither Vail nor the company he headed stinted in cooperation.

His, and the company's, actions had an amazing effect both on the public and the government. Many who had expected and hoped that this control would develop into government ownership began to change their minds, for AT&T was able to prove that what the public interest demanded in time of war, what the government asked it to do, the company would willingly do. And this attitude did not hurt the company. Instead it paid off, for on July 31, 1919, the control of the telephone system was returned to the company.

Had it not been for Vail and his appreciation of the fact that without public permission no business can, in the long run, operate; had it not been for his appreciation that good policies and efficient service were essential, and that no less important was telling the public what you were doing and why; had it not been for his belief in the ability of the public to know the difference between bad and good performance; had it not been for his wisdom in putting the common good first; then the telephone would today be government owned. And the impact of that step would have been to alter materially the balance between the private and government sectors in our economic system.

What kind of man was Vail really? Pendleton Dudley, who knew and worked for him, was a reporter for the *Wall Street Journal* and later set up his own public relations agency. He was retained in 1912 by Vail and was kept as a consultant by AT&T until he died in November, 1966. In 1965, while seeking material for this book, the author asked Dudley, who was then ninety years old, to write his impressions of Vail. He wrote:

My acquaintance with Theodore N. Vail grew out of my work as a reporter on the *Wall Street Journal* during the years 1907-1909. Working with Bill Hazen, a veteran reporter on the *Journal* who covered several important companies, including Telephone, I was occasionally asked to substitute for him in visiting Mr. Vail at 195 Broadway. Although my knowledge of industry and finance was limited at the time, Mr. Vail invariably received me with kindly consideration and I always carried away a story covering some aspect of the Company's operations.

When in 1909 I left the *Journal* to set up my own shop in a very modest way at 34 Pine Street as an independent consultant and had acquired a client or two, I called upon Mr. Vail at his office and suggested a connection. He promptly invited me to spend a weekend with him at his farm in Lyndonville, Vermont.

And so, one Friday evening, sometime during the winter of 1909, I joined him in his car attached to Delaware & Hudson's

Montreal express, which left Grand Central early in the evening, stopping briefly at Lyndonville at 4 A.M.

I still have a lively recollection of leaving the warm Pullman to step out into a typical snowy Vermont wintry landscape. A sleigh and driver behind a couple of lively Morgan horses were awaiting us, and wrapped in heavy furs we were presently hastening to Mr. Vail's farm in the rolling hills several miles away.

As it happened, there had been unusually heavy snowfalls and low temperatures that winter, and his rambling homestead, set amid a cluster of hills all deeply imbedded in heavy snows, presented a Currier & Ives setting which I still recall.

This was Vermont dairy country, and Mr. Vail, who I believe had come from Vermont as a young man to join the U.S. Postal System, becoming in time chief assistant to the Postmaster General, had acquired a considerable acreage of farm lands outside of Lyndonville and was handling a dairy herd of Jerseys and Brown Swiss. I enjoyed his rare hospitality that weekend, skiing over the snowy hills by day and joining him and Mrs. Vail and a few intimates at dinner. Under those conditions it was very easy to develop a working arrangement, which has continued ever since.

No one who ever knew Mr. Vail will ever forget his tall imposing frame and his rosy genial countenance topped with a crown of silky white tousled hair, but, more particularly, his warm responsive personality.

In his knowledge of the nature of public opinion and its influence on a company's affairs, particularly a utility, whose operations, like Telephone's, involve an intimacy with the lives of people, Mr. Vail was far in advance of his time. Long before the management function that we now know as public relations became recognized, Mr. Vail was calling meetings of Telephone companies and exploring with them the Company's relations with its customers; and, as I recall, he sometimes used the term "public relations" at these meetings.

It was characteristic of him, as it has been true of his successors, to think ahead and be prepared for all eventualities—a pattern of management that has been a determining factor in the Company's continuing success.

It is true, of course, that such vast organizations as AT&T cannot be quickly changed by one man. They move slowly. Events, time, and public attitudes have their impact. However, individuals can give direction, develop philosophies, and provide leadership. By force of personality, power, persuasion, and persistence they can make it possible for policies to be carried out even though they are slow to take effect. Vail was such a man. So were two others who developed the modern direction of AT&T and who, over a long, arduous period, strove to have it permeate the entire structure.

Both were of the same age group. Both men graduated from Harvard College the same year and knew each other there. One was the son of the Ambassador to the Court of St. James's and the other became the Ambassador to the Court of St. James's. Both worked together for twenty years to develop and implement their theories, and both were remarkably alike in their concept of how the company should act. They did not begin their joint work until one was forty-four years old and the other forty-two.

Walter Sherman Gifford was born in 1885. Upon graduation from Harvard in 1905 he immediately went to work for Western Electric, the manufacturing arm of AT&T. He became president of AT&T in 1925 and stayed in that post until 1948, when he was chosen chairman of the board. He remained as chairman for two years until President Truman appointed him Ambassador to the Court of St. James's.

Arthur Wilson Page, born two years earlier than Gifford, also graduated from Harvard College in 1905. On graduation he went to work in the family publishing house of Doubleday, Page & Company on the editorial side. From 1913 to 1927 he was vice-president of the company and editor of *The World's Work* except for an army intelligence stint in France during World War I. Page had become editor of *The World's Work* when his father, Walter Hines Page, was appointed by President Wilson to be the Ambassador to the Court of St. James's.

To Gifford, as to other wise managers of other companies since, what the public thought of the company was of great concern. It applied especially to Gifford, for in 1921 Congress passed the Graham Act that, in effect, exempted telephony from the Sherman Anti-Trust Act as far as consolidation of competing companies was concerned. It was clear, for the Graham Act would not otherwise have been passed, that the public had made up its mind to have one telephone service, or a monopoly, in each area. It was realized that it was against the public interest to have competition in telephones. Interstate telephone traffic was under the jurisdiction of the Interstate Commerce Commission. The states and the District of Columbia had commissions which regulated telephone rates and services.

When Gifford became president of AT&T, Ellsworth was publicity manager and advertising manager. Ellsworth, one assistant, and a secretary comprised the entire information operation.

But not only was Ellsworth reaching the retirement age and had, therefore, to be replaced, but there were new rumbles about the telephone company. The war was over. There was a shortage of telephones. There was a shortage of lines, switchboards, trained personnel. People objected to waiting for installation of phones. Telephone traffic was congested. The service was simply bad. When Vail had made his pledge to President Wilson of all-out cooperation in the war effort he had not only meant just that but he acted on it. There was no stinting, no attempt to keep men and materials within the company so that service could be provided at war's end. It was an all-out effort which saw, in 1919 and 1920, more than 25,000 Bell System skilled workers go into the Signal Corps. A telephone system had been set up for the army in France and the newest equipment from Western Electric was sent. There was a dire shortage for post-war civilian use.

The esteem of the company had fallen with the rise of public dissatisfaction. To Gifford this was not only a prime concern for the moment, for the shortage would eventually be overcome, but it meant that more than a publicity program was needed, much more than that, plus an advertising campaign. He knew the company had to have public respect and understanding, so he searched for a man who could help him in the problems facing his new regime.

Page at this time was unhappy with the turn events had taken at Doubleday, Page. He enjoyed his work as editor of *The World's Work*. But F. N. Doubleday, who was of his father's generation, had different ideas on the content of the magazine. He wanted a entertaining picture book, rather than a serious magazine. In addition, Nelson Doubleday, the son, inclined to go along with his father, and it seemed like an insoluble problem. There was no doubt that he could have stayed with the company; if not as editor of the magazine, then in some other capacity. But he had made up his mind that he would look to some other area for a satisfying career.

Page had been writing about the duty of big business in our society. He had been expanding time and again on his theory that corporations derived their right to function from the public. They were incorporated by legislative bodies representing the people and so had to be continuously aware of, and act in, the public interest.

Gifford had read some of Page's pieces and thought well of them, but he wasn't certain exactly what Page could do for AT&T beyond perhaps writing a book about it. As is natural, Gifford was not sure of the details of what he wanted. He knew that he needed a good man to replace Ellsworth; that the company's public problems were serious; that the operation of the company as a big business, a monopoly, demanded a man who understood something of public attitudes; that the new man should have a basic philosophy about the place of the corporation in a democratic society, and could move ahead from the simple information policies under which the company was now operating.

In his recorded talks in 1959 for the Oral History Research Office at Columbia University Page himself tells how he came to AT&T:

> Differences of opinion between the Doubledays and the Pages were always there, but not of any particular importance. You need different kinds of people to make a team anyhow. You oughtn't to all agree. But as time went on, F. N. Doubleday, who was my father's generation, inclined, I thought, more in the direction he ultimately took, which was pretty much opposite to my interests. I think he was the best commercial publisher there's been in the United States in the last fifty years. I think he could do the author more good, because he had a more commercial mind on how to sell books. The publishing business at times has been rather hampered by the fact that the publisher was a literary critic and a lover of books. Well, that isn't his function. A literary critic is a critic, and the author is the author, and the public buys and needs the book. The publisher is supposed to sell it. That's his business. As a publisher you do the public the most good when you sell books.
>
> I think that F. N. Doubleday was the best one there was. Now, if you apply the same thing to magazines, which I didn't exactly, because a magazine has somewhat the responsibility that a teacher has. The author is responsible for the book, but you're responsible for what you say in the magazine, as well as whether you sell it or whether you don't.
>
> I would say from the commercial point of view, both my father and I were more concerned with the success of certain ideas than we were with the maximum of sales, although we understood perfectly that no idea got circulation in a magazine that didn't sell because it had no audience. I don't mean we were not commercial—we were. But Doubleday wanted to leave out the more serious side of the magazine job if you'd call them serious. He

wanted to move into more picture magazines and entertainment. That was all right, except that I didn't want to abandon the kind of magazine we had, because they were what I was interested in.

Well, divergences grew, because as the old gentleman got older, he got somewhat sick. I finally got it into my mind that I didn't want to follow his father for the rest of my life, because his son was a good friend of mine, too, had the same point of view. His son was named Nelson. So I came home here and told my good wife one day, "Now, if you're willing to take a chance, I'm going to quit this thing. I don't know where I'm going or what I'm going to do, but I am going to stop this. But I am not going to jump off this place till I see where I am going to land. I don't want to be in mid-air anywhere."

Well, she said that was all right, go ahead.

So I went back to the office the next day, and about the middle of the day Walter Gifford called me and said, "Are you going to be in town any time soon?"

I said, "Yes, in a couple of days."

"Well," he said, "will you come in and talk to me for a minute?"

He was head of the telephone company. I'd known him some time. We saw each other occasionally. So I went in, and he said they had a problem. Somebody's suggested a book about the telephone, and what did I think of it? I said, "Well, I don't think it'll do you any good, as far as business goes. It may satisfy the vanity of folks in the company, because it'll be a nice book, all very good—but such things don't have much effect upon the public. It won't do you any harm, if you want to have it. It won't do you any good either."

I started to leave. And he said, "Are you wedded to the publishing business?"

"Well," I said, "I hadn't thought about it."

What was in his mind was that I'd been writing editorials about what was the duty of big business in a democracy, and how should they get along, and giving them a lot of free advice. I told him I was interested. What he asked me was to come to the AT&T and see what I could do.

That was a very amazing juxtaposition of things. It all happened within twenty-four hours. So I told him that if they were serious about it—that is, I didn't want to go there as a publicity man—but if they were serious about taking that point of view of the general policy, nothing would please me more than to try to do something instead of telling everybody else to do it. So that's the transition between editorial work and the telephone company, from writing to talking.

So it was that on January 1, 1927, Arthur Page joined AT&T as

a vice-president. It was he who developed corporate public relations as it is practiced by the most enlightened corporations today. It was he who worked out the structure of the first formal public relations department at AT&T and staffed it. It was he who understood so well, and based his practice on, the concept that only by public consent can any corporation survive. And that applies to any other organization that deals with the public in any way, whether it be a business, a university, a trade union, or trade association. His philosophy and its application have major importance for those who have any lingering doubts about the overwhelming importance of the public.

He believed this, had written about it as a magazine editor, and acted upon that belief throughout his career. To him, as he said so often in different ways, "business in a democratic country begins with public permission and exists by public approval." To him, private business had no right to keep its affairs private because of the very nature of its origins. Business had no intrinsic "right" to operate; the American people had given it that right and could take it away.

Page felt that there was, between business and the general public, a contractual relationship that covers a wide range of policies. Since the public has the power to change the terms of the contract, business must in its own interest fully recognize that public's right and power to do so.

Businesses are incorporated by state bodies, which are representatives of the people, and the terms of incorporation can be curtailed, broadened, or changed, depending on what the American public think of what they do and how they act. That is why Page believed that a business had to have a clear policy as to how it intended to act, and then make a reasonable effort to explain this policy to the public. The public could then judge the company, not only by its protestations, or its statement of policy, but by how it performed in the light of the announced policy.

Criticism of big business did not surprise Page. He understood it because, historically, men have feared too much power concentrated in one center, whether that power belonged to big business, big government, or even the church. Power, if it is too great, breeds fear in the individual, and sometimes envy. To Page, because the United States is big—with no trade barriers, a single currency, and good transportation and communications—business has to be big to serve it. Criticism was bound to rise against one company or many, or against large enterprises in general—and Page expected it. That is why it is a duty for a company to tell the public what it is doing, why it is doing it, and what it hopes to do. This follows naturally as part of the Page philosophy, and it entails effort and a reasonable amount of money allocated to informing the public. This, of course, means as many types of publicity as it does advertising. But Page felt that any industry with a large number of employees had, within itself, the biggest single force to explain business and its policies to the public. The effectiveness of the personal element was clear to Page: what the employees said was in fact a testimonial by those who were in a position to know. Page stressed communication with employees as a major factor. What the company did could make them proud, understanding, and vocal.

The company's actions were, therefore, far more important than what it said, and Page insisted there should be no gap between performance and statement of policy. The quality of the product, the service, and the way it was sold or serviced would have a much greater impact than any advertisements or publicity. The public makes up its mind about a company primarily on the basis of its experience with the company, the company's product and/or service, or the company's employees. If this experience shows that the company is generally efficient, courteous, and human, the public will probably be inclined to continue its contract with the business. If the public does not like what it sees, hears, or experiences, it will in time force some change in the contract with the business. The public may even curtail the business's right to operate at all.

Among the many ways of weaving his philosophy into the business, Page believed the most effective was to make the ablest people feel involved. If they were convinced that they were right, they would be the most important force in the company in putting his policies into effect as they moved up the line of command. Basically, that is why he spent so much of his time expanding the public relations department and bringing in specialists in all areas of communication. While working with outside people was not neglected, his essential job was within the business, convincing management that the total work force was the key to good public relations. He knew that the employees were the best ambassadors for the company. They were the ones who could best represent the company, for they knew it by its deeds, not by declarations on paper. Their attitude to the company depended upon how they were treated, and how they saw others treated. And so, employee relations and employee communications, as they have come to be called, were emphasized. In this way all could understand the policies of the company and could answer questions: all could tell why certain actions were taken, why others could not be, and why still others had to be postponed.

It is difficult to assess the full contribution Page made to his company, and to private business generally. But it is easy to give Page his due as the philosopher and most important activist in corporate public relations. Not only did he build, change, and experiment with the basic structure of the public relations department of AT&T, but he convinced the company's leaders that what he recommended and argued for was correct. His contributions were immense in a field so little understood by businessmen and even by corporate public relations directors. Many of them still do not understand, as Page put it, that "public relations, in this country, is the art of adapting big business to a democracy so that the people have confidence that they are being well served and at the same time the business has freedom to serve them well." Page also believed it was essential to be constantly alert to criticisms, not in order to attack the critics, but to learn what public thinking was. Business is not usually condemned for what it did by the standards of the past, but rather by the standards that the public might apply today and tomorrow. By being alert to public attitudes business can, for its own safety, anticipate what the public is going to want to change so that it can itself make those changes.

However, theories, no matter how sound, and practices, no matter how sensible, can never be implemented by a vice-president—and that was Page's rank. A chief executive must be convinced of their validity and effectiveness for the company to give them the impetus to get them off the ground. And in such a massive organization as AT&T, even with the clearest directives and most insistent leadership and command, it takes years before new policies can show their effect. Between top management's acceptance and total performance is the longest of strides.

Gifford was more than convinced of the essential validity of the concepts Page outlined. He acted on his own to implement the ideas. The first step was at Dallas, Texas, on October 27, 1927—some two years after he became president of the company. He chose as a sounding board the Convention of the National Association of Railroad and Utilities Commissioners to announce a policy which was unusual in business history, and perhaps unique. He set out to tell the state commissions that regulated telephone rates within the states, and the Interstate Commerce Commission, which did the same between the states, the fundamentals on which the company was going to act in providing its service to the public. This statement of policy did many things, but it was significant primarily because it was a declaration for everyone—regulatory bodies, general public, stockholders, and employees.

It was the credo of the company, and it was there for all to see. If it were violated, departed from, or not fulfilled, here was the stick to beat the company on the head with. And the stick was put into the hands of the public, the regulatory bodies, the employees, the customers, and the stockholders. Yet it was a simple statement of policies, which, strangely, was at the time almost totally ignored by the press and even the financial community.

In this statement of principles, the Bell System pledged itself to "furnish the best possible telephone service at the lowest cost consistent with financial safety. This policy is bound to succeed in the long run and there is no justification for acting otherwise than for the long run."

The whole policy statement committed the company to many things: an economically run company, lowest possible rates, a financially healthy company, and the promise that all management decisions would be for the long-run benefit of the public, the employees, and the stockholders. There would be, Gifford said, "not only no incentive but it would be contrary to sound policy for management to earn speculative or large profits for distribution as 'melons' or extra dividends." It also meant that payments to stockholders were "limited to reasonable regular dividends with their right, as the business requires new money from time to time, to make further investments on favorable terms."

When earnings were greater than those needed, Gifford said, they were either to be used for improvement of the service or cutting telephone rates. And since the policies on financial safety were a major factor, and success was based on long-run policies, the stockholders would not at any time be seated at a feast-or-famine table. There seems nothing particularly radical today about the Gifford policy. But at the time it was made it set the direction for orderly advance without the often frenzied efforts to make a special showing at any particular period and so hurt the long-term efficiency of the service.

Here then was the frame within which the company was to act.

At the time, it had a greater impact within the organization than outside. Improvement of the service became the first duty of management: more information was provided to the employees about the business; the process of decentralization was continued, but still with strong direction at the top.

It was a year later that Gifford gave further direction to his administration. It was in a speech to the Telephone Pioneers convention in Boston on November 3, 1928. He helped set the tone for the years ahead with one of the bluntest statements by anyone in the company on the recognition that unless the public willed it the company could not long stay in business. It was valid then. It is today. Here is the way Gifford put it: "We must have a satisfactory financial condition if we are to go forward. In addition to that, we must at all times have public approval, because certainly in the United States you can't, no matter what your ability or what your intentions, succeed in the long run without public approval."

That was more than a statement of intention to Gifford. It was a fact of life with him. He knew that good intentions and great ability in the conduct of the business did not, and never could, mean success unless the public approved of company performance. A good profit position for any company, a fine product, satisfied stockholders— these alone did not mean an enterprise could survive. Gifford knew that a business enterprise could, in the short term, act in a way that the public might not approve of, and still survive. That is why he made the distinction between the short and long term. But when the public directs its attention at a company and does not approve of what the company is doing, it means the beginning of the end of that company. This is especially true in the United States, where the public's will and desire can be quickly translated into action by its elected representatives in Congress, state legislatures, or even a village council. The bigger the business, the more immediately this is done.

This means that the corporation—all levels of it, not only the managers—must know that the supreme arbiter for them is public opinion. To have a favorable opinion, much less public approval, a business must be conducted to the public's satisfaction in all its aspects, not only in declarations of high policy. It means also that all the corporation's actions and operations—not just the clearly visible ones—can be exposed to full national scrutiny and still elicit public support. It means that a corporation must so act at all times that it need never fear that any of its decisions, or any of its practices, are of the kind which are in conflict with the mores of the period. Management must always be in a position where it never has anything to hide.

The time may not come often, but it does come, when the public has a hard look at the inner workings of a corporation's practices. It could be during a Congressional investigation or during a long court trial. On these occasions, when the insides of a company are exposed, the facts that are revealed can either be helpful to a company's future, or a long, sharp spike driven into one end of the lid of a coffin.

It was seven years after the Gifford statement at Boston that a joint resolution of Congress authorized the Federal Communications Commission to investigate AT&T. How did Gifford react, remembering that 1935 was part of a period when all big business was suspect? Here is what Gifford said to the inevitable newspaper request for his comment:

> In a business as extensive as ours which so vitally concerns so many people, the public has a right to the fullest information as to how its affairs are conducted. We therefore have no objections to investigations by properly constituted authorities at any time. We have no skeletons in the closet to be exposed.
>
> It is regrettable although perhaps inevitable that public investigations should be disturbing to confidence, at least until all who have criticism to make have made them and the company has had an opportunity to reply. We are primarily concerned with furnishing the people of this country with the best possible telephone service at the lowest possible cost, consistent with fair treatment of employees and of those who have invested their savings in the business. We believe there is no conflict between our aim and the aim of the Federal Communications Commission and we welcome the opportunity to place before that body all the facts as to the manner in which our business is conducted.

Gifford must have been pretty sure of himself when he gave the press that statement. It takes confidence in an organization as vast as his, as decentralized as his, to be prepared to go all the way in an investigation. A company must live clean to enable a chief executive to welcome an inquiry of this kind. As it turned out, the investigation was so dull, the public reputation of the company so good, and "dirt" so absent, that pretty soon the press and the public both lost interest. The only thing resembling a "skeleton" was that the telephone was used by bookies to take bets on horse races.

Gifford's twenty-three-year presidency of AT&T coincided with one of the most momentous periods in America's history. It included the boom of the late 'twenties, the stock market crash, the depression, the New Deal, the rise of Mussolini and Hitler, the attack on Pearl Harbor, the war years, the comradeship with Stalin, the demobilization, the beginnings of the cold war, and the rise of Communist China.

It was the age of bitter ideological conflict and mass unemployment. Fifteen million men—twenty-five per cent of the work force—were searching desperately for a job, any kind of job. Business, particularly big business, had lost the confidence of the nation, and even lost confidence in itself, while its political and moral authority was almost destroyed. President Roosevelt's attack on the "economic royalists," his excoriation of the "unscrupulous money changers," who "stand indicted in the court of public opinion" and who provided "false leadership," was a condemnation of business that reflected the belief of the nation. Desperate men, tired of the vain search for jobs and degraded by public relief, were in a mood of revolt to almost anything that offered them a way out of their bitter plight. The middle class were the new dispossessed. Foreclosures galloped over the farms, cities, and towns, depriving solid citizens of their hope and their homes. A whole country was disillusioned with the ability of capitalism to provide jobs. Wage cuts piled on wage cuts—for those who were lucky enough to be working—and college graduates stood in bread lines, or sold apples, or drove taxis, or scratched for minor civil service jobs—anything so that they could work, maintain their dignity, and stand unashamed before their children.

It was the age of frustration for labor and the drive for unionization of the mass industries. In 1934 there was a general strike in San Francisco and a nationwide textile strike, both of them broken by the militia and vigilantes. In 1937 alone there were more than 5,000 strikes involving more than two million workers. The Committee for Industrial Organization (CIO), which had broken away from the American Federation of Labor (AFL), was a driving force organizing the never-before-organized workers, and after some three years it had a membership of four million, militantly led by John L. Lewis. The seizure of company property and the "sit-down strike" brought court injunctions and violence. The open war continued in South Chicago when police killed ten strikers and sympathizers at Republic Steel's plant, and in the same year United States Steel caved in to the CIO. The Wagner Act, which put the force of the Federal Government behind the drive for unionization of industry, tipped the scale in favor of the unions. The class war became hotter as the newly organized, the unemployed, and the stricken farmer were told again and again that a new economic system was essential since the old one could not work.

It was the age of the growth of radicalism and the intellectual's move to the left. The proletarian novel and theater of protest were in high style. Academicians wrote tracts and learned tomes on the decline of capitalism. Their hearts went out to the aggressive unions and Marxism made a serious impact. The American Newspaper Guild was formed, and newspaper publishers had to raise wages and bargain with their own reporters on hours and working conditions. The clamor from those who said the choice was between fascism and communism drowned out muted sounds from the background from those who said they wanted neither and that reform was the only answer. No one was for laissez faire any longer and *status quo* defenders were minuscule in number. The Communist Party was at its peak when the United Front was the rage. The disillusioned began to leave in droves when the struggle against war and fascism turned into the Hitler-Stalin pact and its defense of isolationism. Then came the holy war when the Soviet Union was attacked—now hours of work could not be too long, nor wages too low, to keep the Russians supplied with arms.

It was the age of extension of government control over business, banking, the stock exchange, transportation, and the hydro-electric power and gas utilities. Odors of unethical practice rose from the Congressional hearings as business leaders followed each other to the witness chair to provide the background for the new Security Exchange Act and the Securities Act. The Tennessee Valley Authority was set up to generate and sell electric power as the government competed with private power companies. It was to be the yardstick for private companies' rates. The Federal Water Power Commission was authorized to regulate the production, transmission, and sale of electric power in interstate commerce, and the Federal Trade Commission was given the same authority over gas, with the right to dissolve holding companies which were against the public interest. The closing of the banks and the almost total paralysis of economic life was followed by the Emergency Banking Act and the blue eagle of the National Recovery Act. Price and wage controls, allocations of men and materials, and stricter government direction during the war all helped to concentrate direction of the economy in Washington.

It was the age of Fascism and Naziism, and of German expansion. When Poland was lost, Churchill's personality and oratory rallied the world to make the stand on the beaches after heroic Dunkirk. Old U.S. destroyers were given to Britain while the great debate of intervention versus isolation roared on, with the America First Committee drawing to it the old-fashioned isolationists, the haters of Britain, and those who thought Hitler was the wave of the future: the argument was ended only by the Japanese attack on Pearl Harbor. It was the time of victory in Europe, the hero Eisenhower, the atomic bomb, the withdrawal of the Soviet Union, and the beginning of the cold war. The Marshall Plan was rebuilding Europe, Germany was rising from the ashes with American direction and help, and Japan was beginning its road back as a hard trade competitor.

How well had Gifford's policies in this age of turbulence worked out? His insistence in 1927 at Dallas that the company had to give the best possible service at the lowest possible price consistent with financial safety, always with the long run in mind; his statement in Boston in 1928 that the company could only succeed with public approval; his annual report in 1929 which outlined the company's responsibilities to its employees and its "aim to pay salaries and wages in all respects adequate and just and to make sure that individual merit is discovered and recognized"; all had their rigorous test. In almost a quarter-century, through the most violent national and international upheaval, the company remained respected and had strong national support because it adhered to its announced and publicly respected policies.

Not even during the most clamorous days of the New Deal was there a serious suggestion that AT&T should be taken over by the government. Nowhere during the Gifford regime were there important attacks on the company even though it was a burgeoning monopoly. At no time was the action of the company, which never cut wages or missed a dividend, such that a politician looking for a popular issue with the voters could successfully make the company his target. This was not an accident or the result of lobbying or devious machinations. It was simply because, to obtain the public approval that was essential to its survival, it acted in the public's interest and the public knew it. Any other course would have meant disaster for this privately owned and privately managed corporation. The stock market crash, the depression, the New Deal, the years of World War II, the postwar readjustments, all of these burned intensely upon the policies and practices of AT&T. At the end of Gifford's career with the company, when he went to London as the Ambassador to the Court of St. James's in 1950, he left behind him a company which was strong in all the areas he had staked out when he took over the top job twenty-five years earlier. Vail built the foundation for AT&T as a monopoly that would serve the nation as a private corporation; Gifford completed the second stage, that of erecting the superstructure. And both, though they came from different backgrounds, had different training, and worked at different times, never forgot who the ultimate boss was. To both it was clearly the public. Both used the same key: performance in the public interest. Both are examples for today's businessmen, who are often bewildered, bitter, or frustrated by the moods of the nation. Both Vail and Gifford are in stark contrast with those of today's titans of industry who believe that it is not in themselves or their actions, but only in the perversity of politicians who rouse the voters against big business, that the trouble lies.

Part of a corporation's getting public approval is telling its story to the public, its employees, its customers, its stockholders, and the Government. This is the reverse of cloaking the operations of the company. It is opening the windows wide. It means an end to secrecy. It means that since the public has an interest—the word "partner" is too wide—it must be informed of all aspects, except trade secrets, of the company. It means full disclosure to the stockholder and an explanation of practices, actions, plans, and even hopes to the public at large and to its customers. In the case of AT&T this means virtually the entire nation. It means informing those who work for the company so that they can first understand the policies and then give witness as to them to all who ask. "None of your business" is an answer which was never effective, and is downright dangerous today.

It is not easy to conduct an effective "telling" policy. Most people are too busy about their own affairs. The children have to be fed and sent off to school; work has to be done on the farm or in the shop or at the office or in the classroom. There are many things more interesting to the public than the story the corporation wants to tell— such as going to a picnic or a ball game or a movie or even staying at home with shoes off watching television.

A policy at the top of providing full information is essential if one wants to do an effective job of informing the public. It needs a skilled staff that understands all the various ways, not only the mass media, of reaching people with its story, men and women who know the difference between simply making the facts and explanations available, and truly communicating them to the potential reader, viewer, or listener.

After Page there was a quick succession at AT&T of those who had the direct responsibility for public relations. Keith S. McHugh had the top job for two years. Clifton W. Phalen had it for two years.

Bartlett T. Miller was responsible for almost five years. Sanford B. Cousins had the post for some four and a half years. James Whitney Cook was public relations chief for six and a half years. Since April 1, 1966, Walter W. Straley has been in charge. In all cases the title for each was "vice-president, information," until 1951, when it was changed to "vice-president, public relations" and the department renamed Public Relations.

Only Miller did not go to college, having entered the Bell System at nineteen after graduation from high school. All worked only for the Bell System. None had any media experience except Straley, who had a minor job for six months at a radio station in Des Moines, Iowa, as a youngster. McHugh had no public relations experience when he came to the top public relations job. Phalen handled public relations and personnel at one of the operating companies, New York Telephone Co., for three years. Miller was public relations vice-president at another operating company, New England Telephone & Telegraph, for a year and a half. Cousins had no public relations experience when he took on the key public relations post for AT&T. Cook had four years' experience in public relations in operating companies, two as a public relations assistant vice-president at Pacific Telephone and Telegraph, and two as vice-president in charge of public relations at Northwestern Bell. Straley worked in the public relations departments at Northwestern Bell and the Pacific Telephone Company, and was for almost three years an assistant vice-president in the public relations department at AT&T. Of the six successors to Page the two men trained most extensively in public relations when chosen for the job were Cook and Straley.

Page, then, was the last of the public relations chiefs at AT&T who had had any worthwhile media experience and the last one to come in at the top from outside. This was the result of the policies he instituted for the department that he built. In the drive to put into practice his theory that everything said and done by everybody in the entire Bell System should be considered on the basis of its acceptability to the public, Page worked to create and maintain a sense of public relations in all officers and employees of the company. This meant that operating personnel from such departments as commercial, sales, plant, and traffic were, from time to time, assigned to the public relations department in various jobs. Usually they worked in customer and community relations, in the speakers' bureau, in public affairs, or as film and lecture aides.

This system had important values to the company. It helped the operating people develop a public relations consciousness that would help them when they returned to their original departments. It also gave the professionals in the public relations department a better idea of the problems in the fields from which the new men came. At no time was this movement intended to give sabbatical leave from an operating job just so that those transferred could meet some new and interesting people. In every case their assignment meant hard work and a chance to produce results in fields outside the areas of their initial training.

It was found that men who had been trained in all sorts of fields— engineering, traffic, commercial, or one of the many other areas— were very good at understanding what was meant by good relations with the public. So they were chosen, finally, for the top post in public relations. The outstanding examples have been Cook and Straley, both of whom understood public attitudes, were able to look ahead for possible changes in views of the public, and knew the history of the company in its search for public approval.

This may not always work out as well in the future for there is often a tendency for those who have never worked with, or in, media to fail to understand the needs of newspapermen, magazine writers, or editors. With their failure to understand often comes fear, for— unlike brochures, annual reports, films, lectures, TV and radio shows, or advertisements—the copy of newspaper reporters and magazine writers cannot be controlled. The result is that stories that may be irritating to management do appear. After seeing a story, the details of which may not be to the wishes of management, the public relations director begins to refuse to make information available even if it is already published. For the same reasons these men who have had no personal experience with news and article writers refuse to permit reporters to see managers, even though these managers are the ones best informed on the subject about which information is sought. And the final step of these frightened men is to close off the very information that the public has a right to know and that the top management of the company has, since Vail's day, been more than willing to make available.

This, of course, does not end the problem. Stories will continue to be written, with or without the cooperation of the public relations people, and before long the gap between the company and media widens, and will ultimately hurt the corporation. Experienced public relations men have not forgotten that the day-in-day-out contact with the public that the company is trying to establish is often achieved through mass media, and the reporter is one of the basic elements of that contact. Indeed it is not too long a step between lack of cooperation with the press, and antagonistic attitudes by reporters that show in their copy. The end result can be to destroy a great deal of the good feeling between the corporation and the public. All this may still happen, despite the wishes of the public relations vice-president, if somewhere on his staff there is an important functionary who stands in the way of the members of the staff to whom press queries are constantly directed. But the greatest fault of all lies in the essential negation of the company's policy of full disclosures, deliberately built in over scores of years.

A look at the careers of Cook and Straley before they were picked for the top job in public relations at AT&T gives a clear idea of the kind of exposure they had to varied company functions.

Cook, a graduate of Yale University, started with New Jersey Bell Telephone Company as a traffic student in 1929. After four months he moved up to assistant traffic supervisor for two years, then traffic supervisor for ten years before he was moved to AT&T's Operations and Engineering Department as an engineer in the traffic division. With three years of that job under his belt Cook was sent to Pacific Telephone and Telegraph Company in 1944 as a traffic results engineer and then moved up to two more years as assistant vice-president, public relations. Then came a shift to Northwestern Bell Telephone Company as vice-president, public relations; then vice-president, general manager; and finally vice president, operations. Next he was transferred back to AT&T as vice-president, administration, for two years; vice-president, merchandising, for three; vice-president, marketing, for six months; and finally, on October 1, 1959, vice-president, public relations.

Cook's experience was as wide as possible, encompassing traffic, operations, administration, marketing, merchandising, as well as public relations. In addition, his work in three different operating companies in three different parts of the country gave him a knowledge of differing public attitudes that was bound to be invaluable to the number one public relations man in the Bell System.

Straley graduated from Grinnell College, at Grinnell, Iowa, in 1933. His first job was with radio station WHO, in Des Moines, where he did relief announcing and some acting, and wrote small plays. In February, 1934, he started as a clerk in the business office of Northwestern Bell Telephone Company. For the next thirteen years he moved through a variety of assignments in the commercial, public relations, and administration departments, until he was sent to San Francisco as a public relations assistant with the Pacific Telephone Company. After three years of that job he was promoted to assistant vice-president in charge of the employee information group. Four years later he was brought to New York to be the assistant vice-president in charge of the advertising section of AT&T. After twenty-one months he was shifted again, this time to be vice-president with the responsibility of organizing the new Southern Counties Area of Pacific Telephone with headquarters in San Diego, and was appointed vice-president and general manager in four months. At the beginning of February, 1960 Straley was elected president of Pacific Telephone-Northwest, with headquarters in Seattle. After seventeen months, when Pacific Northwest Bell Telephone Company, a Bell System company, was set up, he became its president. He remained in Seattle until he was chosen as vice president, public relations, AT&T, almost five years later.

At no time was he far from the direct public relations function, and while president of Pacific Northwest he started *Cascades*, a slick quarterly magazine attractively designed for external as well as internal distribution. He used to write the lead editorials himself.

While Straley and Cook differ in many ways, they have this in common: they both had extensive experience in the Bell System and both had had AT&T training before they were picked for the top public relations responsibility in the organization.

Straley's knowledge of the complex AT&T empire is thorough. But that is never enough. His problem is one all corporation executives face: how to know what is happening so that their judgment can affect all the major decisions before they are made.

AT&T deals with it in this way. The public relations director reports directly to Ben S. Gilmer, president of the company, almost daily—often several times a day. In addition, Straley attends the Monday morning cabinet meetings at which the chairman of the board, the vice-chairman, the president, the executive vice-president, and the sixteen other vice-presidents pose their problems, discuss them, and make the decisions which direct the course of the company. In this way the public relations vice-president is part of the process of decision-making.

Straley keeps his four assistant vice-presidents in New York, as well as the office head in Washington, informed. In turn, Straley is kept posted by these five men on their problems and activities. In addition to the circulation of planning memoranda, there are continuous face-to-face discussions between Straley and these five assistants, as well as numerous staff meetings. To further communication, Straley holds meetings two or three times a year with all members of his department in which trends affecting the telephone business are reported and interpreted.

For better coordination there is an annual meeting at which the public relations vice-presidents of the whole Bell System, that is, those from the associated operating telephone companies, Western Electric, and the Bell Telephone Laboratories, take three and a half days to discuss current and future matters affecting telephone company public relations. This group, which includes key staff members, numbers about thirty people.

All sorts of topics are discussed: the quality of telephone advertising and press services, new concepts in community relations, the effectiveness of employee information, and telephone employee courtesy and reliability. Consideration is also given to the impact of telephone automation on the public and employees and to such significant national issues as civil rights. Studies precede the discussion of a great number of these topics. Authorities from different fields attend the meetings to make presentations and take part in the discussions, usually through extended question-and-answer periods. For instance, there might be present a university sociologist, the head of the National Association for the Advancement of Colored People, and telephone executives who are specialists on the Bell System's vast construction, financing, and research programs. Some of the topics are handled through the panel-discussion method. Often the group probes more deeply by dividing into smaller groups. In fact, the whole meeting is free-wheeling to assure full participation by all those in attendance.

The relationships between AT&T and the associated companies naturally have an important effect on the operations of the public relations departments of the entire Bell System. In simple form the structure is: AT&T owns all the stock of twenty of the operating telephone companies and has some ownership interest in the remaining three. It also owns the Western Electric Company, which together with AT&T, owns the Bell Telephone Laboratories. The operating companies and Western Electric pay dividends to AT&T.

AT&T advises and gives help to the operating companies and runs the long-distance services. Western Electric does the manufacturing, the purchasing, and the central office installation for the whole Bell System. The Bell Telephone Laboratories does the research and development work for the entire system, including Western Electric. The operating companies provide the telephone services and the facilities within their own territories with the help of AT&T.

The same operation pertains to the public relations function. The AT&T public relations people advise and assist on all levels, under license contracts with each of the Bell System companies. These contracts call for AT&T to provide those services which can best be done for the whole system on a centralized basis. And in fact, the public relations department of each component of the Bell System is structured much like the others. They are by no means identical, however, since there are differences in company size and public relations needs.

The AT&T public relations department is headed by a vice-president; so are the public relations departments of the operating companies. Each of these vice-presidents reports to the president of his company and each has a staff of specialists, such as AT&T has. To keep policy lines clear and increase efficiency, the communication between AT&T and the Bell System companies (or the representatives of those companies) is carried on between what the organization calls "coordinates"—people with essentially the same kind of job and responsibility. For instance, the Bell System advertising men deal with each other. So do the press relations men, as do those in public affairs, school relations, films, and the other groups within the public relations departments. Their contacts are often informal. They are continuous. They may be by letter, by telephone, teletype machine, or face-to-face, according to the need for each discussion. The Bell System men in public relations know their coordinates pretty well even though they may see each other only at occasional meetings called to thrash out mutual problems. Almost all of the AT&T public relations staff are former employees of the Bell System companies. Straley, as public relations vice-president, is responsible for coordinating the systems' over-all public relations policy. While informal, these arrangements work rather well.

Straley feels that the chief role of the public relations practitioner in business is to understand the constituencies of business and interpret them to his bosses in management. Sometimes the shadowy reputation of the public relations director derives from a propensity to provide interpretations which his peers and superiors want to hear. Straley thinks, too, that the public relations practitioner is probably put at a disadvantage, for what he hears from the constituents is often irrational and is, therefore, unacceptable at the conference table.

Since the public is made up largely of people who respond in a way of their own choosing, and react mysteriously according to the momentary flow of their emotional juices, this irrationality is the barrier against any permanent success for small or grand plans of opinion manipulation, even though inherently the public relations man seeks to steer opinion. Because the individual's prerogative to make and hold a private judgment—no matter how biased—about a business firm is a freedom to be nourished, public relations can never be truly professional or thoroughly effective. All the practitioner can do, according to Straley, is to hope that the corporation he works for will conduct itself with enough virtue to deserve some bias in its favor. But since virtue lies in the acts of the corporation, not in the telling, it makes many public relations men a trifle self-conscious and somewhat strident in their cries of self-justification. They know that the virtue does not belong to them but to the company they work for.

It may be, thinks Straley, that the most puzzling aspect of relating the public to private business lies in its private status, and that purposeful conduct of private business does not in itself assure the institutional longevity sought by its ownership and management. It is part of management's rationale to know that business survival can only be assured if profits are continuously made. The public relations man knows this, but his irrational instinct tells him that the profit-seeker is at odds with a "spreading ethic which holds that money-making is without virtue." The professional in public relations has failed to convince the curious and indifferent that profit is valuable to society. This, to Straley, is not good enough to assure the perpetuation of private business. The most taxing role of public relations, Straley is certain, is to help management communicate its logic to a world where logic itself has a limited appeal.

In all the twenty operating companies of the Bell System, plus the headquarters, AT&T, there are 640 employees in the public relations departments, exclusive of those at Western Electric and the Bell Laboratories. This does not include secretaries and clerical help. The work force is steady. There is none of the firing and hiring and general instability so characteristic of public relations departments in many other corporations and especially in the public relations agencies. The tenure is solid, for the whole system is interested in the right men. Their average service is 17.3 years; their average age forty-three. Only sixty-eight of them are not college or technical school graduates. As would be expected, the largest single group of public relations people—eighty-six—are in the AT&T operation, for it services so much of the system. In this group, there are seventy-seven men and nine women. The average age is 42.6, which is remarkably similar to the average age of the public relations people in the entire system. Their average service is 16.2 years and seventy-two of them are college or technical school graduates. Forty-two of the eighty-six staffers worked in media before coming to Bell and forty-four have never worked anywhere else except for the company. Their skills are as varied as the whole general and specialized areas in which the public relations department operates.

In an organization so big and continuously growing, with its eighty million telephones serving virtually the entire United States, the functions of these public relations executives are of necessity wide ranging.

Under Straley, each of the four assistant vice-presidents has his own special field to cover. One assistant vice-president heads the programs division; a second is responsible for the advertising division; a third has the responsibility for public and employee information; and the fourth deals with customer and community relations. They all work closely together. On occasion one assistant vice-president may be shifted to another slot with other responsibilities. Sometimes one type of project may be shifted from one assistant vice-president to another. Basically, however, the work areas do not change, although individuals may be moved to some other duty within the public relations department, or to one of the operating companies. For instance, during the New York World's Fair the responsibility for AT&T's exhibit was added to the advertising division of the public relations department.

The community relations section, run by three staff members, coordinates the Bell System's speakers' program, which is extensive and continuously growing. There are seventy-four full-time speakers and about five thousand part-time speakers. Most executives, even though not included in these figures, give a minimum of two talks a year. During 1966, 273,000 talks were given by Bell personnel to about eleven million people. This section also initiates employee participation in community activities and supervises many of these programs. It administers a program that gives information to customers on the use of their telephone; helps in the school relations area through liaison with national education associations and local teachers, and through the use of the Bell System Aids to High School Science, a program that has wide acceptance with science teachers and has won the approval of the National Science Teachers Association for its contribution to science education.

The research group, which has five professionals, coordinates appraisals of telephone service from the customer's point of view. It also initiates flexibility and judgment programs, as opposed to the operating department's stress on practices and measurements. In addition, it analyzes the continuing customer attitude studies, judges internal media performance, tests visual material, and coordinates special Bell System studies and polls.

The customer relations section, handled by five staffers, is responsible for the public relations aspect of customer services, products, and operating practices. Its main jobs are to see that the customer's viewpoint is strongly represented whenever decisions affecting customer services or products are made, and to assist in the information job so that customers can better understand why the company takes a particular course of action. This advocacy of the customer's view is also a function of all Bell System public relations personnel. This section, in addition, gives information on the operating phases of the business, and predicts potential areas of customer problems through analysis of measured customer opinion.

The radio and television section is responsible for all national advertising in the broadcasting media and the Bell Telephone Hour. It also produces some spot commercials, although the associated companies too have this responsibility. It produces the Bell System Science Series. In all cases, this three-man group works with the advertising agencies.

The sales promotion section, run by five members of the public relations staff, works with advertising agencies, and is responsible for booklets, brochures, and product publicity. It is also responsible for special shows and the introductory programs in sales campaigns.

The print advertising section has six staffers who coordinate national advertising in magazines and periodicals. It has nothing to do with newspaper advertising which is the province of the associated companies. Three themes dominate the print advertising program of AT&T: information, sales, and service. Some 350 advertisements are run annually, with the media selection and placement in the hands of one advertising agency. If an example were needed that AT&T does not believe in hit or miss with employees or agencies it is right here. With many companies the length of service of an advertising agency is short. Not only do they change agencies with the ups and downs of sales, but they change with chief executives of the corporations, or for some other reasons which may not have anything to do with performance by the agency. N. W. Ayer and Sons was first retained by AT&T in 1907 and is still the agency handling its work. This must be some sort of record. Ayer does the informative and sales advertising, another group from the same agency handles the Long Lines Department for national long-distance advertising, and a third group from the same agency services the Bell Laboratories. The Yellow Pages program, separate from the other advertising, consists of about two hundred annual advertisements, is serviced by Cunningham & Walsh, and is directed to consumers and directory users. This firm was first retained in 1927 and, incidentally, also handles the advertising for Western Electric. The operating companies of the Bell System use other advertising agencies for their newspaper advertising. In most cases these are local agencies oriented to the territory in which the companies operate.

The exhibits section is divided into two parts. One unit works on special projects. It did the planning, design, engineering and construction supervision of the New York World's Fair exhibit. It also worked on the Seattle World's Fair and on Expo 67, the 1967 Canadian world's fair in Montreal. The second unit is responsible for displays and exhibits of a national or international nature, and in 1966 administered some seventy-four shows as well as maintaining the Bell exhibits at the Franklin Museum in Philadelphia, the Smithsonian Institution, Disneyland, and the Chicago Museum of Science and Industry. There are eight staff members in all in the exhibits section.

Films are an old story to AT&T. This is a function which has been going on since 1915. The film section has eight staffers, plus a full-time projectionist. It produces films and associated materials, such as introductions, leaders' guides, posters, and handouts. The films are of two kinds: training and informative. Some informative films are used for marketing, others tell about the business or are public-service-type films about a subject which is of general interest, not related to the business, but produced to create good will for the company. This group also maintains a Bell System film library of all films produced by AT&T or the associated companies. All the films are made by industrial film producers.

The employee information section, which has seventeen professionals on its staff, plus three artists and two members who run the photo library, is the largest section in the public relations department. This highlights the importance of keeping all those who work for the company as fully informed as possible on all company policies. This section, dealing as it does with internal communications, produces bulletins and magazines, as well as running a photo service for all AT&T workers. It also advises and assists the associated companies, and regularly sends them "syndicated mailings" of material that can be used for bulletins, magazines, and newspapers. The companies in turn send suitable material to AT&T for use at headquarters. Also produced by the employee information section are booklets and the *Bell Telephone Magazine*, which has external distribution. This section also coordinates and supervises the Bell System's part of employee discussion programs.

The personnel and planning section, a one-man operation, handles personnel needs of AT&T's public relations department, spots trends in hiring policies throughout the Bell System, and works on future personnel needs of the various units in the public relations department.

The contributions section, with two staffers, administers the college contribution program. Under this program the Bell System makes contributions annually to privately directed universities, and works on the system's gifts to municipal building programs such as hospitals and schools. It also has a hand in corporate contributions to the United Fund and Red Cross campaigns.

The public affairs section, with four staffers, is a project to keep employees informed on government activities, pending issues, and election campaigns. It regularly issues background and public affairs bulletins. This group also does analyses and trend-spotting in government affairs, and prepares material for speakers in the Bell System.

The press relations group, made up of six people, interprets the Bell System to the public through material to national magazines, New York's metropolitan newspapers, and the major wire services and broadcast media. One of its biggest jobs is to answer queries from reporters and editors of both domestic and foreign publications, and to help them in the preparation of material. It is a decentralized organization. The AT&T press relations group works closely with the news staffers from the associated companies of the system who, in many cases, report to the operating heads of their units. This press relations group also supplies material to the news people from the associated companies for distribution on a local basis. Its whole operation is based on the philosophy of telling the public, the company's customers, about the actions and operations of AT&T that affect them. It works on the "open door" theory and the public is immediately told of important events. It issues few press releases. In 1962 this section sent out forty-two releases; in 1963, thirty-nine releases; in 1964 twenty-nine releases; in 1965 forty releases; and in 1966, seventy-five. But the press, radio, television, and magazine contacts run into the thousands each year.

The news service manager in Washington has a two-man organization. It services the Washington press corps with AT&T information, covers those Federal Communications Commission and Congressional hearings that may interest headquarters, and answers background questions about people testifying at Washington.

The public relations director in Washington is a one-man show. He keeps in touch with public information officers in government agencies; works with Bellcomm, a Bell subsidiary formed to help the National Aeronautics and Space Agency with systems engineering; and supplies information to Bell System companies on government agency actions that affect them.

The largest single group in AT&T's public relations department works to keep the employees informed. The group which deals with the press never pushes for space or notice, and is small. Every one of the functions that the public relations department carries out is vital to the company and, when the company's size is considered, is by no means overloaded with personnel.

The policy of keeping the public informed can be carried out only with skilled people, well trained in their specialties, who know the company, understand its history and have had a real exposure to the problems—both long and short term—of AT&T. But, important as is the public relations department, it can never do the entire job. That is for the whole company, and it is the continuous work of the company to make everyone, from the chief executive all the way down the line, fully appreciative of the fact that to do a technical job is never enough. All in the company have to be aware that wherever they are, or whatever they do, they are representatives of the company. That is the basic reason why it is next to impossible for AT&T to take any course which has not been fully considered from the viewpoint of its impact on the public.

It is no accident that in communities where Bell System people work, there is always a telephone man active in local affairs. It may be the Boy Scouts, Red Cross, local service clubs, Community Chest, Urban League, the committee to keep the streets clean, or a group to raise funds for the local hospital or help in a school bond drive or for urban renewal—a telephone executive will be lending a hand. Nor is this public service limited to the lending of a manager's name. Telephone company practice is for him to participate in these activities himself, not by proxy. In many towns and cities the first call made by any group to improve the local area, or to promote some good cause, is on the telephone company manager. And his answer, if he is a good telephone man, is to respond quickly to the request for help.

Of course, this goes just as much for the man at the top as it does for the minor executive in the out-of-the-way hamlet. Frederick R. Kappel, for ten years chief executive of AT&T until he retired at the end of 1966, did his share of public service in many areas. He was a trustee of New York's Presbyterian Hospital, Grand Central Art Galleries, the National Safety Council, the Tax Foundation, the Committee for Economic Development, the American Heritage Foundation, the University of Minnesota Foundation, Columbia University, and the YMCA of Greater New York. He was also a director of the Boys' Clubs of America, the Academy of Political Science, the advisory board of the Salvation Army in New York City, the Board of Governors of the American Red Cross, the national advisory committee of Tuskegee Institute, and the business committee for the John F. Kennedy Center for the Performing Arts. And he was more than a letter-head name in all of them.

Romnes, even before he became chief executive, was busy serving on the boards of community organizations. His list will increase and probably change, but when he took over the top job at the company his outside activities included being a director of the National Safety Council and the American Cancer Society; trustee of the Westminster Choir College and the Wisconsin Alumni Research Foundation; and member of the advisory board of the Salvation Army, the national corporations committee of the United Negro College Fund, and the National Urban League corporate support committee.

AT&T's reasons for the community activities by telephone executives were underlined when Kappel spoke to the Telephone Pioneers in 1959: "In the years ahead this big industry of ours will grow bigger than ever—much bigger. This makes it all the more important for us to conduct ourselves, in each community, as people who deserve the trust and esteem of our fellow citizens. Our responsibilities are continuously on the increase—and we must measure up."

Slowly, over the course of years, certain changes do take place in an organization, even one as large as AT&T. And it shows up in the type of man who is picked to head the company. Romnes, who became chairman in January, 1967, is a less exuberant personality than Kappel, and is as different from Gifford as Gifford was from Vail. Vail, the civil servant; Gifford, the Harvard man of the liberal arts; Kappel, the electrical engineer from the University of Minnesota; Romnes, the inventor—all have made different contributions to AT&T. But in one area they have been similar: they all understood that success depends on the permission of the public.

Kappel often said, "I am a private enterpriser from my hat to my socks." But that did not mean that he is opposed to regulation of the telephone business by the government. He has said so often, but nowhere more clearly than when writing a series of articles in the *Christian Science Monitor* in 1958. Here is the way he put it then:

> The Bell System is in no way opposed to regulation. We are not merely not opposed to it, we are for it—and this is no lip service. A business like ours, which doesn't have competition in

the same degree as many others, has to be regulated. But this doesn't make us different from other people. We react to incentives and opportunity just as they do. We too need good earnings and ample resources to put in improvements and economies. We too need freedom—under regulation—to do our very best.

Romnes's thinking can be summed up generally by what he said on two occasions after he was made president. On March 7, 1966, speaking in Chicago, he had this to say:

If our experience of regulation has given us any wisdom, it is this: that the best defense against too much regulation or unduly restrictive regulation is doing what's right because it *is* right and not because you're told to. And the best assurance that the public will be on your side when the chips are down is to do the best job you know how to do.

Our customers can't take their business across the street if they are not pleased with our performance. But the very fact that they can't makes it doubly important that we please them. If we fall short of public expectations, the freedom with which we operate, our profitability, the initiatives in forward-looking technology and operations that good earnings permit us, could all be seriously impaired.

On May 17, 1966, Romnes spoke to the Wisconsin Manufacturers Association in Milwaukee. On the relations between private enterprise and the Government he said:

As much as we might yearn for the Jeffersonian ideal of a nation of self-sustaining husbandmen, realism requires that we confront a future in which the public and private sectors will become more and more intertwined. But that this necessarily involves a loss of business freedom I would deny. By freedom I do not mean the license to act arbitrarily and heedless of public consequences. I mean the much more difficult freedom that can only be maintained (and won where it has been lost) by responsibility. To put it bluntly, our experience of half-a-century of regulation tells us that the best defense against too much regulation, unduly restrictive regulation, is performance.

And in the same address on maximizing profits, he said:

There may be some who feel that profit and profit alone is the proper measure of a business's performance and that to accommodate to other considerations is bad business. I don't agree. We

have a responsibility not only for today's profits but tomorrow's—
and a responsibility as well for helping to maintain the kind of
economic environment that will make future profits possible.
More fundamentally, if by our own performance we fail to demonstrate—and demonstrate continuously—that free enterprise provides the best and most effective way to organize and utilize the
productive energies of our country, there won't be any profits
after a while—and there won't be any enterprise.

In these attitudes, different though Kappel and Romnes are in
style from Vail and Gifford, they are in direct succession. Kappel and
Romnes represent the modern breed of company senior executives.
And the chances are that those who follow will be cut the same way,
for the entire organization has been so indoctrinated. Regardless of
the different emphasis others may give, the fundamental is the same.
It will have to be. There will be no other choice.

Kappel was born in 1902 in Alert Lea, Minnesota, a town which
today only has a population of some 14,000. He was the son of a
cigar store and barber shop owner. He had a paper route and through
his high school days he got up before dawn to sweep and clean his
father's store before going to school. At University he waited on tables,
played the drums in dance bands, and did other odd jobs to pay
his fees.

About six months before Gifford became president of AT&T,
Kappel got his first job. It was with Northwestern Bell Telephone
Company as a post hole digger. In twenty-five years with the same
company, he was an interference engineer, a foreign wire relations
engineer, a transmission and protection engineer, a commercial survey
engineer, a transmission and protection engineer, an equipment and
building engineer, a plant engineer, a plant operations supervisor, an
operations assistant vice-president, and then, for seven years, operations vice-president and a director at Northwestern Bell.

In 1949 he became assistant vice-president in the operations and
engineering department of AT&T, then vice-president, long lines department, and, soon after, vice-president, operations and engineering
department, for six years. He then spent some two and a half years as
president of Western Electric before being chosen president of AT&T
in 1956. The chief executive of AT&T was historically the president
but since 1961 he has been the chairman of the board, and Kappel
moved to that office with the new title, although there was no change
in his actual status. So from 1956 until his retirement Kappel had
the main responsibility in the company.

Romnes's background and his early training are remarkably like those of his predecessor. He was born in a small town, Stoughton, Wisconsin, in 1907. He attended the local public and high schools. As the eldest of five children, Haakon Ingolf Romnes—whose origins are Norwegian—did the selling in the family bake shop while his brothers and sisters helped their father stoke the fires of the ovens, knead the dough, and clean the store.

Like Kappel, Romnes worked for only one employer—the Bell System. On graduation as an electrical engineer from the University of Wisconsin in 1928, his first job was with a construction crew for the Wisconsin Telephone Company. He later moved to Bell Telephone Laboratories for seven years as a member of the technical staff in circuit design work. During this period six patents were issued in his name before he moved to AT&T. In the next fifteen years he worked in engineering management before being picked to move to Illinois Bell, where he became chief engineer of the operating company. Two years later he was back with AT&T, where in five years he rose to be vice-president, operations, before his shift in 1959 to the presidency of Western Electric Company. As one of the chosen few, his promotion was still more rapid after his four years with the manufacturing company.

Romnes became vice-chairman of the board of AT&T at the beginning of 1964, then president and a member of the board and the executive committee the following year, with the promotion to chairman only two years later. Romnes brought to the top job in the Bell System intimate experience in all three major functions of the organization—research, manufacturing and operations—training that made him thoroughly familiar with the problems of a company that is quickly expanding and whose public and governmental problems are becoming more and more complex and difficult.

Of all Romnes's jobs, on few does he keep his eye more closely than the company's stockholder relations. To him stockholders are the owners of the business, not just in name but in fact, and they are one of the groups to whom any wise management of a large enterprise will always pay the most careful heed. For the stockholder is many things. He is, in addition to being owner, the source of more capital. He is also a customer, a voter, a friend, an ally. He is an important part of the public who must be kept fully informed on the conduct of his business. And when there are so many of them their impact on the future welfare of the business is immense. It is for these reasons that Romnes directs the stockholder relations of the company although it is, on the chart, under the aegis of the secretary of the company, who has the rank of vice-president and is responsible for day-to-day operations.

AT&T has always been solicitous of the stockholder, even when there were only four of them at the time the present company was incorporated in 1885. As the number of stockholders grew, so did AT&T's care for them. To many companies, the thinking of stockholders, consulting with them, or reporting the facts to them (beyond mailing dividend checks) is very little more than the law imposes on management. This is not so at AT&T, and it has paid off all across the board from increases in numbers to active support in the community, from a bulwark of the economic system to suggestions for improvement of service, from interested followers of company activities to defenders of the maintenance of the telephone company as a privately owned and privately operated business.

Today, AT&T has more than three million stockholders and the growth has been phenomenal. In 1920 there were 139,488; in 1930, 567,500; in 1940, 630,000; in 1950, 986,000; in 1960, 1,911,000. Their profile is an interesting one: forty per cent of them are women; thirty per cent are joint accounts of man and wife; about fifty per cent of the stockholders own fewer than 30 shares. More than ninety-nine per cent of the stock is held within the United States with better than half the stockholders living in New England, New York, Pennsylvania, Maryland, New Jersey and the District of Columbia. Yet despite their numbers, every possible effort is made to keep close to them, to let them know what is going on in the company and its plans for the future.

There are seven basic information pieces mailed to the stockholders: the annual report, the report of the annual meeting, the quarterly statements, the proxy material. Through advertising and statements to the news media, which are widely used because of the importance of the company, more information reaches stockholders. But the newest development is what AT&T calls its Share Owner-Management Visit Program in which stockholders are visited in their homes by middle-management personnel of the company.

This program began as a pilot project in 1954 and became full-fledged in 1956. This is the way it works:

In all the Bell System companies, middle-management people take courses on AT&T's financial structure and the objectives of the company. The type of question that stockholders may ask are studied in advance. Material is provided for homework for those attending the course, which runs from two to five days. This is done during company working hours. Stockholders' names are chosen at random; letters go out to them from AT&T's corporate secretary, telling of the management-visits-with-stockholders program and that they will be telephoned to arrange an appointment to their convenience. The manager who has been given a stockholder's name calls, makes an appointment to see him in his home. Usually the session involves the stockholder and his family. The company representative hears at first hand the questions that are in the minds of the stockholder and his family, their opinions of the company and its service, and their criticisms. Where an answer to a problem can be given immediately it is done. If not, when the answers are later obtained by the manager he writes, phones, or again visits the stockholder. After the manager has finished his work with the stockholder, he writes a report to the person in the associated company who is in charge of the Share Owner-Management Visit Program.

Stockholders respond warmly to these visits. They feel that the company treats them as more than a name and number. They also get answers to all their queries, which usually center around earnings, growth, construction, and the long-term prospects of the company. There are no overtime charges. It is an inexpensive program for the company and has been so valuable that visits by managers to stockholders now run to more than 100,000 a year. It is the newest, and probably the most effective, aspect of stockholder relations at AT&T.

There is value to these visits beyond the immediate advantages to the stockholders as customers and as members of the general public. Also, the "feedback" here can help improve telephone service itself, for the stockholder develops an interest in the company that is deeper than the dividend check and the growth of his stock.

Letters to the company from stockholders are always carefully answered, not only as a simple courtesy, but because management wants them to know more and more about AT&T. For instance, all those letters, except the routine ones, that are addressed to Romnes go to his office. The important ones are put on his desk, with copies made and sent to the secretary of the company for the preparation of an answer. Often Romnes will dictate his own answer. He signs all letters which go from his office. Monthly reports of all stockholder letters, with a breakdown of their questions according to the area of inquiry, are made to the chief executive, and during the proxy period the volume of mail increases sharply. Before the annual meeting Romnes gets weekly reports that give the attitudes and subjects of stockholder queries.

As more and more people have bought stock in AT&T, the annual meeting itself has grown and changed. Until 1924 the annual meetings were held in the board room at 195 Broadway. The attendance in that year was under forty, although there were some 345,000 stockholders. The year 1925 was the first in which there was a large stockholder attendance at the annual meeting. There were about 300 stockholders present and the meeting was moved to the assembly hall. The attendance began to climb until, in 1954, the last year the annual meeting was held in the assembly hall of 195 Broadway, there were almost 1,000 present.

In 1955 it was necessary to move the meeting to 50 Varick Street, and the attendance began to run between 2,000 and 3,000. In 1961 the annual meeting was shifted to McCormick Place in Chicago and the attendance rose to 20,109. In 1962 it shifted to Kingsbridge Armory in the Bronx, and the attendance was 3,254. It was held in the same place in 1963 with the attendance 3,751; at the same place again in 1964 with an attendance of 4,411. In 1965 it went to Convention Hall in Philadelphia and Cobo Hall, Detroit, in 1966—attendance each time more than 4,000. In 1967 it was held at Civic Center in Baltimore with 4,801 stockholders present. Stockholders are not provided with a lunch because the feeding problem is unmanageable with crowds running this size. The annual meeting, except for the intrusion of those who are exhibitionists, continues to be an important part of keeping the owners of the company informed.

In recent years, these meetings have been disturbed by those who use them as platforms for personal showmanship. The antics of these publicity seekers have antagonized the stockholders who come to listen, ask questions, and learn. The problem has become so bothersome that Kappel, in his last report before retirement, wrote to stockholders about the annual 1966 meeting: "The meeting lasted a little over four and a half hours. More than two hours, or some three-fifths of the total discussion time, were taken by the remarks of three share owners and by their questions and answers thereto. Several other members of the meeting came to the microphones to express their annoyance over this, and before adjournment came most of the shareholders had left."

While the public relations department of AT&T is not responsible for stockholder relations, its members are often called in for writing chores as well as for other help. The annual report and the report of the annual meeting are both prepared by a vice-president, Prescott C. Mabon, who is the assistant to Romnes. The proxy material is prepared mostly by the legal department, with the treasury department maintaining all stock records. AT&T acts as its own transfer agent and handles from 350,000 to 600,000 contacts a year, from letters to telephone calls to requests for changes of address by its 700 full-

time employees. The number of persons in the company who spend all
their time on stockholder relations is surprisingly small: there are four
professional and three clerical people in the office of the secretary of
the company; letters from stockholders number between 6,000 and
7,000 a year.

All business is involved with government, and the trend is that the
involvement will intensify rather than diminish. With AT&T, government has always been an important factor since governmental
agencies—the regulatory bodies—set the standards for service and
rates. It is important for all large business enterprises to see that their
relations with governments at all levels are good, but for the telephone companies it involves survival as privately owned and privately
run businesses. The policies of AT&T in its government relations
remain basically the same under Romnes as they were in Vail's time:
to so conduct its operations, all aspects of them, that there will be no
credit to any government official or office-seeker in harassing or attacking the company. Kappel put the company's position this way in
a talk to The Bond Club of New York on November 20, 1958:

> Let us once and for all get over the habit of going to people in
> government when we need something, and ignoring them when
> we have nothing to ask for. Let's never ignore them. And I mean
> never. Let us rather, as their constituents, invite them on all
> suitable occasions to tell us what they have been doing. Let us
> tell them our plans and take a sincere interest in theirs. Let us
> by all means increase our understanding of their problems, as we
> hope they will gain insight into ours.

Since 1935, AT&T has kept a Washington office, run by a vice-
president, which devotes itself to government relations. It is responsible for coordinating telephone service for the agencies of the Federal
Government but it also provides the information about the communications business to the Executive Branch and to Congress. In addition, it keeps the Bell System informed of everything happening in
the government that may affect the operations of the system. At every
opportunity AT&T will appear before open hearings and testify about
legislation that may affect the telephone companies. Investment tax
credit, excise taxes, overtime pay: the whole range of possible subjects that concern AT&T are openly discussed before Congressional
committees. The Washington office also keeps the government informed by answering all questions, sending material to officials who
may be interested, and, when the need arises, interviewing members
of Congress and their staffs.

To keep informed on what is being done in Washington, all sorts of official and semi-official publications are carefully checked for items, speeches, or notices of actions that may in some way affect AT&T's operations. The government relations staff in Washington has twelve management people. Five are registered lobbyists and handle legislative and legal matters. The others provide liaison with government agencies and departments on communications problems. No outside lobbyists are used although, on rare occasions in the past, outside counsel has been retained. Testimony before governmental committees is prepared by the witnesses who, prior to the presentation, review it with those departments that may be affected by what witnesses may say. There is no involvement here of the public relations department.

In the field of regulation at the national level, since the Federal Communications Commission supervises the activities of the Bell System which cross state boundaries, AT&T has a regulatory matters department under a vice-president. Its primary responsibility is to coordinate all Bell System activities with the FCC. When the system has a new offering, such as Wide Area Telephone Service, air-to-ground telephone service, or "after 9 P.M. lower rates," the regulatory matters department prepares all materials needed to present the company's position. Periodic meetings are also held with the FCC to review operations of the Bell System, its earnings, construction program, and capital needs.

When it comes to state regulatory bodies that deal with service and rates, the individual telephone companies are responsible. To do this job each company has a staff which can make the required written reports to the regulators and help coordinate the company's witnesses when there are formal or informal hearings. These state regulatory bodies have an association—the National Association of Railroad and Utility Commissioners—with a Washington office. The five major federal regulatory agencies are represented in this association's board of directors. And here is where the regulatory matters department of AT&T again comes into the picture. It answers requests from N.A.R.-U.C. for material, expert witnesses, or for a Bell System position on some aspect of regulation.

In the days following October 27, 1965, AT&T learned what surprise, haste, frustration and anger can do to affect its relations with the public. Though organized to act rationally at all times and trained to be continuously aware of the impact of all management decisions on the nation's thinking, on that day the top leadership of the company forgot its traditions and ignored its history.

How Kappel lapsed from the Vail and Gifford dicta can be seen from his statement issued following the Federal Communications Commission announcement that day of an investigation of the Bell System's interstate and foreign telephone rates:

> The action taken today by the FCC is totally unwarranted and unnecessary, and in the final analysis the telephone-using public will be the loser.
>
> There are no interstate problems confronting the FCC that could not be resolved faster and with far less expense by means other than the sweeping action taken by the Commission. Without resorting to such a painfully slow and costly investigation, the Commission over the years has effected rate reductions which now amount to savings of about $1 billion annually to the American public. The latest reduction of $100 million was made only a few months ago, and interstate telephone rates today are twenty-two per cent below the levels of 1940.
>
> The Commission, by this course of action, will be casting aside regulatory policies that have been most effective and have produced excellent results through a minimum expenditure of time and money to both the Commission and the users of telephone service.
>
> The energies of the many telephone people required to work on a case like this could be better expended to help keep our economy growing.

The following morning, the newspapers carried the Kappel answer within the story of the FCC announcement. *The New York Times* reported that the chairman of the company "denounced the planned investigation." Other newspapers used similar descriptions of Kappel's statement. Editorially, the *Milwaukee Journal* said on November 4:

> The investigation is likely to be "painfully slow and costly" as Chairman Frederick Kappel of AT&T says. Yet a comprehensive study would seem to be warranted. Without it FCC has no realistic bench marks on which to base realistic rates or carry on future negotiations with the company. In the public interest and under the law, the FCC has a clear right and duty to look into the affairs of AT&T.

The St. Louis *Post-Dispatch*, on October 29, took this position:

> The Federal Communications Commission deserves special commendation and support for its decision to make a comprehensive investigation of telephone rates on its own initiative. One of the

most serious shortcomings of the regulatory agencies generally is that they assume a passive and piecemeal role. . . . We trust the company will give complete cooperation in the work at arriving at these determinations.

On the same day the New York *Daily News* editorially supported the company's position this way:

You'll pardon us if we take a dim—an exceedingly dim—view of this AT&T probe by a commission which up to now has been chiefly distinguished for small-minded hectoring and bullying of the television and radio industries.

On January 4, 1966 *The New York Times* insisted that:

The investigation can be particularly useful if it provides some real ground rules for operation of a regulated industry in an era of swift technological change. But this will require the Bell System's full cooperation. So far the company has been acting as if the FCC were off the track in calling for a thorough study. In our view the commission is simply going about doing the regulatory job that it was set up to do.

And on June 8 the *Times*, in an editorial headed "The A.T.&T. Investigation," took this position:

There is no telling what the outcome will be. But there is no doubt at all that the investigation itself is worth holding. The system requires a thorough and open examination to demonstrate that it is giving the public fair value. Even more important, the FCC must show that it has the capacity and the will to regulate effectively. The investigation should provide as useful an appraisal of the regulators as it does of the monopoly it is charged with regulating.

To *Fortune*, in its June, 1966 issue,

AT&T's first public reaction to the commission's decision to hold a formal investigation was one of outrage. Since then the company has moderated its attitude, but it still questions (unsuccessfully) the fairness of the procedures the FCC will follow in conducting the inquiry.

Every step of the way after the first statement was issued, in answer to the FCC announced investigation, AT&T was more moderate in its approach. Almost immediately following Kappel's initial release, Romnes, then president of the company, tried to make the company's hard line softer, at least at the edges, and this continued right through the end of Kappel's reign. In his last report to the stockholders, following the April 1966 annual meeting, he wrote:

> Regulation of our rates and earnings is nothing new. We have long been regulated by state commissions and our interstate and international service have been regulated by the FCC for more than thirty years. Soon after the FCC was organized in 1935, it conducted a thorough investigation of our business. We said we had no skeletons in the closet and the investigation showed this to be true. In fact, we have demonstrated under continuous regulation that our business is conducted in the public interest and we are confident that the current proceeding will reaffirm this.

There is no doubt that the FCC announcement had a depressing effect on the market price of AT&T stock. For instance, between October 28, the day following the FCC statement, and February 2, 1966, the price of the stock fell from 66⅞ to 58⅝, a loss of $4.36 billion on paper to the company's investors. And before the end of 1966 the stock went as low as 50½. But how much of this lack of confidence in a booming company was due to the general slide of the whole market—particularly the blue-chip stocks—how much to the FCC, and how much to the Kappel statement, no one can tell. But it is reasonable to assume that the Kappel reaction to the FCC statement did the market price of the stock no good. If anything, an investor might well say that if AT&T is so bitter about the investigation by FCC, something it could not stop, perhaps he had better be cautious. This view was underlined in a *New York Times* report of December 27, 1965, when it was noted that members of the FCC felt that much of the adverse effect on the market came from the company's failure to simply advise the public that it disagreed with the FCC approach "instead of acting 'like a stuck pig.' "

The question then naturally arises: why did Kappel—so thoroughly aware of the company's policies in its relations with the public, so clear in his thinking about the effect on the nation of what the chief executive of the company says and does, so successful in building AT&T to its position of eminence—act in such a precipitous way? What lay behind the Kappel statement, so out of keeping with the company's imbedded policy of always offering to cooperate with all governmental bodies in all investigations?

Part of the answer lies in the fact that Kappel has a low boiling point. He was a vigorous chief executive, aggressive in his expansion of the company, and certain that his views were right, as they usually were. He obviously reacted against the FCC announcement as harshly as he did because he was taken by surprise, had no inkling that such a move was in the offing. And while the responsibility has to be Kappel's, since he was the chief executive, there are others who had a hand in the policy decision and the statement.

What happens when a press statement is prepared for release is governed by many factors, including length of time available for preparation and the complexity or technical nature of the subject. If there is ample time, a draft is written, circulated to company people who work directly with the subject, revised if there are comments for changes, and then, only then, is the statement issued. Where the time is short, when for instance a reply has to be issued within an hour, the people directly involved meet in an office, talk over the policy and then draft the statement. In either way the public relations department has a part in the discussion. If it is a policy statement, a member of the public relations department drafts it. At a minimum he gets a chance to comment on it, or in the case of a short-fuse assignment, he participates in preparation.

This case was a short-fuse one. Without advance notice, the FCC released its statement at 3:15 P.M. Kappel did not know about it until 3:30 that afternoon. A meeting was immediately called in his office. Present were the top company authority in regulatory matters, a representative from the legal department, a member of the public relations staff, and one or two others who were called in for the discussion and drafting. They were offended by the FCC action. Obviously the tradition of Vail and Gifford had been so far in the back of the group's mind that it did not register until after the statement, released at 4:45 P.M., had been reported by the press, radio, and television the following morning.

Both 1965 and 1966 were unusually profitable years for AT&T. The company grew remarkably, the increase in number of telephones breaking all records. Long distance calls in 1966 were fourteen per cent higher than in the previous year. The service is growing much faster than the country as a whole. Since 1950, for example, with a population increase of thirty per cent, the number of Bell System telephones has more than doubled, and long distance calls have tripled. If the growth continues, even at the same rate during the next fifteen years, AT&T will continue to grow even more quickly in proportion to the population. The business has also grown faster than the nation's economy. Since 1950 the Gross National Product has risen about fifty per cent, while the Bell System's business has nearly tripled. The company is lusty and growing solidly. AT&T will survive this investigation by FCC, no matter what changes are made in the rate structures. But what this incident showed above all was that even a Kappel, forgetting history, piqued by an act he was certain was wrong, could overlook the public impact of a statement which announces company views.

All in all, the whole Bell System is fully responsive to the legislators and regulators for information about company views on everything affecting it, and it is equally active in giving testimony on the impact of any government measures on telephone customers, employees, and stockholders. The views of the governmental bodies—what they think and the trends they are taking—are woven into the heart of management's daily tasks. None dares forget them. Nor could management, if it wanted to, for government relations are far too important. Government so much represents public thinking that what is public objection today can mean government action tomorrow. It is not an exaggeration to say that governmental bodies are both the watchdog and the instrument of public will. The relationship is direct, immediate, and there is not one telephone manager worth his pay in the whole Bell System who does not know it. He is born into it when he enters the company and grows up with it. Everything done internally with the employees is directly related to the impression their daily actions have on the public and so, ultimately, on government.

A large part of the continuous employee orientation is by the written word, but by no means all of it. AT&T uses the spoken word extensively, for it is often a more effective communication tool. Some of the oral communication is one-way: lectures, closed-circuit television, or recorded messages. The development of this phase of the employee information program varies from company to company within the Bell System, for the primary responsibility is at that level. For instance, in the recorded message field, twelve of the companies have "communicator tapes" which carry company news and other news affecting AT&T or the operating company. By dialing a local telephone number the employees can hear about personnel changes; on- and off-the-job activities; new developments that have a bearing on the work of the company; Washington news that may affect operations. For the special use of telephone operators, fifteen of the Bell companies have a similar message system available at the switchboard. During a lull in handling telephone calls the operators can plug into a special jack on the switchboard and hear about activities that may interest them.

This has been carried a step forward by the New England Telephone and Telegraph Company, one of AT&T's subsidiaries. It uses a closed-circuit television set-up. When there are valleys in the calling volume, which follow an up-and-down pattern throughout the day, operators get together in small TV lounges right in their office and watch training films; live or taped video presentations; and slide talks.

But the discussion meeting, or two-way communication, is the newest and in many ways the most promising of the means of people within the company developing a better understanding of the issues with which they are involved. Two of the companies, Northwestern Bell Telephone Company and Southern Bell Telephone and Telegraph Company, have been holding discussion meetings since the late 1950's. Other Bell companies have started programs more recently, and, as the programs grew, innovations have been added to make them more effective.

The best of these discussion meetings have been those which have been held on a regular basis. Catch-as-catch-can meetings, held without organization or focus, are ineffective. The meetings have to be held in a relaxed atmosphere and must be informal. Experience has shown that only under these conditions, will people speak up and begin an easy flow of ideas.

In these discussion meetings, eight to twelve people meet with their immediate supervisor to explore a subject previously suggested by the employees after earlier talks. The meetings usually last about an hour and, ideally, each employee attends a minimum of four times a year. The supervisor uses a discussion guide, which has an outline of the subject and some background information. There are almost 100 of these guides, prepared over many years, to cover almost any subject in which the employees are interested. They may be on automation, taxes, pensions, benefits, wages, "the spirit of service," new equipment and services, interdepartmental relations, the work of the Bell Laboratories, direct distance dialing, customer views of the company, or all-number dialing. In some companies short films are used as discussion starters and in others a skip-level technique is used where, for a change of pace, the boss's boss conducts the session.

This discussion meeting has many values aside from the increase in knowledge by both the supervisor, who has to prepare for the discussions, and the employees. The supervisor gets a better understanding of his employees, their informational needs, and their job problems. The employee gets a fuller understanding of the telephone business and of his supervisor, as well as recognition, if he has not had it before, that he is important to the company as an individual.

By feeding employee questions and problems up the line, and management's answers and plans down the line, a sort of two-way communications highway is built. It can be used up, or down, to deal with the most complicated, difficult, or controversial subjects, and the rapport built by the discussion meetings makes normal, day-to-day communication easier. In addition, it has been found that employees become more interested in the printed material the company distributes.

In any study of the internal operations of AT&T one theme is seen as overriding. It is stressed by the top executives of the headquarters company. It is underlined by the presidents of the operating companies. It is repeated by all managers in talks with employees and reiterated in all training manuals. It appears consistently in all company publications until, like an article of faith, it is imbedded in the consciousness of all who would be considered for promotion. And that theme is that the company operates only by public permission, and that the base of public acceptance is service. Time and again it is hammered home that public attitudes are grounded on personal experience with service, and that incidents connected with telephone service, both favorable and unfavorable, can make decided and lasting impressions on people's attitudes toward the company.

The personal element—the actions of those who work for the telephone company—is of immense importance, yet the opportunities for friendly personal contacts between employees and the customers are getting fewer and fewer. The opportunity of the "voice with a smile" to reach the subscriber is limited and is becoming more so with automation of the telephone system. Dialing, direct long distance dialing, the recorded message, and additional new developments in telephony, make the chances of the subscriber talking to a live person in the company smaller and smaller. For these reasons, where there is still a chance for the customer to talk with someone at the telephone company, the role of this company employee becomes more central than it has ever been.

One of these few keys to good relations between the telephone user and the telephone company is the service representative. Her selection, orientation, training, and development are of prime importance. She (and until the new Federal law against discrimination on the basis of sex, there were virtually no males in this field) is the object of a continuous hunt. She is hard to find and, when she is trained, is considered a jewel deserving the most infinite care. Her job is one which can, with many customers, make or break the reputation of the company. She is becoming the major link between the company and the subscriber, and her way of answering queries, her tact and courtesy, her knowledge and ability to deal with unusual problems, her manner of saying "No," and her explanation of why it is a No are of continuing concern to management.

The telephone representative is the person you talk to when you order a phone, question an item on your bill, want the service turned off and on at vacation time. You call her when you want to change your listing in the directory or want to know the charges for a color phone. She answers your letters, collects bills, meets you face-to-face in some offices, and does the clerical work involved so that what she promises will be done when promised. She has understanding, tact, judgment, and knowledge of the company's operations. She must be friendly, have a sense of humor, be resourceful, and have initiative so that she can "go by the book" and yet know when she can depart from it. Above all, she must know that every customer is different.

There are some 25,000 service representatives in the Bell System and they handle some ten million customer contacts a month, each of which can affect customer attitudes. Her average age is thirty-three, and she is a college or high school graduate. She comes from many types of backgrounds and may be a former telephone operator whose children are now grown sufficiently and who wants to get back to work. She likes talking to people and likes doing clerical work, for both are essential to her job. Of those who apply for these positions, only one out of a hundred is chosen, and some fifteen per cent of these are dropped in training. Finding this unusual person is the job of each operating company and by the time she is trained the company has invested $2,000 in her.

Even after a qualified person is told what the job is, she sits with a service representative for half a day. To be certain that she really would like to do this type of work, she is shown a film that explains the job. Then begins her training, in a group of three, under the tutelage of a supervisor. This training ranges from twenty-two days to as many as forty, according to the operating company and the particular group. In this course the service representative learns what she has to do and how she is to do it. Since her feelings about the company are projected to the customer, she is completely oriented according to the highest possible standards of personnel practice. The more she feels the company is interested in her welfare, the more she will be concerned with the welfare of the customer. The recruiting, the orientation, the training, the continuous concern about her understanding of the company and its policies as well as the respect for the service representative herself as an individual, are some of the proofs that AT&T fully appreciates that good public relations practice is no trick or sleight-of-hand operation, but a solid understanding that those inside the company must be happy at their jobs if those outside are to think well of it.

Nonetheless, of the 800,000 Bell System employees only a tiny handful—some 56,000 installers and repairmen—routinely get a chance to go into the customer's home. And when one of them does, he is the telephone company to the housewife. She has never heard of Romnes and really could not care much if she did hear his name or saw his picture. She judges the telephone company—what it is like, what kind of people work for it—by the man who comes into her home to install the telephone, or move it, or add an extension. His actions, the way he does his work, his courtesy, his advice on the best place to install the telephone, how he cleans up when his job is done— these are the ways she knows if the telephone company is made up of the kind of people she can trust and whether or not they are reliable. The way he answers her questions, the way he leaves her home, how he identifies himself when he enters it, and even his "good morning" and "goodbye" help or hurt the reputation of the telephone company.

The installer or the repairman—often he is the same man, a repair-man-installer—has always been considered by AT&T as an important factor in the good will of the company. For that reason, the stress on his training, not only in the area of his mechanical competence, but as the representative of the company, is increasing. The company knows his value for its relations with an important part of the public.

Back at the turn of the century the installer-repairmen were called "troublemen." The basic philosophy behind their training has not changed a great deal since October 28, 1911, when the Chicago Telephone Company, as it was then called, issued a memo to its troublemen. It was a series of twenty-three rules for their behavior. Except for the rule about making "the liveryman wash and oil your wagon and harness, and do not tie the harness up with wire longer than is necessary to get proper repairs and the same may be said of your suspenders and buttons," they stand pretty solidly today.

Rule 1 of the 1911 memo is: "Put up a 'good front.' It is not neces-sary to advertise any tailor shop, neither is it necessary to go about your work looking like a coal heaver. Over-alls can be as respectable as anything else, but they must at least show that they are on speak-ing terms with the laundryman; and shoes must have a bowing ac-quaintance with the bootblack."

Rule 5 is: "Go about your business cheerfully and quietly. When you enter a residence don't overlook the footmat. If requested to go around to the back door, don't consider yourself insulted, but try to realize that the lady of the house may not have a maid and is only trying to save work for herself. Say 'good morning' or 'evening,' it doesn't cost anything and shows you started out right at home."

Rule 10 is: "If you ever believe that a subscriber is a crank, forget it. All of them are wise enough to tell when a telephone is not working right. Not every troubleman can do this."

Rule 18 is: "Cultivate the friendship of the people with whom you do business: it makes friends for the company and friendship is essential to true success."

Rule 19 is: "Carry yourself with dignity and others will accord it to you."

Who is this man who is more important to the public acceptance of the company today than he ever was? He is a high school graduate, is intelligent, and has, of course, mechanical ability. He rarely starts work as a telephone installer. He ordinarily begins at a lower level craft job which does not involve contact with customers. It may be as a mailboy, a frameman, or splicer's helper. Early in his working career he associates with older, experienced craftsmen and he picks up from them skills related to the job and an attitude toward the customer which the successful craftsmen have.

Since he works for an operating company there are variations in the training he gets in policy, the procedures when in a customer's home, and his general approach as an important representative of the telephone company. For instance, Southwestern Bell Telephone Company has an eighteen-minute color film that it shows to installers. The film points up the importance of politeness and efficiency when working in close contact with the customer. The same company has a sequel, which runs twenty minutes and shows how the little things done by contact people can affect the attitudes of the customers. These films are of course available to other operating companies.

The best way to get an idea of the whole orientation and training programs of the installer is to look at one of the operating companies closely and see what it does. A good example is the Illinois Bell Telephone Company's program. From the day the serviceman starts on his job until the day he leaves, every attempt is made to make him feel that he is an important part of the company. A continuous effort is made to keep his attitude toward the company favorable, so that he will reflect that attitude to the customers into whose homes he goes.

The installer is given information about Illinois Bell and the Bell System, the departmental relationships, his job benefits, the traditions of service, and the answers to any questions he may be asked. The principle here is that the more he knows about the company, and its history and policies, the better an employee he will make. And this goes on all during his job training. The company wants this man to be a part of the company, a participating employee.

The installer is told early in his training how his good performance benefits him and how a favorable public attitude toward his job helps him protect it. Neat appearance, concern for a workmanlike, clean job—these are taught in the classroom and through examples of supervisors and co-workers. The new installer is at first paired with an experienced man whose work habits and general approach to the job make a good model. And while there are booklets for him to read, the example set by his older and more experienced co-worker is more effective. The beginner's work is frequently checked by his supervisor, and during the regular evaluation periods he has a chance to discuss his strengths and weaknesses.

To underline the need for installers to re-check their work, to make certain that every detail is properly handled, Illinois Bell even uses a cartoon character, Double-Check Charlie, as a symbol of the program. Posters, slide presentations, and talks are part of the course to make sure that errors are avoided. Never forgotten at any time during the continuous orientation of the installer is the vital part he plays in the success of the company. The objective of all this is to have the man know that he is working for good people who are interested in him and are concerned about his working conditions, his chance of promotion, and his opportunity to move into other and higher fields. And when that is done, Illinois Bell has an installer who is proud of his company and so makes the best kind of ambassador for it.

Extensive as are the functions of AT&T's public relations department and those of the affiliated companies, there is little resting on oars. There is, instead, a full realization that public opinion can alter quickly. Like gusts of wind, it can sweep all before it and change what is a satisfaction today into trouble tomorrow. For these reasons there are continuous assessments of public attitudes. A great deal of this is done through the use of polls taken by the headquarters and by the operating companies. Each has a heavy responsibility for what is happening in its own province. While the research group at AT&T coordinates all the appraisals of telephone service from the customer's point of view, evaluates the customer attitude studies made by the operating companies, assesses the internal media for effectiveness, tests all the films and other visual material to see if they are filling the purposes for which they are intended, its work does not stop here. It also coordinates the special Bell System studies and polls.

There is no attempt to seek confirmation of an existing point of view by using polls. Rather, there is a hard search for weakness, for customers' objections, for complaints about service, and for comparisons with the results of previous polls. For instance, in the polls made by the operating companies, the number of customers who have one complaint about service or costs are compared with national averages to provide a measuring rod of performance, and to determine whether or not the customers think there has been improvement. There are also surveys of what the employees think of the company, their interest in sickness benefits, accident benefits, group life insurance, or the pension plan. These are broken down into management and non-management categories. Every publication for external or internal company use is surveyed to see if there is true communication with the reader or if the editors are talking to themselves. While there is bound to be some "flying by the seat of the pants," every attempt is made to check the theories of those who are responsible for publications. Whether it is an exhibit at a world's fair, a brochure, a television or radio show, or a film shown to installers or long distance operators, continuous checks are made for effectiveness and acceptance. Without this continuous concern for what the customer and the employee think, a company as vast as AT&T might well go off on a tangent. It is perilous to be unaware of possibly harmful changes in public opinion. Nor would the publications intended for internal and external use be anything more than a waste of stockholders' money if they did not fill the purposes for which they were established. These are the big reasons why continuous studies, polls, and self-questioning are necessary. Without this persistent probing of the effectiveness of all the material prepared, management is flying blind, and few things are more dangerous.

The number of programs in which the public relations department is involved is large and covers almost every field of importance. Yet, on occasion, some new, previously non-existent problem protrudes and demands a re-assessment or an extension of a program. This was the origin of the Bell System's Aid to High School Science program. It rose out of a need and resulted in the best program of its kind in the country.

It all began when the Soviet Union launched its *Sputnik I* in 1957. Until that time the Bell System had a program of science education in the schools, limited though it was by present standards. It will be recalled that *Sputnik*'s launching raised a storm in the country. The quality of U.S. science education was questioned by political and education leaders. Newspaper editors and the general public were concerned. The Soviet Union was supposed to be far behind the United States in scientific development, yet it was able to send a satellite into orbit before the United States. "Why?" was the persistent question. It bothered not only the President, but educators on all levels. When President Eisenhower pointed out that the Russian high school graduate has had five years of physics, four years of chemistry, one year of astronomy, five years of biology, ten years of mathematics and trigonometry, and five years of a foreign language, there began the kind of search for answers that was bound to force changes. And collateral to these questions came others: Why had not more American youngsters been encouraged to study science? What was the reason for lack of motivation?

The dire shortage of scientists and engineers was underlined by the National Science Foundation as it was stressed by individual scientists and those concerned with American engineering and science education. The public pressure for results was acute. It was in this environment that the Bell System's public relations people began to ask themselves questions. The school relations sections of the public relations departments had long emphasized training in the use of the telephone, safety programs, visits to central offices, grants of obsolete phone equipment, and career direction days. These were fine in themselves, but was this enough for a company employing thousands of engineers and scientists? Was this all a company, whose researchers and engineers produced new knowledge in many fields of science and technology, could and should do? Was there any obligation for a company whose laboratories often made technological progress faster than it could be put into the textbooks to get this significant information, and more like it, into the schools?

To get answers to their own questions AT&T's public relations people set up a task force to make its study a basis for recommendations. The task force visited thirteen operating companies, interviewing 132 telephone executives in all departments involved with school contacts; obtained answers to a detailed questionnaire from fourteen telephone company operating areas; met with forty educators representing twenty-three school districts in different parts of the country, interviewed representatives of four major industries concerning their school programs; and obtained additional information on the school activities of other industries in reply to letters sent to eighty-five companies.

The task force drew these conclusions: every educator interviewed believed that industry had a place in the schools; school administrators were tired of classroom gimmicks—bits and pieces of surplus, unrelated equipment; educators were feeling the pressure of public opinion and wanted improved science education in the schools.

The result of the task force study was that the Bell System reappraised its objectives for aid to the schools. It was certain it had an increased responsibility to American education and that one great need it might help fill was in secondary school science education. To do this, teaching aids in certain areas of science had to be developed. So was born the Bell System's Aid to High School Science program, a major public relations project for AT&T, carefully designed to answer the needs of educators, and not those of the company.

The task force found that while science teachers could use help from the industry, there were many restrictions. The aid had to serve the specific needs of teachers and it had to come from those competent to give it. Educators needed material to bolster the weak spots in school texts, and to help them raise their own level of teaching competence and so narrow the gap between the laboratory and the classroom. They also needed materials that could be used in teaching the class as a whole, something beyond their own resources. They wanted materials that either illustrated important physical concepts or provided information in areas where the teachers' was slight. They wanted material to stretch the imagination and thinking power of those better students whose talents put them ahead of their class. Also badly needed were projects which tied together some of the disciplines the student was studying—exercises in problem solving.

The Bell System came up with two kinds of teaching aids. One was a teacher-oriented unit for use with the class as a whole; the other was a self-contained science experiment for the gifted student. Both were first offered in 1961.

The teacher-oriented classroom units dealt with similarities in wave behavior, the theory of ferromagnetic domains, the physics and biology of speech and hearing, semi-conductor physics, and crystal growing. The gifted-student experiments enabled budding young scientists to create a solar-powered, transistorized audio-oscillator; turn silicon slabs into working solar cells; produce speech electronically; and experiment with crystals and light.

Both units were designed to provide information in areas of science where textbook and teacher information was incomplete or outdated. The developed units covered a wide range of subjects and took advantage of new knowledge gained from Bell Laboratories research. The classroom units generally consisted of a textbook written by a scientist who worked for Bell Laboratories, a correlated motion picture, and the necessary demonstration devices.

Some of the Bell Laboratories' leading scientists contributed their time and knowledge to this program of encouraging youngsters who showed an interest in science. A wave demonstration machine was devised by John Shive, inventor of the photo-transistor and the Lab's director of education and training. An expert in magnetism, E. A. Nesbitt, prepared the materials on ferromagnetic domains. George Frost, a member of the Education Aids Department, designed the "From Sun to Sound" experiment. A co-inventor of the Bell Solar Battery, Daryl Chapin, contributed the Solar Energy experiment. Teaching units on the physics and biology of speech and hearing were developed by three specialists in the field, Peter Denes, Eliot Pinson, and Cecil Coker. Three other experts, Elizabeth A. Wood, Alan Holden, and R. H. Thompson, wrote materials on crystallography.

In no case did the company provide teaching aids merely because, in their own opinion, they thought they would be useful. In every case the teachers themselves were queried. To be certain that what was being developed would be exactly what the teachers wanted, special meetings were held for teachers. They were individually interviewed. Bell people read their publications, took part in their conventions, studied their curricula, and, on occasion, hired them to assist in the day-to-day development of the materials. In addition, every year, formal presentations of possible subjects were made to groups of educators. One year, for example, three such meetings were held, in New York, Cleveland and San Francisco. At each of these meetings, twenty-five leading teachers and administrators were invited from the nearby territory. In each case, the local Bell telephone company was the host and representatives of Bell Laboratories and AT&T made the presentation.

In the final running there were six subjects. When the three meetings were over and the year's subject was chosen, the educators were again asked for their advice. To do this best, a meeting was held in Washington, D.C. attended by nationally recognized educators, including staff members of the National Science Teachers Association and the U.S. Office of Education. This time, the Bell Laboratories people presented the practically developed teaching aids that they were working on. This was a final check to see if they were on the right track. The educators said they were, and made several useful suggestions that were used in the final development.

There was still a further trial of the equipment by teachers and students. In this way, by their participation in the formative stages of a project's development, the company made sure that its aid to education was truly an aid and not something the company felt that the teachers and students should have whether they found it really helpful or not.

Then came the problem of letting the high school science teachers throughout the country know that the aids were available for them. Beyond the word-of-mouth method of spreading information, which by the time the projects were completed was pretty extensive, the executive secretary of the National Science Teachers Association endorsed the program to every high school physics and science teacher in the country. The telephone companies, as a matter of information and not promotion, let the teachers know what the materials were and that they were available. They did this by inviting teachers to meetings where the year's offerings were described. Meetings were chosen as the means of presentation because the science subjects presented were difficult and the teachers knew little about them.

These meetings meant a great deal of hard work for the teachers, the telephone engineers, and the public relations staffs of AT&T's companies. But they were worth it, for the response of the teachers was widely favorable. Comments from school science administrators were strongly in support and often highly laudatory.

The demonstration devices are not entirely free, but the schools are happy to pay the low unit manufacturing cost set by the private suppliers, as well as the costs of the books supplied by the publishers. The films are loaned to the schools by AT&T without charge, while the advanced-student experiments, single copies of the books, and some of the other materials are provided free to teachers and administrators. It is left to the teacher to decide which students, at which stage in their studies, can best benefit from the materials.

To motivate junior high school students to develop an interest in careers in science and engineering, AT&T has a series of career guidance publications. They have a wide popularity and teachers are glad to have them available.

As often happens, success brings additional development. Since 1960, special visits by high school students and their teachers to Bell Laboratories in Murray Hill, New Jersey, have been continued. Every month during the academic year Bell companies sponsor a visit by some thirty science students and their teachers to a two-day program at the Bell Laboratories. They attend lectures, take in round-table discussions with some of the Laboratories' leading physicists, chemists, mathematicians, and engineers. The students are picked by their schools, not by the Bell System. The goals of this program are simple: to give the students and teachers a feeling for the work done by scientists and engineers in a large research and development organization; to help bridge the gap between the science class and the research and engineering laboratory; and to encourage students to continue their studies in science and engineering. At the same time the teacher gets a chance to see and discuss "work in progress" in his teaching field.

What have been the results of all this? A study covering four states was made among 269 teachers and administrators, most of whom had attended telephone company meetings introducing the teaching aids. Seven out of ten teachers had used at least one of the aids in their classes, and many of those who had not, planned to use them. So one of the first objectives of this program was obviously achieved: the teaching aids are being used. By the time the program was six years old in 1966, about 75 per cent of all the high school science teachers in the United States were using these experiments.

What does the Bell System get out of this program, one that is ? antithesis of self-serving press agentry, a function so widely fused with public relations? Out of a desire to fill an urgent need ?ience educators, and do a service to the public, it has brought will to AT&T. But there is another factor. As a company which that if it is to benefit from science and engineering it must ?cate scientists and engineers, AT&T has, by advancing the ?ood, furthered its own. By sharing the results of its work and technology with the schools, it has made a long-term in its own future, for many of the best men and women science and engineering go to work for AT&T.

g time since Theodore Newton Vail started in Boston ?ager of the company out of which grew AT&T. The ricans of 1878 have become 200 million. The United ?ed the convulsions of two world wars, the rise and ?ism, and now confronts the upsurge of an ideology ?oviet Union and Communist China toward world China angry at the Soviet Union for not being ?. Man seeks to land on the moon as his satellites back to earth sound and pictures. From the ?—AT&T now has the picture phone in which ? person with whom you talk; has two com-?lstar I and Telstar II, in orbit; markets

Touch-Tone, the push-button telephone which also may be used for low-speed data transmission; provides the electronic larynx for those without vocal cords; and developed the *Nike-X* missile defense system and the command guidance system that orders the missile to go, change direction, speed up, or slow down.

Political systems have changed. More than one hundred nations raise their voices in the United Nations. The world is better fed, better housed than ever before—yet millions are hungry and live in the streets and fields, without shelter. Dictatorships increase. Through all this, the public is more articulate and more insistent that its will be done. The people of the developing nations demand that they be obeyed, and those leaders who are deaf pass from power. In this country, politicians are more responsive to the public will than at any time in history, listening carefully for the murmurs of discontent and the sounds of approval.

It is in this context that AT&T operates now. In the future the wish of the public will become even more quickly the command of the politicians. Business and government will be even more closely interwoven than they are now and the public interest, or what the public believes to be its interest, will continue to be the dominating factor. The easy days when the chief executive of a corporation could have a pleasant little chat with the President and so solve all problems has long gone. The vestiges will be whittled away as a more educated, more sophisticated voter will insist that his voice be heard sooner and his wishes be heeded more quickly.

As today's world is different from yesterday's, so will tomorrow's be different from today's. But the basics will be the same. As Vail said: "In all times, in all lands, public opinion has had control at the last word," and that a public utility is "dependent on public consent to operate." The structure built so carefully on Vail's principles, developed during the long Gifford regime, and nurtured since, has kept AT&T privately owned and privately operated. But this is no guarantee for the years to come should some new chief executive forget that the stockholders, the subscribers, the employees, the general public are the bosses, not he. It takes decades to build the kind of public acceptance AT&T has. It takes very little to destroy it. All the past service for the common weal will mean little if a new group takes command of the company, a new group which knows not its history, which does not appreciate that the very size of the company makes it a larger, not smaller, target for those who believe it is not well and faithfully serving the public. As AT&T can operate if the public permits it; so will the public, thinking serving well, support it against those who would make it into a branch of the government.

A series of thoughtless or deliberate actions which offend the public —an arrogance which forgets that AT&T is the servant, not the master of the public—can shatter the whole structure, turn a private enterprise into a government department. The chances of this happening are remote, for built into the very fiber of all managers of the company is the belief that the public interest is paramount. So long as this is remembered, so long as it remains a daily concern of management, so long will the world's largest privately owned corporation remain so.

e
y
a
ws
the
eve
only
it is

IN A BIG GLASS HOUSE

It was 1931 and Alfred P. Sloan, Jr., was perplexed. He was fifty-six years old and had been president of General Motors Corporation for almost eight years. He had molded an inefficient and loose collection of diverse automobile manufacturing firms into a cohesive whole. Sales, profits, and dividends—beginning with his first year as chief executive officer—had steadily risen, except for the year just ended.

The figures for 1930 had been appalling. Sales had dropped more than a third, from 1929's $1.5 billion to $983 million. Almost three quarters of a million fewer cars and trucks had been sold in the United States and Canada. Profits and dividends had tumbled. To Sloan, "the downward steps were gigantic."

The year 1931 was one of political and economic convulsion. Fighting had started on the Manchurian border as Japan attacked; 160 Hitler deputies in opposition shook the government by a boycott of the Reichstag; after nine months in prison Mahatma Gandhi and 50,000 of his followers were granted an amnesty by the British; the Soviet Union announced a new Five Year Plan to begin in 1933; Secretary of State Henry L. Stimson apologized to Mussolini's Italy for a denunciation of fascism by Gen. Smedley Butler; and President Hoover proposed an international moratorium in war reparations and war debts to ease the burden of the European governments, and told Congress that the chief influence affecting the state of the Union had been the continued world-wide economic disturbances—that "within two years there have been revolutions or acute social disorders in nineteen countries embracing more than half the population of the world."

It was a year of accelerating economic depression following the panic of October-November, 1929, when the stock market crash cut the paper value of stocks by $30 billion, almost as much as the total cost of American participation in World War I; when nearly seven million out of a total work force of 48 million were unemployed, with sixty per cent of the organized workers in the building trades jobless; when membership in trade unions fell so badly that the loss of revenues forced the laying off of organizers; when there were no serious strikes; when the unemployed sold apples on street corners; when private charity couldn't begin to meet the needs of the hungry and President Hoover said he was "opposed to any direct or indirect government dole"; when the American Federation of Labor opposed any form of compulsory unemployment insurance as contrary to American ideals and American needs and a menace to the labor movement; when bankers pressed for wage cuts and Hoover called leaders of the largest industries to Washington and asked them not to cut wage rates; when United States Steel, months later, announced a ten per cent cut in the wages of 220,000 workers followed by Bethlehem Steel, General Motors, and U.S. Rubber; when banks representing three per cent of the nation's total deposits failed; when prices continued to fall; when wheat was selling at fifty cents a bushel with all exports for the last quarter down to $606,000,000 and imports at a low $540,000,000; when the depression had not hit its worst point and those unaffected were certain that prosperity was "just around the corner."

Sloan was puzzled as to how "to cope with the unbelievable course of events." He had been pessimistic after the stock market crash and was more pessimistic in 1931. He was concerned, as he said in his annual report to stockholders at the close of 1930, for the future position of General Motors, "not only from the standpoint of the confidence with which it is regarded by the public, which is a measure of its goodwill, but likewise from the standpoint of its future economic development." He ordered "the most searching analysis of all problems."

One of those problems was the state of mind of the shocked nation. It had begun to question a system in which men who desperately wanted to work could find no jobs of any kind. Business, especially big business, was beginning to feel the attack for its failures to provide work; for its layoffs; for its wage cuts; for its supposed unconcern with what was happening to its depleted work force; for the insecurity of its workers; for the speed up on the assembly lines. Should these cries remain unanswered? Should public opinion just be ignored since management had so many other problems that needed emergency treatment?

Sloan knew something was needed to somehow establish contact with the great number of people who bought cars, went to baseball games, voted or sent their children to school. He was not quite certain what he wanted, but he felt he should know more about the millions who had been hurt in the aftermath of the stock market crash. He did know that the public ought to have more information about General Motors policies, the reasons for its actions, and an explanation of what large scale business meant to the economy.

There was no pressure in 1931 from unions. General Motors had not yet had any dealings with labor unions except for a few craft organizations in the construction field. Big industry had never been organized. There was no United Automobile Workers. Walter Reuther, twenty-three years old, was working at Ford as a tool and die leader while attending Wayne University at night studying economics and sociology. Nor was there a New Deal to harass business; New York Governor Franklin D. Roosevelt, with the advice of Louis Howe and James Farley, was beginning to feel out his chances for the Democratic presidential nomination a year away.

Sloan believed that the period of public turmoil would be long-lasting; and decided that he would look for a man who would be able to interpret the corporation to the public, and, in turn, help him try to understand what the country was thinking. He sought out Paul Willard Garrett, financial editor of the New York *Evening Post*, a conservative daily newspaper which sold for three cents while all other New York City newspapers sold for two cents. It had a heavy interest in business and finance, and was quite different from today's *Post*. Sloan offered Garrett the job.

What were the factors which motivated Sloan to hire a man to take charge of public relations at a time when few industrial corporations were interested; when the general attitude of businessmen, when dealing with the public, was "tell 'em nothing"? Sloan's answer was:

Up to that time there was very little consciousness of the significance of public relations either to expose to the proper degree the operations of an enterprise, or from the wider point of view, to expose what the enterprise contributes to the general economy. It was a new idea. When Paul was appointed, it was my feeling that we ought to move in that general direction. But until that time public relations counselors were really unknown. It was a new feature as far as I can recall. I am quite certain that I visualized at that time the evolution and significance of a move into public relations.

Garrett was forty years old and ready for the move when the chance came on May 1, 1931, to go to General Motors. His father was a Kansas farmer. His grandparents had trekked west by covered wagon. He was a Phi Beta Kappa at Whitmore College, in Walla Walla, Washington, and on graduation went east, and enrolled for graduate work at Columbia University so that he could be in New York. He took his master's degree, working in political science, economics, and public law. After jobs with the Bureau of Municipal Research in New York and the War Industries Board in Washington in 1917-18 he went to work for the *Post* as a financial columnist. The newspaper was then owned by Thomas W. Lamont, head of the J.P. Morgan Company. In 1924 it was bought by Cyrus Curtis, owner of the *Saturday Evening Post*. Garrett's column, "The Investor," was syndicated. By 1925 he was financial editor—the youngest in New York—and began an additional daily column, also syndicated, called "Business Today." He had covered the automotive industry, was read by businessmen, and had developed a fondness for them. By the time the call from Sloan came, he was fully prepared. Wider fields in business attracted him.

Prior to Garrett's appointment as public relations director of General Motors, Carl Ackerman was listed as assistant to the president on the organization chart of the corporation. He was hired on January 1, 1931, to write a book about Sloan but lasted only four months. From the aborted job at General Motors he went to Columbia Graduate School of Journalism as dean. No one before Garrett had had the public relations responsibility, and the new hand from the *Evening Post* decided to learn about the company, as well as what he could about public relations, before he started to function.

For some six months Garrett did nothing but study the company and its problems. He visited its plants, had long discussions with the executives, and wrote notes to himself about ideas which struck him. There were no instructions from Sloan. He had told Garrett to do the job as he saw fit. Garrett's approach was entirely different from what is so often done these days. Today, a new man works out a public relations plan of operation—often in detail—then appears before management to explain what he proposes to do, includes a timetable and tries to have the plan as a whole accepted.

Garrett never pushed for a new program or decisions from management until he thought the time was ripe. While he had a general plan in mind he felt that timing was all important in presenting each part of the whole program separately. He did not expect management to be public relations authorities. He himself was learning as he went along about the needs of the company, the various groups affected by it, and the changes that would meet the volatile demands of the public. Nor did he ever present his ideas for the development of a new aspect of a program until he had so well prepared the way that the request he made to his management would appear to be the most reasonable answer to a problem that was then acute, or that might become acute under the pressures of changes in public opinion. During the first six months, which he insisted be his orientation period, he worked out his fundamental approach to General Motors' problems.

Garrett knew instinctively what others later learned the hard way: that, to be effective, the public relations director must operate at a policy level with the full support of top management. He believed no public relations program could be any better than the policies of the corporation; that good public relations could only work from the inside out; and that corporate policies in the public interest were the beginning of any public acceptance of the corporation. Further, he believed that, unless management was fully behind such thinking, a cloak would be the result, and no cloak could ever take the place of well-thought-out, carefully implemented policies that in themselves carried public support because of their intrinsic worth. Declamations of good intentions could never hide inadequacies for long, or replace worthwhile policies. From the beginning, Garrett knew the value of opinion leaders and their influences on the various segments that made up general opinion.

Before Garrett's arrival at General Motors there were no public relations programs or press relations programs. Lockwood Barr, who had left the corporation when Ackerman had joined it, had for thirteen years handled the corporate financial publicity. He worked out of General Motors' New York office, seldom went to Detroit or visited the plants, and made no attempt to broaden the scope of his work. Product publicity was under the advertising department, and Barr reported to a sales executive. Reporters on newspapers and the magazines dealt with the advertising department, which did not in the least feel ashamed of working on the implied, and on occasion expressed, principle that if there were no publicity the advertising would be cut. Campbell Ewald, the advertising agency, had all the motor car accounts with one publicity man attached to each account. This was an easy reminder to the press that publicity was related to the volume of advertising received. And as far as community relations programs were concerned, they were simply non-existent. The theory was that a plant manager's job was to run the plant, not waste his efforts or his time in what was considered to be outside his area of concern.

Garrett started with one secretary as his entire staff. There was no department, nothing. A month later he hired Kenneth Youel, who had been a financial writer working for Garrett on the *Evening Post*. There was no quick staff build up. That would have to wait until there was a program accepted by management. Then, and only then, would he recruit staff. Until he was certain of the direction he was taking in each area, he saw no purpose in hiring staff members. Nor did Garrett worry very much in which department some of his programs developed. If they were accepted, and the work was to be done under some department other than public relations, that was fine with Garrett. Then, with his advice, the other department could do the job and the budget costs would be assigned to it as well. Many of Garrett's most effective ideas were carried out during his twenty-five-year regime by departments other than the one he headed and had responsibility for.

Sloan told the author, when asked what was done when the corporation had something to say to the public: "When anything happened in the corporation we thought we should say something about, somebody would write out a notice and it would be discussed and it would be issued as one, two, three business statements as circumstances developed. There was no coordination. There was nothing of that kind existing in General Motors until Paul came along."

Not quite six months after Garrett started his job, Sloan gave him a chance to speak to the annual Executive Conference. This is a closed meeting of the leading executives of General Motors at which the major problems of the corporation are discussed. It was the new man's first chance to explain his work, his ideas, and any general plans he had for the company. Garrett was not meeting an over-friendly group: to them, this new idea of Sloan's was not wholly acceptable. However, they gave Garrett the hearing that Sloan's backing assured him. He talked to them in their own terms: about the growth of the company, its future, and what would help the company sell more cars. He was careful to underline that what he was proposing was a general approach, not specifics that they would have to accept simply because he said they were good. He made his points in a way they could understand, for he keyed what he said, every step of the way, to the profits of the company.

It was at this confrontation, for that is what it was, with these hard-driving executives assembled at the Greenbrier Hotel in White Sulphur Springs, West Virginia, on October 3, 1931, that Garrett outlined his basic public relations thinking. Many of the suggestions that he made were accepted in course of time, and formed the under-structure of General Motors' position in its relations with the public. He explained that there could only be public confidence when General Motors' products were good, but that the growth of the corporation could be hastened if the road to good relations were clearly marked. He underlined his belief that, while good relations outside could only come from good relations inside, the improvement of external relations ought to go along at the same time, and not wait until perfection had been achieved inside the company. He emphasized that it was essential to have good relations, not only with those who were in the market for motor cars, but with the whole country; all were potential customers. That they be assured, through performance, that General Motors was a good company was basic to economic growth.

When Garrett felt that he had at least softened the attitudes of General Motors' leading executives he then, and only then, made some suggestions in the areas that badly needed improvement. Because of lack of coordination, there had been conflict on the part of the divisions of General Motors in the statements made to the public on corporate policies. To overcome this, he suggested that those who had functions that touched on the relations of the company with the public should meet from time to time in Detroit for an exchange of views, for discussion of policies, and to develop an effective overall plan. That way, they would at least all speak in the same tone, discuss policies from a unified position, and make certain that there were no conflicting announcements. He stressed the importance of the car dealers to the company, for they were direct representatives to the public. He touched on the advantages of a well-organized program of dealer education, to develop better service, courtesy, and an awareness of the public interest. In this way Garrett said, profits could be increased.

He also suggested better corporate identification in the selling of cars. As it was, General Motors would be running institutional advertisements, and in the same issue of the same magazine there would be advertisements by Cadillac and Chevrolet that did not mention their connection with General Motors and advertisements by

Buick and Pontiac that did. There were positive profit values to all divisions of adopting one General Motors insignia to show they were part of one corporation. In this way they could all benefit from the public's acceptance of all General Motors products as being of high quality. He suggested that accurate and complete statistical figures be collected and provided for financial analysts and newspaper editors since this would make General Motors more attractive to investors. At the same time the publication of these accurate and complete figures would enhance both the reputation of the automotive industry and that of the company itself. He made two other suggestions: that an objective history of General Motors be written for use in libraries as a source of information for opinion leaders; and that talking pictures, new at the time, be used as a public relations medium. He favored inaugurating a three-year film program for public, stockholder, dealer, and employee education.

In keeping with his usual approach when proposing programs Garrett made it clear on his first appearance before the senior management group that he did not have all the answers to all General Motors' problems; that he was making proposals which he thought might have merit; that he was not critical of what was being done or left undone, for he did not know all the difficulties involved; and that he hoped that he was stimulating ideas rather than giving pat answers to knotty problems.

To Garrett the early months with General Motors would set the pattern for his operations. In keeping with his theory that he would not be able to do an effective job unless he had the full support of Sloan, plus all the top command of the company, he refused a large office on a floor below Sloan's and asked for a small one which was on the same floor—the 24th—at 1775 Broadway in New York City. Garrett knew that proximity to the center of power would have its influence on others in the company. With the same thinking, Garrett suggested to Sloan that a public relations committee that would include the leading executives be organized. Sloan went along with Garrett's plan, and out of it grew a valuable means of policy discussion and clearance of plans that was of immense value to Garrett and to his successor.

In many corporations, the public relations director has difficulty getting access to the chief executive. Since Garrett knew that access, not only to Sloan but to his top managers as well, was the *sine qua non* of policy acceptance, the formation of the public relations committee was one of his most basic and far-reaching accomplishments.

It immediately gave notice that public relations was not a fringe activity but one in which the highest echelons of General Motors were deeply involved.

Sloan's directive, dated December 9, 1931, issued little more than seven months after Garrett started with General Motors, was an earnest indication of the company's commitment to public relations. It is probably the most fundamental directive Sloan issued for Garrett and was sent to all officers and top divisional and staff executives.

As a basic policy of his organization of General Motors, Sloan used the technique of committees for high-level policy matters, and this one on public relations was an alert to those who managed the company that the new function was considered of major importance. The membership of this committee was an added sign of the backing Garrett had from Sloan. Members appointed were Edward R. Stettinius, a vice-president of General Motors who later became U.S. Secretary of State; Donaldson Brown, a director of General Motors, a vice-president, and chairman of the finance committee, and who was a Du Pont representative; R. H. Grant, a vice-president; John L. Pratt, a company director and a vice-president; Alfred H. Swayne, a director and a vice-president; Alfred P. Sloan, Jr., president and a director; and L. R. Beardslee, secretary of the executive committee, operations committee, and finance committee. Garrett was named chairman of the committee.

The directive gave the committee general supervision in these areas: public relations; the press and all publicity relationships as well as those with the stockholders of the corporation; trade association representation; the development of good will; institutional advertising; radio broadcasting; "and such other functions as may properly be considered in this connection."

This committee met regularly once a month. It was an active committee. Garrett brought before it his ideas, plans, and programs. To it he explained, each step of the way, what he was doing and why. This, of course, did not take the place of Garrett's discussions with Sloan, nor did it inhibit him from exploring projects with others in the company who did not have the exalted status of membership on the committee. To Garrett, the committee was invaluable. It eased his way throughout the corporation, and was one of the best guarantees that when he met with others in the corporation he would get a receptive hearing. There were those in the company in Garrett's early days, as there are in many companies today, who had a reluctance to think in terms of public reaction to corporate policies. For them, Garrett carried on a continuous educational effort, explaining that everything a company did, every decision made, had an impact on the relations of the company with the public.

To Garrett, the educative process, explaining why good relations with the public were vital to the success of General Motors, never ended. He made speeches to groups within the company. He worked closely with those executives in the divisions who understood why a favorable public opinion was important to the corporation, then labored with those who were willing to understand, and finally with those who were opposed to the entire concept. And during all this period not only did Sloan give him full support, but became one of the strongest advocates of what Garrett was doing.

A simple, yet important, aspect of Sloan's belief in the merit of Garrett's activities is shown in the annual report to stockholders for the year ending December 1933. Stockholder relations were always an essential part of Sloan's business life, and the annual report was something he labored over long and hard. He believed that the stockholders, as owners of the company, had a right to know all that was happening to their investment; that the company could not exist without them. Full disclosure was a must. At the suggestion of Garrett, Sloan began to include in his reports information about public relations.

Under the heading of "Public Relations" in the 1933 annual stockholders' report dated March 15, 1934, Sloan wrote:

> It is apparent that there is a growing realization in this country that nothing is more vital to the maintenance of a corporation's position in industry, and to its future development, than a satisfactory relationship with the public or good public relations.
>
> Public needs and viewpoints must be interpreted by the Corporation through its engineering, manufacturing and sales organization in the form of satisfactory products and services. This in turn places a definite public relations responsibility upon every General Motors employee and General Motors dealer, each in his or her own particular sphere, to build good will for General Motors by being public-minded members of a public-minded institution.
>
> In addition to furnishing satisfactory products and services, it is of equally vital importance that the public should have an understanding of the motives that actuate the Corporation in everything that it does. In harmony with this conception the

Corporation makes every effort to keep the stockholders and the general public properly informed as to the Corporation's policies in dealing with the various problems that arise.

He followed these words by outlining in the report what he called "a new activity" to keep in closer contact with the public thinking. This was "Customer Research." He said it was now possible for General Motors to gauge, with a high degree of accuracy, public thinking on many questions which were of great assistance to the company, both in the manufacture of its products and the formulation of its policies.

Sloan ended his discussion of public relations with these words:

> Thus to insure a satisfactory relationship with the public, emphasis is placed not alone on what management may think but on the correct interpretation of what the public actually thinks. This is the point of view of General Motors as a public-minded institution.

Garrett, who was given a General Motors vice-presidency in 1940, headed the public relations activity for a full twenty-five years. He went through the entire New Deal period with President Roosevelt's attacks on "the economic royalists"; the legislation which business did not like but had to learn to live with; the organization of General Motors by the CIO; the violence and the sit-down strikes of 1937; the rise of Walter Reuther and the United Automobile Workers; the preparation for World War II; the conversion to a war footing and the production of arms; the war years; the strike of 1945-46 which lasted 113 days; the reconversion to peacetime operations; and the fluctuations of public opinion, which ran from simple anti-business to anti-capitalism and then, latterly, to a recognition that business could adjust itself to the public will and serve the public interest.

In this quarter-century Garrett developed one of the few effective public relations departments in the country. From establishing a Detroit public relations office out of which the Detroit newspapers could get reliable information about General Motors when they asked for it, to the start of the annual automobile show for the corporation; from the development of the exhibit for the corporation at the Chicago World's Fair to helping Sloan become a public speaker; from encouraging the setting up of divisional public relations departments to the inauguration of plant city programs; from establishing field relations to giving institutional advertising a new approach; from traveling shows such as the "Parade of Progress" and "Preview of

Progress" to the employee magazine *GM Folks;* from the Futurama for the New York World's Fair in 1939-40 to the nurturing of a staff of men who could think for themselves and understand his concepts of public relations; from the stress on stockholder relations to the beginnings of the General Motors Management Clubs; from the education of General Motors managers in public relations to the missionary work with other corporations who asked help. In all these Garrett had the prime responsibility. His was the labor of setting the tone of General Motors' attitude toward public opinion.

It took an unusual man to perform as he did during the periods of depression, war, and cold war, through labor upheaval, and the continuous expansion of the world's largest industrial corporation, which now has 750,000 employees, 1,400,000 stockholders, sales of $20 billion and profits of $2 billion. One measure of his ability is that he was successful under three different chief executive officers: Sloan, Charles E. Wilson and Harlow Curtice. In this field, where the chief executive must have personal confidence in the public relations director, and where a rapport between them is so vital, it is one of the amazing facets of Garrett's methods that he worked so intimately and well with them all, vastly different in approach and temperament though they were from one another. He usually moved indirectly, made many speeches, and cared little for personal credit.

What was Garrett's philosophy of public relations? What was his view of the function of management in its relations with the various groups which make up the public as a whole? What, in Garrett's belief, makes for good corporate public relations? An analysis of his views, based on interviews with executives, conversations with Garrett, and a study of his speeches, articles, and programs provides one of the most useful outlines of how a corporation ought to conduct itself. What Garrett said, wrote, and did for twenty-five years is as fundamentally valid today as it was during the period when he was developing his theories. These were based on close observation of his own company and of the often wildly changing moods of the public.

Garrett made scores of speeches and presentations. He explained to General Motors' management exactly what public relations was, and what it was not. He explained to large organizations and small assemblies outside the company what his experience had taught him about a corporation's dealings with the public. He devoted an active and fruitful quarter-century working in the field with an amazing, powerful, and successful company. Yet the single speech that best explained what he thought business ought to do, in fact had to do, for survival, was made before the American Association of Advertising Agencies at its twenty-first annual meeting in 1938. The surprising thing is that it was given only seven years after he joined General Motors. It remains one of the best documents for those who want to know what public relations can do, what it cannot do, what it is, and what it can never be. Even though Garrett had another eighteen years in harness at General Motors he most simply explained his views in this speech, which he titled: "Public Relations—Industry's No. 1 Job." It received wide distribution at the time he made it. Sloan had it sent to every stockholder. The newspapers gave it exceptional coverage. Editorials were written about the speech. It was reprinted time and again. Even though it might be called an early distillation of his thinking, it still stands as the best summary of Garrett's views.

To Garrett, if business is to survive it must interpret itself by deeds and words that have meaning to those outside the company. That management thinks it is worthy of public support—that it is certain it makes a contribution to the economic advancement of the country—is not enough. Business's future depends not on the return on the capital invested, nor the wages it pays, but on the benefits to those outside the company, particularly the consumer, who is both inclusive of all groups directly affected by the company and so larger in number than any. Business has to learn that people are interested in more than the product and the price. They are interested in the way things are done, in what he calls the "social by-products" of business.

Garrett believed "public relations" is a synthetic term which to many is nothing more than a tony appellation from common press agentry. To some it is putting over insidious propaganda; to others its function is to present only the "favorable" side of business. To gain some understanding of public relations is to think of it as an institution's relations with the public. It is not something that can be applied to a particular phase of business. It is not a panacea. It is rather a fundamental attitude of mind, or if you will, a philosophy of management, which deliberately and with enlightened selfishness puts the broad interest of the consumer first in every decision, not just key ones, affecting the entire operation of the industry. Nor can good relations with the public be achieved through publicity or through what one particular department of a corporation can do.

To Garrett, what really counts is removing the causes of trouble, not putting out fires of public antagonism caused by bad corporate policies. Press agents, hack writers, publicity hounds, lobbyists, psychoanalysts, pseudo-scientists, straw vote experts—none of these can change public opinion. Public relations is not a program of defense or experiment in mass psychology, but a philosophy of management which must concern itself with satisfying the public's wants.

Garrett felt that the public means people who are members of many overlapping groups. They include those who build the product, distribute it, buy it, own the business, live in a plant community, supply the materials, and also those who do not directly fall within these categories but who, with the special groups, make up the entire consuming public. Public relations does not turn on the needs of industry, but the needs of the consumer. In its broad sense, public relations is not a specialized activity like production, engineering, finance, or sales. It cuts through all these as the theme for each. It is an operating philosophy that management must apply in everything it does and says. Patching up past mistakes or providing temporary or soothing substitutes for sound management policies will never do the job. Industry will only solve its public relations problems if it puts as much serious effort into their solution as it does in solving financial, engineering, and production problems. And business must stand "for" some things and not so often only be "against."

Garrett stated that good relations outside a company can only grow from good relations inside. If you want to be well thought of in the plant community the beginnings must be in the plant. To be favorably regarded throughout the nation the beginnings have to be in the plant community. If those who work for the corporation are not happy, those whom they meet outside the shop will not be friendly, for outsiders judge a corporation by the people they know who work for it. Nor do high wages alone assure good internal relations, important as good wages are. What the employee needs is the feeling that he is being fairly treated. Grievances, even if they are imaginary, must be met. The failure to explain company policies and why they were adopted can cause trouble. This is true for both the white- and blue-collar worker. In addition, management, while explaining its policies to its employees, must provide machinery for communication upward as well.

Garrett maintained that a company's public relations must always be firmly rooted in its plant community. This is where it lives and this is where the employees and their neighbors notice and talk about what is going on. Employees are the most articulate spokesmen for the company's policies. But being a good employer is not enough. The company, since it gets the benefits of the community, must shoulder its community responsibilities. Here again two-way communication is important: local management must make certain that the community understands what the company is doing and why, and must at the same time understand the community's wants.

Garrett believed that living right, however, is not enough. People must know you live right. To let them know, there must be communication that is effective. All media must be used to tell the corporation's story clearly and simply, without blurring facts. This demands a system of informing people who are directly involved and reaching beyond them. It demands the proper use of all means of communication to multiply the effect of good policies. Whether it be through stories in the local press or in a national magazine, or through films, speeches, brochures, open house for visitors to the plants, or round tables with teachers and editors, communication is vital. But the impact of all this is meager unless the basic policy of sound practices in the public interest is there to begin with.

Garrett insisted there is no place for public relations that connives, distorts facts, squirms, or is not frank and honest. It must have vigor, be open, and pervade the entire business from top to bottom. And it must interpret the practices and beliefs of industry in terms of benefits to others, not to itself. Public relations can only serve its purpose if it convinces the public as a whole that the public's good is being served at all times.

Enormous as was Garrett's contribution to General Motors in implanting the concept of public relations and in its practice and in building a department of competent practitioners, and valuable as he was in advancing the understanding of public relations with business leaders other than those in his own corporation, little could have been done without fullest support from Sloan. No corporation's relations with the public can be better than the sophistication of the chief executive. No matter how able the public relations director may be, no matter how good he is at understanding the corporation and the public, he is strapped without the continued insistence by the man who heads the corporation that the public relations policies be implemented. This is particularly true in the early stages of its development in any corporation. Only after public relations is established as a way of life in a company—only when all decisions by all managers are considered for their impact on public sensitivities as well as on economic growth of the company—does the active backing of the chief executive become less essential. That Garrett's work was of immense benefit to General Motors is not doubted by anyone. It was recognized on his retirement by the board of directors of General Motors, in a resolution: "He has effectively emphasized in General Motors Corporation over the years the importance of early recognition at the policy making stage of the public relations aspect of any management step."

It was lucky for Garrett and General Motors that his period as public relations director coincided with the Sloan regime. For thirty-three years Sloan was president (1923 to 1937) and chairman (1937 to 1956), and for twenty-five of these Garrett was public relations director. For twenty-three years Sloan was the chief executive officer, fifteen of them while Garrett was public relations director. One can only guess at what might have happened had Sloan not been in that exalted post during the Garrett years. If there had been someone who was not as perceptive as Sloan, who did not realize the importance of public opinion to the success of the corporation, Garrett would never have been able to make the impact he did.

William S. Knudsen, for three years, Charles E. Wilson, for twelve years, and Harlow H. Curtice, for five years, were presidents of General Motors. While Garrett was public relations director, Wilson was chief executive for seven years and Curtice for three. Their views were important, of course, and were of major influence in the corporation. It was essential that Garrett have their trust, so basic to a public relations director's success. But they would not, even had they wished, run in the face of the established Sloan policy in the corporation's relations with the public.

Garrett's successor is cut out of his own mold. Anthony G. De Lorenzo came from inside the public relations department. He had had long newspaper and wire service experience and six years under Garrett. One of those years, as public relations director, was for orientation in anticipation of his appointment as vice-president. This was in Garrett's last year with the company. The quiet, soft-spoken De Lorenzo, Wisconsin-born and a 1936 honor graduate of Wisconsin in journalism and political science, was forty-two years old when he became vice-president, public relations, of the corporation in 1956—seven years after he joined General Motors public relations department. For five years before that he was with the Kudner advertising agency as public relations counsel to the Fisher Body division of General Motors and the Buick Motor division in Flint, Michigan.

For more than a decade, De Lorenzo had been a newspaperman. After a year with the Racine *Journal-Times*, he moved to the United Press, working in Madison, Milwaukee, Chicago, and Detroit. In the three years in his last UP post he wore three hats: automotive editor, Detroit bureau chief, and Michigan manager. As Michigan manager he supervised the agency's coverage throughout the state. It was the Detroit assignment which led to his particular interest in the automotive industry since he covered every major development of its mobilization for World War II as well as innumerable other automotive stories. He had better than a front row seat; it was a first-rate chance to get a close look at the competing motor car manufacturers and their topmost brass.

It was in Curtice's era at General Motors that De Lorenzo shot up quickly. In three years, from 1955 to 1957, he received three promotions: to director of press, radio and television relations; to director of public relations; to vice-president, public relations staff. He moved into the top job seasoned in General Motors policies, knowledgeable in shirt-sleeve operations in the public relations department, with the full confidence of Curtice and the respect of his staff for quick decisions. He had a thorough knowledge of media and an appreciation of the need for management's continuous acceptance of the overwhelming power of public opinion.

De Lorenzo's first achievement as Garrett's aide—and one of the most important in his career—was to bring about the separation of General Motors' divisional public relations operations from the advertising agencies representing the various divisions. It was not easy or done overnight, because for many years General Motors' divisions had relied heavily on their advertising agencies to handle a multitude of public relations problems. Even in cases where there was a designated public relations director on the divisional payroll he normally reported to the advertising manager, the general sales manager, or the personnel director. De Lorenzo, with the strong support of Curtice, pressed hard for a divisional public relations director who reported directly to the general manager. Today, the direct line between the divisional general manager and his public relations director is standard practice in all General Motors divisions.

It was in 1954, while Curtice was president and Garrett vice-president, that De Lorenzo saw the results of an overquick decision, taken in anger, and without proper consideration of possible results. It made a lasting impression.

In 1953, some major publications carried stories describing the following year's car models. In the sharply competitive automotive industry the sales departments are certain that premature announcement of model changes cut sales. The whole concept is that advertising for new cars in magazines, newspapers, on radio and television, along with dealer showings and publicity be coordinated for maximum impact. The GM organization was disturbed by these advance leaks but saw no way to prevent them.

Then, in 1954, the *Wall Street Journal* ran a story with a sketch of a 1955 General Motors model months before the release date. The caption to the sketch noted that the drawing was from a blueprint obtained from an industry source. Curtice hit the roof. Without consulting Garrett, Curtice immediately accepted a suggestion from his sales chief and ordered that no more news be released to that paper and that its allocation of $250,000 in advertising be cut off at once. To Curtice, publication of the picture was a violation of General Motors' property rights. In his anger he didn't think of the effects of his move.

Garrett, as soon as he heard of Curtice's order, went to his president, told him that it was a mistake; that the news flow ban should be removed and the advertising allotment be restored. Naturally the *Wall Street Journal* defended running the sketch. Other newspapers joined in the cry of alarm and *The New York Times* editorially took after General Motors in an attack in which it said, in part, that "General Motors needs a 1954 model for its public relations." Strong newspapers quite naturally thought that if this could happen to the *Wall Street Journal* they could be next. The withdrawal of General Motors' advertising as punishment for a real mistake might very soon become punishment for a fancied affront. The whole idea of using the advertising bludgeon was insufferable and completely contrary to any policy of consideration of public attitudes or good sense.

Of course, the advertising was restored to the *Wall Street Journal*. The lesson was clear to all General Motors executives. It underlined that good judgment, without which a public relations director—or a chief executive either, for that matter—is useless, is the rock upon which good relations with the public rests. De Lorenzo never forgot what he saw and heard. It was equally salutary to others in the corporation, and has been one of the many reasons why managers today know that all their decisions must be carefully weighed for their impact on the public.

Curtice, who began as an accountant, and later managed two General Motors divisions—AC and Buick—was an outstanding salesman and served the company well at a time when salesmanship (because post-war car shortages were over) was badly needed. During the years of World War II and in the immediate post-war period, when there were more buyers than cars, and other goods, companies had forgotten how to sell.

Curtice enjoyed personal publicity. His successor as chief executive, Frederic G. Donner, is a very different person. Studious, prudent, and an omnivorous reader, he is a man who always does his homework.

He shuns personal publicity, even though any industrialist who heads a corporation so essential to the health of the American economy cannot stay out of the public prints no matter how much he may desire to do so. A Phi Beta Kappa from the University of Michigan, where he majored in economics, Donner came up through the financial side of the corporation. He was fifty-six years old when he was chosen chairman and chief executive of General Motors in 1958.

Donner's thinking on public relations is important, for during his tenure dollar sales, profits, dividend payments to stockholders, and world-wide unit sales of cars and commercial vehicles established new records. Much of General Motors' present expansion abroad is due to his foresight. Much more of it will probably not show on the income statements for years to come, since the time-spread between overseas development and profits is long.

In stating his views to the author Donner said:

Our public relations efforts are concerned with publicizing our products and particularly the new developments that our scientists and engineers bring forth. They are concerned with explaining our policies and our actions as they relate to people—customers, employees, stockholders, suppliers, dealers, Government and the public at large. They are concerned with telling what General Motors stands for and giving evidence of our competitive spirit, alertness, efficiency and high standards of moral integrity. The end of all this is to make the buyers of our products want them because they are built by General Motors.

These are the objectives of public relations as they relate to the larger goals of General Motors as a whole. The public relations executive contributes towards achieving these public relations objectives by the competence he brings to his job. He contributes through drive and determination and plain hard work, coupled with a capacity for growth and development. He must exemplify in his own life and conduct the high standard of qualities generally associated with General Motors.

The public relations executive has the continuing task of helping his associates in General Motors become effective representatives of the Corporation in their contacts with others. He has the responsibility of keeping management informed of the shifting winds of public opinion, of giving advice on public relations matters and of taking appropriate public relations action in support of corporate policies and actions. This responsibility, if carried out, is one that raises a public relations executive's value beyond an ordinary day-to-day one of carrying out what others ask him to do.

Donner outlined his thinking about public relations in an unusual talk some four months after he became chief executive of the corporation. It was made to a divisional public relations conference in Detroit. He said then that deep as are the roots of General Motors' public relations policies, going back to the Sloan-Garrett early days, the principles are as timely today as they were then. But what has happened is that their application has become more difficult. Just as life is more complicated for the individual, so is it for the corporation. In frontier days, a man provided food, clothing, and shelter for his family by hunting, felling trees, and raising crops and cattle. Today, in most cases, his job bears little relation to what he and his family consume. Even so, his major objective is still to provide food, shelter, and clothing. The same holds true for the corporation which too has come a long way from its "frontier" days when its only concern was to produce goods or services and earn a profit. Earning a profit is still the primary concern of the corporation, but it also must consider many things that "seemingly" have little to do with the primary function of profit-making.

Donner went on to underscore the word "seemingly," and told the public relations practitioners that he was convinced that in the long run everything the company did must have a relation to the primary function of producing goods and services at a profit and that every decision must be made with due consideration for the profitability of the business; that every activity must be judged in the light of the degree to which it strengthens or weakens the corporation's earning ability. The point, Donner said, was that today the corporation is concerned not alone with the immediate profitability of the business but equally with its prosperity over the long pull, and while many of those long term concerns are not essentially public relations concerns, they all involve public relations in a greater or lesser degree.

Donner explained that because public relations considerations enter into almost every decision, some companies have yielded to the temptation of letting surface public relations pressures control decision making.

I am glad to say that General Motors has not been among such companies. We have always been careful not to make unbusinesslike decisions because someone thought they were smart public relations—just as we have always been careful not to make un-

sound financial decisions because they appeared to be smart for
the short pull from the tax standpoint.

Stating this point positively, it appears to me that what is
sound from a business standpoint can also be expected to be
sound from a public relations standpoint. A sound business decision necessarily takes cognizance of the public relations aspects
involved. In fact, a decision is not soundly conceived if it does
not do this. It then becomes the job of public relations an
activity to make sure that the public understands why the decision is a sound one. This basic contribution in the public relations area is most important to any business.

Since General Motors is the largest industrial corporation in the
world, it is hard for many to grasp the dimensions of its operation
through figures. In other terms then—the corporation's sales in 1966
were larger than the national budget of France. The total population
of New Zealand is just about the same as the number of General
Motors employees and their families; while the net income of the
corporation was roughly the same as the national income of Ireland.
General Motors, which is not a holding company, but an operating
company, has 127 plants in seventy communities in eighteen states.
It has seven plants in Canada and assembly, manufacturing, or ware-
housing operations in twenty-two additional countries. It is generally
known as a manufacturer of passenger cars and trucks through its
Cadillac, Oldsmobile, Buick, Pontiac, Chevrolet, and GMC Truck and
Coach divisions; more than ninety per cent of civilian sales are in
automotive products. But it also makes diesel-electric locomotives and
diesel engines for marine, highway, and stationary use. It made a
significant contribution to the development and production of advanced
types of prop-jet aircraft engines for military and civilian use. It manufactures household appliances and other products built around an
electric motor or electrical controls, and heavy-duty earth-moving
equipment for off-highway use. Defense products accounted for more
than $552 million in sales in 1966. Overseas it employs more than
150,000 people; makes the Vauxhall cars in England, Opels in Germany, Holdens in Australia, and Chevrolets in Argentina and Brazil;
Frigidaire products in Australia, Brazil, France, Mexico, New Zealand,
and South Africa; and Euclid earth-moving machinery in Scotland.
General Motors relies on more than 36,000 suppliers to whom it paid
more than $9.56 billion in 1966, which was 47 per cent of its sales
for the year.

General Motors, a veritable dukedom, many parts of which are themselves bigger than good-sized corporations in the United States, naturally has a sizable group working directly in the public relations area. The structure of the public relations staff is accordingly built to suit the corporation's purposes. Unlike the practice in some corporations, the top management is directly involved in public relations policies and plans. The public relations staff's operation fits into the committee method used by other staffs of the corporation.

At the very top, the Personnel and Public Relations Policy Group of General Motors operates under the executive committee of the corporation. This group, an outgrowth of the committee Sloan set up on Garrett's advice in 1931, has alternating chairmen, Louis G. Seaton, vice-president, personnel staff, and De Lorenzo, vice-president, public relations staff, depending on the subject to be discussed. Meetings of this group are scheduled for every third Tuesday of the month in Detroit, usually at 2 P.M. The measure of its importance can be best gauged by the list of its members: D. L. Boyes, vice-president, components group; E. N. Cole, executive vice-president, operations staff; H. E. Crawford, vice-president, marketing staff; F. G. Donner, chairman and chief executive officer; R. C. Gerstenberg, vice-president, financial staff; S. E. Knudsen, executive vice-president, Dayton household appliance, engine, and overseas and Canadian groups; R. M. Kyes, executive vice-president, automotive components group and defense divisions; P. J. Monaghan, vice-president, Dayton household appliance and engine group; J. M. Roche, president and chief operating officer; E. D. Rollert, executive vice-president, car and truck, body and assembly group; George Russell, executive vice-president, finance; H. G. Warner, vice-president, body and assembly group.

It is at this meeting that actions demanding decisions are discussed: institutional advertising campaigns; new programs; progress and assessments of old ones; new model announcements and promotion; general policy approaches; public opinion trends; review of films before release. This committee assures the direct involvement of key executives of the corporation. Here they keep in close touch with all basic activities of the public relations department, and in turn De Lorenzo, in an organized way, learns of the thinking of those who have the final operating responsibilities for the corporation. It is both a learning and participating process for the entire group.

Nor is this the only, or even the principal, contact De Lorenzo has with the corporation's top executives. He sees or talks almost daily with both Donner and James M. Roche, who has been General Motors' president and chief operating officer since June, 1965. There are no doors barred to the public relations director; he has an opportunity to know what major decisions are being made. He reports directly to Edward N. Cole, one of the five executive vice-presidents, who is responsible for staff operations. The public relations staff is one of seven central staffs which make up the operations staff of the corporation. The others are marketing, engineering, personnel, manufacturing, research, and styling. This too is a measure of the status public relations holds at General Motors, for it ranks as a management function on a par with the others that are generally recognized as making up management's responsibility. Each of these operations staff activities is run by a vice-president, who acts in an advisory capacity to both the management of the operating divisions and the corporation's executives, including the chairman and the president.

Since no department can be any better than the people hired to do its job, General Motors carefully selects those who work in De Lorenzo's department. Excluding secretarial and clerical workers, there is a total of eighty-three people based in Detroit, New York, Washington, and the regional offices. Of these, 90.4 per cent have a bachelor's degree; 15.7 per cent a master's degree. A total of 30.1 per cent have degrees in journalism; 20.5 per cent in business administration and economics; and 39.8 per cent in various disciplines in the liberal arts and physical and social sciences. Their average age is 43.7 years, and 21.7 per cent have been at General Motors for more than twenty years.

Their backgrounds, beyond academic training, are varied, for there is no one source of those who prove capable in public relations. Prior to joining General Motors, 42.2 per cent of them had newspaper or wire service experience, and in many cases both; 10.8 per cent had a background in teaching; 4.8 per cent in advertising; 3.6 per cent in government; 2.4 per cent in radio and television; 8.4 per cent in public relations agencies.

A total of 30.1 per cent of the staff worked for other divisions or units of General Motors before joining the public relations department, and 18.1 per cent of the men worked for other industrial corporations before being hired. A total of 25.3 per cent joined the corporation's public relations activities directly out of college or the armed forces.

Some of the jobs these men had at General Motors before being recruited by the public relations department were: assembler, tool and die maker, tool inspector, machinist, safety engineer, salesman, labor relations specialist, parts representative, cost accountant, financial analyst, manufacturing foreman, stylist, researcher, engineer.

In looking for recruits, General Motors seeks, in addition to the right kind of academic training, those who are diligent, sociable, and creative, and have promotional ability, good judgment, and a facility in speaking and writing. Intelligence, poise, and tact are qualities at the top of the list of qualifications. Those who come directly into the public relations department from college usually are assigned as lecturers for the traveling science shows, "Previews of Progress," which cover almost all of the country.

The members of the public relations department of the overseas division, operating abroad, are, with only one exception, hired in the country in which they work. In fact, of the 150,000 GM employees stationed overseas in all categories, little more than two hundred are home office personnel assigned to locations outside of the United States.

The organization of the public relations department is never static. To meet changing conditions the structure is continuously altered and staff workers move from regional to divisional jobs, from divisions to regions, from both to the central office in Detroit, and back again to a region or a division. But even as the emphasis of the department varies, the job to be done remains constant to carry out three basic objectives: giving advice, disseminating information, and listening for the public's moods.

As advisor, the department calls attention to the public relations implications of management decisions, and suggests ways of making the public impact of these decisions of greater benefit to the corporation. As disseminator, the department uses all avenues: newspapers, magazines, wire services, radio, television, films, personal contacts, speeches, exhibitions, stockholder reports, educational booklets, and technical papers. As listener, it collects, evaluates and summarizes what is said and thought about General Motors and its products.

The department always keeps in mind the groups with which the corporation deals, as well as the general public. The goal is to build a reservoir of good will. Stockholders, employees, plant community residents, customers, dealers, suppliers, mass and specialized media, and, of course, the public at large are continuously informed. The customers are expected to look for quality and value in the products they buy; the employees for fair treatment, good wages and benefits; the plant communities for responsible conduct; the press for cooperation in covering newsworthy aspects of the business; and the general public for behavior in the public interest.

Mostly this means continued, low-key activities. But on occasion special events are set in motion, like the Motoramas, which introduce new cars, the Futuramas at the two New York World's Fairs, the celebration of General Motors' 50th anniversary in 1958, or the 1964 announcement by Donner of a $2 billion expansion program timed to coincide with the dedication of the new and vast assembly plant in Fremont, California.

General Motors' public relations function includes institutional advertising, and product advertising when it has an institutional flavor. Product promotion is done only at the divisional level. In addition, the department services other department staffs by writing reports, preparing presentations, or aiding in the promotion of an exhibit or a show.

In keeping with the general corporation policy of decentralized operations whenever it is most effective, the divisional public relations directors report to the divisional general manager, not to De Lorenzo. He does not hire, and has no authority over, the divisional public relations directors, although there is no problem of keeping a close liaison on policy.

The pragmatic approach of the public relations department is made clear by a look at its organization. It is partly set on functional patterns, partly on "publics," and partly on geographic lines. There are four major sections: institutional operations; news relations; communications; and field operations.

These sections, as well as the Washington office, report to De Lorenzo through his executive assistant, William E. Hamilton, a Boston University graduate who started as a field representative with General Motors Acceptance Corporation in 1931 and moved ahead through various jobs until he was given his present post in 1963. He takes the day-in-day-out burden of administration off De Lorenzo's back and rides herd on the section chiefs.

The institutional operations section is directed by Waldo E. McNaught. He began with Buick as divisional public relations director in 1950, after fourteen years as a newspaperman, all of it—after graduation from Marquette University—with the *Detroit Times*. He has been in his present job since 1963. This section is responsible for four areas: educational relations; institutional advertising; divisional relations; and special projects.

The objective of the educational relations activity is to make General Motors favorably known to students and teachers in secondary schools, colleges, and universities—the source of both future customers and future employees. Educational relations helps educators by keeping them in touch with major developments in industry that are directly related to their interests and with which General Motors is concerned. It also provides educational aids ranging from automotive parts and components to classroom booklets such as "Mathematics at Work" and various career booklets. In addition, it puts out driver, drafting, and design training kits, and *General Motors Engineering Journal*, a quarterly technical magazine, with articles by General Motors' scientists and engineers, written for college educators in engineering and allied sciences.

General Motors holds annual conferences for educators at both the high school and college level at which staff executives make presentations and during which educators visit General Motors laboratories and operating units. The oldest of these, begun in 1952 and lasting for a full week, is for college and university administrators, and teachers in engineering, physical sciences, and industrial design. By the end of 1966, 411 men and women representing 178 institutions of higher education in the United States and Canada had attended. During summer vacations General Motors divisions and staffs hire between forty and fifty local high school science and mathematics teachers for jobs related to the subjects they teach. Late in August, these teachers attend a one-week conference in Detroit.

Also, every year, at least one three-day conference is held in Detroit for the high school vocational guidance counselors who are located in General Motors plant cities. Carefully selected state directors of guidance, and college and university educators who are responsible for training high school counselors also participate in these meetings. The corporation's personnel, employment, training, and recruiting philosophy and programs are discussed.

The educational relations staff members also, cooperating with General Motors divisions, arrange local educator conferences and promote student-teacher visits to General Motors plants. Every month a newsletter summarizing trends and developments in education is sent to 524 General Motors management members and to 227 General Motors employees serving on local school boards.

The institutional advertising category of the institutional operations section is responsible for the corporate advertising campaigns. These advertisements sell no specific products. Instead they tell the public what General Motors is, what its policies are, the kind of people who work for it, and the contributions it makes to the country as a whole. In so doing they give support to the divisional product ads. Since ideas are usually harder to sell than goods, these ads are difficult to create successfully. The emphasis in these institutional advertisements shifts with the climate of the times. They are keyed to the particular audiences of the individual magazines and newspapers. Here the quality magazines have a special value, for through them the chances of having the ads read by the intellectual community is greater than in the general magazines. Science journals, teacher publications, and literary and public affairs magazines are all used for selected messages to selected groups.

Institutional operations also produces and distributes films, booklets, and a bi-monthly magazine, *American Youth*, which is sent to newly licensed drivers. This magazine's underlying purpose is to encourage safe driving. The bulk of its readers are youngsters who get the magazine for a full year. It has twenty-four pages, runs letters, articles, cartoons, and other features keyed to teen-age readers, and each issue carries two articles on safe driving plus a back cover message, in advertising format, on car safety. Its circulation is some 1,800,000.

The corporation, a pioneer in the use of films to inform the public about its policies, products, and activities, provides prints to any group which asks for them, with schools and colleges the most extensive users. Currently there are thirty-eight subjects covered by these films with an inventory of 8,100 prints. The booklet program, started in the research laboratories in 1934 with "Chemistry and Wheels," covers a wide range of subjects.

The purpose of the divisional relations category of institutional operations is to coordinate the central office and divisional public relations efforts so that there is no conflict. Each of the divisions runs its own programs, in addition to the product publicity for which it is responsible. These programs cover a wide spectrum: Fisher Body Craftsman's Guild, which has enrolled more than eight million boys and paid more than $2.5 million in awards and scholarships since 1931; Buick Open Golf Tournament; Buick's "Factory Whistle" radio program for Buick employees and others in communities where Buick plants are located; Chevrolet's Soap Box Derby, started in 1933, which registers just under 50,000 boys each year; Allison Division's "Power-ama," a permanent manufacturing and engineering museum which in 1966 attracted 93,947 vistors; Oldsmobile's annual sponsorship of Miss America; Guide Lamp Division's annual Junior Firemen's Day, a fire prevention program beamed at young people.

The special projects category has the onus of putting on events which attract public attention. These have included stockholder meetings, the dedication of General Motors' Technical Center, the travelling "Parade of Progress," caravan, the Milford Proving Ground's 40th birthday celebration in 1964, and the public relations events involving Motoramas.

The news relations section, with offices in Detroit and New York, has the primary responsibility for the release of information about General Motors to the general public. It deals with the editorial staffs of all news media: newspapers, magazines, radio, and television. The post of section head demands a director who knows media and understands news, the demands of journalists, and the operations of the wire services. It has one in Thomas E. Groehn, a graduate of the University of Michigan. He worked as a reporter on the *Detroit Times* for a short time, then moved over to the *Detroit News* as a reporter. He was labor editor there for seven years before being hired by General Motors in the press relations section. He moved up steadily in the same area until in 1963 he took over his current post. Groehn's section functions much like a news room on a metropolitan daily. Each man is assigned to a regular beat, is responsible for reporting the activities on his beat, must know and work closely with executives of the corporation he covers. Since every man in this section has had extensive experience in news media before being hired, the system is flexible so that one man can move quickly into areas where help is needed. The major beats are General Motors' executive offices and central office staffs—financial, personnel, manufacturing, marketing, legal, research, engineering, and styling.

The news relations section initiates and develops stories which may interest news media. Its members, in addition, work with other public relations sections; write summaries of executive speeches and statements for public distribution; arrange interviews for newsmen with General Motors executives; answer queries by news media on policies and activities of General Motors; and, in 1966, handled more than 2,800 written and telephoned questions about General Motors. In all cases, the news relations section works with other sections of the public relations departments on the news aspects of activities which are primarily the responsibility of those sections. This work may include news stories on special projects, the annual stockholders meeting, or the dedication of a new plant.

It also works closely with the thirteen regional public relations offices in getting information and clearing it for stories needed for news media in their local areas. The news relations section, in addition, assists General Motors' divisional public relations directors in getting clearance for publication of divisional information involving the corporation's policies. Another major function is to keep central office top management in Detroit and New York abreast of major developments abroad and at home that might affect their planning. This is done by providing the *Daily Digest* by noon each day to 125 leading corporate executives. Whenever necessary, special management bulletins are issued made up of material from the Dow-Jones ticker, UPI's radio wire, or other news sources in Detroit, New York, and other major news centers. These are hand delivered, as are the *Daily Digests*. News of special interest to these same executives is provided directly off the ticker or in clipping form. The entire news relations section works at high speed when necessary, with the fullest recognition of the problems of a newsman with an urgent deadline.

The communications section is directed by Swiss-born Maurice Wyss, who came to the United States when he was seventeen, went to night school in Philadelphia, graduated from the University of Pennsylvania's Wharton School of Finance and Commerce, and has been with General Motors since 1938, except for U. S. Army service. He has been in his current job since 1965, running a section which has three categories: editorial writing, shareholder relations, and editorial research and services.

Editorial writing's major field is in drafting speeches, presentations, statements, memoranda, and letters for General Motors executives for both public and internal consumption. The public speeches range from those given at annual stockholder meetings and major addresses before such groups as the Society of Automotive Engineers and The Economic Club of Detroit to short talks for civic luncheons. Those for internal use may vary from presentations to the board of directors of the corporation to short talks at dinners for retiring executives. In all cases the writers must have a thorough grounding in General Motors' policies, procedures, organizations, and objectives. Other writing assignments include help for other central office staffs and the divisions; articles for newspapers or magazines; presentations before governmental bodies; and letters to influential Congressmen.

The shareholders relations category is of infinite importance to General Motors, for it has always been stockholder oriented. It works like a two-way transmission belt, with information from management to stockholders and comments from stockholders to management. It is responsible for preparation, printing, and mailing of all stockholder publications, and handles the stockholder correspondence and the preparation of material for the annual stockholders' meetings. It gets the help of other sections, such as art and production, of the public relations staff, and from the financial, marketing, and legal departments. It gets out ten regular mailings a year to General Motors stockholders: the annual report, three quarterly reports, the report of the annual meeting, the automotive product booklet, and the four transmittal slips which go out with the common stock dividends. An eleventh mailing, a non-automotive product booklet, which is enclosed with the first quarter report, is sent out every other year.

Work begins on the annual report, published around March 1, during the early part of the summer with the evaluation of possible color picture themes. Color photos of cars are taken as soon as new models are ready in the fall, with the first drafts of the text being written in the late fall. Proofs of the report are checked by scores of executives. As part of the development of General Motors' interest in overseas operations, French and German language digests of annual reports were started in 1964, with Spanish and Portuguese editions added in 1965. These are sent to government officials, and business and financial leaders abroad.

The shareholder relations section also reports on annual meetings of other companies so that General Motors' managers can prepare for the kind of question asked by that new breed of annual-meeting-goer, the "professional stockholder." To keep management abreast of stockholder thinking, it also writes a monthly report on stockholder correspondence, including a tabulation of types of complaints, excerpts from representative letters, and charts showing trends of monthly correspondence.

The editorial research and services section assists in setting out broad policy guidelines and objectives for the public relations staff, prepares meeting agendas, reports these meetings, and is in charge of opinion surveys. It also supervises two libraries, in Detroit and New York, keyed to serve General Motors executives and their staffs. The libraries examine periodicals, books, and government documents for material of special interest to executives; clip all kinds of general and specialized publications; and get new books and reports for executives. The section also covers meetings and conferences on antitrust and economic issues, writes daily reports on Congressional hearings that have a bearing on the corporation, and handles a good deal of the correspondence sent to the corporate executives.

The field operations section's main concern is community relations. Its two basic jobs are to transmit General Motors' institutional policies and public relations programs to plant cities, and to report to central management the reactions to General Motors' policies, programs, people, and products. The section is run from Detroit by Edmund Steeves, a University of Nebraska graduate, who worked with United Press for sixteen years before joining General Motors in 1954 in the press relations section. He has been in his current post since 1962.

The principal vehicles for this two-way flow of information are the thirteen regional offices, located in Atlanta, Buffalo, Chicago, Cleveland, Dallas, Dayton, Detroit, Flint, Indianapolis, Kansas City, Los Angeles, Newark, and San Francisco. They are staffed by a manager, sometimes an assistant, and two or three secretaries. It is their job to anticipate local public relations problems; report public attitudes; keep local General Motors executives aware of corporate activities; maintain close working relations with the area's press, radio and television; localize and distribute General Motors' national news releases and initiate local news stories; help divisions and plants on local public relations problems and encourage local executive participation in community affairs; keep good relations between the corporation and schools, colleges, and community organizations; handle executive visits, news conferences, and local arrangements for such special events as GM Motoramas and auto shows; schedule the corporation's science shows and films; distribute booklets; and update civic mailing lists.

Through these regional managers the field operations section services the fifty-seven plant city committees. These committees, working in centers where the corporation has plants, are appointed by the president of General Motors from the top local plant managers. They meet regularly, discuss community problems and decide courses of action which have the full support of all General Motors units in the areas. They deal with charitable contributions, plan open houses and plant tours, and are responsible for relations with service clubs and other local groups as well as with the home governmental bodies.

The field operations section also keeps an eye on the forty-eight field relations committees, whose membership comes from divisional sales offices and plant managers in plant cities. These committees coordinate local planning of General Motors' management club programs. The thirty-five management clubs have as members zone and branch office personnel down to the level of department head, in addition to plant managers' and general managers' staffs. These clubs have nearly four thousand members. The clubs meet for lunch or dinner five times a year and give the General Motors men of different divisions a chance to know each other and their problems, and talk about corporate policies and programs.

The field operations section is responsible as well for the seven "Previews of Progress" science shows. These educational science demonstrations, conducted by two men, are presented at junior high schools and high schools throughout the country. More than a million students a year see these shows.

The speakers' bureau is another responsibility of field operations. This bureau, set up for state-wide, regional, and national organizations that ask for speakers, fills some five hundred requests a year, turning away nearly four times as many. To take the burden off the corporation's executives who cannot begin to make the appearances, eleven outside speakers are used; six are educators, three are clergymen, and two are retired General Motors personnel. They are chosen, not because they know the corporation, for they do not talk about GM or its policies, but because they are good speakers. These speakers work for their expenses and a fee per speech and their subjects are largely inspirational.

To reach small town and rural America, the field operations section has set up community relations chairmen in 2,400 towns, mostly with populations under ten thousand. These chairmen are generally General Motors car dealers who work in three areas: dealer relations, farm youth organizations, and safety. The chairman serves a three-year term for his county during which he arranges the showing of General Motors' films, keeps lists of opinion leaders in his area for mailings of material from Detroit, distributes booklets, and sponsors the Green Pennant safety program. Safety, an overriding theme— safety at home, at work, at play, on the highways—takes much of the chairman's time for it means working in schools, with 4-H clubs and the Future Farmers of America.

No corporation of any size can do without a listening post in Washington, and this is the primary purpose of General Motors' Washington office. Its manager, Ernest L. Barcella, is a thoroughly experienced Washington hand, with twenty-one years in the nation's capital for the United Press, the last eight of which were as bureau manager. A Dartmouth College graduate who worked for UP for thirty-one years, he knows Washington's politics and its leading figures. Barcella also worked in Philadelphia, Albany, Boston, and Chicago. He has been with General Motors since 1961, and was appointed to run the Washington office in 1965. Six men, including the manager, make up the staff. He has an assistant manager, a staff assistant, and a general assignments man. The manager and his assistant are responsible for government relations. The assistant manager, Warren R. Jollymore, has been with General Motors since 1953 and is a solid backstop for Barcella.

The Washington office gathers information, which it sends to the corporate executives concerned; is General Motors' liaison with the government, acting as the general Washington information center for the corporation's central office and divisional executives; maintains proper and useful relations with government officials, members of Congress, military authorities, national business associations, representatives of other corporations, Washington community and business leaders, and, of course, the capital's correspondents.

It also suggests procedures and makes arrangements for special General Motors Washington activities, such as Congressional committee appearances, and meetings between the corporation's executives and government officials and legislators; provides General Motors information to news media, congressmen, and government officials; and helps the corporation's divisions with their Washington problems.

General Motors does not use outside lobbyists. All representation to government officials and agencies is carried out by the corporation's own people, with the manager of the Washington office registered as a lobbyist. When an executive outside of Washington wants to see a government official, appointments are set up by Barcella or Jollymore. A staff member usually goes along with the visiting executive. For a Congressional hearing, the Washington office makes the mechanical arrangements and assists with background information on the subject of the hearing. In addition, it answers queries, which run about seventy a week, from Detroit, New York, and the divisional plants, and it can quickly get in touch with the right government official or legislator on any problems of the corporation.

Important corporate statements, speeches, committee testimony, and other material are sent to congressmen, cabinet officers, and other officials with a covering note from the Washington manager. In some cases only members of interested Congressional committees are sent material. Nor is this a one-way thoroughfare: the Washington office gets frequent calls from government people about policies, products, or service. These are either answered directly or are referred to the corporation divisions directly involved.

The Washington office sends daily reports of hearings, proceedings, and other activities of the Federal Government by mail, teletype, and telephone to General Motors' other offices. These range from short memos to copies of bulky government documents. To do its job better the Washington office keeps close contact with trade associations and business organizations that have headquarters or branch offices in Washington. To keep this large establishment working closely, to make certain that De Lorenzo is not riding horses racing off in all directions, and to prevent false moves which can cause serious trouble demands a good deal of coordination. The first step to assure that the policies of the public relations department are understood and that the men down the line know about its plans is the public relations planning committee. On it sit De Lorenzo, Hamilton, McNaught, Groehn, Wyss, and Steeves, plus the managers of education relations, institutional activities, divisional relations, special projects, Detroit news relations, business management (who handles all budgets, personnel records and general office management in Detroit, New York, Washington, and the regional offices), editorial writing, editorial planning and services, field relations, and plant city and regional activities. The committee meets once a week in Detroit, is chaired by De Lorenzo, and has a permanent secretary who keeps records and distributes minutes of the meetings to all members.

Current and planned projects are discussed at this meeting. Progress reports are scheduled frequently. Since the public relations activities are not compartmentalized and revolve around projects, and since some of the staff sections' work overlaps on occasion, assignments are made at these meetings. A member of the committee has to be asleep not to know what is being planned or what is being done by his colleagues. The system works. But then comes the problem of letting others in the department know what is happening. Most of this is done by word of mouth, unless it is a key decision. Then a memorandum is sent by De Lorenzo to all department members. In addition, to keep the divisional public relations staff on top of what is happening in divisions other than their own, a weekly, single-spaced, four-page newsletter is sent from Detroit to all divisional people and key members of the Detroit central staff. Another weekly newsletter, *Regional News*, is based on items sent to Detroit by all regional managers, runs from three to four pages, single-spaced, and carries the doings of divisional men, regional men, the central office, and changes in media personnel in publications they may deal with. Policy statements, reports, and general information are also continuously sent. Quarterly meetings are held in Detroit for the public relations chiefs of the five car and truck divisions; key central office staff members attend. Occasional regional or area conferences in plant cities are convened for local public relations staffers.

Another means of keeping the far-flung public relations executives from working at cross purposes is the corporation-wide annual conference. The first was held in 1947. It was dropped for a time but was revived in 1957 by De Lorenzo. Conferences have been held annually since and serve many purposes. The men get to know each other. Policies are outlined. Techniques are discussed. The issues which may affect the corporation for the coming year are reviewed in the two-day conference, and there are speeches by Donner or Roche or one of the executive vice-presidents. There is no rigid pattern and the program, tightly scheduled, is diversified and attuned to topical interests. Presentations are made by line and staff men about particular areas that need clarification for those far from the central office; and, when labor negotiations are about to take place for the three-year UAW contract, the chief General Motors negotiator discusses issues which may arise. These conferences are chaired by De Lorenzo. On occasion invitations are extended to outside speakers who are specialists in some area of public policy that needs elucidation for those in attendance. It is at this event that the divisional men, responsible as they are to their own general managers, get in depth what the central office thinks, what it believes are priorities, and, in many cases, what the planned projects are.

Keeping the overseas staff informed is another and quite different problem. Bringing the public relations men to Detroit from all parts of the world is expensive and difficult. Instead, the public relations department of the overseas operations division in New York attends the conference and in turn sends memoranda reporting on it abroad. This department, which acts as a service staff to the twenty-two overseas subsidiaries' public relations men, sends additional information on what is happening in the plants in the United States and Canada, provides germane data on U.S. products and projects, and answers queries about trends in the United States. The objectives of General Motors' public relations operating overseas are, quite naturally, the same as those at home: to assure public acceptance and good will for the corporation and its products. They help the overseas subsidiaries act in the interest of the host countries.

De Lorenzo, as part of keeping abreast of what is going on in the corporation, is a member of the board of trustees of the General Motors Institute, the fully accredited engineering college at Flint. He also belongs to the employee benefits plans committee, the committee for educational grants and scholarships, and the General Motors administrative safety committee. Other members of his staff sit on the interstaff review committee and the committee on labor negotiations.

To keep in touch with other automobile manufacturers on items of public relations which affect the industry as a whole, contact is maintained through the public relations committees of the Automobile Manufacturers Association. Problems of smog, safety, and state and federal legislation are discussed. When action is necessary, it is either done directly by each company or as a whole through the AMA, whose public relations director is in Detroit.

Every good public relations director has his own emphasis on what effective public relations principles and practices should be. De Lorenzo, different as he is in outlook and personality from Garrett, naturally has his own views—even though he is fully in agreement with his predecessor's fundamentals and has built on the solid base he inherited. As times change, as new stresses appear caused by social adjustments and shifts in public attitudes, new methods, or variations of the old, are used. And as the corporation grows older, as more and more executives have lived with the policy of viewing their decisions for the effect they may have on the public, the orientation and practice of those who are in the public relations department shift.

To De Lorenzo, a company has to be concerned with the impressions created by its corporate behavior, by the behavior of its individuals, and by the behavior of its products, because all of these impressions affect the sale of its products and its ability to earn a profit. Whatever can be done to heighten and increase the company's good impressions or correct and counteract the bad impressions will eventually be shown in the firm's balance sheet. This is where public relations as a staff activity makes its contribution in a large company.

De Lorenzo feels that large corporations should be reconciled to being unloved. They are not supposed to be loved and the best that they can ever get is respect. A corporation cannot expect even to be liked at all times, nor should it try to be. A legitimate objective is to be respected, and it should be satisfied if it reaches this position and maintains it. Some of the things management of necessity does for the over-all good of the business are bound to displease one group or another. It should strive, however, to achieve and preserve a net balance of good impressions, because this good standing, solidly based, pays dividends in increased sales and in ability to attract good employees. A company should also want a good public standing for the same reason that an individual wants a good reputation—as evidence that it is a good citizen, good neighbor, and good employer.

A business enterprise operating in today's competitive economy, says De Lorenzo, has to observe two basic essentials if it is to get lasting public approval: it must serve society effectively, and must let people know—and get them to understand—what it is doing and what it plans to do. The second is the primary role of public relations in modern management. To handle this job with any degree of competence a public relations man must first understand the corporation and its goals. Understanding means more than a technical knowledge of its products, its organization, its financial position, or the various day-to-day problems of the business. It is essential for those responsible for interpreting the company to the public to know the corporation's history, traditions, plans for the future, the reasons for its basic policies, and the development of its guiding principles.

To De Lorenzo, the public relations man must also understand the corporation's weaknesses, as well as its strengths, and must be as well informed about the arguments of the company's critics as he should be about the compliments of those who admire it. He should be saturated with his company, but not brainwashed. He must be able to look at his company objectively, knowing where it is most vulnerable to at-

tack so that he can be ready to defend it. As a member of management he must share responsibility for correcting his corporation's
faults as well as directing public attention to its virtues. Few people
in public relations can consistently strike the balance between objectivity and company identification, but the real professionals come close
to it most of the time; and when they swing too far in either direction
they are likely to find themselves in trouble.

De Lorenzo believes some of the confusion about public relations
stems from the fact that it has been surrounded by a mumbo jumbo
of mysterious phraseology—phrases like "engineering of consent," "per-
ceptual context," "propulsion of motivation," "social lubricity." Additional confusion arises from the illusion that public relations can dress
a company in any costume it selects. He cites as examples one public
relations agency in New York which even offers "Image Management"
and others which have promised "the fabrication of a corporate profile," as if a company could pick out an attractive profile and public
relations could then proceed to create it out of thin air. There is no
such thing as a single profile or image, for every company is many
things to many people and the bigger the company the more things
it is to more people. It may also be many things to the same person—
a product, a job, a neighbor, a dividend. Nor can public relations
"fabricate"—it must reflect, and you cannot create images without
having something to reflect. Of course, reflected images can be dis-
torted, but sooner or later the distortions will be recognized for what
they are; but by then the damage has been done and it is too late for
repairs. It is far better to reflect honest images, even if they win few
popularity awards, than to take bows for flattering reflections whose
phoniness will later become apparent to the public. Too many practitioners in the public relations field have helped surround it with an
aura of mystery with the misguided intention of giving it a more professional appearance.

De Lorenzo points out that, not many years ago, a corporation's
relations with the public were presumed to be good until they got so
bad that sparks were flying. At this point the company president would
get a bit worried, call in the fire brigade, and say he thought he
detected a faint aroma of smoke. The whole place was ablaze by then
and often there was nothing to do but rebuild it from the ground up.
Even today, some public relations practitioners are required to try to
make a silk purse out of a sow's ear but, by and large, the public has
learned to recognize a pig, even in a poke. Public relations must—
there is no other way—build on a sound foundation of good deeds.
Then, and only then, can telling about the company have an enduring
value. To communicate is essential: there is no beaten path to the

door of the better mousetrap builder who hides his light under a bushel.

Public opinion is a complex thing; the product of many, and often opposing, influences. And polling to understand it is a tricky business. For one thing, it assumes that the public always has an opinion. Unfortunately, the sad fact is that people are opinionless on many subjects and issues. Even more unfortunately, some won't admit this to the pollster. That is why you can always get expressions of conviction on non-existent issues. The label on the public opinion poll package should always read "handle with care." Even so, the polling technique is useful in measuring attitude trends, and, in some cases, for exploring specific public issues.

To De Lorenzo, building and protecting a corporation's public reputation is an integral part of modern business management—part of its day-to-day job. Here are his ten simple rules of thumb, what he calls a working guide for managers:

1. Don't consider public relations the sole job of Public Relations. The public relations specialist can't do much without the help of everybody else in the management organization.

2. Do remember that public standing is built from the sum of all impressions. However small an individual's public relations contributions may seem to be, he should make sure that each one is positive, not negative.

3. Don't expect a company's public relations standing to stand still. At any one moment only one thing is certain: it's either moving up or down.

4. Do consider public relations each time a decision is made. The best time is before a decision is made, although many people wait until afterwards—and usually regret it.

5. Don't think the most effective public relations results necessarily from projects or stunts. They're the banquet, but people have to eat three meals a day.

6. Do bear in mind that what is done is even more important than what is said. The pen may be mightier than the sword, but the deed is mightier than the word.

7. Don't make the mistake of thinking that relations with the public can be avoided by doing nothing. Doing nothing—of itself— can create an impression—usually a bad one.

8. Do the right thing from the standpoint of the business and most often it will be the right thing from the standpoint of good public relations. If at any time this does not seem to be true, the fault probably lies in taking the short, not the long-range, view of what is right from the standpoint of the business.

9. Don't hesitate to step up to bad publicity—unless "bad" means "true." If the shoe fits, the remedy obviously lies in correcting the policy or action that caused the bad publicity.

10. "Do unto others as . . ." still spells out the best approach to public relations. Try as we may, there is really no substitute for the Golden Rule in any phase of living.

Not all the concern with public relations is by any means concentrated in De Lorenzo's department. Good relations with employees, one of the fundamentals of a corporation's policies, is the province of the personnel department. Plant recreation facilities, payments for employees' suggestions, recruitment and training, and provision for hiring handicapped workers, all fall under personnel. So does the foremen's training program which General Motors stresses as one of its bases of successful operations. So important did Sloan consider this area that, in 1934, foremen were put on a salary basis and in 1941 the corporation established the rule that their salaries had to be at least twenty-five per cent higher than the earnings of the highest paid group of employees they supervised. They are paid for overtime work, a practice adhered to since the early days of World War II. In addition, the personnel department handles labor relations, employee programs, and all publications that go directly to those who work for the corporation.

The most thorny of the personnel department's work is in its labor negotiations. More than 400,000 General Motors workers belong to trade unions, mostly the United Automobile Workers of America, whose leadership is determined and hard-driving. It is as progressive a union as General Motors is a corporation. Walter Reuther, UAW's president, understands, as few other union leaders do, that the final court in negotiations is public opinion. He is himself a public relations expert who understands how to appeal to the public and use media, and knows instinctively how to couch his demands in terms of the public's interest.

General Motors accepts unions. It works with them. It makes every effort to meet every reasonable demand of the unions. It is anxious to keep its workers satisfied, for it operates on the principle that it must have a work force that knows that the corporation is fair, is

anxious to do the decent thing, and does not niggle on a contract. In
that way, it can keep production schedules, and turn out a product
that the consumer will buy. There is no name-calling or attempts by
General Motors to denigrate the union and its leadership. Irritants
that make some corporate managers fire back shot for every shell from
those old-timers in the union who forget that the union-busting era
is over, do not excite either the personnel department or General
Motors' corporate heads. General Motors has learned to live with
unions. The issue of unionism was settled a long time ago. To General
Motors, a worker can be a loyal employee and at the same time a loyal
member of the UAW just as he can be a loyal member of his church.

But one thing that General Motors will fight over, will refuse to
give up, is its basic right to manage, including pricing policy. Essential as it is to avoid strikes, General Motors is convinced that it is just
as essential to keep management in charge of managing the business.
It is not an easy job to do both, and the troubles in labor negotiations
will only be serious when this balance cannot be maintained. Walter
Reuther and his top command are as aware of this as are the personnel
department of General Motors and those to whom it reports.

It was not always an easy road. It has been smoothed by hard
experience on both the union's and management's side of the bargaining table. There was a time when General Motors opposed union
organization of its plants with every weapon it could use. The events
leading to the sit-down strikes at General Motors in 1937 are not the
best examples of statesmanship on management's side or the leadership
the unions had at that time. It is, however, important to go back to
those days to see how far labor negotiations have come since this
period, and to understand how the force of public opinion has changed
conditions so that such events could never be repeated today. And
with the change of public attitudes has come the respect that management and the union leadership have for each other.

Domestically, 1937 was one more year of depression, bitterness,
and social unrest. Franklin D. Roosevelt had been re-elected the previous November in a landslide victory over Alfred Landon, the Republican candidate. Both houses of Congress were overwhelmingly
Democratic. The fear of unemployment, the frustrations of job
hunting, the pressures for better working conditions in the plants, and
the demands for better pay gave rise to demands for union organization far beyond the competence of the leadership of the American
Federation of Labor, with its emphasis on craft unionism, to satisfy.
The new element, which the AFL's heirarchy just didn't grasp, was
that industry had so changed that masses of workers could not qualify

for membership in craft unions. The urge for industrial unionization was strong, and John L. Lewis, the United Mine Workers' leader, and others who understood the trend of their times, formed a new group, the Committee for Industrial Organization, which was expelled from the AFL in 1936 and became a competing organization. It moved with great speed to organize the unorganized workers in the steel, rubber, automobile, and other mass industries which had previously escaped organization by the AFL. It also moved quickly into politics, contributing nearly $500,000 to Roosevelt's campaign against Landon. No organization can of course come into being without organizers, but the demand from the unorganized for the protection of unions was insistent and the time was ripe for their unionization.

The Wagner Labor Relations Act had been passed and, with it, the heavy weight of the Roosevelt administration came down on the side of unions. As the burden of the law had once been in favor of industry so it now shifted to favor unions. With the law at their back, and the all-out support of the governmental machinery and the President to help them, organizers went to work with the kind of zeal that great crises bring. The Congress of Industrial Organizations—as it later became—brought into this new kind of trade union those workers in mass industries who had not previously been in unions.

Sloan's comment on the Wagner legislation when it was before Congress, was that "industry, if it has any appreciation of its obligations to future generations, will fight this proposal to the very last." At the time it seemed a revolutionary proposal to Sloan and other industry leaders, and to such commentators as Walter Lippmann, who wrote that "if the bill were passed, it could not be made to work." It was both a "legal monstrosity," he said, and "one of the most reactionary measures of our time." General Motors' own lawyers had said it was unconstitutional.

Sloan was fearful. In *My Years With General Motors* (New York: Doubleday & Co., 1964) he states his case, not "to revive the bitter controversies that arose over these early encounters with labor organizations" but "merely to suggest one of the reasons why our initial reaction to unionism was negative."

Sloan writes:

One is inclined to forget that unionization in large industries was not then the custom in the United States. The significance of large-scale unionization was not yet clear to us. We know that some political radicals regarded unions as instruments for the attainment of power. But even orthodox "business unionism" seemed to us a potential threat to the prerogatives of management. As a businessman I was unaccustomed to the whole idea. Our early experiences with the AF of L unions in the automobile industry were unhappy; the chief issue with these unions became organizational. They demanded that they represent all our workers, even those who did not want to be represented by them. Our initial encounter with the CIO was even more unhappy; for that organization attempted to enforce its demands for exclusive recognition by the most terrible acts of violence, and finally seized our properties in the sit-down strikes of 1937.

The troubles had been building up for several years before the sit-down strikes. To block the CIO's attempt at organizing its workers, General Motors rushed through a series of company union elections. It set up an extensive spy system to report on workers who joined or spoke favorably of unions, and fired and blacklisted workers to break the union before it became strong. The official summary of the La Follette Committee of the Senate stated flatly that during the period between January 1, 1934, and July 31, 1936, General Motors Corporation "paid $994,855 to detective agencies for spy services." While doubtless much of this sum was expenditure for plant protection in its normal sense, a good deal of it was spent to trail union leaders, and report on their activities and the views of those in the plants who expressed favorable feelings about unions or intended to join one.

Edward Levinson, who, Walter Reuther says, "almost single-handedly" was responsible for the creation of the La Follette Senate Civil Liberties Committee, wrote in *Labor on the March* (New York: Harper & Brothers, 1938) that the "speed of the belt lines and the conveyor system sapped them [the workers] of their strength early in their manhood. Improvements in machinery increased the length of seasonal layoffs, created a reservoir of unemployed to fill the places of the workers who 'slowed down.' "

Levinson, former labor editor of the *New York Post* and who in the early '40s became public relations director of the UAW called the strike of General Motors workers in January and February of 1937 "the most significant industrial battle since labor's defeat at Homestead. It held in its hands the future of the CIO and the new labor movement which was soon to sweep millions of American breadwinners into its ranks." Levinson wrote further that it was more than a strike; it was a momentous struggle between the aroused forces of labor and the third largest corporation in the country, typifying years of unchallenged anti-unionism and involved the seizure of industrial plants worth more than $50 million and "the failure of the owners, vigilantes, courts, police, and military to recapture them."

Over and over again, writes Levinson, the 1937 strikers summarized their chief complaints as being two: "We don't want to be driven. We don't want to be spied upon." The mood at this time in the plant towns was ugly. The social historian Frederick Lewis Allen describes the attitude of workers in industrial centers this way in *Since Yesterday* (New York: Bantam Books, 1961):

> Men who had suffered acutely during the Depression had lost all respect for the princes of industry who hired and fired them; were ready to make trouble just as soon as they had full stomachs and a glimmer of hope. With labor in a rebellious mood, many unions inexperienced and undisciplined, racketeers and adventurers making hay as union organizers, jurisdictional disputes frequent, the labor high command divided, the status and meaning of the law uncertain, the attitude of the government shifting and ambiguous, many employers openly heedless of the law, and conflicting propaganda misrepresenting the issues, there was confusion everywhere. Anger deepened and strikes mutiplied.

Homer Martin, a former Baptist clergyman, was then head of the United Automobile Workers Union, which had affiliated with the CIO in 1936. Martin was a strange man of many sides on many issues. Levinson views Martin's principal asset an extremely effective style of oratory, as an emotional man with little administrative ability at a time when the union badly needed a strong leader to unite its many factions. Martin's attempts to negotiate with General Motors failed. The fury of the workers in the plants steadily mounted. Finally, they sat down in their plants, took possession, and refused to leave.

The strike lasted forty-four days. It closed sixty plants in fourteen states. It involved, directly and indirectly, 150,000 workers. General Motors recognized the union as the bargaining agent for its members in seventeen of its plants. The cost in dollars to the corporation was incalculable. The victory gave industrial unionism a tremendous boost. Yet there is no doubt that the strike was illegal, that the strikers had occupied property which was not their own. The first attempt to evict them brought violence and failure. Nor were the court orders to the strikers to leave the plants implemented.

The Governor of Michigan, Frank Murphy, had been swept into office in the Roosevelt landslide. He, in concert with President Roosevelt and Labor Secretary Frances Perkins, brought pressure on General Motors and Sloan to accept the union. Murphy did send the

National Guard to Flint, but ordered the men not to evict the strikers, despite court orders and the decision that they were trespassing. Murphy's reasoning was that under the circumstances, with the workers, their families and supporters in Flint and Detroit in a frenzy of emotion, enormous violence and bloodshed that would leave scars for generations would result. Reports of the period underline how the sit-down strikers would not be budged; that their morale was high; that they were in a kind of euphoria that would have driven them to face the fire of the National Guard had it been ordered to shoot. Sympathizers from other plants and other industries marched, drove trucks and cars and came by train to Flint and Detroit in thousands in a demonstration of solidarity that awed commentators of the era. The only way, Governor Murphy believed, was settlement, despite the illegality of the strike.

Management and the public relations department were both bewildered by the sit-down strike. They had no previous experience with either unions or strikes. How to proceed, what to do, how to get their side of the story to the public was a mystery. The union leadership ran rings around them. It could, and did, make all sorts of statements, often contradictory, but they suited the mood of the moment. The least of General Motors' worries was an answer. And when answers did come, generally several days later, they were written in style suitable to rock-bound corporate lawyers who had no concept of what was usable by the press or understandable to the public. To complicate the problem, the answers had to be cleared by innumerable executives who had not the foggiest notion of the deadline needs of media, and who were editing for the long-term court record, not for immediate use and effect.

Today the public relations and the personnel departments work together prior to and during labor negotiations and during a strike if one is called. They confer frequently, plan strategy and tactics and try to anticipate what the UAW will say and do to obtain public support. The union has, from the beginning, known that public backing is essential, and long before the end of a contract to lay the background for its demands, it begins to appeal to the country at large in addition to its own members. The corporation now operates on this principle as well.

Louis G. Seaton, General Motors' chief negotiator, is the director of the personnel department. Like Reuther, he attended Wayne University and did not graduate. His experience at General Motors, starting with his assignment to the sales section in 1928, includes the dealer organization department and industrial relations section. He had ten years' experience as director of the labor relations section before his appointment as vice-president, personnel staff, in 1957. He is a hard bargainer, a man of his word, who knows the UAW almost as well as he knows General Motors; has the fullest support of his superiors and can speak for the corporation on a day-to-day basis without having to run back to the chairman or the president before answering the query of a newspaperman—nor does he need a public relations man at his right elbow.

During contract negotiations he sees the press frequently, is available to newsmen at all hours, and immediately after a negotiating session will hold a press conference and answer questions for the press as well as for radio and television reporters. He knows the newspapermen who cover labor for the general press, the business press, and the labor press, and they consider him a straightforward informant. One of his many strengths is his understanding that it is essential to get the corporation's side of the story across, and here he works intimately with De Lorenzo and the news relations section. Before labor negotiations begin he briefs the public relations men at the annual public relations conference on the potential issues and what he thinks the union's demands may be.

The general responsibility of the news relations section is to have General Motors' position and views reported as fully as possible by the news media. Seaton welcomes its help, for, over a period of some twenty years, news relations has built a solid relationship with the corps of Detroit-based newsmen that report labor news.

The 1964 negotiations for a new three-year labor contract with UAW is a good example of how the public relations department works in this specialized area. Immediately after the 1961 labor contract was signed, the planning began. During the 1961 negotiations the UAW tried to draw the public's attention away from the economic demands by accusing General Motors of tolerating poor working conditions, and the phrase "gold-plated sweatshop" was used. From that phrase the General Motors' public relations people guessed that UAW would use the same tactics in 1964 and decided that the best answer they could possibly have was to invite the public to visit its plants and see for itself.

The plant-visits program that the corporation normally runs was expanded. The divisions were encouraged to step up these visits and to the usual open invitations were added special invitations to those who were opinion leaders in the communities in which General Motors had plants. From 1961 to 1963 General Motors held more than 500 open houses with a total attendance of more than a million visitors.

The special groups invited added close to another million who could see the assembly lines in operation and the conditions under which the men worked.

Then, at the beginning of 1964 the plant-visit invitations were accelerated once again. Editors, clergymen, city councilors, teachers, service club groups, and others were particularly asked to see conditions in the shops. Targets were set so that those who had an effect on public opinion would be asked to visit plants at times of their own convenience. This added another million visitors, for the campaign to get visitors was intensive. Then, as 1964's labor negotiation time grew closer, editors and labor reporters in General Motors communities were asked to see the plants. The working press was given carte blanche to talk to workers on the assembly lines, query them without any manager or public relations staffer from GM listening. The personnel and public relations people in every area of the country worked on the campaign of "come see for yourself." Some three hundred editors, labor writers and reporters came, saw conditions, asked questions, wrote stories.

Then—because the guess that the UAW would again use the theme "gold-plated sweatshop," plus a variation "chained to the assembly line like dogs," proved right—the continuing background and off-the-record briefings on the labor situation and the forthcoming negotiations were intensified. These were for the influential news media representatives, both the working press and those who were in policy positions. These briefings, held on an individual publication basis, were begun in the fall of 1963 and included more than thirty-four major newspapers, wire services, magazines, TV, and radio outlets. At these sessions the corporation spokesmen were Seaton, De Lorenzo, and director of labor relations Earl R. Bramblett, who is on Seaton's staff.

These briefings were effective. As the grapevine spread the word of them, additional publications called General Motors to ask for similar briefings. The three objectives set out in advance were attained: to counter the expected line of the UAW about "inhuman working conditions"; to establish General Motors' own position; and to develop a rapport between the news media and General Motors' bargaining group. On the local level, the same thing was done, except that it was not as intensive.

Before the negotiations began, Seaton's department wrote, and sent to every hourly rated employee and to management, a brochure headlined "Sixteen Years of Progress Through Free Collective Bargaining." In the 36-page publication, the theme of cooperation between General Motors and the UAW was stressed. On the inside front cover was a reproduction of the introduction of the first General Motors-UAW national agreement in 1940, which has been used in all such agreements since:

> The management of General Motors recognizes that it cannot get along without labor any more than labor can get along without management. Both are in the same business and the success of that business is vital to all concerned. This requires that both management and the employees work together to the end that the quality and cost of the product will prove increasingly satisfactory and attractive so that the business will be continuously successful.
>
> General Motors holds that the basic interests of employers and employees are the same. However, at times employees and the management have different ideas on various matters affecting their relationship. The management of General Motors is convinced that there is no reason why these differences cannot be peacefully and satisfactorily adjusted by sincere and patient effort on both sides.

The booklet, by the use of charts and line drawings, showed that, according to published data of the U. S. Bureau of Labor Statistics, the current earnings, including overtime premiums, of the average General Motors employee were twenty-seven per cent higher than those for the average U. S. manufacturing wage earner; that, in April of 1964, General Motors wages averaged $3.01 an hour; that, in addition, the costs of the extra benefits to its employees went from 18¢ an hour per employee in 1947 to 94¢ per hour per employee in 1963; that a typical employee had $6,500 of group life insurance or $9,750 in case of accidental death; that sickness and accident benefits ranged in 1963 from $55 to $110 weekly, with the typical employee weekly benefit $65; that, in 1963, General Motors employees, retirees, and their families received $93 million in hospital, surgical, and medical expense benefits; that the average monthly General Motors pension for employees retiring at or after the age of 65 in 1963 was $74 in addition to social security benefits; that General Motors pays one-half the cost of hospital, surgical, and medical expenses for retirees and their families; that the supplemental unemployment benefits plan, first agreed on by General Motors and UAW in 1955, provided payment for a maximum period of fifty-two weeks; that $172 per month per employee is the cost to General Motors of these benefits.

The booklet also pointed out that UAW membership grew from 164,000 in 1947 to 352,000 in 1963 and that in the same year the check-off remittances by General Motors to UAW were $20,491,284. It underlined that all these arrangements help provide for GM industrial peace, dividends for stockholders, and the ability to operate at a profit which makes progress possible; for UAW they provide strength, growth, stability, and added stature as a progressive union.

Neither Seaton nor De Lorenzo had any illusions that this well thought out, reasonable statement of facts would stop any union demands for more money and benefits. The best they expected was that the UAW member might say to himself, "I'm sure I want more and I'm sure the union is going to get it for me, but I am not doing badly right now." Its value as a reminder to the union members that General Motors was fair, that it wanted stability, and that it was anxious to continue to grow with the union was important for the future as well as for the present. It certainly would help prevent wild talk of "union busting," still the theme of so many depression-minded union leaders.

When the open contract negotiations began between UAW and General Motors on June 30 at General Motors Central Office Building in Detroit, which is not entirely occupied by the corporation and is considered neutral grounds by both parties, General Motors opened a press room on the fifth floor. While paid for by the corporation, it was used by both the UAW's and General Motors' public relations men. The union is happy with the arrangements, for here the newsmen get the releases from both sides and use the radio and television facilities. Press conferences, statements by Reuther and Seaton, singly or together, for live or taped radio and television are made from the same offices. Both the union and General Motors press relations men have their separate quarters for mimeographing statements and for their own huddles; but when it comes to meeting newsmen, both work out of the same center.

On August 17, after UAW had presented its contract demands and they had been discussed on and off for forty-seven days, General Motors offered its economic proposals to UAW. They included increased wages, vacations, continuation of the cost-of-living program, broad improvements in the retirement program, the supplemental unemployment benefits provisions, and additional benefits for General Motors employees. But a new problem arose. How was the General Motors offer to get to all the union members? The UAW's own publications, as a matter of practice, downgrade or pooh-pooh, company offers until the final settlements are made. Only then are they given full coverage. The mass media would not, naturally, carry the whole offer. General Motors' public relations department's answer was a letter sent to the home of every union member, signed by Donner and John F. Gordon, then president of General Motors. The mechanics of the operation had been in preparation for some time. Packages of these letters were sent to all regional and divisional offices and hand-carried to the plants where addressed envelopes were kept in readiness for the mailings. UAW members could then judge for themselves the company offer in its entirety.

After two extensions of the contract, which had run out during the negotiation period, UAW on September 25 announced "selective" strikes against General Motors and ordered 260,784 members in eighty-nine GM plants to leave their jobs and instructed 83,826 UAW members in forty-one other General Motors plants to remain at work. Bargaining broke off after a marathon session, and then resumed two days later with the activities pointed to speeding up settlements of local issues. Then, on October 5, General Motors and UAW reached a tentative agreement on all economic and national contract issues for a three-year period ending the eleven-day national strike.

It looked like it was all over. The money package was satisfactory to UAW's leadership and to General Motors' management. It also looked like another three years of industrial peace. Donner left Detroit to fly back to New York. Reuther was certain he had a good deal. But then the roof fell in.

The rank and file of the union members revolted. The revolt wasn't in complaint against the money package that UAW's leadership got for them. It wasn't because the raises were not enough, or because the benefits were poor, or the hours long, or the bosses bad, or that they worked in a "gold-plated sweatshop," or for any of the other issues that were being negotiated for in the national contract. It was simply because they wanted little things that had been ignored by Reuther and his top leaders and had been overlooked by General Motors in all its carefully laid plans for industrial peace. The local issues bothered the members of the local units of UAW and they had a wide range. Local issues in 117 of the 130 General Motors bargaining units included demands for change in the local grievance procedures; bulletin boards in the plants for the union's use; more drinking fountains; the same right to smoke in washrooms that management had; more floor mats for employees to stand on; doors for all toilets; better designed aprons and coveralls; more gloves and shoes; relocation of vending machines; and more entrances to and bigger employee parking lots. The parking lots provided by General Motors for employees cover 1,700 acres of free parking space for a quarter of a million cars, and, in exceptionally high periods of employment, are crowded.

What was basic to all these local complaints was more than the articulated grievances that could easily be settled, and finally were, between Seaton and Leonard Woodcock, head of UAW's General Motors department. It was the feeling that they were too far away from the union's top managers, from those who did the negotiation for the national contract. This sense of remoteness from the center of action by the rank and file gave their local leaders, competing with leaders of other locals for prestige, the chance to capitalize on this neglect.

These local issues resulted in a needless strike for thirty-four days, ending on November 9. And while it cost the workers a good deal of money—$7 million a day in wages—it was important enough for them to pay for it, because it meant recognition for them as individuals. The best national contract in UAW's history was beside the point to the workers in the locals. What bothered them now was the loss of identity, and Walter Reuther missed understanding this as much as did General Motors' management.

This could almost be a classic case of the failure of communication from the bottom up, so essential in good public relations whether it be in a union or in a corporation. The men on top just missed grasping that times had changed: that while pay and hours were important, and pensions and vacations vital, there was a new factor in a period of affluence, the extra little bit that made the workers more than a small cog in a vast organization. And while Reuther and his top men were dismayed by what they had failed to grasp, and should have known about their own members, it was cause for General Motors' dismay as well. A strike was the last thing management wanted. Donner above all had hoped to have a settlement that would avoid a strike. As for "the labor bosses," they couldn't boss their own members, so remote were they from their inner wishes, so little had they understood the changes which had taken place in their membership.

The strike was of course costly to General Motors. Cars were in short supply although many customers waited until the strike was over. The newspaper comment was overwhelmingly in opposition to the strike, or bewildered that the men in the plants would lose pay for grievances that seemed so trivial. But commendations from media were no answer to General Motors' management for the holdup in car production. It began to assess the causes of the strike and the result was an unusual position for the corporation, as different from the era of the sit-down strikes as 1967 is from 1937. On Donner's insistence, after a thorough study of the facts, a new tack was taken in an attempt to prevent a recurrence of the 1964 strike.

The choice of the person to speak to all management on the new

approach was James E. Goodman, the executive vice-president responsible for the automotive and parts divisions of the corporation
until he died on January 15, 1966. As a production manager who had
been through the mill himself, Goodman was just the person to speak
to the hardhanded production men to whom meeting production quotas, and no excuses, was always the objective and to whom talk about
human relations often seemed so much gibberish. They would listen
to Goodman for he started in 1925 as a worker on the assembly line in
the Fisher Body division in Norwood, Ohio. He became plant manager
in Norwood, Oakland, and Flint. During World War II he was assistant director, then director, of the tank section for Fisher Body. Later
he was assistant factory manager of all Fisher Body assembly plants,
and in 1948 general manager of the Buick-Oldsmobile-Pontiac assembly division. He continued to move up in production until in 1961
he was appointed to his last job. He was certainly the man to be
heeded by managers in the plants if they would pay attention to
anyone.

The vehicle for the delivery of Goodman's policy statement was a
14-minute color film. It was shown early in 1965 to the entire management group, from foreman up, all 20,000 of them, plant by plant,
region by region, division by division, and at the central offices in
New York and Detroit. There was no doubt left in anyone's mind that
this was not playing games; it was policy from the top, to be followed.

The film began with a black-and-white newsreel clip of the principals in the General Motors-UAW negotiations of the previous fall.
Seaton and Reuther were before the cameras to announce that negotiations at the national level had been postponed until local issues
throughout the country could be settled.

The scene changed. It was now in color. Goodman was at his
desk. He began by saying that the introductory scene had been taken
after General Motors had been shut down for five days. He told the
managers that it took an additional five weeks before enough local
grievances could be settled to start production again; that the shut-
down period cost General Motors millions of dollars in profits, the
employees millions of dollars in wages, the union millions in strike
benefits, and General Motors' dealers and suppliers untold amounts;
that a prolonged strike at General Motors puts a pretty big hole in the
nation's entire economy; and that the prevention of a strike from
happening again deserved a lot of time spent on it.

The fact is, said Goodman, that a great change had taken place in
the corporation's relations with its people over the past quarter of a
century and that a new period of greater change was beginning. He

called it a "new era for management" that needed better ways of handling relationships with GM people.

Goodman then went on:

Actually we're dealing with a very different kind of employee today. Many have moved to the suburbs and live in fine houses. As they have become property owners, they have also acquired a relatively conservative attitude. They have the same stake in stability and orderliness that all of us have. They are no longer class conscious. They think, feel, and act like everyone else in the American mainstream. In fact, you might say they *are* the mainstream. GM employees rank in the upper one-third of the nation's income group. They are better educated and informed than their predecessors were fifteen years ago. They read the same newspapers, same magazines and watch the same TV shows that we do. They often own two cars, and maybe a boat, many take vacations in faraway places. They expect their children to go to college as a matter of course. In short, they have the same values, goals, desires that we and our neighbors do.

The new man we're dealing with is so unlike the old concept of the mass-production worker that even his own union leadership is surprised. His liberated state of mind has actually provided what might be called a third force in the labor movement. Now he questions not only the traditional antagonist—the company—but he also questions his own union leadership. And the pressure he exerts, has, in my opinion, been the underlying cause of the local issue strikes that shut down General Motors this past year.

Now no reasonable person is going to predict an end to big unions like UAW. But changes taking place now indicate that local leadership is assuming a bigger place in our labor-management relationships. It's important for us in management to recognize this, for it focuses attention on the local level—the level where grievances occur. These are the grievances that have held up negotiations between the corporation and the union in the past.

The time has come for us to re-examine the relationship between the corporation and the employee. All levels of supervision must give greater attention to individual needs. Problems of local grievances should never be allowed to pile up the way they have in the past three years. Most of these should be settled and out of the way when our contract negotiations begin.

Even the top UAW officials agree with this. Both Reuther and Woodcock have said it. Everyone benefits when local disputes are settled at the time and place they occur.

Now what can *we* in management do to see that they are settled? Well, I'd say we can all begin by putting ourselves in the other fellow's shoes for a moment.

Too many times we tend to become isolated from the people who work for us—forget about things from their point of view. But I'd like every member of management to think of himself as a plant employee. Look at his situation through his eyes, with your body being his body, and to say to yourself, "Is this the way I'd like to be treated?" Management must take this point of view if we are to work harmoniously with our employees.

This is the only way we will ever know whether or not honest grievances really do exist. You must ask yourself, is the employee performing a work load that you would readily perform, assuming you had his same health and age?

Are his personal needs being met the way you would expect yours to be met?

How about housekeeping? Is management meeting its responsibility in this area?

Is the employee able to conduct himself with dignity, in the kind of environment you would expect if you were in his shoes?

These are the questions management must ask in the new era to come. For we must recognize our employees as the individuals they are—and work with them accordingly.

Goodman went on to tell the managers that the old fashioned "out the door" type of discipline was no more; that all levels of supervision must stay close to day-to-day dealings with employees and show personal interest in labor-management problems; that better communications, written and oral, must be geared to the new era; and that a prime job was to assure harmonious relations between management and employees.

Old-timers would, doubtless, call this appeasement. General Motors as a highly profit-oriented corporation will probably find, as time goes on, it has made another long-term investment which will bring returns; this one in labor peace.

General Motors has always laid heavy stress on the stockholders' interest. To Sloan, the stockholders' point of view was continuously uppermost, and it has remained so with all his successors as chief executive of the corporation. Yet General Motors does not hesitate to spend stockholders' money in areas not directly related to the manufacture of its products if it feels it might advance the long-term interests of the corporation. The field of aid to education is one example. Many corporations, even after the decision in the Smith Manufacturing case in 1952, which ended the doubts of corporate directors about the legality of giving stockholders' money to higher education in unrestricted gifts, still do not make contributions which are not directly related to the corporation's business. To General Motors, there is no conflict between management's responsibility to the stockholder and its executives' giving time and company money to the advancement of the public good.

Sloan told the author he could see no conflict here but

> rather on the other hand there is a responsibility. I think that in the last ten or fifteen years, along the lines of public relations, executives of large enterprises have devoted an increasing amount of time to public welfare. They've become directors of foundations. They've engaged in all kinds of things to promote a more satisfactory relationship between enterprise and the public at large. And also from the educational point of view, there's a tremendously increased recognition of the responsibility of corporate management to support higher education. That's the most selfish one because it's their interest to have trained people and plenty of them. Also, it's a public thing because it helps the public relations of the corporation and provides a more satisfactory recognition of the broader aspects of corporate management.

General Motors has an extensive program of aid to higher education and is the largest corporate contributor of funds for institutions of higher learning. For 1966 its grants were $11,400,000, a sum in excess of the money contribution of any other corporation. How this money is spent provides a sidelight on the pragmatic approach of the corporation, even in its support of higher education.

The program is divided into five basic parts: direct grants to institutions; indirect grants through associations; fellowships; special projects; and scholarships. Run by General Motors' committee for educational grants and scholarships, it is chaired by the vice-president, personnel, with six members: the vice-president, public relations; the vice-president, engineering; the vice-president, marketing; the vice-president, research; the executive vice-president, finance; and the director of personnel relations, who also acts as executive director of the committee. All policies and the allocation of funds are decided by this committee, and the stature of those on the committee in the corporation are a measure of the importance General Motors gives this function.

Many other corporations that have a sense of social responsibility are substantial contributors to higher education, but not many of them like to make gifts which go for bricks and mortar of college construction. General Motors does not draw the line. It gives direct financial aid to major fund drives of colleges and universities for endowment, equipment, fellowships, and research, as well as for the construction of new buildings. The criteria here are the accomplishments of the institutions at graduate and professional levels plus the number of their graduates who work for General Motors.

The gifts, given indirectly to colleges, are channeled through regional associations of private colleges whose members are 500 private institutions of higher education. An annual contribution of $50,000 is also made to the United Negro College Fund for help in meeting operating expenses of thirty-three Negro colleges. In addition, because the need is so urgent, General Motors contributed $400,000— in yearly installments of $100,000—for the fund's drive for capital funds. Grants are also made to the National Fund for Medical Education and to the National Fund for Graduate Nursing.

The graduate fellowship plan of the corporation is for employees who are college graduates. This is for a full school year, and may be renewed for a second and even a third year. Single employees get $1,800 for normal expenses and married workers $2,400. General Motors also pays the educational institution for the tuition and fees of the students, all of whom work in the fields of engineering, science, and business administration. A research allowance of $1,000 goes to each private college for the completion of a research project for each one-year fellowship, and $500 to a tax-supported institution.

The special programs vary from scholarships to foreign and Canadian colleges to an extensive tuition refund plan through which employees may continue their education in their own time. This is to encourage those who work for General Motors to improve their skills and knowledge. The courses must be taken at a college level school approved by local management. The tuition costs, up to a maximum of $250 a year, are refunded when the student-employee completes his or her studies with a satisfactory grade.

But in many ways the most interesting of all General Motors' aid to education programs is in the scholarship field. Curtice, who was then the chief executive of the corporation, had several reasons for moving into this area in 1955. General Motors is dependent for its progress on the accumulation of knowledge in virtually all fields of the arts and sciences, and the developments in technology have their roots in the fundamental knowledge developed in the colleges and universities. General Motors also has an increasing demand for college-trained people as employees. There was also another factor: the financial problems for both students and the colleges created by the increasing enrollments while the normal sources of funds were insufficient to keep pace with the needs. Since these were the concerns of the average citizen they were of concern to the corporation.

Three hundred of these scholarships, for four years each, are awarded every year to high school graduates, men and women, in the United States and Puerto Rico. The scholars are chosen by 133 private and eighty public colleges on standards they set, with as many as six scholarships a year at each. There are 1,450 currently in attendance on these scholarships. Students make their own choice of college, subject of study, and career. The stipends vary from a minimum of an honorary award of $200 a year to $2,000, depending on the assistance the students need. The yearly renewal of the scholarship is entirely up to the college, just as it is the college's sole responsibility in picking the scholarship winner. Students are expected to work for pay during their vacations and during the school year, if it does not interfere with studies. There is no obligation on any scholarship winner to work for General Motors or enroll in courses which may have any relation to the corporation's operations. And to help colleges as well as exceptional students, General Motors gives the private colleges unrestricted grants from a minimum of $500 to a maximum of $800 a year for each scholarship. This program cost General Motors $2,400,000 in 1966, made up of $1,800,000 in stipends and $600,000 in unrestricted grants.

The corporation is not satisfied simply to provide the funds and sit back. Instead, General Motors' three full-time professional staff members who work in the education field visit the colleges; interview the students and their teachers; and discuss the scholarship winners' progress. Often a senior executive of the corporation will go along to his alma mater with the scholarship administrator to see how the plan is working. Reports are then made to General Motors' committee for educational grants and scholarships. The results tell a story of their own.

These scholarship winners are an unusual group, having leadership qualities as well as scholastic ability. For instance, the class of '66, which numbered 285 men and ninety-three women, in 191 participating colleges and universities, had seventy-one per cent finish in the top quarter of their class, half of whom placed in the upper five per cent. Nineteen of them were valedictorians, ten salutatorians and eight were third in scholastic performance. Sixty-two were elected to Phi Beta Kappa. Seventy-four per cent of the men and forty-four per cent of the women enrolled in graduate schools. To cap this record, 260 scholarships, fellowships, and assistantships were offered to these General Motors graduates, including thirty-one National Science Fellowships; twenty-five Woodrow Wilson Fellowships, and two Rhodes Scholarships.

That General Motors' purpose is being met can be gauged from this: from 1955 to 1966 inclusive thirty-seven per cent of the General Motors scholars chose teaching as a career. Engineering was chosen by fourteen per cent, ten per cent chose medicine and nursing, and eight per cent chose law and government service. Of the sixty career areas represented, that of the ministry and the priesthood has forty-eight students.

After the Higher Education Act of 1965, with its $66 million annually for opportunity grants or scholarships for some 130,000 students, was passed by Congress there was serious questioning by many corporations whether corporate scholarships were any longer needed. Some corporations dropped their scholarship programs and diverted the funds to other education fields. General Motors' approach was the usual one when faced with a problem.

George A. Jacoby, director of personnel relations for the corporation and also in charge of the education grants program, decided to find the facts. He questioned all the colleges and universities in the corporation's scholarship program. A careful analysis of the Higher Education Act was made. The conclusion was that General Motors' program would be continued for these reasons: historically, the purposes of scholarships were to recognize high academic achievement; the Federal Government's purpose was primarily to help the needy, and not necessarily the most able; General Motors' scholarships were not in conflict with the federal program, since high achievement was the first consideration and need the second. The colleges and universities came to the same conclusion as the corporation.

While General Motors' scholarship program is not directed to its own direct needs for better educated personnel, another and rather unusual project, the General Motors Institute, is. This institute's purpose is to train men for engineering and managerial jobs in the corporation. Started in 1919 as an evening school by a group of Flint factory workers, it grew until, in 1924, it developed an emphasis in industrial engineering. In the summer of 1926 it became part of

General Motors and an extensive development program was started, including its chartering as a degree-granting engineering college under the laws of Michigan.

Today the General Motors Institute is an accredited engineering school granting bachelor's degrees in mechanical, industrial, and electrical engineering. It is probably the most successful, and definitely the world's largest, industrial educational institution: 2,900 students are enrolled in the five-year engineering program.

The first four years operate on the cooperative plan, in which all students, who are high school graduates, become employees of a unit of the corporation. These General Motors units pay the youngsters the going rate for the work they do. They work for six-week periods in the sponsoring General Motors units, then study at the Institute for six weeks, alternating for the full four years. During their work periods the students make enough to pay the costs of their academic studies and, with careful budgeting, can cover their living expenses as well. After deductions, the working student earns about $2,600 a year. His tuition and fees come to $774 a year.

For the fifth year, which must be completed if the student is to get his degree, he works full time on a project problem related to his sponsoring unit, and writes his thesis on the subject. During this final year the same sponsoring unit pays his salary.

But no ring is put through the student's nose. General Motors would like the graduate to work for the corporation, but if, after graduation, he thinks he can do better for himself with Ford, Chrysler, or a corporation not in the automotive field, there is no attempt to prevent him from making the move. About a third of all General Motors Institute graduates do not work for the corporation. But of those who do, there are a great many who hold high posts. One executive vice-president, two group vice-presidents, and seven general managers, as well as the president of General Motors of Canada and the president of Frigidaire Products of Canada are Institute graduates. In the engineering sector of the corporation there are seven chief engineers, ten assistant chief engineers and two chief metallurgists, all graduates of the General Motors Institute, as are one regional plant manager, twenty-five plant managers, seventy-four plant superintendents, six works managers, eight manufacturing managers, and eleven production managers.

The cost to General Motors of the Institute runs to some $4 million a year and the total higher education contributions have consistently gone higher, year by year. In 1954, General Motors' aid to higher education was $2,500,000. In 1956, it was a little above $4 million. In 1960 it was $7,100,000 and in 1966 it was roughly $12 million. Since the corporation needs educated workers, and since it also takes its responsibilities seriously for the improvement of education generally, the grants will increase as both the country and General Motors grow. The Sloan belief in the values of this corporate aid to education has never been questioned by his successors. Nor for that matter have the stockholders, except the recent breed of professional noisemakers, raised their eyebrows. The vast majority of stockholders have never been critical of the managers of the corporation for giving their money away to colleges and universities, a large part of it in unrestricted gifts unrelated to the normal operations of the company. They know of the corporation's program of aid to higher education because the annual report always discusses its development, as well as the totals of the money spent on it. There is no push to gain credit from the general public for what General Motors is doing in higher education. General Motors simply takes what it thinks is the proper course, and the stockholders approve.

Early on Tuesday evening, March 22, 1966, the country watching the three television network news programs saw the gentle-faced, quiet, fifty-nine-year-old president of General Motors. They heard him apologize to a thirty-two-year-old attorney whose book, *Unsafe at Any Speed* (New York: Grossman Publishers, 1965), had devoted the first forty-two pages to an attack on the safety of the Corvair. Roche, thirty-seven years with the company, testifying before the Senate subcommittee on traffic safety, was admitting that Ralph Nader, whose book had helped raise the issue, had been investigated on the orders of General Motors' lawyers, and that it had been done without his knowledge. Said Mr. Roche:

> I deplore this kind of harassment . . . . I am shocked and outraged. . . . I hold myself fully responsible. . . . I did not know of the investigation when it was initiated and I did not approve it. . . . I am not here to excuse, condone or justify in any way our investigation of Mr. Nader. To the extent that General Motors bears responsibility I want to apologize here and now to the members of this subcommittee and Mr. Nader. . . . To the best of my knowledge—and I have made every effort to obtain all the facts since learning about this some two weeks ago—the investigation initiated by General Motors, contrary to some speculation, did not employ girls as sex lures, did not employ detectives giving false names, did not employ Allied Investigation, Inc., did not use recording devices during interviews, did not follow Mr.

Nader in Iowa and Pennsylvania, did not have him under surveillance during the day he testified before this subcommittee,
did not follow him in any private place, and did not constantly
ring his private telephone number late at night with false statements or anonymous warnings. . . . At the time the investigation
was initiated last November, Mr. Nader's book had not yet been
published, he had not appeared nor was he scheduled to appear
as a witness before this subcommittee and he was not regarded
to anyone's knowledge as a consultant to this subcommittee. . . .
There has been no attempt by, and it has at no time been the
intention of, General Motors Corporation, or any of its officers
or employees to annoy, harass, embarrass, threaten, injure or
intimidate Mr. Nader, to invade his privacy, to defame his character, or to hinder, impugn, coerce or prevent his testimony
before this or any other legislative body. Nor was any attempt
made along these lines with respect to any other critic of General Motors. I personally have no interest whatsoever in knowing
Mr. Nader's political beliefs, his religious beliefs and attitudes,
his credit rating or his personal habits regarding sex, alcohol
or any other subject. Nor for the record was any derogatory information of any kind along any of these lines turned up in this
investigation. While I do not personally know Mr. Nader, I am
informed that he is an articulate attorney and citizen who is
deeply interested in traffic safety and has written and spoken
extensively on the subject.

The morning following Roche's testimony all the newspapers highlighted his apology. *The New York Times* in a four-column headline
at the top of page one, said: "G.M. Apologizes for Harassment of
Critic" above a picture of Mr. Nader and another beside it of Roche
with his lawyer, Theodore C. Sorensen, Special Counsel to President
Kennedy, at his side. The *New York Herald Tribune*'s two headlines
ran: "Big Business Caught Snooping; GM Apologizes to Author"
with pictures between them of the principals. The *Wall Street Journal*
on the same morning ran this heading over two columns: "GM Con-
cedes Detectives That It Hired Shadowed, Harassed Auto-Safety
Critic." And *Time* ran a three-column, full-page story in its April 1
issue with the heading: "The Spies Who Were Caught Caught Cold,"
while *Newsweek* of April 4 carried almost two pages, including pictures, under the heading, "Private Eyes and Public Hearings" and
wrote that the "scene had all the fascination of a public whipping."

Editorial comments were harsh. *The New York Times*, under the heading, "What's Good for G.M.," wrote: "The Ralph Nader affair smacks too much of the philosophy that 'what's good for General Motors is good for the country,' even if the late Charles E. Wilson never put it exactly that way. Here was the nation's biggest corporation paying $6,700 for an investigation of a private citizen who had the audacity to criticize the lack of safety devices in American automobiles."

The *New York Herald Tribune* said, "General Motors' apology to critic Ralph Nader came belatedly, but better late than never . . . Luckily, GM was caught, as the saying goes, flat-footed. It was a good lesson."

The *Detroit Free Press*, under the heading, "GM's President Is Upset," had this to say: "From start to finish, if the finish has come, GM's handling of this episode has been incredibly bad. Its shadowing and harassment of Nader and snooping into his private life smacks of tactics alien to the U.S. Its false statement on the nature of its investigation compounds its error. Its eleventh hour hiring of Ted Sorenson to sit at the subcommittee hearing, many will suspect, was prompted less by recognition of Sorenson's legal talents than by appreciation for his Washington contacts. GM's president is very upset by the whole affair and so are we."

Editorial comment in the rest of the country was no gentler.

How did General Motors—so jealous of its reputation, so careful that its decisions take into account their impact on the public, so highly organized to make certain that all actions are carefully thought out beforehand—get into this mess so deeply that it came under violent attack throughout the country with no voices in Congress to defend it and only a scattering of commentators taking up its cause?

It began with the lawsuits which rose out of accidents in which the Corvair was involved. The claim had been made by the lawyers for those suing General Motors that the Corvair was faulty in design and unsafe on the road, and that the accidents in which the car was involved were due, not to the negligence of the drivers, or the condition of the highways, but to the car itself. There was a flood of lawsuits that, before the investigation of Nader was begun, totalled more than one hundred involving up to some $40 million in claims. These all related to the Corvair, particularly the 1960 to 1963 models. The American Trial Lawyers Association publications were calling Nader an expert on Corvair affairs and there was a suggestion that those who had an interest in Corvair litigation get in touch with him. He made speeches, wrote articles, appeared on television and radio, and dealt with the lack of safety of cars, underlining the Corvair as a prime example of dangerous design.

Roche told the Senate subcommittee, whose chairman was Abraham Ribicoff, long interested in highway safety, what lay behind the thinking of General Motors' general counsel, Aloysius F. Power, in starting the investigation of Nader. Here is what the testimony shows:

> Troubled by what appeared possibly to be a concerted effort on the part of a few trial attorneys handling most of the Corvair cases to stimulate both additional cases and the kind of sensationally adverse publicity that might influence juries against the Corvair—and troubled further by requests from shareholders as well as from both satisfied and worried Corvair buyers that the corporation counteract the harsh attacks on this product which had been continuously made outside the courtroom—our general counsel felt called upon, first, to ascertain whether any actions for libel of the corporation or its products or bar association grievance procedures, based on violations of the Canons of Ethics, should be instituted against members of the Bar (including Mr. Nader) who publicly discussed pending or anticipated litigation; second, to ascertain whether any witness, or author of any book or article which might be offered as evidence in any court (including Mr. Nader) was entitled to the legal definition of "expert"; and third, to ascertain whether any of the individuals (including Mr. Nader) who were most often said to be cited or consulted by these attorneys, or to be publicizing their allegations, could properly be cross-examined in any trial in which they might appear as expert witnesses to show bias, lack of reliability or credibility, if it were a fact that they had a self-interest in the litigation or had been attempting deliberately to influence public opinion.

Then, in mid-November, 1965, without the knowledge or consent of any member of General Motors' governing committees, Power began to check on Nader's credibility, reliability, qualifications as an expert witness, and any possible ties with the Corvair case attorneys. To do this he felt he needed an outside private investigating agency and asked a reputable Washington law firm to hire one. It did so. The reports were channeled back to General Motors, via the Washington law firm, and the testimony shows that the Washington firm did not even bother to read the reports of the investigators before sending them on to General Motors' legal department in Detroit. The Washington law firm acted simply as the hiring agent of the investigating agency and the conduit for the reports on Nader.

Had General Motors any right to make this check of the critic-author? The law is clear that it had. In fact, during the Senate hearings, Senator Robert Kennedy, who with Senator Ribicoff was an active examiner of Roche, made this statement:

> Now, let me just make my own position clear. I think that you were justified, if you felt the protection for your own company, your stockholders and the good name of your automobile the Corvair, and feel justice on your side, to conduct an investigation of the kind to determine whether Mr. Nader was in fact in the employment of some of these litigants and that there was an effort, a conscientious organized effort to try some of these cases in the newspaper rather than to try them in the courts, and from what I have learned, there has been some of that effort in the Midwest and some on the West Coast rather than just doing it through the courts.
>
> There have been a good deal of public statements in connection with this matter. So, I understand your concern. I can understand the fact that you would feel an investigation to determine about Mr. Nader's connection and association with these individuals, particularly if he was going to be an expert witness, was completely justified. That part of it I don't find any fault with.

What Senator Kennedy was concerned with, as he said, was "whether that investigation went on to the area of harassment, intimidation, and possibly blackmail. These are some the questions that were raised by the investigators. I think this is a matter that is of concern to us and a matter of concern to the general public."

There is no doubt that the investigation, started by General Motors' general counsel, did go far beyond fair bounds. For this, Roche apologized. That it showed sloppy supervision, to say the least, in General Motors' general counsel's office, is equally clear. It is surprising that the investigation was not closely checked and stopped the moment the reports arrived in Detroit.

The public knew nothing of this until an article in the *New Republic* in the issue dated March 12, 1966. It was titled "The Dick" and signed by James Ridgeway. It told of the investigation of Nader by private agents and how "the auto makers, who first ignored Nader, have now turned on their most vigorous critic. This is precisely the sort of knockdown public fight Nader was hoping for, but instead of open battle, he finds himself suddenly distracted from the task at hand and locked in a subterranean struggle against an uncertain enemy." The article also told of what looked like an attempt to entrap Nader by women used as lures. The *New Republic* article was distributed to a number of sources over the weekend beginning March 3.

On March 6 *The New York Times* carried a story headed, "Critic of Auto Industry's Safety Standards Says He Was Trailed and Harassed; Charges Called Absurd." The *Times* story was datelined Detroit, March 5, and carried many of the essential details which appeared in the *New Republic*. In neither story was the source of the investigation mentioned, which only deepened the mystery and made it first rate copy. Here was a young Princeton and Harvard Law School graduate, author of a book attacking the automotive industry, being followed by private detectives, having his phone tapped, and being lured by blondes. Close friends were being asked all sorts of questions totally unrelated to auto safety. It was David versus Goliath, with spokesmen for all the motor car manufacturers denying they had any part in the snooping. In fact, it was not established that General Motors was involved until two weeks before Roche appeared before the Ribicoff Senate subcommittee. That it made for sensational reading and public involvement is easy to understand. The nation's normal feeling for the underdog, plus its new interest in safety, kept the stories steadily on page one. And while Roche's clear, complete apology to Nader was the only, and indeed proper, course of action, it did not end the hearings. General Motors' general counsel's lack of control over what might have been a simple, and perfectly acceptable investigation, became overnight what seemed to be an attempt by the biggest industrial corporation in the world to entrap and muzzle a lone critic. It was the mystery of who was responsible for the investigation as well as the dramatic qualities of the stories that both made Nader a martyr to the public and a best seller out of his book, which up to that time was just rolling along at a slow pace despite generally favorable reviews.

That the whole episode began with the story in the *New Republic* is clear, not only from the external evidence, but also from the magazine's own circulation promotional material. In the *New Republic*'s direct mail campaign for new subscribers in mid-August, 1966, this paragraph appeared in its four-page letter under the title "Exposé Without Sensationalism": "This year, too, our editors broke the story of General Motors' efforts to intimidate Ralph Nader for his attacks on the safety of the American automobile—a revelation that made front page news for weeks. (The original story of the Corvair's safety problems appeared in the *New Republic* more than a year ago.)"

As the hearings of the Ribicoff subcommittee were ending Roche said:

> Such errors will not happen again. It was not done and it has not been, and will not be, our policy in the future to undertake the surveillance or broad background investigation of those persons who write or speak critically of our company and our products. On the contrary, what we do in General Motors as a matter of basic policy is aimed at earning the public respect and confidence for our corporation and our policies, and we would hope that we would enjoy this kind of respect on the part of everybody. If we can't earn it from our critics, certainly we have no intention of trying to counteract any of the criticism in any way along the lines that have been suggested here today.

At the annual meeting of stockholders on May 20, 1966, Donner, who was abroad when the Senate subcommittee hearings on safety were held, reiterated that "we do not and will not undertake surveillance or broad background investigations of our critics in the future. . . . We undertook to set up procedures to assure it wouldn't happen again. And we have undertaken to assure that assignments of this sort in the future would be undertaken only under the direct supervision of the president of the company."

Donner, who as chief executive officer was presiding at the meeting, also said that he wanted to emphasize that Roche's apology was "not a rhetorical or an hypocritical device," that the error made was an "honest error and it was done in the spirit of protecting General Motors in a very difficult situation."

On March 31, nine days after the Senate subcommittee hearings were ended, what is called a "blue letter" policy statement on the use of outside investigators or investigating agencies was sent to all GM executives. It was signed by Roche as president. The assignment of duties for matters of this kind was reviewed, and safeguards established, under the direct supervision of the corporate president, to make sure there would be no repetition in the future.

Great harm was done to General Motors' reputation by the lack of control of the investigation of Nader instigated by Power. Among many other things, this whole sorry business is proof that no matter what system is set up for proper consideration of all corporate decisions so that their impact on the public is fully considered, there can be a breakdown. Relations with the public can, of course, never be the province of the public relations department alone, or of the chairman alone, or of the president alone, or of a committee alone. They must be the responsibility of all executives who in any way make decisions which can have an effect on the thinking of the public. Power is a serious, thoughtful man who had been with General Motors for thirty-nine years when he made the decision which was unwise in the context of the time and who did not insist that when the investigation was set in motion that it be properly controlled. Corporate lawyers are a special breed. Too many of them believe that to win a case in court is all that they need do. To think of winning it in the court of the nation's opinion is not very often in the front of their minds, and is often foreign to them. That public attitudes always have to be considered is one of the lessons of the case of the investigation of Nader.

The entire hearings of the Senate subcommittee, and public distress at the time, show once again that public opinion is volatile. For many years safety was not what the buyer of the motor car wanted. He wanted speed. He wanted attractive design. He wanted excitement. He could not be persuaded to buy seat belts or be concerned with safe design—as Ford's experience showed in 1956. Even today when cars all must have safety belts as standard equipment, they are probably as often left unbuckled as they are buckled. But suddenly the slaughter of the highways became a deep public concern and instead of three basic elements, the car, the highway, and the driver, being blamed, only one was picked as the villain—the car.

What then is the obligation of General Motors, Ford, Chrysler, and American Motors? Is it to stress and engineer a safer car even though the public does not want to hear of it? The answer is yes. It is, of course, the obligation of the industry to provide the safest engineered cars it can possibly produce. For if it does not, it will be under the kind of onslaught that struck not only General Motors but all the motor companies. The result is that the government steps in and insists on legislating safer cars when the industry has lacked the drive to provide them on its own.

The fact that the legislation, properly administered, that grew out of the Ribicoff hearings can be lived with by the industry does not mean it can stand too many of the blows to its reputation for safety. Of course, it is unfair to blame all accidents on the motor car. Many other factors, including the very important one of the competence of the driver, are vital elements in cutting the death toll on the highways. But this does not absolve in any way the failure of the industry to, on its own, assure that its product is so engineered that it is the safest possible. And, unless the industry does everything necessary on its own, it will find that the kind of legislation passed by Congress is only a taste of what can happen in the future.

For decades the motor car industry was a sacred cow in Congress. But when the public was truly aroused and the voice of the nation was heard, then the members of the House of Representatives, the members of the Senate, and the President himself listened and bent to its will. In many ways, this was the important lesson repeated once again: Common consent is essential for business's health, no matter how powerful, pure, and influential it may be with the politicians, with the press, and the other media of mass communication. When the public mood is ripe, then one man, working alone on a book, can make a tremendous impact on even the richest industry in the land.

General Motors has many sources of strength that help it live in a big glass house in the highly competitive automotive industry. Since every major decision has some impact on the general public, the very manner of management decision-making militates against snap judgments that can be harmful. Major policy actions are only taken after discussion in committees and policy groups. That way there is less chance that some headlong course will be taken that will bring down on the corporation's head the wrath of a special group or the country as a whole. Corporate policies are not made by one man, nor implemented as the result of an individual's impulse. The strong tradition of the corporation compels the proponent of an idea to convince his peers and his seniors on a committee that he is right. In the course of doing so, every aspect of the proposal is discussed and the fullest relevant information gathered. Before it gets a "Yes" or a "No," the policy is so thoroughly explored that the public relations aspects are reviewed time and again.

Another source of immense strength is that there are few changes at the top of the structure; the men who have risen to be chief executives have all spent a lifetime in the corporation, learning its ways and meeting its short- and long-term problems. Since May 10, 1923, General Motors has had only four heads: Sloan, Wilson, Curtice and Donner. Donner's successor will also come from within the company. All have had the advantages of knowing the history of the corporation, the kind of mistakes it has made, and what must be done to assure that they are not made again. General Motors never has had the trouble which can arise from the hiring of an outside chief executive who has to make his mark quickly with his board of directors, and therefore is prepared to take the chance of neglecting the long-term effects that may come from too-slick short-term actions.

Since 1931, General Motors has had only two public relations directors. Since 1931, the public relations policy group has had as key members all the most responsible executives in the corporation, as well as the public relations director. No man can rise to great heights in the hierarchy of the corporation without a thorough exposure to the fact that the public is looking over his shoulder and over the shoulders of his colleagues; that the corporation is too big to hide its actions or escape from their results; and that the only worthwhile policies are those based on the public interest and taken for their long-term results.

General Motors' top managers are fully aware that in times of sharp change, public moods change; that what the public thinks is in its interest today it may condemn tomorrow; that there is nothing static about public opinion. General Motors' executives know that the corporation is so central to the nation's life, and that it impinges on its welfare at so many points, that it can forget these facts at great peril. General Motors can only remain a profitable corporation as long as the general public permits it to operate with the measure of freedom its success demands. And to do that it must continue to act in ways the public finds acceptable, remembering that every important action makes imperative public explanation, and that self-restraint and responsibility are marks of good management.

THE TIPTOEING GIANT

IT WAS A DAY TO REMEMBER IN THE HISTORY OF STANDARD OIL Company (New Jersey). On Thursday, March 26, 1942, 109 days after Japan's assault on Pearl Harbor, Thurman W. Arnold, assistant attorney general, at hearings of the Senate Committee on National Defense, said the patent agreements between the company and Germany's I. G. Farbenindustrie A.G. were the principal reasons that the U.S. had not made synthetic rubber. He pointed out that the Jersey company had invented butyl rubber, but had, after giving the information to Germany and Italy through I. G. Farben (before United States' entry into the war), refused to tell its processes to the United States Navy and the British Government. He said that the whole purpose of what he called the Jersey-Farben cartel was "an attempt on the part of Standard Oil to get a protected market, to eliminate competition and finally to restrict world production in order to maintain control"; and that the entire arrangement was against American interests. Immediately on completion of Arnold's testimony before the Senate committee, its chairman, Senator Harry S Truman, told reporters that, if these were the facts, then, in his opinion, the company's action constituted "treason."

It was a day to remember in the history of the war. On that day, Japanese troops in Burma—preceded by parachutists whose job it was to stir native rebellion—moved northward in force about forty miles below Prome, on the road to the Burmese oil fields a hundred miles beyond the city. In the Philippine Islands, the Japanese kept

the initiative with a six-hour, forty-four plane bombing raid on Cor-
regidor Island. In Canberra, Gen. Douglas MacArthur promised
Australian members of Parliament that "we shall win or we shall die."
Shortly before that, he told the Australian War Cabinet that the
United States pledged all its resources in the common struggle. In
London, Winston Churchill reported that the Battle of the Atlantic
had turned once more in favor of the Axis with German submarines
off the American coast taking a heavy toll of war-supply shipping. The
Ruhr Valley was bombed by hundreds of Royal Air Force planes in a
new offensive, while Germany continued its air attacks on English
cities. In Rio de Janeiro, a spy ring was broken up with the arrest of
more than a hundred Axis subjects, including a German Army colonel
and a Japanese admiral disguised as a farmer. In Washington, President Roosevelt, alarmed because U.S. shipments to the Soviet Union
were falling behind schedule, sent sharp letters to the secretaries of
War and the Navy to clear all barriers to the sending of supplies to
Murmansk. William Green, president of the AFL, and Philip Murray,
president of the CIO, together pledged to Congress that there would
be no strikes for any cause during the war, the first time in organized
labor's history that the right to strike was voluntarily given up.

The day following the Arnold testimony and Truman's offhand
accusation, the press played the story big on page one. "Treason"
was in the headlines. The stories became extensions of the testimony.
The New York Times, more careful than some of the other newspapers, gave the hearings a front-page play with a two-column headline: "Arnold Says Standard Oil Gave Nazis Rubber Process," leaving
Truman's charge to the fourth paragraph.

As the nation screeched in outraged protest, the *New Republic*, in its
issue of April 6, proclaimed on its cover, "Standard Oil: Axis Ally,"
by Michael Straight. In the same issue, the magazine's "Washington
Notes" said: "Arnold told the Truman Committee that Standard gave
Hitler the benefit of its experiments with synthetic-rubber production
while withholding the same information from the U.S. Navy and from
other American companies." The magazine's lead editorial, describing the last week in March, said: "The Standard Oil Company of
New Jersey was pictured as having voluntarily bound itself hand and
foot to Hitler's chariot wheel pursuing profits with apparently no
thought for the protection of this country."

PM, the now-dead New York City newspaper that was edited for
exposes, ran a series of open letters to John D. Rockefeller, Jr., claimed
that the company was in effect "an ally of Hitler, an economic enemy
agent," an aide to the Axis war machine whose executives put profits

ahead of patriotism, ethics, or morals; and it asked stockholders to throw out the company's directors.

The executives of the Jersey company were devastated. The agreements made for technological and economic reasons with I. G. Farben dated back to the 1920's. They were loyal businessmen. They had an enormously complex story to tell explaining their actions. They had no machinery to tell it; no people on the staff who understood media and its needs; no one to translate complicated agreements into language laymen could grasp. So lost were they that, after the Arnold testimony, they told the press they had "no comment," and would wait until they were called to testify before the Truman committee to give their answers. *The New York Times*, on the same day the paper carried the Arnold accusations on page one, ran a story on page twelve with this one-column headline: "Standard Oil Men Silent On Charges." Only during his appearance before the Truman committee, several days after Arnold's, did W. S. Farish, president and chief executive officer of the Jersey company, say that any charges that the company or its officers had in any way been disloyal to the United States were unwarranted and untrue.

"Within one month after Europe went to war and more than two years before America went to war we had eliminated all foreign interests in the rubber process," he told the Senate committee. He went on to testify that whether or not the contracts with the German company fell within the anti-trust laws, "they did inure greatly to the advance of American industry and more than any other one thing made possible our present war activities in aviation gasoline, toluol, and explosives and in synthetic rubber."

Farish dealt with the accusations in detail, denied that the company had "delayed, retarded or stifled the development of synthetic rubber in this country," and testified that the Arnold statement had "not a shadow of a foundation." As for butyl rubber, the company—under arrangement with I. G. Farben—had told the German company of its discovery but Germany did not have the petroleum gases essential for making butyl.

In fact, the company had tried to stir up interest in the United States in the production of synthetic rubber. Discussions had been held with U.S. rubber companies and with the government at Washington. But synthetic rubber in those days was not a very satisfactory product. It could not easily be worked on the machines that handled natural rubber. Tires made of it flattened out on a car left standing overnight. Its costs were so high that its commercial production was impossible unless subsidized, and there was not a single office or branch of the government that had the budget for it. As for withholding information about butyl from the United States Government—in November, 1939, the Navy completed tests on it that the Jersey company had suggested, and for which it had supplied samples. The Navy was simply not interested in the manufacture of synthetic rubber.

After the Jersey company did present its case to the Truman committee *The New York Times*, in its lead editorial on April 2, evaluated the testimony of all parties and said: "In the light of this evidence Mr. Arnold's charges that the Standard Oil Company is responsible for the shortage of synthetic rubber simply evaporate. It is apparent that he did not have the facts."

And the report of the Truman committee itself, when it was finally issued in May, stated that "there was no question of moral turpitude or of subjective unpatriotic motivation on the part of Standard or any of its officials."

What then happened? How did Standard Oil of New Jersey get caught in this squeeze of political misunderstanding?

The decision not to embark on a large-scale synthetic rubber program was made by President Roosevelt himself long before Japan's onslaught on Pearl Harbor. The reasons seemed valid at the time: the expense of the program and the view held by both political and military thinkers that Japan would not attack and that, even if it did, it could never conquer Southeast Asia, the American-British source of natural rubber. Singapore, the gateway to Malaya, was considered impregnable; the British and American Pacific Fleets were believed to be separately stronger than Japan's, and together overwhelmingly superior in every way.

Instead, not only did Japan grievously wound the Pacific Fleet of the United States Navy at Pearl Harbor, it also destroyed a large part of the British Pacific Fleet. In quick time Japan took Hong Kong, Indo-China, the Philippines, Singapore, Malaya, and the Dutch East Indies. The battles of the Java Sea and the Coral Sea were disastrous for the Allies. The British ships *Repulse* and *Prince of Wales* were sunk, the first capital ships to be sent to the bottom by land-based aircraft.

In North Africa, Rommel was driving ahead. In addition, there were reverses in Europe and in the Atlantic. The Germans continued their bombing of British cities; their submarine warfare was highly successful along the eastern coasts of the United States and Canada; Axis infiltration into Latin America was increasing; the German armies had moved deeper into Russia. For at least six months after Pearl Harbor the war was going badly, very badly, for the Allies.

The great debate on intervention versus non-intervention being over, the American public was agonized at the setbacks. The realization that, in addition to its being thoroughly unprepared for war, the country now seemed to be on the brink of an internal breakdown because of a shortage of rubber, seemed the last straw. The voters, humiliated, frustrated, and angry, demanded the heads of those responsible. It was a time when villains, or at the least scapegoats, were needed. It was also a time when Thurman Arnold, the assistant attorney general in charge of the anti-trust division, was intent on new enforcements of the laws, and had fresh fears that cartels, if not broken, would do untold harm to America.

It was in this atmosphere that Standard Oil Company (New Jersey) came under attack. It was in this atmosphere that Senator Robert M. La Follette, Jr. could say: "The people are not in a frame of mind to be gentle with industrial treason at home while American boys die on battlefields scattered all over the globe" and not be rebuked. It was in this atmosphere that the Truman committee held its hearings.

The Jersey company was the perfect target. It was huge. It was powerful. It had had agreements with the enemy. And it was inarticulate. When the blows came the company staggered like a heavy-footed giant moaning through the gag he had insisted on stuffing tightly into his own mouth. Never in the history of the company had the public attacks on it been more severe. Never in its history was it less prepared to answer them. As it remained silent, the strident voices of those who condemned it became more and more believable.

The Jersey directors seemed incapable of learning that the company could not isolate itself from the public; that what it did and said and thought were important to the nation; that every man and woman had a vote; that the voters' will could swiftly become the country's law; that if it were to continue in business it would have to win the acceptance of those it chose to ignore; that no matter how right, honorable and patriotic it believed itself to be, those outside the company could not possibly agree if the company's actions were not explained. As long as the public did not believe the company was acting for the national good it was endangered.

As Jersey was beginning to learn, good products sold at fair prices with satisfactory profits for the stockholders were not enough. A telling of its story; a frank exposition of reasons for its policies; some actions that governments would agree were in keeping with public policy—all these essentials of large scale enterprises had not been concerns of the directors of the company. Now, for their failure to understand, they stood condemned in the eyes of the nation.

It was not the first time that Jersey's directors had had their feet put to the fire. Neither the depression, the rise of the New Deal, the onslaught on private business, nor the attacks on profit-oriented management by President Roosevelt seemed to be danger signals to the Jersey company. Jersey simply did not take the nation into its confidence. It seemed to operate on some kind of out-of-this-world thinking that somehow, perhaps because its executives' hearts were so pure, Jersey was different from the other large corporations that were being forced to become aware of their relations with the public.

In the period from 1870 to 1892, Standard Oil was under violent public attack. It epitomized to the public all the evils of big business. Its playing of one railroad against another for rebates from the published freight rates, its overwhelming power, its very size and the fact that it was a trust at a time when trusts were feared as stifling private enterprise, brought attacks by politicians and writers. In 1892, the Supreme Court of Ohio dissolved the trust. This was an unwholesome period in which many of the evils attributed to Standard Oil were general business practice, carried on by the company's competitors. A great deal of the company's success was due to economies, improvements in marketing, better service to customers. But the company's directors did not bother to explain their actions, again on the theory that their services and their products would in the long run be the best answer to charges of monopoly. It did not stop the dissolution of the trust; nor did it enhance the reputation of the company in the country.

In 1911, the company, which, after the Supreme Court of Ohio decision, had incorporated in New Jersey where the laws regarding holding companies were more lenient, was hit once more. This time it was broken up, forced to get rid of thirty-three subsidiaries, and restricted in its operations to narrow, specified areas. The directors still did not seem to grasp that public attitudes were important. Strict adherence to the letter of the law, in their opinion, was all that was needed. The 1892 court decision and the popular dissolution in 1911 seemed to teach few lessons. The directors continued unaware that their competitors could and did appeal to the voters and the legislatures to restrain the company. Even when the company had a good case with which to go to the public, it did not. The legal department was supreme. What it said should be done was done. Strict legal interpretations, without peripheral and valid considerations, had brought infinite trouble. But instead of reassessing its practices, instead of trying to understand why the public was objecting, and instead of adjusting to public will, the general corporate attitude was that it was only yellow journalists and cheap political demagogues who were critical of the company.

So, as was to be expected, when the Truman Senate committee hearings were held in 1942, Jersey, with a solid position to defend and a satisfactory answer to give, was totally unprepared. Not only was there no department whose job it was to make available the company's position, or people trained in the needs of media or with an understanding of public opinion, but there was only one small, internal publication. This was *The Lamp*, which was started in 1918 by Victor Ross who had come to New York from the company's affiliate in Canada, Imperial Oil, for a short stay. *The Lamp* was not geared to quick publication of answers; it was nothing like the widely read magazine it is today, with an 850,000 circulation that includes stockholders, employees, and opinion leaders throughout the country.

But 1942 was not 1911 or 1892. This time the nation was at war against skilled and ruthless enemies. The struggle was going very badly; the American public was in a dangerous mood, unwilling to brook organizations—business or any other—that they thought were acting against their welfare. The board of directors had finally and reluctantly come to understand that briefs read before Congressional committees were not enough to answer the persistent attacks, which did not show any signs of subsiding. There were other factors which forced the hands of the directors: John D. Rockefeller, Jr., hurt by the press criticism and distressed by what he had been reading, told the directors that he hoped they would act to improve Jersey's relations with the public. Sales had been falling, stockholders complaining.

What may have been the biggest single push came from an unusual, talented, intelligent executive, Robert T. Haslam. As a vice-president of Jersey's principal domestic affiliate, the Delaware Company, and responsible for the sales of the so-called Esso Marketers, he was a great deal closer to public thinking than were the board members. Haslam thought there was worse to come, and he finally told the directors that he could not be responsible for improving sales unless the company took constructive action to develop its public relations. He freely admitted, however, that he knew almost nothing about the techniques of doing so.

Haslam was one of those men who on occasion rise to great heights in corporations despite a background quite different from that of most of his colleagues. Haslam, who had graduated from Massachusetts Institute of Technology and then taught chemical engineering there, was a rare combination, a professor who was business oriented. He had great insight into the problems of large enterprises, and a solid educational training that enabled him to assess difficult situations without getting himself emotionally involved. To these qualities must be added exceptional ability in understanding human behavior.

He had been a consultant to one of Jersey's affiliates, Humble Oil & Refining Company, while teaching at MIT. His first full time job with the company was when he was brought into Standard Oil Development Company in 1927 to direct the development of the high-pressure hydrogenation process that was then under negotiation for purchase from I. G. Farben. He led a group of technicians in exploring the application of this chemical process to the oil industry. This group has been credited with several new and improved products. One of them, 100-octane gasoline, became highly valuable during World War II.

Haslam got involved with the marketing side of the business through the back door. The earliest commercial application of hydrogenation was in the chemical improvement of lubricating oils. He started by giving technical advice to Jersey's marketing executives on these products and became increasingly immersed in marketing, until he rose to be general sales manager for the Esso Marketers.

Haslam, almost immediately after Arnold gave his testimony before the Truman committee, became deeply involved in the controversy for two reasons: he knew as much as any other single person at Jersey about the arrangements with I. G. Farben, and he had an organization, the Esso Marketers, that had an audience, or, at least, a public to which it could send material that gave the Jersey company's position. Haslam organized the writers of his marketing staff to prepare and send a "Dear Customer" letter, written in question and answer form. Then the directors of Jersey asked him to set up a task force to defend the company. Immediately he reached both inside and outside for writers and for advertising men and raided the Esso Marketers for sales personnel who would be useful. He set up a speakers' bureau to train and send out speakers who could answer the questions the public was asking.

When Haslam started his defense force, there was no intention by the directors of Jersey to do more than put out one fire. Some directors were reluctant to do even this, on the theory that pretty soon the public would forget everything the politicians, the editorial writers, and magazine editors were saying. Once Haslam had the signal to go ahead, he moved with speed to present the company's case before stockholders' meetings that were quickly arranged in a number of cities in the east. He also set out to get professional public relations help.

The first man Haslam called on was Thomas J. Ross, head of Ivy Lee and T. J. Ross, the public relations counsel. Lee, who was a pioneer in the business, had established his reputation with many corporate heads and had advised the first John D. Rockefeller. Ross, who had been Lee's partner, took over as head of the firm in 1934 when Lee died. He was the obvious one for Haslam to turn to. After the first meeting with Ross for exploratory talks, Haslam invited Ross to the Jersey offices and offered to retain Ivy Lee and T. J. Ross. Ross turned down the Haslam offer pointing out that the counselling firm had Socony Vacuum as a client, and that it never took conflicting accounts. Ross did, however, suggest two names to Haslam: John Hill, who founded the Hill and Knowlton firm, and Earl Newsom, who had a small agency of his own. Haslam interviewed both Hill and Newsom, and late in April, 1942, decided on Newsom as advisor to the *ad hoc* group set up to get Jersey's defense across to the public.

With the Jersey employees Haslam had organized, and a group Newsom had assembled, an intensive campaign was started to first put the Jersey company position on the record and then answer all new attacks—and they were multiple from all directions. Carefully documented, clearly written material was prepared, but there seemed no end to the attacks. The policy then changed from a purely defensive one to a positive one. A press conference—the first ever—was held for critical journalists. The directors of the Jersey company announced the completion of the first fluid catalytic cracking plant. The officials, frightened of the forthcoming ordeal, had balked several times; but Haslam, with Newsom's help, persuaded them that this was a first and essential step.

The press conference was a success. The newspapers carried stories of the contribution the company was making to the war effort, and, when difficult questions were asked by the newspapermen, the directors, who knew more than the questioners, handled them well. The results gave the directors greater confidence in Haslam's judgment on public attitudes and the press. It was an important step in the education of those who ran the Jersey company.

Haslam's conception of the relationships of corporations to the public was clear, and far removed it was from the thinking of the Jersey board. To Haslam, the machinery for a modern corporation's contacts with the public mind had always been hopelessly minimized in Standard's setup, and he was certain that the first job for him and Newsom was to lift the company's management out of its traditional concepts. He wanted a comprehensive organization to meet the problems of the future, as well as to handle the current attacks, and he wanted it to work like "a well-oiled machine." He wanted studies made of public attitudes, both those of a general nature and those that more immediately affected the company. He wanted trends of public opinion reported to the top managers, research men, chemists, patent executives, and others. They would, in turn, report to "the public relations office" any incorrect statements about the company. He also wanted news released to the press and contacts with news-papermen and writers established. Opinion formers were a key to Haslam's approach.

Newsom's own thinking was in tune with Haslam's. In a memorandum to Haslam discussing a possible public relations department, Newsom outlined his own views, and warned that the establishment of such a department would not of itself solve the company's public relations problems. "Only management can do that," Newsom wrote Haslam. "The president of the company and the board of directors are responsible for the company's public relations whether they like it or not. They decide company policy. From that policy flow company actions which make the news—actions which, when reported, determine the company's reputation among its employees, its stockholders, its customers, its other 'publics.' "

Both men were in complete agreement in basic philosophy. Their work dovetailed. Together they set out on a course of action that could not help but result in the establishment of a public relations department at Jersey. On Newsom's suggestion, Haslam hired Elmo Roper and his opinion polling organization to make a study of what the public thought of big business in general, profits, the Jersey company's contribution to society, and its responsibilities to the country.

Meanwhile, changes were taking place in the board of directors of Jersey. There was a shift toward new men, men who were prepared to break with company's encrusted traditions. One of the new directors, elected on December 1, 1942, was Haslam. The promotion foretold the changes that had to come. It wasn't long after Haslam's elevation to the board that the announcement came, on February 17, 1943, of the establishment of the public relations department. Its job was to "assume responsibility for assisting the board and the president in public relations matters" and to counsel subsidiary companies in the public relations field.

In September, 1943, little more than six months after the start of the Jersey public relations department, three organizations were retained on a regular basis by Haslam: Earl Newsom & Company, Elmo Roper and Associates, Arthur G. Newmyer & Associates.

Newsom, who had been in business for seven years, had been working steadily with Haslam for the emergency defense period. Former high school teacher and graduate of Oberlin College who had worked on the promotion side of the now-dead *Literary Digest* and had been in book publishing, he had impressed Haslam. It was on Newsom's recommendation that these other firms, each with a specialty that Jersey needed, were hired.

Roper, too, had done some work for Jersey before he was retained on a regular basis as consultant on opinion research. He had been in business for ten years, had extensive experience in market research and as a public-opinion analyst, and could provide the advice and service that was complementary to Newsom's.

The third factor was the newest: Arthur Newmyer had been in business in Washington, D.C., for four months when Haslam retained him as Jersey's Washington public relations consultant. Newmyer had been associate publisher of the *New Orleans Item* and the *New Orleans Tribune* when he returned to his native city, Washington, as publisher of Hearst's *Washington Times*, and, later, associate publisher of the *Washington Times-Herald*. His contribution to Jersey was to provide daily information on Washington trends and developments that might be of interest to the company's managers or of potential public relations significance. He did not act as a spokesman for Jersey before the government, but provided an advisory and information service.

Unlike most other corporations, Standard Oil Company (New Jersey) had at that time and until May 18, 1966, no outside directors on its board. All its members were full-time employees of the company with no other posts. They met every week and had special areas of responsibility. Haslam became the contact director for public relations. This was a major step in Jersey, the proof that the company had finally accepted the principle that its relations with the public were important, important enough to have a director whose responsibility was the company's relations to the public and to whom a full-time, properly structured department would report.

Haslam, to whom public relations was a way of life, not a group of techniques, felt guidelines were necessary for this new department. He wanted it clearly understood what good public relations were from the company's point of view, and what actions the company should take to reach this position. These were the company answers to Haslam's requests for a policy declaration: "Good public relations is deserving and achieving a climate of opinion in which our company can continue to exist as a privately-owned competitive business earning a reasonable profit." To have good public relations it is necessary "to maintain constantly the position where all the company's acts are in the public interest; to report and explain the company's actions so thoroughly that the public readily and continually identifies them with the public interest."

One of the most productive periods in Jersey's relations to the public began. New ideas, both from Newsom and his men and from the group Haslam surrounded himself with in the company, were sought and implemented. Techniques that had proved effective for corporate public relations were used, from an improved annual report to an expanded company magazine, from slides and film strips to good full-length films, from better internal communication to public speeches by officers of the company. A new spirit seemed to possess the company. It opened its doors to newsmen who asked questions and began to provide fuller reports to the press of the activities of the company. At the same time the search went on to find a manager for the public relations department of the Jersey company.

The choice was George H. Freyermuth and he came from inside the company. A mechanical engineer from the University of California with a master's degree from Massachusetts Institute of Technology, he had been with Jersey since 1928. He had worked for a research affiliate, Standard Oil Development Company, and the sales engineering department of the Delaware Company, and was one of the men that Haslam had secured when he organized a crew to answer charges before the Truman committee. Freyermuth knew Jersey and many of its problems, and had been exposed to the hectic aftermath of the troubles that had arisen because the company had cared little for the views of the public. He had another qualification: he was from inside the company, assistant manager of the sales engineering department.

To back up the new public relations department's manager, Stewart Schackne was brought in from the Newsom organization as the assistant manager. He had worked with Newsom and Haslam as one of the outside members of the task force formed to answer Arnold's accusations. He had been a reporter for the Scripps-Howard papers, had experience as a house-organ editor and an associate editor of a Hearst trade publication, and was for six years the publicity director of the Sonotone Corporation before being hired by Newsom in 1942. A native of Toledo, Schackne attended Yale, then moved to Dartmouth College where he was elected to Phi Beta Kappa before graduating in 1927. To Freyermuth's technical knowledge and understanding of Jersey was added Schackne's experience in media and in public relations.

To carry out an effective program, Freyermuth needed men. Some came from the Esso Marketers; others came from other areas of Jersey. Skilled writers and public relations men were hired from outside, often filtered through the Newsom agency. None of the staff was fresh out of college. All had skills which could be put to work at once, because if there was going to be training in company policy and operations, it had to be on the job. The ability to write clearly, an understanding of media, and some conception of public moods were part of the equipment that the outsiders brought with them. It was a good, enthusiastic group. It had a long way to go, knew it, and was full of the excitement that comes from building an organization from the ground up in the midst of a crisis. Added to that, they had a willingness to try new approaches and the support of management.

Freyermuth's ideas of public relations are as germane today as they were when Jersey's department was established. To him, the orthodox concept that a business, to survive, had only to provide a good product and good service at a reasonable price was no longer so, at least for a corporation the size of Jersey Standard. The company's business activities touch on many basic things—discovery and development of natural resources; making of investments so large and important as to be significant factors in the economy of many lands; development and advancement of industry and industrial life; providing of skilled knowledge derived from experience in all parts of the world; employment, directly and indirectly, of many thousands of people. In addition to such critical elements as foreign exchange and balance of payments, it is involved very heavily with people's living standards and the economic future of the many countries in which the company operates.

To Freyermuth, the business ability of a large corporation is one aspect. Its right to do business is another matter which used to be taken for granted. This right is dependent on contracts, charters, concessions, laws, constitutions—all of them derived from the will of the people. And when these contracts, no matter how solemn, are in basic conflict with the will of the people, they are subject to change. This means that the people themselves must be convinced that the company, in addition to providing good products and good services at a reasonable price, is doing its job better than anyone else—better even than governments could. The people must want the company to keep on doing business this way. These are the points that make up the basic concept of public relations and should remain so at Jersey if it is to stay in business. They are of fundamental importance and have nothing to do with fancy publicity or stunts.

To Freyermuth, the establishment of public relations as a functional operation of Jersey does not, nor should it ever, mean that it intruded into, or supplanted, other well-established corporate activities. Public relations organizations and personnel are set up to supplement and strengthen the over-all operations of a company, and there are no secret formulas to be called upon to solve public relations problems. The job is like any other in the company in that it is part of the hard work of business.

Under Haslam's direction, and the prodding of urgent need, the directors of Jersey began to accept fully the public relations department. They started to realize they had to act for the good of the community in which they did business if they were to be allowed to be in business at all. Freyermuth was able to do his job because the directors realized that the privately owned, profit-oriented company had to act as a public institution if it was going to develop the good will it needed to sell its products.

When Haslam appeared before the Jersey board to say that he could not accept the responsibility for the sales of the company's products unless a conscious effort were made to improve its relations with the public, he had the support of one of the newer directors, Frank W. Abrams, appointed in 1940. Abrams had been with Jersey since 1912, the year he graduated from Syracuse University. He had an instinctive appreciation of the value of public support to the company. Cautious as a new director, he more and more began to influence his colleagues until, by the time he became a vice-president in 1944 and chairman of the board in 1946, he had developed into one of the strongest advocates of public relations that the company ever had.

Abrams, in the nine years of his chairmanship, was a leading figure in the development of public relations at Jersey. To him, there was no doubt, as he said in 1946 shortly after his choice as chairman, that the future of American business depended to a large extent on the intelligence and understanding with which business leadership recognized and adapted itself to the thinking of the people of the nation and of all countries in which American companies did business. Abrams was a strong believer in the theory that all executives of a corporation always had to keep in mind the public interest when they were making decisions. To him, the public relations department's job was to be the liaison between the company and the public, and to interpret one to the other.

In 1947, a year after he became chairman, at a conference of Jersey's public relations staff, he said of his board of directors: "I think all of us are conscious of the fact that millions of people in this country and elsewhere are in a very real sense looking over our shoulders as we discuss and deliberate. Although not physically present, there are a lot of people in our board room whenever we meet."

Abrams was distressed because corporate officers and executives, as they rose in position and affluence, tended to lose touch with all but a few of their own kind. The isolation of the senior executive from his origins, from the lives of those in other fields with whom he used to associate, and even from lower echelons in the company, tended to make him forget the wishes, desires, and aspirations of the public. Abrams felt that businessmen could not win much needed support unless they kept up their personal contacts with the kind of people from whom they came. Businessmen had to reorient their outlook to face the facts if they were to understand social changes that were bound to affect business. Identification of Jersey with society as a whole, not simply with one group, was necessary if business was to be acceptable to those who, in the final analysis, ran the country—the voters.

Abrams, too, was highly influential in persuading his fellow directors and other senior executives of the company to take active part in developing better relations with the public. They were encouraged to make speeches before special groups, meet journalists, talk to educators, and visit Washington for conferences with government officials and congressmen. Abrams himself took the lead in this field. When a newspaperman or magazine editor was critical of Jersey or of business in general, Abrams asked to meet him. He enjoyed learning the reasons for criticism and found great pleasure in explaining why Jersey took certain actions. He did not send others to do this when he felt he himself would be the best one for what, in many cases, seemed like confrontations rather than quiet discussions.

Probably the best expression of Abrams's views was in the annual report of Jersey to its stockholders in 1948:

> No business exists in economic isolation. It is part of the social climate of its time. Its policies and actions affect the character of that climate. In turn, that climate—which is, after all, simply the ideas and goals of large numbers of people—influences any business importantly. It can even determine whether the business is to prosper and survive or decline and disappear.
>
> Corporate citizens have, therefore, come to accept many of the obligations traditionally imposed only upon the individual citizen. Today companies concern themselves with employee and community welfare, and with many other activities going beyond

a strictly economic concept of business functions. The management of this company is devoting an increasing share of its attention to the social problems affecting its business. We believe that in this way the continuity of the enterprise may best be assured and its economic health sustained.

There can be no better example of Abrams acting on his own theory of corporate responsibility than what he did to aid education. Abrams's actions rose from a number of motivating drives. He had hoped for a better relationship between business and the educator. He deplored the lack of rapport between leaders in industry and those who taught in the colleges and universities. Since educators are important thought-leaders, Abrams wanted corporations to be closer to colleges and universities than they had been. He was certain that the gap between them was harmful to both. He also was aware of the crisis in education, which was particularly severe with the privately directed institutions. The state-supported colleges had a strong base in the appropriations by state legislatures; but the private colleges, which could more easily experiment and which offered the diversity so essential to good education, needed a great deal of help, and the support had to come from the voluntary donor. There was also the demand from business for educated men and women, without whom no large enterprise could survive. Abrams also knew that the low pay of academicians deterred many of the best college graduates from going into teaching.

One of Abrams's first steps was to persuade his directors to study the possibility of Jersey supporting the social sciences in colleges as it had chemistry and physics. Then, outside the company, he set his course to rouse businessmen generally to support education, with the argument that the future of the nation depended in a large measure on the way teachers were treated. To Abrams, "education helps to build a more productive society and better markets, and provides the foundation of America's greatness as a nation." He made several widely reported speeches, to stimulate action, and announced at the same time that Jersey was prepared to carry its part of the load.

But there was a legal barrier that concerned directors of corporations. A good deal of doubt existed that corporations had the legal right to give financial aid to education that was not directly related to the business itself. Many directors feared that unrestricted gifts to colleges might open them to successful stockholder suits.

The opportunity to test the legality of such gifts came in 1952. It was a stockholder suit in New Jersey. The A. P. Smith Manufacturing Company, a small company with some 300 employees, incorporated in New Jersey, which manufactured valves, fire hydrants, and special equipment had made an unrestricted gift of $1,500 to Princeton University. Stockholders sued the Smith company, claiming it had no right to give away their money for purposes that did not involve the work of the company. The Chancery Division of the Superior Court of New Jersey upheld the legality of the gift, and the highest court of the State, the Supreme Court of New Jersey, unanimously affirmed the ruling. In October, 1953, the Supreme Court of the United States declined to hear an appeal because of the lack of a substantial federal question.

During the case, which was as important to college presidents and the general public as it was to corporations, Abrams gave testimony. He also asked Irving Olds, who was a former chairman of the United States Steel Corporation, to do the same. Abrams's position before the court was that corporations are expected to acknowledge their public responsibilities in support of the essential elements of the free enterprise system. He went on to say it was not "good business" to disappoint "this reasonable and justified public expectation" nor was it good business for corporations "to take the substantial benefits from their membership in the economic community while avoiding the normally accepted obligations of citizenship in the social community."

Olds supported Abrams when he told the court that corporations have a self-interest in the maintenance of liberal education as the bulwark of good government. He said, "Capitalism and free enterprise owe their survival in no small degree to the existence of our private, independent universities," and that, if American business does not aid in their maintenance, it is not "properly protecting the long-range interest of its stockholders, its employees and its customers."

Justice Jacobs, who delivered the opinion of the Supreme Court of New Jersey, wrote:

> There is now widespread belief throughout the nation that free and vigorous non-governmental institutions of learning are vital to our democracy and the system of free enterprise and that withdrawal of corporate authority to make such contributions within reasonable limits would seriously threaten their continuance. Corporations have come to recognize this and with their enlightenment have sought in varying measures, as has the plaintiff by its contribution, to ensure and strengthen the society which gives them existence and the means of aiding themselves and their fellow citizens. Clearly then, the appellants as individual

stockholders whose private interests rest entirely upon the well being of the plaintiff corporation, ought not to be permitted to close their eyes to present day realities and thwart the long-visioned corporate action in recognizing and voluntarily discharging its high obligations as a constituent of our modern social structure.

It was as much a victory for Abrams and Jersey as it was for colleges and the general public, for Abrams had campaigned hard for corporate aid to education. His views coincided with the judgment. Even the terms of Justice Jacobs' decision sounded like Abrams. Of course, he did not rest with the decision in the Smith case. He persuaded Alfred P. Sloan, Jr. of General Motors, Olds, and several other business leaders to join him in organizing in 1953 what became the Council for Financial Aid to Education. It was set up as a non-profit membership corporation, to be the unofficial arm of business in stimulating gifts to higher education. It was one of the special concerns of Abrams during his years as chairman of Jersey. After his retirement from the company in 1955 he continued to press for business assistance to education and remained a director of the Council.

Today corporate aid to higher education is running at the rate of about $250 million a year, an increase of some 280 per cent over the 1954-55 period. Based on reports of senior colleges only, 71.1 per cent of corporate support goes to privately controlled colleges and universities and 28.9 per cent goes to those publicly controlled.

Considering the vast amounts spent for all education in the United States, the business support does not seem overwhelming. But when it is put into the proper context, that of voluntary support, it is fairly substantial. Of the voluntary support 24.2 per cent comes from alumni, 23.4 per cent from general welfare foundations, 26.1 per cent from non-alumni individuals, and 16.1 per cent from business corporations. All signs point to the fact that business giving to education will increase as more corporations decide to move into this sector.

The Esso Education Foundation, set up by Jersey in 1955, had contributed $22,074,000 by 1967. This aid to education is greater than the dollar amount, for it is creatively given. Every dollar provided to aid higher education has a multiplying effect. Jersey is among the top dozen corporations in its contribution to education in the country today.

Abrams's contribution to Jersey's acceptance of its obligations to society, beyond the operations of the enterprise itself, was vast. His leadership in persuading the company that good relations with the public are essential to its ability to perform effectively is one of the reasons that Jersey's reputation in the country as a whole is as good as it is.

M. J. Rathbone, who retired as chairman and chief executive officer of Jersey early in 1965 after nearly twelve years as president and chairman, used to insist that no one could be a good executive if he did not appreciate the importance of public opinion. He even told his company managers so at a meeting in October, 1962. At that time he said: "I do not think it would be possible for a senior executive of Jersey to reach any position of high operating responsibility unless he has developed a very great sensitivity in the public relations field."

Rathbone was no dreamer. He was an intensely practical man. The profit position of the company was of prime importance. Waste was always poison to him and in his five years as chief executive he ran a tight ship. He made up his own mind on the indispensability of good public relations. In his decision making, the profit motive alone was not enough; it had to be tempered with the desire to appeal favorably to many groups in other ways.

Rathbone made public relations the subject of a full dress speech to the Wharton School Alumni Society on October 31, 1962. It was an interesting statement, and, coming from him, it had far more impact than if it had come from a practitioner whose immediate job depends on the acceptance of the public relations department by management.

A manager, Rathbone told the business school graduates, must always tune in on public thoughts and attitudes, and, as far as possible, consider them in all decisions and actions. While this holds true for corporations generally, the larger and more complex they are the more essential such tuning in must be.

He outlined the groups that concern modern management: stockholders, customers, employees, governments, educators, and the general public. While each has particular points of interest, there are other factors. For instance, while the stockholder is essentially interested in profits, earning records, dividends, and future growth possibilities, he is also interested in good treatment for the employee, civic performance, and social responsibility.

To Rathbone "business does not function by divine right, but like any other part of our society, exists with the sanction of the community as a whole and the interests of the community are in turn expressed through governments." That is the basic reason for management's attention to public opinion, "for today's public opinion, though it may appear light as air, may become tomorrow's legislation for better or for worse. Therefore a wise firm makes public relations a function not simply of a staff department but of top management, so that every major business decision is considered from the standpoint of its public impact."

The press, radio, and television—which Rathbone calls "public opinion in concentrated form"—are essential to tell the story of business and free enterprise. However, to do so properly media must know the facts; and that is why management must talk to media representatives often and frankly. Nor should media's comments on subjects that management does not like mean a withdrawal from contact with these means of reaching the public. Rathbone's stress on involvement with the education field, he said, had many reasons; not only because educational institutions provided business with future employees, but also because educators "to a great degree shape the future thinking of the public."

The present chief executive and chairman of the board of Jersey, Michael L. Haider, who stepped into the top job in March, 1965, has been with the organization since 1929, two years after graduating from Stanford University in chemical engineering. In addition to his experience in the United States, he was with the Canadian affiliate, Imperial Oil, as a director and a vice-president; and was president of International Petroleum Company, whose main spheres of activity are in Colombia, Peru, and Venezuela. His international experience, which was bound to color his approach, gave him an extensive orientation in the governmental and public problems in Latin America as well as in problems in the United States and Canada.

His work in the United States and abroad convinced him, as he told a public relations orientation course in September, 1963, that "good public relations is primarily good performance; that good performance alone is not enough, the public needs to be informed if we are to get the benefit of good performance." Now, as the chief executive, he has amplified his earlier belief this way:

The first responsibility of corporate management has always been to make a profit for its stockholders, but in driving for this profit the company becomes involved with customers, employees, the public, and governments, and all these have to be taken into consideration to make certain that the stockholders' interest is served over the long term. And while maximizing profits is vital it does not mean getting into the market, making a big killing and getting out fast. In our free market economy the chances of doing this are few and far between; and they are rarely useful to a company whose success depends on long term operations, since the sound modern corporation's success is based on providing a present profit in dividends as well as in future growth. It expects to be around for a long time.

Haider maintains that, in our free society, a corporation is a legal person. Like individual persons, it has all the responsibilities that go with freedom. Each of its basic relationships entails particular responsibilities and an obligation on the part of management to report on performance. This means, says Haider, that shareholders are entitled to management's best efforts to produce a return on their investment and to protect their equity and increase its value. The customers are entitled to their money's worth, as measured by the competitive market—and in our system the customer is always right. Employees are entitled to fair wages and working conditions, the personal respect of their superiors, and a chance to develop their skills and leadership qualities on the job. The public is entitled to an over-all performance by the corporation, both in the market place and as a corporate citizen, that is beneficial to the community. And finally, says Haider, government is entitled to lawful taxes on the company's business, and to a scrupulous observance by the company of all the laws affecting its activities. Government itself has a reciprocal responsibility to use its vast powers with restraint, lest the freedom and the responsibility of the corporation—and its contribution to the economy—be impaired and destroyed.

All these elements are interrelated. Haider believes that no corporation that wants to do profitable business over the long term can afford to neglect its responsibilities or its communications with stockholders, customers, employees, public, and government. It is thus, he says, that private enterprise, wisely carried on, will always serve the public interest.

Like other executives in other highly competitive and aggressive corporations, Haider continuously questions the activities of all operations. Each has to justify itself in dollars and cents. This is easier for others than for the public relations department, which can never fully measure its contribution in the sense that producing, or marketing, or research can. But a reassessment of a public relations department is always useful, for it can have the effect of strengthening it, giving it new direction, new support, and, often, a fresh impetus to what it is already doing well.

Haider's review of Jersey's public relations department in 1966 made him conclude that a variety of changes were necessary to meet the problems that the changing company has to face in a changing environment. But never at any time did Haider depart from his belief that Jersey must operate in the public interest and keep the directly concerned groups and the general public fully informed of the reasons for the company's decisions. Haider, with the larger stress Jersey has been laying on its international operations, has faced the opposition to foreign investment in developing countries, and in older and fully developed countries as well. The new nationalism which has so grandly increased the nation members of the United Nations is bound to influence Jersey's overseas operations even as it has the United Nations. As his regime gets older, the result will be even a stronger stress on public relations activities in all the affiliates in countries abroad.

The public relations of a corporation can be no better than management's understanding of the context within which it does its business. Those chosen to head a public relations department have a key role to play. Beyond knowing the mechanics of their field, they must advise management of public attitudes, and here the wisdom of the public relations head is the key to his success. His assessment of the effect that changes in society may have on the corporation can help the corporation make the adjustments it must to survive. Since 1943, Jersey has had four public relations heads. Freyermuth, who was in charge from 1943 to 1954, was an engineer. Schackne, the public relations deputy chief who succeeded Freyermuth, ran the department for the next six years.

To Schackne, a creative practitioner, the aim of a corporate public relations head is to seek out and to cultivate means for reducing friction and for increasing harmony between the company he represents and the elements outside the organization. Because of specialization and the technological development from which it springs, the number of friction points have increased. As the employee relations department seeks to achieve harmony between two groups within the organization—the managerial and the non-managerial employees—public relations directs its attention between the organization and outside elements.

Schackne contrasts the activities of the public relations department and the company's legal department. Like public relations men, the lawyers aim to avert conflict or, if it does arise, to resolve it. But the difference between the public relations department and the legal department is that the corporate lawyers' advice deals with how far the client can go in the direction of possible conflict without actually crossing the line, while the public relations man tries to find out how far his principals can reasonably move in the opposite direction. To Schackne, the law resolves conflict through the application of statute and common law, operating through the highly organized instrument of the courts whose judgment can, if necessary, be enforced by physical power. But the public relations efforts to resolve conflict, if it should arise, do not employ arguments based on the law, but use any kind of statement or communication that imagination can conceive to appeal to the antagonist's sense of justice or to his self-interest. When a conflict is resolved by the operation of the law, one party is likely to be be left resentful, and tension may be greater than at the outset. When conflict is resolved by public relations actions, the aim is to achieve at least increased tolerance between the contestants and to reduce tension.

Schackne believes the performance of the public relations department is basically the same as that of any other staff department in the over-all operations of the corporation. Simply, he says, it is to make it easier for a company to fill its economic role. If a corporation wants to stay in business as a private entity, manage its own affairs, make its own decisions and earn a reasonable profit, it must function with the conviction that the way it does business must serve the nation as a whole. Good products and good service are not enough in themselves, for a company can provide these things and still be harried and hampered. Efficiency is no guarantee against nationalization or fragmentation. Public relations, as Schackne sees the function, is to help make it possible for the company to fill its profit-making role, something that is impossible without the support of public opinion.

Schackne's successor, Robert H. School, was a lawyer who had been executive vice-president of Esso Standard Oil Company before his appointment in 1960. He retired from Jersey in 1965. His successor, Henry B. Wilson, is an engineer, a graduate in petroleum engineering of Oklahoma University. For four years before taking on the chief job in public relations, he had been the Washington representative of Jersey's government relations department, and had been with the company in this country and abroad since 1929, the year of his graduation from college. Overseas, he worked for Jersey affiliates in Argentina, Venezuela, Colombia, Peru, Brazil, and Spain. He was sixty years old on his assumption of the public relations manager's job.

Clearly, Wilson's appointment is a signal of the greater emphasis on government relations in the United States and on the development of Jersey as an international company. Both are related to the broad public relations problems of the company. The shifting political scene in Washington and the often-revolutionary changes throughout the world are fundamentally the result of changes of public opinion. In an attempt to meet and anticipate these, Jersey picked a different type of public relations head, one without any experience in the normal public relations operations but with a strong, practical company background, wise in the ways of foreign governments, and with an alertness to U.S. governmental realities.

A company's public relations structure and programs are designed to meet its own particular needs. Jersey's needs are varied, operating as it does in more than 100 countries. The biggest company in the oil industry with world-wide assets of more than $13.8 billion, sales in 1966 of $13.6 billion, and profits in 1966 of $1.1 billion, it has 738,000 stockholders, none of whom holds more than three per cent of the stock. The largest holdings are not in the names of individuals but belong to insurance companies, investment companies, pension funds, and banks.

Standard Oil Company incorporated in New Jersey, its legal name, is a holding company which itself does not carry out industrial operations. This work is done by its affiliated companies which operate in most countries of the free world. Jersey owns all of the stock of many of these companies, most of the stock in others, and varying lesser amounts of still others. Each operates as, or under, a regional organization, with a high degree of independence: each has its own officers and directors who run the business. Decentralization is an old and honored policy, in many ways essential, for management decisions demand an intimate knowledge of the region or country of the affiliate.

Although the Jersey organization includes a large chemical affiliate, well over nine-tenths of its business is in the energy field. One out of every six barrels of oil and products used throughout the non-Communist world come from the company's operations. In 1966, Jersey had 149,000 employees, 45,000 of these in the United States, about the same number in the rest of the Western Hemisphere and some 59,000 in countries of the Eastern Hemisphere. With more than half of its investments outside the United States, there is increasing emphasis on foreign operations. In 1966, of the $1.2 billion invested in new plant and equipment, slightly more than half was abroad, one-quarter of which was in the less-developed areas of the world.

More than $200 million was spent in 1966 for exploration of petroleum and $400 million for inventories, trade credits, and other working assets. A good additional measure of the company is that in 1966 again, Jersey paid a combined total in world-wide operations of $4.7 billion in taxes and royalties, and of this about $1 billion went to the less-developed regions. These payments to governments were more than twice as much as the payments to employees and stockholders combined.

The size of Jersey can be more clearly grasped when it is seen that the Houston-based Humble Oil & Refining Company, embracing most of Jersey's U.S. operations except research and certain special functions, and which is owned 100 per cent by Jersey, had sales of more than $4 billion in 1966. This makes Humble one of the ten largest companies in the United States. And Imperial Oil in Canada, which is seventy per cent owned by Jersey, is a billion-dollar company. So is Creole Petroleum Corporation, ninety-five percent owned by Jersey, operating in Venezuela.

The entire Jersey company is run by a board of directors of sixteen men, twelve of whom are full-time employees long experienced in the oil business. Almost all of the twelve have come up through service with the affiliates. The board's executive committee meets almost every day and its decisions are reported to the full board every month. Management's job is carried out through committees at all executive levels. Directors are assigned to special areas, one director being a primary contact for each department and another, since Jersey's directors are frequently on the move, acting as the alternate.

The fundamental function of Jersey is to give its affiliates the help, advice and the services they may not themselves be able to supply. It makes studies of economic trends; carefully assesses the political climate in the United States and in all the countries where the affiliates are; supplies research and technical information; reviews their financial affairs, operating results and management performance; develops management techniques which can be applied throughout the organization. It is through the cooperation of Jersey that the day-to-day interaffiliate buying and selling relationships are coordinated. The actual operations involved in finding, producing, refining, transporting, and marketing oil and its related products are carried on by the affiliated companies themselves.

It is for this holding company that Jersey's public relations department does its job. Naturally, the objectives of the public relations department, the methods by which these are met, and its organization, are all keyed to serve Jersey, and only indirectly the affiliates—most of which have their own public relations organizations.

Jersey's very nature and size raise major public relations problems. As a company incorporated in the United States, predominantly owned by Americans, it is bound to be involved in American affairs. As a company which has extensive business interests abroad, its investments and operations are also of major importance to the welfare and development of the host nations. Jersey is also a focal point of criticism, partly for historic reasons, partly because of the oil business itself. As the world's largest oil company, Jersey is quite understandably the target of those who believe that size by itself results in wielding undue power. As a holding company, Jersey seems very often to be remote.

Also, Jersey operates in the midst of a brutal ideological struggle; of fervent nationalism and of strong political and social pressures. Issues such as trade, foreign investment, propaganda of the cold war, struggles for power in unstable nations—all these affect and disturb people everywhere. The war in Vietnam, the pressures of the draft, the antagonisms to the United States by other nations for many—and sometimes conflicting—reasons, make the problems of adjustment to public opinion extremely difficult, and the general conduct of business even more so.

The problems are particularly complex in the area of foreign investment. In some countries it is equated with foreign control. In other countries a wild nationalism is simply opposed to foreign investment of any kind, especially American. In still other countries, there is a demand for such rigid controls of foreign-financed industry that effective operations become almost impossible.

These are only some of the basic difficulties which affect the company's relationships to the public throughout the world. Others, like sharp gusts of public anger directed toward a government or political system, can have enormous effects on the company itself or one of its affiliates.

For these reasons, a clear definition of Jersey's public relations objectives and activities is desirable, as are periodic reviews by the board of directors. They are necessary for another and very human reason: far too many executives in the company (and not only those abroad) are personally so removed from the public and so little aware of the historical crises that the company has survived, that they refuse to believe that public opinion should be their concern. To them it is only something which gets in the way. To these insensitive managers, who will sometimes only heed an order by the board of directors, a declaration of objectives is extremely important and can be pretty close to being a directive.

So, in January, 1966, Jersey's board reaffirmed the company's three major public relations objectives and summarized them in these words:

1. To demonstrate through its actions the constructive role filled by a responsible, privately operated international company.

2. To explain how Jersey Standard fills this role.

3. To work for a climate of opinion at home and abroad that will encourage fair opportunity for its operations.

These primary objectives might be illustrated this way:

Jersey wants people to know the company. If they do, and have some knowledge of how it conducts its business, it is likely they will have confidence in Jersey and will give the company a fair hearing.

Jersey wants people to think of the company as an ethical, socially desirable enterprise, made up of men and women of character, human understanding, and unusual knowledge of world affairs. Jersey wants people to know that its executive and management groups are interested in the problems of nations and are deeply conscious of the public interest.

Jersey wants people to think of the company as a leader in the business world because it is enterprising, efficient, progressive in research, a good employer, advanced in inventing, developing, and making available new products and processes. The company also wants to be thought of as a leader because of the positions it takes on public and industry issues, and because of the willingness of its senior executives to speak out where it is appropriate and natural for them to do so.

Jersey wants people to feel that the products and services offered by the operating affiliates are of top quality, and that both the prices and profits are fair.

Jersey wants to be recognized as an important national and international asset. In the United States the company wants people to feel that as one of the largest international enterprises it is working toward goals which the vast majority of Americans approve—such as the economic strength and progress of the United States, the economic development and strengthening of friendly countries, the promotion of education, and a recognition of the interdependence of the nations of the free world. Abroad, the company wants people to understand better the constructive function of international capital investment; to realize that Jersey's operations and experience are important contributions to economic expansion; to be aware of the stimulation that comes from the importation and exchange of ideas, people and techniques; and to know that Jersey provides employment and opportunities for the personal advancement of many of their compatriots.

The duties of the company's public relations department is clearly outlined in Jersey's management guide in these words:

It advises and assists management in matters relating to the public interest to the end that company policies and activities may merit and attain public approval.

The department examines public opinion, both of the company itself and on broad social, political, and economic issues, and reports its observations to interested executives and departments. In these examinations it regularly scans news media and journals of opinion, studies general public opinion surveys and current work in the social sciences bearing on public opinion and communications, and when desirable, initiates surveys of its own. In gathering, analyzing, and evaluating public opinion data, it also draws upon the help of outside consultants.

The department serves as a source of information about the company to the public in general and to special groups. It answers inquiries made concerning company affairs and through news releases, publications, and other communication material, disseminates information aimed at increasing public knowledge and understanding of the company, its actions and objectives. The department plans and carries out special activities designed to increase knowledge about the company, improve its acceptance by influential groups, and enhance its reputation generally.

The department counsels and advises the affiliated companies with a view to effecting a general coordination of public relations policies throughout the Jersey family. It keeps them informed of significant actions taken by any of the company interests and of important developments in the field generally. Personnel of the department are available to assist the affiliates, as well as the Jersey management and individual executives, on public relations aspects of particular activities.

To carry out these duties, the public relations department is structured so that it can serve management, serve the affiliates, and serve the particular purposes of the holding company. Wilson, the public relations manager, reports to the contact director of the board, Emilio G. Collado, an executive vice-president whose three primary concerns are finance, government relations, and public relations. Collado, a 1931 graduate in business and engineering administration of the Massachusetts Institute of Technology, is a Harvard Ph. D. in economics. He was with the U.S. Treasury Department and the Federal Reserve Bank of New York before he joined the State Department, where he was special assistant to the undersecretary and deputy to the assistant secretary for economic affairs. He was also the United States executive director of the World Bank before he was hired by Jersey in 1947.

The department reports to management, and, in turn, keeps in touch with management's plans through weekly conferences with Collado and Wilson. When necessary, there are telephone conferences and *ad hoc* meetings on day-to-day developments. In addition, Wilson is in frequent, though irregular, contact with Haider and the president of the company, J. K. Jamieson, who also serves as the executive committee advisory contact director for public relations. Further, Wilson goes before the executive committee or the full board on public relations problems, both to present his proposals and to report on what his department is doing. There is no barrier to Wilson's opportunity to express his views to top management or to know the directors' thinking. Unlike what happens in so many other companies, Jersey's public relations head has the ear of management.

The department is organized in two broad areas—planning and advisory, and services. The latter, in turn, has these principal divisions:

The creative services division is headed by a manager, whose main job is to prepare materials for Jersey and its affiliates in a wide range of communications media. The writing and publishing of *The Lamp* and other periodicals, the annual report and other stockholder publications, speeches, background memoranda, booklets, television and magazine advertising, exhibits, motion pictures, and still photographs —all are creative services' responsibility.

The Lamp is itself a major project. The company magazine is a quarterly, with a fine reputation as a periodical designed primarily for stockholders' reading. It is well written and handsomely designed, and makes effective use of color reproductions of paintings and photographs to illustrate the articles. The inside cover usually carries a signed statement by Haider explaining some aspect of Jersey's business or enunciating Jersey's views on an economic or social problem important to the company. It is not dull, the failing of so many publications of this sort. One of the reasons for this is that it is written and edited by an experienced magazine staff, and is continuously being reviewed to make certain that its content is bright and informative, and its format attractive.

This creative services division also produces Jersey's annual report, although stockholder relations generally are the province of the office of the secretary of the corporation. This report, with a print order of more than 1,200,000, is prepared in cooperation with the comptroller's and the secretary's departments, as well as others. It is extensively used in colleges and schools of business administration as case history material as well as by security analysts and others who have more than a passing interest in Jersey's business. The size, contents, charts, and illustrations are all under regular study for readability and effectiveness, for it is one of the most valuable documents Jersey publishes.

This division also has a hand in designing and producing the *Jersey Shareholders' Quarterly* and *Report of the Annual Meeting*, as well as assisting with exhibits at the annual meeting.

Speeches are always an important means of reaching special sectors of the public—and often the general public—with management's views of its own problems and of general issues that involve Jersey. The editorial section of creative services, which is headed by an editor, researches and helps prepare these speeches. Often they are distributed in printed form to special lists of people who have an interest in the speeches' subjects. Frequently this distribution has a greater impact than the original speech, for the booklets reach a greater number of people than heard the speeches in the first instance, or read news reports of it. Even though the forums before which speeches of this kind are made are really sounding boards for larger constituencies, Jersey is very careful to develop topical and newsworthy statements in its selection of the platforms.

Creative services is also responsible for the writing and production of policy statements, position papers, booklets, and brochures to meet special public relations objectives. It revises existing publications. For instance, there is an almost continuous revision of a short history and general description of Jersey Standard to keep pace with developments in activities and organizations. Another project may be a new brochure on Esso in Europe, done at the request of European affiliates, or an updating of a pamphlet on Esso research. These publications are first distributed to carefully selected lists, and then become stock items used to meet the requests for information about the company.

The creative services division also writes and designs—or may only design—other publications ranging from programs and menus to complex presentations. The design and production section headed by an art advisor, stresses the appearance of a publication—its stock, color, size, type face, and illustrations—so that its readership can be extended and it can be more easily assimilated. There is another value: clean, modern design in publications is part of the impression the reader has of the company's character.

Television—an area in which Jersey has done some noteworthy work—and institutional advertising for the company fall under this division as well. Paid space has many advantages. There is control over subject matter. This holds as true for television commercials as it does in print advertisements. The audience can then be selected and the information is controlled. What Jersey wants to say is said, therefore, in the manner it desires—not, as in the case of news or feature stories, filtered through the writer or editor who may or may not understand what he is writing about or what he is editing. In choice of audience, whether in print or television, Jersey seeks those who are the more serious readers or viewers. And the company has found that properly done TV commercials and carefully presented advertisements with copy that does not offend always bring a good response.

Just as Jersey selects its outlets carefully for its television shows, so it just as carefully uses magazines for explaining the company and its policies. While the magazines Jersey uses for its institutional ads vary, they pretty much run to *Harper's Magazine*, *The Atlantic*, *The Reporter*, *Time*, *Newsweek* and *Saturday Review*. Messages are directed to those whose opinions and influences are especially important to the company.

Films also come under the direction of the creative services division. Almost from the beginning of its public relations department, Jersey has fully realized the power of the film as a medium of communicating ideas and impressions about the company. An unusually successful beginning was *Louisiana Story*. Another was the story of energy, *Energetically Yours*. More recently, Jersey has produced a film on Esso's research, *The Human Element*, told in terms of its benefit to the world with an emphasis on the spirit of research. This was followed by *Life in the Balance*, which stressed the growing problem of food supply and oil's part in helping solve it. Foreign language versions of these films were made and distributed through affiliates throughout the world.

Still photography is also the province of creative services. Photographs are an important means of letting the public know what a company is doing, and so Jersey has an active library covering all phases of the oil industry for use both within the organization and to supply requests from newspapers, magazines, book publishers, and schools. New developments are documented by photos and these are used in company publications and in feature stories that may be used by syndicated feature services or newspapers.

Every large public relations department sets up exhibits. Jersey is no exception, and the exhibits, done by creative services, are as much help to affiliates as they are to Jersey as a whole. This work includes cooperation with outside agencies such as museums. An oil exhibit at the Museum of Natural History in New York drew millions of visitors during the years it was on display. Those created for the affiliates in Italy and Latin America to be travelling art shows in the United States were of special help for the countries involved.

Jersey has always fought against the tendency to overwhelm media with press releases or unnecessary publicity activities. The idea of "getting some publicity" usually leads to frivolous and phony events intended to force public attention; they can, in the long run, have a bad public relations effect not only on the press, but, through the press, on a wide public that can tell the difference between news and stunts. This does not mean that publicity is not an effective and proper tool for providing information in its proper place. It may be even necessary and desirable to gain public attention by some special tactic in some cases. To Jersey, however, getting public attention is not the purpose of the public relations department.

Maintaining a sound relationship with the trade, financial, and general press, and radio and television stations is important to Jersey. This function falls to the press services division, with a manager and staff that answers innumerable questions every day from all kinds of news outlets. It develops and distributes press releases on earnings, elections of executives, speeches, feature stories, and new developments. When the occasion demands it, this division arranges press conferences to give the press a chance to ask questions for clarification of a major news announcement. When it is necessary to develop important stories in depth, interviews are arranged between reporters and members of management. Press services also arranges press trips to newsworthy company installations, and provides facilities for the working press at stockholders' meetings and other large occasions.

Press services regularly scans the more important papers and news magazines, and indirectly monitors radio and TV broadcasts, for mention of Jersey and of matters of interest to Jersey. When the significance of the item demands, Jersey may undertake a rebuttal, a fuller explanation, or a correction.

Cooperation is given to the press when it is researching features on senior members of Jersey's management, or when the financial press is interested in doing background articles. Stories which appear in *The Lamp* are often developed for the newspapers, and special stress in keeping with the development of Jersey as an international company is given to stories about the affiliates abroad. Often announcements which have to be made abroad first will be distributed in the United States and other countries. In turn, Jersey affiliates work with Jersey's press division in handling press releases within their own area to get better local notice.

The press division will sometimes invite publishers, editorial writers, and business editors to join company executives at lunch where they can get to know each other better. Newspapers are also given fullest cooperation when they invite Jersey's managers to their editorial board discussions to deal with special issues or for background purposes. In late 1966, to make the press relations function more effective, an office of the press services division was opened in Washington. It is staffed by one man whose purpose is to service the Washington media, which have become even more important to the company than in the past.

Jersey runs an annual New York press dinner, started in 1944, which is attended by news, television, and radio writers, and where company executives and guests meet informally. These "no work" affairs are helpful to both sides, provide valuable background understanding for the press and give the executives a chance to meet newsmen in a relaxed atmosphere. But the most important single continuing job for the press services division in its relations with media is to add to the reputation of the company by giving the press fair treatment, and quick and straightforward answers to its queries, so that media will know that legitimate information is not withheld.

The research and analysis division—whose head has the title of advisor—reviews, researches, and analyzes economic and other information concerning the company and the oil industry. Particular emphasis is given to the public relations aspects of this information and recommendations are made to the department management for public relations action. The division keeps itself informed on developments within the company and the oil industry and develops background data on subjects of importance to the company's public relations program.

The division prepares analytical and interpretive reports and papers on issues of concern to the company. For example, it recently prepared a background paper on European attitudes toward United

States investments in Europe. This paper dealt with the major arguments—most of which were of an economic nature—made by Europeans against United States investments in Europe, and presented the company's views and position on this issue.

As part of its advisory job, the division reviews new books, speeches, editorials, and articles that may have an effect on the company, and, when necessary, summarizes books for quick executive reading. The division is alert to public and industry issues on which Jersey executives may want to speak, and it provides research material for speeches, articles, booklets, films, and other informational material required by the creative services division. In all, it acts as an advisory and service division to the entire public relations department.

An essential part of Jersey's public relations department is the counselling of its affiliates, both in the United States and abroad, on public relations programs and issues. While this is done by the management and by all divisions of the department, the day-to-day job belongs to the planning and advisory division, which consists basically of the three area advisors who cover the areas where Jersey operates—Europe, Africa, the Middle and Far East; Latin America; and North America, including affiliates based in New York.

Regional companies are responsible for the operating affiliates in various areas: for example, the affiliates in the United Kingdom, Germany, France and Italy, among others, report to a regional company, Esso Europe. The latter in turn conducts the advisory and service function. In this setup, the planning and advisory division, as well as the public relations department management of Jersey, deals primarily with the regional organizations.

The counselling is done through personal visits, correspondence, and regional public relations meetings. Company information, public relations material, speeches of Jersey managers, policy statements— all are sent to the affiliates by this division, which, also, because of its special knowledge of the public relations staffs of the affiliates, helps the department's management evaluate personnel and public relations programs run by the affiliates. This division also organizes public relations orientation courses to keep staff members of the affiliates in touch with new development and Jersey's thinking. It also recommends rotational assignments of public relations personnel among the affiliates and it lends staff members from headquarters for special public relations assignments with affiliates.

It is relatively easy to keep in close touch with public relations departments of affiliates in this country, the telephone being the handiest means of answering questions and giving advice. The affiliates overseas present special problems; language, differing mores, political systems, economic and social problems, and levels of competence of public relations staff. In some countries, public relations is such a relatively new field that it is often difficult to find competent people, or even those who would like to be trained in this field. However, with the growth of Jersey as an international company, the stress has increased on establishing competent public relations departments and worthwhile programs overseas, particularly in the developing countries. In older, more economically matured nations, people who understand public relations, or who can be taught to function effectively in this field, are not a major problem.

Fifty-four Jersey affiliated companies overseas now have public relations departments, and, in every case except one, the manager is a national. With one exception, these departments have been in operation for at least five years and in most cases for ten or more years. There are about seventy senior staff public relations people in the Latin American operations, more than eighty in Europe and North Africa, and more than fifty in the Far East and Australia. Some of these departments are fairly small operations and devote most of their efforts to press and community relations. Others have extensive programs covering a wide range of traditional public relations activities. In Latin America, yearly public relations expenditures by Esso companies run to more than $4 million, in Europe and North Africa in excess of $5 million, and in the Far East and Australia about $1,500,000.

Of the senior men in the public relations departments in the Jersey affiliates abroad, approximately sixty per cent have had previous press or other media experience; fifteen per cent have had other public relations experience; fifteen per cent worked in some other department of Jersey or one of its affiliates; and some ten per cent held some college or university positions.

All affiliate public relations departments report directly to their local managements and are responsible to them. The regional operating companies in Europe, Africa, the Far East, and Latin America have public relations departments responsible for coordinating the public relations activities of the operating affiliates in their areas. In turn, the departments of these regional operating organizations are in close touch with Jersey's public relations department in New York. Close consultation has to be maintained between the regional operating company's department and Jersey's so that decisions can be made quickly on how best to inform affiliates about parent company activities and policies. Any crisis or unusual development concerning the company, its affiliates, or the industry are matters of concern to Esso companies around the world and action is taken to assure that affiliates are prepared to answer questions or meet criticism on these developments. In addition, general information about petroleum industry developments, and relevant political, economic, and social developments are sent to affiliates when necessary.

Occasionally, disputes with a host government are of interest to audiences in other parts of the world. Then background memoranda are prepared to explain the history of the particular issue and the company's position in the dispute. In the past few years such papers were developed on issues arising from operations by Esso companies in Peru, Argentina, Ceylon, and Indonesia. Speeches by Jersey executives and testimony before Congressional committees on subjects of possible interest to Esso companies around the world are also sent to them.

These affiliate public relations operations have an influence of sizable importance on the businessmen running locally owned enterprises in the countries where Jersey companies operate. Through Jersey's example, they often pay more attention to the needs of their own people and the advancement of their country beyond the progress which may come from the successful running of a single company. The U.S. concept, as represented by Jersey, of contributing to the general welfare of the nation as a whole is rather new to many businessmen in some developing countries. For them, their own company's profit position seems the only worry, for either the long or the short term.

In addition to originating material which eventually finds its way to affiliate public relations departments, Jersey's public relations department receives—via the public relations departments of the regional operating companies—information about affiliate public relations problems and programs. Sometimes this information is of obvious interest to other affiliates—for example, the imaginative use of display material by the Indian company to illustrate the theme, "Esso is Oil and So Much More"; the development of seminars for financial writers in Germany and Italy in which Esso management participated; and the sponsorship of contests designed to encourage a greater appreciation of local art and cultural traditions by the International Petroleum Company. By informing affiliates in other parts of the world about these programs, they often can be adapted to local needs. Esso companies in East Africa and South Vietnam have in the past few years sponsored contests for local artists based upon the success reported by other affiliates in carrying out similar programs.

The importance of close liaison between Jersey's public relations department and its operating affiliates is shown by the way in which *The Lamp* calls upon affiliates to help its writers in collecting material for articles. In turn, the affiliate magazines often adapt *Lamp* articles for use in their local publications. There are twenty-six affiliate publications throughout Jersey's world empire, and most of them model themselves in large measure on *The Lamp* in their literary and artistic contents. The combined circulation of these overseas magazines is more than 400,000 copies. These are sent to government officials and opinion leaders. In addition, more than thirty thousand copies of *The Lamp* are distributed by affiliates to opinion leaders in their countries. A lesser quantity of the *Jersey Annual Report* and other publications are also distributed by affiliates.

Just as there is an effort to keep a to-and-fro flow of information between headquarters and the field, so there are also assignments of personnel from headquarters to the field, and vice versa. Public relations men from New York are often sent to affiliates to assist in recruiting and training new personnel, to lend a hand in coping with some special problem that has arisen, or to broaden the experience of headquarters staff. Such assignments have been made recently in Southeast Asia, East Africa, Brazil, and Argentina.

In turn, Jersey's public relations department has been host to staff members from affiliates for one- or two-year working assignments designed to give these high-potential people an appreciation of the parent's operations and problems. Esso Philippines' most senior national, a skilled professional, spent a year with Esso Standard Eastern's New York headquarters prior to being appointed to an important position in the management of its new fertilizer company in his country. Others from France, the United Kingdom, and Italy have returned to senior positions with their companies or other affiliates following a tour of duty in New York with Jersey's department. In addition, affiliates participate from time to time in programs of lateral assistance. Public relations executives from Esso Petroleum Company in London have been assigned to East Africa, Pakistan, and India. All of these efforts in the field of talent development aim at creating a flexible cadre of professionals who are available for assignments in any part of the world.

In any large organization, administrative responsibility has to be placed in one locus if a department is to be run efficiently. For Jersey's public relations department this job is done by the administrative and special services division, headed by a manager. It handles the administration of the staff and its budget, is charged with cost control, personnel matters, salaries, office facilities, and the business details of public relations projects. The manager is privy to all that is being done in the entire department, as the controller of the purse strings should be. In addition, this division handles Jersey's educational projects, exclusive of the work of the Esso Education Foundation, the distribution of all public relations materials—including the maintenance of highly selective mailing lists and such special projects as company history.

Jersey itself has no community relations department since it is a holding company whose only physical facilities are offices in New York City. It has no "community" in the sense of the community in the environs of a refinery. The affiliates, however, all have community relations divisions as part of their public relations departments. Employee relations—another key function, for employees are certainly an important public—are handled by an employee relations department which antedates the public relations department, having been set up in 1915 after a violent strike in Bayonne, New Jersey.

For the rather extensive operation which is carried on by Jersey's public relations department there is a relatively small staff. It fluctuates little, about twenty-five professionals, exclusive of clerical and secretarial help. It is a seasoned staff, whose average age is forty-seven. Seventeen of the staffers are college graduates with at least a bachelor's degree or the equivalent, and the others have had some college training. Six of the public relations staff have master's degrees; one has a Ph.D. Three members of the staff are women, one an executive working on educational projects, one the managing editor of *The Lamp*, the third a research and production assistant.

The career backgrounds of these people are varied, yet clearly related to their jobs: six in general writing and editing; five in journalism; two in public relations and advertising; three in art; two in education; three in magazine design and production; one in sociology; two in engineering; and one in economics.

The total of all public relations staff professionals for the entire organization, including the public relations staffs of all the affiliates throughout the world, numbers about 325. In some African countries the public relations staff consists of half a man since he only puts in half his time on the public relations job. At the other end of the scale is Humble Oil & Refining Company's public relations department, where there are more professionals than in the holding company—thirty-six—including the community relations men stationed at refineries. And Imperial Oil, the Canadian affiliate, is not far behind.

It is no surprise that so many public relations professionals working for Jersey and its affiliates are communications specialists, for one of their chief functions is to communicate. The ability to write simply and clearly is one of the essential qualifications for almost all members of any well-run public relations department. Jersey and its affiliates are no exception. Nor is it any surprise that few youngsters get hired at Jersey, for when a job is open a specialist is sought and the chances of newly minted college graduates being specialists in this field are not great. In addition, maturity of judgment is essential and maturity cannot be won except by living longer than new graduates have. The type of experience in some kind of work where public reaction to events is seen at close hand is often essential and this still further restricts the areas from which Jersey can recruit its staff. There is, however, recruiting from inside the company, especially among the affiliates, from those who work in sales, research, producing, and refining.

There is not much turnover in the affiliates' or Jersey's public relations departments, but several new people are hired every year. This means special training, either in understanding the company and the oil business, or in public relations, because every new man must have a sound, if not detailed, knowledge of company organization and operations, of basic company philosophy and policies, and of public relations techniques.

Full use is made of the regular employee training courses run by both the parent and affiliated companies for general orientation and indoctrination. In addition, Jersey has found from experience that a specialized public relations training course helps give new employees in this field the specific tools and knowledge they need, and gives them a chance to understand better the economic and social philosophy of the company.

These courses are given in New York, usually every other year. Included are lectures, discussion periods, office visits, and field trips, covering three weeks. Because of the international character of Jersey, there is a clear world-assembly look. The stage is set for the courses by having a Jersey board member discuss top management's views on public relations; this is the best way to show the trainees the importance the company gives to public relations. Jersey's organization is covered in a general way with a close explanation of how the holding company's public relations and government relations departments are run, what they do, and the services they provide for the affiliates. Included in these courses are talks on the main phases of the company's business—exploration, producing, transportation, refining, and marketing. These are given by members of the involved staffs. Descriptions of stockholder and employee relations are given, as well as of industry and company economics, by the company executives who hold the prime responsibilities in these areas.

Following this, general background phases of the public and government relations departments' activities are explored in detail by members of Jersey's staff.

A typical course might include preparation, distribution, and timing of news releases; news photographs; use and handling of press conferences; helping company executives deal with press contacts; radio and TV activities; editing and exploitation of speeches and policy statements; preparation of the annual report to stockholders; letters to the public; cooperation with magazine editors and use of company material in magazine articles; special events; photographs, motion pictures, displays and visual aids; contacts with schools and educators; preparation and production of institutional magazines; and production and distribution of other publications.

Public opinion surveys may be discussed, with reviews of data from recent company surveys. The significance of these surveys in developing a public relations program is stressed, as are the effects of changing public moods on company activities.

Visits are made to refineries, laboratories, and offices of domestic affiliates to let the trainees see how community relations problems are handled, for this is an area in which many of them will be involved and all of them have to understand. The trainees are given, usually in Texas and Louisiana, an idea of oil industry operations, oil fields, pipelines, over-water drilling, and natural gas plants. On the way back to New York, the new employees see Washington, where they receive an explanation of how the government affects the oil industry, and meet legislators and government officials.

The final day of the conference is taken up with a critical evaluation of the orientation course in which all the trainees participate. Plans are then discussed for improvement of future courses, based on what the newcomers have learned and the gaps they feel should be filled for those who may take future courses.

Convincing the public that Standard Oil (New Jersey) is operating in the public interest is difficult. The special groups, stockholders, employees, customers, government officials and legislators, are relatively easy to tell a story to for they have natural interest in what Jersey is or may be doing. Through these groups the opinions of others are influenced, for good or ill. But what of the general public which has no more interest in Jersey than it has in any other large corporation? How can this vast group know what the company does? How can Jersey hope to tell every American of its programs and actions?

Politicians, who are the people most experienced in dealing with the opinions, moods, prejudices, and diverse interests of a whole nation, know that all cannot be reached with what they have to say. There are a surprising number of Americans who would not today know the name of the Secretary of State, despite the fact that it appears almost daily in newspapers and news magazines, and on television and radio. Never does the entire nation listen to even the President of the United States, no matter how important or august the occasion.

In 1945, President Truman gave his VJ-Day address on radio over all networks. It had the kind of advance notice that no corporation is ever going to have for anything it says or does. Yet despite the nation's concern with the war in Japan and its end, that it involved the lives of husbands and sons and brothers, that it would influence the entire course of the world, only 49,000,000 people listened to the broadcast out of a population of 130,000,000.

The major political parties spend several hundred million dollars during the presidential election campaigns to let the people know their candidate and his views, yet they actually reach only a small percentage of the voters. The 1960 presidential election campaign was a clear example of this. John F. Kennedy, who knew the value of public relations techniques, had an amazingly effective buildup prior to his winning the Democratic party's nomination for President. He had been across the country making innumerable speeches, had written a book which advanced his name and had had others written about him, had been on all kinds of national television and radio programs, and after the convention was the cover subject of all news magazines. His exposure was fantastically wide, yet before the series of debates with Vice-President Richard Nixon, Kennedy suffered severely from the fact that millions of Americans had not the faintest idea of who he was.

The Nixon-Kennedy television debates on all three networks had a vast audience. The first one was watched by 75,000,000 people; the second by 69,900,000; the third by 72,000,000; the fourth by 68,-300,000. Yet there were 180,000,000 people in this country at the time of the debates.

And when President Johnson delivered his State of the Union address in January, 1966, he had 66,600,000 viewers even though it was given in prime time, on all networks simultaneously, and repeated by NBC and CBS for the west coast later in the evening. That is a long way from reaching 196,700,000 people, the population of the country at the time.

There is not the slimmest hope of a corporation reaching even the smallest portion of this kind of audience at one time or, for that matter, even with any kind of public relations story over a long period. For these reasons, the efforts of the wisest public relations directors are spent reaching the opinion formers among the general public. This is what Jersey does. From its first steps after the public relations department was established, Jersey has worked on the principle that opinion is formed in most cases through the community leaders or the opinion leaders in key fields. With that in mind it becomes clear—whether it is in institutional advertising, or use of television for public relations as opposed to sales purposes, or use of films—why Jersey insists on doing a quality job or not doing it at all.

The intellectual, the writer, the syndicated columnist, the news reporter, the magazine editor, the television news editor, the radio and television commentator, the schoolteacher, the legislator, the senior civil servant—these lead and form public opinion; it is to these the public relations programs are directed. It is, in most cases, the favorable or unfavorable opinion of these individuals that affects the reputation of a corporation. In a period of crisis they can attack the corporation or defend it. It is these natural leaders throughout the country who are likely to have good taste and a sense of proportion, to whom a quality television show, a pleasant commercial, a fine film, or a creative education program for aid to colleges, will appeal most. In size this group is small; in influence, great. Without its members' understanding and support, little general opinion can be influenced.

This seeking to reach the opinion-former is clearly shown in Jersey's first full-length film, *Louisiana Story*. Robert Flaherty, the patron saint of documentary film-makers, whose *Nanook of the North*, produced in 1922 under the sponsorship of a fur company, Revillon Frères, attracted world attention to his work, was given the assignment by Jersey's public relations department. The picture was four years in the making. No strings of any kind were attached to the assignment other than the general theme of the search for oil. Before the film was shown, it had cost $325,000. The setting was the bayou country of Louisiana and the story line was built around a family of Acadian descent whose land Humble Oil Company had leased to search for oil. The cast was non-professional, as was the lead, a boy of twelve. One of the most exciting scenes, which in some ways stole the show, was a blowout of a wildcat oil well.

The film had original music by Virgil Thomson based on Cajun folk themes. It was played by the Philadelphia Orchestra under Eugene Ormandy. There was no credit line for Standard Oil Company (New Jersey) but Humble was mentioned in the credits for its cooperation. The film's reception was truly sensational. Press notices gave Jersey high praise for the production of the film that had such artistic merit. The association in the critics' minds of Humble and Jersey was so clear, and their enthusiasm for Flaherty's work so great, that they were happy to credit Jersey as the sponsor.

The launching of *Louisiana Story* was in keeping with the merit of the film. After a series of private previews in Louisiana and New York, it opened at a small art house, the Sutton, in New York in September, 1948. The reviews overseas were as enthusiastic as they were at home, again with nods of appreciation for Jersey for its sponsorship.

It was shown at the Venice Film Festival, the Edinburgh Festival, and the Cork Festival. It is praised by Richard Griffith, curator of films at the Museum of Modern Art, in his *The World of Robert Flaherty*. It was picked by the British Film Academy as the best documentary film of the year and noted by the Venice Film Festival judges for its "lyrical worth." Arthur Knight, in *The Liveliest Art*, a history of the movies (New York: New American Library, 1959), deals with the film in these words:

> When Robert Flaherty's feature length documentary *Louisiana Story* began playing the art-house circuits, it seemed to presage a whole new era. Financed by Standard Oil and produced with unprecedented freedom at a cost of a quarter of a million dollars, it was a model of institutional film making. Its sponsor neither asked nor received credit or mention in the film—simply the good-will that might accrue from its unaffected account of the discovery of oil in a Louisiana bayou and its effect upon a Cajun family. The picture's warm reception and the sponsor's expressed satisfaction added to the general optimism of the documentarians. They felt that the value of their kind of film making, their approach to reality, was at last receiving public recognition and support. They looked forward to the day when such enlightened public relations programs would be the rule and not the exception.

The music of the film, "Louisiana Story Suite," was featured during a European tour of the Philadelphia Orchestra and was made into two widely sold recordings. To cap this, Virgil Thomson was awarded the Pulitzer Prize in 1949 for his music for the film. The choice of Flaherty, the music itself, its performance by the Philadelphia Orchestra, the conducting by Ormandy, and the film as a whole merited all the time, effort and money spent by Jersey. *Louisiana Story* is still being circulated and is considered an important milestone in the history of the documentary film.

Thought leaders are not easy to impress. Slick tricks and gimmicks repel them. It is accordingly often difficult for a corporation to make a contribution appropriate to the times which will draw support from intelligent, thoughtful citizens, fill a need and at the same time build good will for the company. To do all this through the use of television is even more complicated, for television is a medium which seeks out ever-larger numbers of viewers and which, in thus reaching for a lower common denominator, often offends those who enjoy entertainment of high quality.

Jersey aimed at this selective audience and hit bull's-eyes consistently. It all began early in 1960. The "Play of the Week," an ambitious two-hour program of classic and Broadway drama, was being broadcast by WNTA, an independent TV station based in New Jersey and covering metropolitan New York. The plays, presented seven evenings a week in prime time with a change of show each week, had fine critical reviews and established for themselves an exceptionally faithful audience of theatre lovers. But artistic successes though the full-length plays were, and even with such established stars as Helen Hayes and Judith Anderson accepting the minimum payment permitted by Equity, the actors' union, "Play of the Week" was in danger of being dropped because the program was too heavy a financial burden to the station. It had not attracted a regular full-time sponsor and the raucous "hard sell" spots failed to cover production costs.

The announcement that WNTA, now the educational station WNDT, was about to drop the show because of lack of sponsor support brought wild expressions of dismay from television columnists and viewers in New York. Jack Gould, *The New York Times*' television critic, set out on a campaign to keep the show alive and wrote a series of columns about the plight of the one outstanding dramatic show then on the air. The response was quick: voluntary contributions from viewers, adding up to several thousand dollars, and more than 27,000 letters and postcards went to the television station seeking to save the show.

Jersey recognized that here were all the elements necessary for a good public relations approach. The audience was of first rate quality. The need for this kind of entertainment was in demand; to provide it would be performing a public service. At the same time Jersey could, under the best of conditions, reach a highly articulate group of viewers in the nation's communications center whose opinion was important to the company. Jersey undertook the sponsorship of "Play of the Week." The first purchase was for thirteen weeks, later extended to eighteen weeks.

Rathbone, who was president of Jersey at the time, in his announcement of the company's sponsorship of the show, said:

> At Jersey's request, one clause of our contract with WNTA specifies that we will have no voice in the subject matter, scripts, production techniques of each week's play or choice of actors. This is a hands-off policy that we have traditionally followed in our long sponsorship of daily newscasts on the Esso Reporter on radio and television.

In the same announcement Rathbone gave Jersey's rationale for its action:

> From its beginning, The Play of the Week has attracted an audience of mature and thoughtful people in the world's largest metropolitan area. . . . This is an audience which Jersey Standard wishes to reach with institutional messages about its policies and activities. Thus, we feel our sponsorship represents sound business. I consider it a part of enlightened corporate citizenship for American industry to encourage the theatre and the arts as it has encouraged education and science.

The sponsorship of the plays and the "no interference" clause brought laudatory editorials from New York's major newspapers, from magazines, and from commentators across the country, although the "Play of the Week" was being shown only in New York and later was broadcast on a single station in Washington.

The hands-off policy was particularly important at that time, for it came on the heels of the television scandals of 1958 and 1959. Some of these revolved around sponsor interference in television program content, and the insistence of account executives and advertising managers that they control not alone the theme of a play and the actors, but also the lines of each character lest they offend a potential customer.

Jersey did take full responsibility for its commercials. Here it again showed the good sense necessary when dealing with a quality audience that, while accepting the need for commercials, did not want to be hit on the head with "Hurry, hurry to your nearest Esso station." The allowable time for commercials on these two-hour shows was twelve and a half minutes. A maximum of nine and a half was used on any one show. All commercials were simple, documentary in character, in good taste, and pleasant to watch. Jersey's world-ranging affiliates provided the subjects for the commercials, which the show's host narrated with low-key good humor. One of the commercials highlighted a failure by documenting the expense and dry-hole hazards of wildcat drilling in Utah. Another traced the supply line of kerosene from Venezuela to a remote Arctic village in Lapland via boat, truck, aircraft, and reindeer. Anthologies of Esso commercials produced abroad were presented in their original languages without subtitles. Excerpts of *Louisiana Story* were also used. What really had high viewer appeal was the placing of the commercials at the intermissions between the acts of the plays. One intermission was devoted to ad-lib interviews with theatre personalities including Guthrie McClintic, George Axelrod, Otto Preminger, Anita Loos and Blanche Yurka. Their role was to comment on the plays, playwrights and performers.

Because of television's split-second timing, another unusual commercial was used. It was simply an Esso oval equipped with an electric clock's sweep-second hand which marked off a one-minute intermission of soft music with no talk. All these commercials were so different from the usual drive to sell goods on television that they received warm applause from viewers as well as from press critics.

The plays themselves, the most important ingredient of all during the eighteen-week run of 126 telecasts in New York and eighteen in Washington, were: *Tiger at the Gates; Don Juan in Hell; A Very Special Baby; Volpone; The Rope Dancers; The Climate of Eden; The Master Builder; The Grass Harp; Palm Tree in a Rose Garden; The Enchanted; Girls in 509; Mornings at 7; Night of the Auk; A Piece of Blue Sky; Archie & Mehitabel; Grand Tour; Mary Stuart;* and *House of Bernarda Alba.*

The cost to Jersey for the "Play of the Week" was $850,000. What was its return? Neither the station nor Jersey had rating surveys made during the show's run, but trade estimates placed the audience at about ten per cent of the potential. Some 6,500 letters and postcards—entirely unsolicited—came to Jersey from viewers, of which fewer than 100 were critical, and these mostly because the themes of some of the plays were looked on by the viewers as too adult for home entertainment. Some twenty per cent of the writers asked for Esso credit cards. Magazines, newspapers, columnists, and academic observers of the social scene praised the company for its sponsorship. But what most convinced Jersey's directors that the stockholders' money was well spent was the certainty that the sponsorship of performing arts on television was the vehicle it wanted to reach a thoughtful audience of adults interested in the arts, sciences, professions, and government.

In 1961, the company tried another type of quality entertainment, "An Age of Kings," a fifteen-week series of Shakespearean dramas which traced eight-six years of the fifteenth century and the turbulent reigns of seven English monarchs through Shakespeare's dramatizations. Each of the episodes, some of which ran an hour in length and others an hour and fifteen minutes, were broadcast twice a week at prime evening time by a single channel in New York, WNEW-TV, and by WTTG in Washington. It was an unusual series. Performed by a permanent repertory theatre group in London and produced for the British Broadcasting Corporation, it had been broadcast earlier over the BBC network in Britain; this was the first time these eight historical plays were presented in chronological succession by one theatre group. It was the first time a commercial sponsor had ever undertaken a Shakespearean series on television. This cycle of plays, retelling the story of the bloody and glorious years between the deposition of Richard II and the coronation of Henry VII, was the kind of series that commercial sponsors would normally back away from as if it were loaded with new and dreadful poisons that instantly killed television audiences.

Once again, Jersey did not attempt to influence presentation. Once again the commercials were gentle, the kind which would interest the viewer instead of sending him into the kitchen for another snack. Once again the full commercial time, in this case six minutes, was not used. Only three minutes were devoted to commercials, which told brief stories on the use of oil in everyday life, and did not interrupt the plays.

The cost to Jersey was $385,000. The response was overwhelming. More than 50,000 commendatory letters and postcards were received by the company, again with a high percentage asking for credit cards and telling of their switch to, or continued use of, the company's gasoline—although there was no intention of using these broadcasts for sales purposes.

Critics, educators, editorial writers, and scholars of Shakespeare were overwhelming in their praise, not only for the presentations but also for the program guide produced by Jersey for the fifteen broadcasts, which helped students and teachers to follow and better understand the plays. It was the most spectacular response imaginable to a television show of this kind. Students of Shakespeare were more than thankful for the chance of seeing this complete cycle, which had not been presented consecutively since it was performed in one week at Stratford on Avon in 1905.

One of the offshoots of this successful television programming was that the National Educational Television and Radio Center (NET) came to Jersey's affiliate, Humble Oil & Refining Company, with a proposal. The series had been sold to NET by the British Broadcasting Corporation for use in the United States. It would be broadcast over forty-nine affiliated educational television stations. There could be no commercial sponsorship, but would Humble be associated with the presentation through a grant to NET? If so, it would assure the series a broadcast of three years. Humble said yes.

Humble's reasoning was that the corporate name would be identified with good works; it would give it exposure throughout the country; it would enhance the prestige of local educational stations; it would have favorable acceptance by the very people in education a major corporation often wisely seeks. This was especially true at a time when television had been frequently described as "a vast wasteland."

Humble made a grant to NET of $80,000 for the three-year broadcast period, contributing $30,000 the first year, $25,000 the second, and the same amount the third. It promoted the program by paying $150,000 for tune-in advertisements in 112 daily newspapers and institutional advertisements in *Harper's Magazine*, *The Atlantic*, *Editor and Publisher*, *Broadcasting*, and *Saturday Review*. It also paid $20,000 for Humble titles for the beginning and end of the broadcasts. And it provided copies of the program that had been originally prepared by Jersey for the broadcasts on the New York and Washington commercial stations.

The shows run full length with no interruption by credits. Only at the beginning and the end the audio and video pointed out ". . . 'An Age of Kings'—made available in the United States under a grant from Humble Oil & Refining Company." And to add to the educational value of the shows, NET and Humble arranged to have Dr. Frank Baxter, an English professor who was already well-known for his commentaries on Shakespeare, as host and narrator for the specially filmed introductions and closings. By the use of diagrams, charts, and maps he provided animated notes on the historical, geographical, and genealogical backgrounds of the plays.

The results? "An Age of Kings" ran three program years, 1961-62, 1962-63, and 1963-64. Beginning with forty-nine stations, it ran on fifty-four the first season, sixty-seven the second season, and eighty-two the third. On many of the stations it ran more than once each season. It brought commendations from all sorts of viewers—customers, Jersey stockholders, employees, and educators. In total, slightly more than 50,000 letters and cards were received and hundreds of letters to the stations enclosed contributions to educational television. In this highly commercial age it is interesting that more than 10,000 of the letter writers praised Humble because no sales or product message was included in the broadcasts.

For commercial television stations in 1962, Jersey came up with the

"Festival of Performing Arts," a ten-part series that featured well-known performers of stage, the recital hall, and opera. The range was from vocal and instrumental music to literature and comedy. All the programs, produced specially for Jersey, ran a full hour and were shown twice each week in prime time in New York and Washington. Paul Scofield, who was then appearing in *A Man for All Seasons* on Broadway, and his wife Joy Parker opened the series with a program of dramatic sketches and poetry. The others were: Rudolph Serkin and the Budapest String Quartet; Dorothy Stickney in *A Lovely Light*, a dramatization of the poems and letters of Edna St. Vincent Millay; George London in a concert recital of German lieder; Isaac Stern playing Bach and Mozart violin concertos; Margaret Leighton in Dorothy Parker readings; Andrés Segovia in classic guitar solos; Michael Flanders and Donald Swann in *At the Drop of a Hat;* Pablo Casals, with violinist Alexander Schneider and pianist Mieczyslaw Horszowski; Cyril Ritchard and Hermione Baddeley in a musical review.

Again the response was highly favorable, with more than 30,000 people writing to Jersey to say thank you. Again the full commercial time was not used, only four of the six minutes allowable was taken up, this time with institutional messages telling of the activities of Jersey's research affiliate, Esso Research and Engineering Company. The cost for this program was $859,000.

In 1963, Jersey decided to broadcast another "Festival of Performing Arts." Under the pressures of the demand from viewers outside of New York and Washington who wanted to see the kind of programs they had read so much about, seven cities were chosen for the shows: Boston, New Haven, Rochester, Philadelphia, Raleigh, New York, and Washington. Once more it was a ten-week schedule of one-hour shows. Again the performers were tastefully chosen: Yehudi and Hephzibah Menuhin in a program of Bach, Beethoven, and Bartok; Robert Morley in a program of readings; Cesare Siepi singing Mozart, Fauré, Lully, Ravel, and Verdi; Jason Robards, Jr. in F. Scott Fitzgerald's *The Crack-Up;* Robert and Gaby Casadesus in a program of Debussy; Joyce Grenfell, the singer-satirist; Miriam Makeba, the African folk singer; Zero Mostel, fresh from *A Funny Thing Happened on the Way to the Forum;* the Robert Shaw Chorale; five members of the Stratford Shakespearean Festival of Canada doing *The Disease of Love*. Again the response was good: 10,500 letters. Again the commercial time used was four minutes of the allowable six; again the commercials were institutional and in good taste. This series cost Jersey $1,120,000.

For the following year, 1964, there was a switch. Instead of a third festival there was "Esso World Theatre," a series of programs from eight countries reflecting their national heritage in literature and the performing arts. Each one-hour show was produced in the country featured. Internationally known performers and directors, natives of these countries, presented anthologies of drama, music, poetry, and dancing. The countries represented, in addition to the United States, were England, France, India, Nigeria, Japan, Greece, and Sweden. This time eight cities were covered. Again the same type of commercial was shown, and once more only four out of the allowable six minutes of commercial time was used. The budget for this one was $1,140,000. It brought in 5,850 letters of commendation. Jersey affiliates made use of these shows in Canada, the Netherlands, Greece, India, Denmark, Finland, Australia, East Africa, Libya, West Africa, West Germany, the United Kingdom, Ireland, and Japan. Still another use was made by these government agencies: U.S. State Department; Central Intelligence Agency; the Peace Corps; the Department of Health, Education and Welfare; United States Information Agency; the Armed Forces Radio-TV Service; the Embassy of Japan; the Embassy of Greece; and the Nigerian Mission to the United Nations.

For 1965 there was once more a change of approach, still with the idea uppermost that quality cultural programs on television are an effective avenue to those who have an important influence on public thinking. The program was "Esso Repertory Theatre." Thirteen of the top community theatre groups in the United States presented plays from their repertoires of modern and classical drama in one-hour television shows. The telecasts ran for thirteen weeks and these videotaped shows were chosen to provide a balance of comedy and serious drama. Most of these had never been seen on television before and each repertory company was generally accepted as being of high standard, operating full seasons with active professional directors and actors. The narrator, who commented each week on the play, theatre, featured actors, and director was Walter Kerr, then the *New York Herald Tribune*'s drama critic. This time, television stations in these nine different cities were chosen: New York, Washington, Baltimore, Rochester, Richmond, Boston, Philadelphia, Syracuse, and Albany. Again only four of the six allowable minutes were used for commercials, all of which were documentaries of the operations of Jersey companies overseas.

The programs, picked by the resident companies themselves, were: *Irish Triple Bill* (Yeats's *Calvary;* Shaw's *How He Lied to Her Husband;* Beckett's *Act Without Words II*) by Cincinnati's Playhouse in the Park; Norman Corwin's *The Rivalry* by Cleveland's Play House; Sean O'Casey's *Bedtime Story* by Seattle's Repertory Theatre; Harold Pinter's *The Dumb Waiter* by Chicago's Hull House Theatre; Richard Brinsley Sheridan's *St. Patrick's Day* by Boston's The Charles Playhouse; Moliere's *The Forced Marriage* by Princeton's McCarter Theatre; August Strindberg's *Creditors* by Abingdon's (Va.) Barter Theatre; William Saroyan's *The Beautiful People* by the Pittsburgh Playhouse; George Bernard Shaw's *Don Juan in Hell* by The Association of Producing Artists at the Phoenix in New York City; Anton Chekov's *A Wedding* by the Milwaukee Repertory Theatre; Luigi Pirandello's *Chee Chee* and *The Man With the Flower in his Mouth* by The Theatre Group of the University of California Extension, Los Angeles; Euripides' *Trojan Women* by the Alley Theatre, Houston, Texas; Shakespeare's *Variations* by the Stratford (Conn.) American Shakespeare Festival.

The cost for this series was $1,625,000. Commending letters and cards to Jersey from viewers totalled 3,800. This experiment in showing the work of community theatres in the United States gave a rather valuable helping hand to the entire cause of the repertory concept.

Jersey did not sponsor television of this kind in 1966 for one main reason: it could not find shows which were up to the quality of those produced six years in succession.

In the six years, Jersey spent—including the cost of "An Age of Kings" for educational television—a total of $6,229,000 for televising quality entertainment. Was this worth the stockholders' money? Jersey thinks the money well spent. Stockholders these days expect their company to fill its obligations to the community as a whole. By aiding higher education through grants for the liberal arts and the sciences, by making all corporate decisions in the public interest, the narrower stockholder interest is served. Broadcasting these shows was good business for Jersey because it provided, under the best of circumstances, something that was needed and wanted by viewers the company was anxious to reach. This objective of good public relations programs, when carried out, always redounds to the benefit of the company, and therefore the stockholders. It is to the benefit of the entire system of private business in our mixed economy as well, for the company knows that to do less than accept its public responsibilities is to put in jeopardy its very permission to exist.

Antagonism between big business and the academic community is of long standing. It grows and wanes as social and economic conditions change. Some of the most trenchant attacks on business have come from writers who teach at the universities. Businessmen have, in turn, often thought of university professors as a special breed put on this earth for one reason: to harass them. The New Deal period highlighted this bitterness between business and the universities, neither thinking the other worth speaking about except in terms of contempt. The lines of communications have never been really good between the two.

Recognizing that the academicians make up a group both articulate and influential, Jersey decided that some sort of dialogue was essential. Out of this decision came the Jersey Roundtable, an annual meeting between leading executives, including directors of the company, and members of college and university faculties in the social sciences, humanities, law, and business. The company made no attempt to mask its purpose: to explain what it was doing to men who have long-term influence on the nation's thinking. In turn those from colleges and universities were interested in why the company acted as it did; what its philosophies were; and the problems of large business enterprises here and overseas.

At the first Roundtable, held in 1947, eight educators attended. The informal meetings went on for two weeks; no record was made of the discussions. At first, the company's representatives were on the defensive, and the guests were afraid of being brainwashed. Gradually, even though there were disagreements, the two sides began to understand each other better. It was a good enough start to make the visitors happy that they had seen and heard the businessmen, and the Jersey managers in turn found many of the professors stimulating, and not quite the devils some of them expected.

Since that first meeting, the Roundtable has been an event of some importance to Jersey. Many of its executives, including directors, look forward to them. They are held for three days, usually early in June, scheduled to avoid conflicts with commencements, summer jobs, and travel. They are held in New York, in an auditorium in an office building close to Jersey's headquarters. The participants are selected by a committee of company people with the advice of previous participants. The guidelines of choice follow these policies: wide geographical representation, variety of disciplines, no two from the same college or university in the same year, high professional standing, and a variety of status—that is, professors, instructors, deans, and presidents.

The number of academic guests runs between fifteen and twenty, with about the same number of executives from the company. This core group meets the evening before the conference and breaks up into smaller dinner groups at different restaurants to get to know each other better. At the conference itself, attended by more of the top executives of the company than are part of the core group, half a day is usually given to orientation. The rest is spent on case studies running from fifteen to twenty minutes presented by executives of the company or its affiliates. Wide-open discussions follow which are carried forward at lunch, coffee breaks, during the evening, at dinner, and later. All questions are frankly and fully answered by management. The talks range far beyond the subject matter of the papers delivered by the company's managers.

The Roundtables, organized by the public relations department, invite no members of the press. No publicity is sought. The guests' transportation to and from New York is paid, as are hotel expenses. There is a per diem of $20 to take care of the meals not taken as a group, and for incidentals. The average annual cost to the company, exclusive of employees' time, runs to about $10,000.

The agendas of these Roundtables are as topical as current business problems. The 1963 theme was "The Role of Private Investment in the Development of Nations." In 1964 the theme was "An International Oil Business in a Changing World" and in 1965 the theme was similar to that of 1963: "U.S. Private Investment as a Factor in World Development." The case study was based largely on Jersey itself. The three-day program included on its first day an orientation to Jersey Standard by an executive vice-president after J. K. Jamieson, the president, set the general stage on the company. The manager of the coordination and planning department dealt with "Making Investment Decisions" in the Jersey company. He was followed by his deputy who gave a paper on "Oil's Role in the Resurgence of Japan and Europe," with an emphasis on the "Postwar Demand for Energy." Later in the day one of the directors of Jersey spoke on "Investing to Meet Consumer Needs in Europe." For the second day papers were given on "Finding the Raw Materials"; "Investing to Meet Consumer Needs in Japan"; "Creole Petroleum Corporation and the Economy of Venezuela"; and "Political Problems Faced by an American International Business." For the third day the subject was: "The Impact of Oil Investments on the U.S. Balance of Payments," followed by a panel discussion. After lunch there was a review of the meeting and a request by management for suggestions for future conferences.

From 1947 through 1965, about 150 universities and colleges were represented at the Roundtables. They were as varied as the originators had hoped, and included faculty members from Harvard, Chicago, the University of Michigan, Columbia, Northwestern, Dartmouth, New York University, the University of Texas, Yale, Duke, Stanford, MIT, the University of Pennsylvania, the University of California at Berkeley, Princeton, Michigan State, The New School for Social Research, Brown, Cornell, Ohio State, Swarthmore, Fordham, Fisk, Brandeis, Williams, Tufts, Smith, Radcliffe, Oberlin, Georgetown, Brooklyn, Haverford, Johns Hopkins, Bowdoin, Skidmore, and three theological seminaries.

The disciplines at the Roundtables were economics, sociology, political science, business finance and management, history, science, English, law, education, theology, philosophy, and psychology. Almost every state was represented as well as three Latin American countries. Most of those from the academic world who attended have felt the meetings worthwhile. Criticisms are asked for by Jersey and they deal mostly with details helpful in improving succeeding Roundtables and in choosing themes for future discussion. The present pattern has developed more from the suggestions of the educators than it has from the company although new approaches are continuously sought to increase direct discussions between these two important groups, and so help each to get a clearer concept of the ideas and actions of the other. That there has been no criticism from those attending the Roundtables on this objective is perhaps the clearest proof of their value. There have been a few professors who have declined invitations because they felt it would be a "waste of time" or because they thought they would be "exploited." There have even been those who refused to go to the Roundtables because they would receive no "consulting fees." But the majority of the professors have been satisfied with the Roundtables and have said so.

In the end, the major public problems of Jersey—and other large commercial enterprises for that matter—are political, and the politicians who make the decisions affecting company operations depend on public opinion. This has always been generally true in the United States and other countries where the voter has a freedom of choice of candidates for office; it is almost as true in newly developing countries where the democratic processes are primitive or half-learned. For Jersey, operating as it does in more than a hundred countries, the problems of government relations are of almost a hundred different varieties. From Jersey's first incorporation its managers have had to deal with governments—but the complications were few; governments were largely glad to stand aside and let business have its way. But with the growth of the areas in which governments concerned themselves and the consequent intervention in business operations, management began to face new areas of difficulty that have often been frustrating.

Abroad, Jersey has to contend at times with governments whose views of private business are overshadowed by a militant nationalism that is basically opposed to foreign, and particularly U.S., business, or with a philosophy of government that would sooner leave resources unexplored than see them developed by private capital. Other nations favor private investment, but only by their own nationals who have not yet been able to accumulate the capital necessary for large-scale enterprise. Nearly all of the developing nations are short of capital, so it is simply not possible for the local private sector to expand the economy as rapidly as would be possible with the help of foreign private capital. Yet these nations seek the higher standard of living their people demand without the understanding that it will be postponed indefinitely unless private capital is imported, or attracted.

The result is that chief executives of Jersey have had to spend more of their time on political problems and government relations than ever before. Necessarily, Haider's work is more onerous in this field than that of any of his predecessors' for he has to deal with more governments than Jersey has ever been involved with before. This is true of the United States as well for, since the days of the New Deal, governments—national, state and local—have become more deeply committed to meeting the growing needs of their voters through legislation, all of which affects the operations of private enterprises.

The clamorous hostility between business and government, so intense from President Franklin D. Roosevelt through President Truman, and modified under Eisenhower and Kennedy, is beginning to soften. For almost thirty years, the government voice in favor of industry was rare. And even rarer was the leader in industry favorable to government. He often spoke as if the government in Washington were some alien thing out to destroy the economic system. But this is changing as large business has learned that there is no going back; that there will not be less, but rather more government involvement with, and regulation of, business. Wiser business leaders realize this and are beginning to understand that Presidents are not simply perverse creatures out to give corporate heads a hard time, but are acting in response to their people who are happy to retire anyone to the sidelines, no matter how eminent, if he does not carry out their will. The war between government and business is ending, and Jersey is one of the large U.S. enterprises which recognized advantages in this long before most others. Its managers realize that politicians have their problems too and that they can no more stop the wave of public demand for greater and still greater services than Canute could halt the incoming tide. It then becomes a matter of adjustment, of making certain that the private sector is not choked to death, that it be allowed enough breathing space to carry on profitably. And this demands an acceptance that the United States has an economy in which the public and the private sectors both function.

The adjustment of large business to the facts of economic and political life—its clearer understanding that its goal must be to act in keeping with public policy always, even though it means a profit motive cushioned by other factors in decision making—has made the climate for business much better. The proof of this is that for the first time in decades, the 1964 presidential election was fought without any attacks on business or private profit by either of the parties. In addition, the national platforms, for the first time since 1932, were free of planks belaboring business.

Under President Johnson, the pugnacious union leader, the bitter big-company official and the anti-business politician have all been receding. In place of antagonism at the White House, the welcome mat has been put on the threshold by the President. Thoughtful company managers, including Jersey's, have not hesitated to see its meaning, even though working with governments is no bed of roses, as Jersey knows. Jersey knows that it has no other choice. Its management understands, as Rathbone said in June, 1961, that a real effort is needed for business and government to understand the problems of the other, and that

> business and government must make the effort, and then, patiently, firmly and thoughtfully work out joint solutions. This cooperative approach to solving our nation's problems is, however, no one-way street. Government must cooperate as much as business. Distrust and suspicion, petty political harassment, unwarranted attacks, and the belief that bigness is badness, can have no place in our government's share of the cooperative approach. . . . In many areas of public policy, business and government must be and are both involved.

Jersey, like any other big company, has always had some kind of relations with the government, even as it had relations with the public. Relations are ever-present, even though little may be done about them. It was not until early in 1959 that the company established a government relations department in its present form. Before this, there had been a government relations counselor who shared with one of Jersey's affiliates the services of a Washington representative. His responsibilities were much narrower than those of the present government relations department.

The government relations department is headed by a manager, Luke W. Finlay, a 1928 graduate of West Point and a magna cum laude graduate of Yale Law School in 1933. After service with the Wall Street law firm of Davis, Polk, Wardwell, Gardiner and Reed, he joined Jersey in 1938 as an attorney and rose to his present job in 1963. He served in the U.S. Army during World War II, had special assignments with the Defense Department after the war including fifteen months in 1952-53 as a Deputy for Defense Affairs to the U.S. Special Representative in Europe, with a base in Paris and the rank of minister. Finlay reports to Collado, with another executive vice-president, Howard W. Page, as the alternate contact director. Haider himself is the executive committee contact.

Fundamentally, the government relations department's job is to help the board of directors establish and keep proper governmental relationships; to coordinate contacts made with the federal government; to keep in touch with what the affiliate companies are doing; and to make sure that there is both consistency and continuity in approach. It tries to avoid duplication as well as conflicting statements, particularly in over-all policy. It follows legislative developments that may affect Jersey and is responsible for direct contact with Congress. It also coordinates the contacts in the United States with the government representatives of countries in which Jersey affiliates operate.

It keeps in touch with what is going on at the United Nations and other supranational agencies such as the European Common Market, the Organization for Economic Cooperation and Development, and others that have a bearing on Jersey. It keeps a steady stream of information on these organizations going to key people in the company on any issues that may have an impact on corporate policies. While each affiliate looks after its own local government relations, the holding company's government relations department, together with the corresponding group in the regional organizations, provides advice and help.

Of the six government relations department staff members, aside from clerical and secretarial help, four are in New York and two in Washington. New York group members specialize in particular areas as well as working in the general field. For instance, the senior government relations counselor, who has had long experience in Latin America, takes on the government relations aspect of Latin American affairs as part of his responsibility. In the same way, one of the two government relations counselors in the New York office spends a good deal of his time on United Nations affairs that may be of company interest, while the other spends much of his time working on those activities of the European supranational organizations that concern Jersey. He also has a hand in the formation of company policy on the issues in his field.

The head of the Washington office, while a member of the government relations department, is general Washington representative for Jersey. His most important duty and that of his assistant, the associate Washington representative, is to represent Jersey on Capitol Hill. They keep the company in touch with legislative developments, express its views to Congress or help the New York executives do so. They keep extensive contacts with offices and bureaus of the executive department that concern the company, alert the company to new developments in this area, and often represent the company before executive departments or go along with executives from New York who do so. The head of the Washington office himself handles all queries about the company and the industry from congressmen and the executive branch, or passes them on to New York for answering. He also works closely with Newmyer Associates, which keeps the government relations and other departments current on all developments of company interest whether they be in Congress, the executive department, or independent agencies. He also answers queries from New York. The Newmyer firm follows and reports on legislative and executive hearings and administration trends, and helps with statements and testimony. This is in addition to what Newmyer does for the public relations department, which is serviced with special information. Newmyer's work, and that of the Washington office head, are not in conflict. Instead they are complementary. Newmyer never speaks or lobbies for Jersey. The firm only looks, listens, and advises. In turn, of course, the staff of the company's Washington office and the Newmyer firm are continuously told what is going on at Jersey's New York headquarters. A member of the public relations department works closely with the head of the government relations Washington office. His primary function is to provide a channel of information between the company and the Washington press corps, but he also works closely with government relations.

Jersey does not use outside lobbyists. All lobbying is done by the Washington representative or his associate, both of whom are registered. In this way they are able to represent Jersey, actively and openly, on Capitol Hill without having to be worried whether or not something they are doing may or may not demand registering under the Federal Lobbying Act. The decision to have a company man registered as a lobbyist dates back to the department's establishment in 1959. Sometimes lobbying on some subject in which Jersey is interested is done by one of the many trade associations to which the company belongs; on other occasions a large number of firms, including Jersey, may join in a common effort. Then a lawyer or law firm, who may or may not lobby, is retained to advise on a legislative matter. But Jersey itself never—and this is fundamental—uses any outside lobbyists when it presents its case.

Naturally when the work of the government relations department and the public relations department are in special cases interwoven, they collaborate fully. Whichever has the primary interest in a particular case leads, for they are completely separate departments. To make certain there is maximum coordination, the two departments meet regularly every week so that they are fully informed of what each is doing. Both departments are consulted when testimony is being prepared for Washington hearings and appearances by top Jersey executives. The division of labor is often done in this way: aid in research by the government relations department, aid in drafting by public relations.

In the democratization of the ownership of Jersey since its founding in 1882 with twelve stockholders, most of whom were owner-managers, a whole new area began to open—that of the development of better relations with the investors. It was slow in coming to the company, tradition-bound as it has always been. At the time of the dissolution of the old Standard Oil Company in 1911 there were 6,078 stockholders and by the time of U.S. entry into World War I there were only 7,850, certainly a slow growth. But by the end of 1949 there were some 200,000 owners of Jersey's stock, and they have steadily increased as the holdings of the Rockefellers and other founders of the company gradually decreased through sale, distribution by inheritance, and gifts to institutions and philanthropies. Ninety-nine per cent of all stockholders live in the United States; the other one per cent live in more than ninety countries abroad.

As in other fields, the growth of stockholder relations at Jersey was a combination of events and an individual. As the company—after the explosion following the Truman Senate committee hearings in 1942 —turned to improve its relations with the general public, more stress was given to its relations with investors. One of the key individuals in this course, besides Haslam, was Adrian C. Minton, the secretary of the company from 1933 until his retirement in 1955. A thoughtful man, a 1916 graduate of Rutgers College, he was a member of the first Jersey training class, and worked in marketing in the United States, Germany, Poland, Switzerland, and France.

It was not until 1944 that he was given the job, in addition to being secretary of the company, of directing stockholder relations, and here he made an extraordinary contribution. He began by making a thorough study of the problems he was bound to face, and prepared an analysis with recommendations for action. The board of directors

largely accepted his recommendations and on them the present shareholder relations activities are principally based. Minton's views were
that a corporation should do more than comply with the statutory requirements in its relationships with stockholders, even though it is
easier to do only what the law demands and leave it at that. And while
it is true, Minton used to argue, that a stockholder may be a customer,
employee, government representative, and supplier, as well as a pro-
vider of capital funds, he could also be a friend whose sympathetic
understanding of management's problems were highly desirable. For
these reasons, Minton felt the stockholder ought to be sought out to
build up "an atmosphere of mutual confidence and good will between
stockholders and corporate managements." For managers who thought
the small stockholder a nuisance, Minton had advice, which he expressed publicly before a symposium on public relations held by Massachusetts Institute of Technology's department of business and engineering administration in 1949. It was that "management needs to keep in
mind that 999 out of 1,000 stockholders who seek information or
raise questions are exhibiting a completely proper curiosity. Such
inquirers do not go to all the trouble to make a nuisance of themselves;
they are expressing their sincere viewpoints and welcome clarification."

That advice is exceptionally relevant today because of the distaste
of many corporate heads for the antics of some stockholders at annual
meetings. To sharply curtail these meetings might make it easier for
chief executives to avoid those who make mischief for mischief's sake,
but it would be a long step backward, for Minton's "999 out of 1,000"
are serious investors to whom what management does is of infinite importance.

Minton also said, on the same occasion, that

> stockholders need to keep in mind that modern business enterprise
> moves within a complicated structure of government relations,
> employee relations, customer relations, stockholder relations and
> social and commercial customs. It is a heavy task for management
> to conduct an enterprise successfully within that framework and
> at the same time appropriately interpret the affairs of a company
> to *all* the stockholders so that *all* the stockholders may obtain an
> understanding of those aspects of the business which interest
> them most.

Minton never felt there were any great secrets in the development
of sound relations between management and stockholders. Instead
he felt they were rather simple. They needed first the frank and fair
recognition of the rights and obligations of both parties, and the

broad observation of them by the criteria by which all persons of intelligence and good will instinctively govern their attitudes toward one another. In keeping with his philosophy, Minton was also responsible for the holding of periodic meetings with small groups of large stockholders which were started in 1945.

Today, the shareholder relations division, which is part of the secretary's office and has been a separate unit since 1952, is run by a manager, Matthew F. Kane, who is also an assistant corporate secretary. With the company since 1946, Kane is a Fordham graduate who has handled a variety of jobs in the secretary's office and with an affiliate in Europe. He is responsible for the programs and for communication with stockholders and the investment community. To do his job he has a staff of nineteen people, ten of whom are professionals. Some of the professionals have at least ten years' experience with the company and have worked in technical, sales, financial and accounting fields with other departments and affiliates of Jersey. Kane has two assistant managers, each one handling one specialized aspect of stockholder relations: institutional investors and financial analysts, individual investors, and special projects.

A mark of the importance Jersey's management puts on this stockholder relations field is that the contact directors on the board of directors of Jersey are Haider and Jamieson. In addition, the directors get regular reports giving all significant information of the stockholder picture, including a resume of all topics of stockholder worry that come to light in the mail and in personal calls. Special reports are also made to keep the board abreast of new programs of activities and what stockholders think about the annual meetings. Long-range analyses of the composition of Jersey's stockholders are also sent. This division has, since 1958, acted as the contact point with institutional investors as well.

The shareholder relations division, working intimately with the public relations department, sends stockholders *The Lamp* and the *Jersey Shareholders' Quarterly*, a pamphlet which is enclosed four times a year with dividend checks. This gives interim financial and operating data, and carries short articles about new products and current doings of Jersey and its affiliates. The stockholders also get, along with the annual report, a proxy statement asking for support by their proxies for the annual meeting with sketches of the nominees for directors. Instead of being a dry legal document, this is, with the help of the public relations department's graphics specialists, made attractive and easy to read. A printed summary of the annual meeting is sent to stockholders if they ask for it. To keep all the publications readable for stockholders, surveys are continuously made of both format and material. The emphasis in all the publications is to let the stockholder know that there is an open door policy on information he might want.

When it comes to the special groups of institutional investors and financial analysts, every query is answered in all possible detail. And while there is no information provided for these two groups that is not available for all stockholders, financial analysts obtain company data in more detail and far beyond the needs—and desires for that matter—of most individuals. There are also periodic informal luncheon meetings held in various cities where there are heavy concentrations of institutional holdings. These are kept small, with a maximum of thirty guests and a small group of company executives, including Haider or Jamieson and several other directors. In this way, a rapport is developed between Jersey's top management and the senior executives of institutions that hold large blocks of Jersey stock. Over the past twenty years, contact has been kept by this technique with investors in some ten different cities. When it comes to speaking before security analyst groups, only members of top management participate. This, of course, limits the number of people who are available for speaking dates, but makes each of the meetings of high importance to these analysts and assures exceptional attendance.

Jersey now places a great deal of stress on the annual meeting of stockholders. This too has been a slow growth. In the 1943 stockholders' report of the proceedings of the annual meeting—which was then a stenographic report—R. W. Gallagher, the president of the company, proudly proclaimed in this, the third year of this report, that even though a "heavy rainfall throughout the forenoon restricted attendance somewhat" there were 225 people in the Grange Hall in Flemington, New Jersey, when he called the meeting to order at 2:00 P.M. on June 1, 1943. Free transportation by train was provided for stockholders in or near New York. In the stenographic report of the annual stockholders meeting held on June 6, 1944, also at Flemington, Gallagher again was proud to point out that some 400 stockholders were present. These reports show that a great deal of time was taken up, at both these meetings, with resolutions and arguments which followed the Truman committee hearings on Jersey's agreements with I. G. Farben as well as stockholders' demands that no such agreement be made in the future.

By 1949, attendance at annual meetings had grown to 1,235. In 1950 the figure was up to 1,600 and by 1957 had risen to 3,600; from 1958 to 1960 it ranged from 4,000 to 4,500. It was in 1960 that the Jersey stockholders accepted a management recommendation that the certificate of incorporation be amended to permit the holding of these meetings anywhere in the U.S. because the "rapid growth in the number of Jersey shareholders has been accompanied by an equally significant change in the geographical pattern of ownership, paralleling the national population shifts."

So the annual meeting went on the road. The 1961 meeting opened in Boston with an attendance of 3,800. In 1962 it was held in Chicago with 2,200; in 1963 in Houston with 2,800; in 1964 in Lawrence-ville (N.J.) with 4,600; in 1965 in San Francisco with 1,800; in 1966 in Cleveland with 1,150; and in 1967 in Houston with 1,570. It was a hit all the way.

Going to stockholders in different parts of the country has been another effective means of reaching those most interested. At the same time the local press is given a chance to cover these annual meetings itself, instead of using the wire service stories. These annual meetings belong to the stockholders. The better the job management does, the more information it provides, the more closely it listens to those who spend time seriously thinking of the actions of the company since the last meeting, the more valuable does this become to management itself as well as to investors. Often, management will get from these meetings the first, faint notice that certain changes might be in order, even if the stockholders' timing may be a little off or their requests premature.

Time was when an American corporation abroad could do its specific job, remain aloof from the host country, make a fair profit, and all would be well. It is far different today, for the American corporation overseas is more than a privately owned company tending to its own knitting. Both the corporation and its personnel must now not only show a concern for the people and institutions of the host country, but must also make a contribution to the country's general welfare. The better-managed U.S. corporations know this. They run their enterprises with a constant consideration of local interests. This means more than employing indigenous personnel. It means more than scrupulous obedience to all laws and customs of the host country. The U.S. corporation, besides making a profit, must convince the overseas country that it is interested in the advancement, and attuned to the aspirations, of the local nationals.

In one crucial respect, the responsibility of American corporate management is greater overseas than at home. Abroad, a corporation represents the United States as well as its own stockholders. The reputation of the United States depends heavily on the manner in which U.S. businesses are run and the extent to which they show an awareness of the desires and needs of the countries in which they operate. In many ways, the attitude toward the United States is more influenced by the practice of the U.S. company abroad than by the U.S. embassy, for the immediate impact on those who run the affairs of the host country is greater when a company does important business there. In these overseas countries, the U.S. presence is even more immediately felt when an industry employs large numbers of local workers. The United States is judged by the conduct of the U.S. corporation, for it is here that the local people see this nation first hand.

Jersey has had almost a century of experience working in foreign lands. Long before the establishment in 1888 of its first foreign affiliate, the Anglo-American Oil Company, Ltd., it had marketed oil abroad. The Jersey holding company and the predecessor companies had learned, often through harsh and unhappy means, that constructive actions to help the host countries in which they explore for or extract oil helps themselves as well as the countries in which they operate. The activities of the affiliates abroad today go far beyond any obligations imposed on them by the local laws. Jersey acts on the principle that to gain a better profit position it must seek a higher standard of living for the peoples in the countries where its affiliates are located.

With more than two thirds of its business done beyond the borders of the United States, Jersey not only appreciates that its own long-term interests and those of the host countries in which it has affiliates coincide, but it acts on that understanding. While believing that it has a heavy stake in the outcome of the ideological conflicts which now beset the world, Jersey feels that the role it plays in this field is of necessity limited. To Jersey, the U.S. corporation is not an arm of government, nor does it believe that it is the function of business to serve as a medium of propaganda.

Jersey's policy abroad is that it can best serve the interests of the United States, as well as its own, by being a responsible citizen of the country in which it does business. It is convinced, and practices its theories, that, like any other segment of society, it exists only with the sanction of the community as a whole. Therefore, constant care is taken to be sure that the affiliates abroad are in harmony with the national interests of the overseas countries; that they not only comply with local laws and regulations and adjust to local mores, but scrupulously seek to avoid any involvement in political activity of any kind.

This political neutrality—for that is what it is—is essential, for any other course would involve Jersey's affiliates in grave peril. In some cases, were the company to lose in any political situation, it would bring restrictions on its operations that might cripple its ability to function. In extreme cases, it could result in confiscation of the holdings of the affiliates. However, this hands-off policy on politics does not mean that the affiliates neglect their government relations activities. Jersey continually seeks to keep these relations friendly, based on the common interest of the company and the government.

In many countries, particularly in the developing ones where the need is greatest, the overseas affiliates are committed to improving living conditions. This is true in health, education, the arts, highways, and welfare. They help build strong national economies, encourage stability, and develop natural resources other than oil itself. Experience has shown that this works in the interests of Jersey as well as the host countries. This fundamental approach, Jersey has found time and again, is the only one that makes sense. However, the extent to which this is carried out varies with the countries in which Jersey has interests. It varies as well with the extent to which the host country desires Jersey's help.

In the developing countries Jersey's activities stem from three broad policies. The first is developing and utilizing local resources of manpower and materials to the fullest practical extent. The second is assisting the host country in as many ways as possible in its economic and social development. The third is to recognize and support the cultural traditions of the country, and the aspirations of its people.

In developing and utilizing local resources, Jersey uses not only raw materials and manufactured goods but the skills of the inhabitants. The affiliates provide training that extends from welding and analytical laboratory work to sales techniques and the operation of refineries. Training centers are run to teach nationals accounting, sales, engineering, and business management. During the past seven years, Jersey has trained more than 2,500 indigenous employees. More advanced training in management is provided at the offices of Jersey in New York, and at university facilities at home and in the United States. Jersey finds that two objectives are served here: the development of more efficient employees who can rise to all levels of management in the company, and the enrichment of the nationals as more effective citizens of their own countries. The importance Jersey places on this training concept can be gauged from this fact: of the 100,000 employees in the overseas affiliates, fewer than two per cent are U.S. citizens.

Jersey's policy in developing local resources can be seen from what happened in Venezuela. There it recognized that the shortage of investment funds for industrial and agricultural development was tending to inhibit maximum growth of the economy. So Creole Petroleum Corporation, Jersey's affiliate, set up in 1961 a subsidiary company, the Creole Investment Corporation, to provide new risk capital for ventures outside the oil industry. This subsidiary company, to insure local involvement and control, is so structured that Creole limits its interests in these projects to less than fifty per cent. Up to the end of 1965, the Creole Investment Corporation had invested more than $8,000,000 in 20 companies. These are largely in manufacturing and agriculture. They have proved themselves by increasing productivity as well as saving foreign exchange for Venezuela. Similar mechanisms have been developed in Colombia.

In Saudi Arabia, the Arabian American Oil Company, or Aramco, which is thirty per cent owned by Jersey, dealt with a local problem of stimulating the economy in this way: Large quantities of fresh foods had to be imported since little was being grown. Aramco worked out a program to encourage Saudi Arabians to go into farming, including the growing of fresh vegetables. Out of these crops Aramco buys about half its needs.

Another example of Aramco's help in solving local problems involved sand migration. Around the Al-Hasa Oasis, sand dunes had drifted so dangerously that at one time it looked as if the oasis would be covered. Aramco brought in specialists to work with local authorities to stem the sand movement. At another oasis, Hofuf, specialists were again hired by Aramco who developed a date-packing plant. The towns of Damman and al-Khobar were both without a decent water supply and adequate sewage disposal. The company lent the local officials several million dollars to enable them to modernize facilities to meet the need. The same happens in the construction of roads by many Jersey affiliates in developing countries. And even though these roads are built mainly for the affiliates' use, they have helped open parts of the country for development that would otherwise have remained closed, perhaps indefinitely.

In the sector of social development Jersey has also shown its concern, education and public health being prime fields of improvement. All the Latin America affiliates of the company have programs of scholarships and direct aid to education. In the past few years, hundreds of students from these countries have been sent to the United States for higher education. The affiliates also made a local university education possible for many men and women who otherwise would not have been able to afford it. In Pakistan, India, Thailand, Vietnam, Kenya, Tanzania and Uganda, scholarship programs have also been established. The Creole Foundation, set up in 1956, has regularly contributed about $1 million every year to aid education in Venezuela at all levels, as well as giving financial assistance to social welfare agencies in their educational works.

Teacher-training has been another field of Creole's involvement. In cooperation with the Venezuelan Ministry of Education, it set up rather large programs of teacher training. It has done this not by financial aid alone, but by having the members of its own staff—who had special skills not available in the country—teach as well. In one case, where Creole found that the school facilities were quite inadequate for the company's local employees it built a new school that provided schooling for the general public as well as its own employees. In primary education, Creole has provided facilities for more than 8,000 children. Several years ago, when Creole found that it no longer needed the land and buildings of a community which it had established in a producing area in eastern Venezuela, it did not abandon it. Instead it gave the land, the buildings and all the other facilities to the government to aid it in founding the University of the East.

In Libya, the Jersey affiliate provided for the first professorship of geology at the University of Libya. Jersey's affiliate in Italy, working with the government, started an agricultural school and a school for mechanics. In Dharhan, Aramco built and paid for Saudi Arabia's first television station. It still supports the station, which is used part of the time for the teaching of Arabic. When it comes to the public health field, Jersey's affiliates have been active. Aramco contributed $500,000 to the Harvard Medical School for a five-year research program on trachoma, the eye disease that, according to the World Health Organization estimates, afflicts some one-sixth of the world's population. In 1960, when the money originally granted for the study ran out, a larger sum was contributed. The result of this research was so encouraging in tests made in various parts of the world that a trachoma prevention campaign using a newly developed vaccine was started by the Saudi Arabian Ministry of Health.

In Venezuela, Creole helped the government in its attack on malaria. Through an extensive spraying program, malaria in many large sections of the country was almost entirely wiped out. To look after the needs of its own employees, Creole built and equipped hospitals. These hospitals also served the surrounding communities and were then turned over to other groups to run. In Colombia, Jersey's affiliate contributed a hospital to the city of Cartagena where it has a refinery. In Argentina, the company's affiliate founded one of the best nursing schools in the country, and today Aramco supports a school for nurses in Saudi Arabia.

In keeping with its policy of supporting the cultural activities of the host countries, Jersey's affiliates have long been active. This needs the kind of imagination and understanding that business is often incapable of supplying. Jersey tries to pick people who really make an effort to learn the local language, take part in community activities, and who do not segregate themselves in American ghettos. Jersey searches for managers who will be accepted by the local leaders and these, so carefully picked, have been able to establish a rapport with the cultural life of the countries and their artists, writers, and historians.

In line with this thrust, Jersey's Colombia affiliate sponsored an exhibition of 3,500 years of Colombian art. The first attempt to show this collection outside the country was at the University of Miami. It was so successful that it was exhibited at the Pan American Union building in Washington. Since that time it has been shown in Italy, Sweden, Germany, and Spain. In every case, the exhibition was sponsored by Jersey affiliates in the countries concerned.

Attempts of the same kind, though far less impressive, have been made by affiliates in Africa, the Far East, the Caribbean area, and parts of South America. The affiliate in Peru sponsored a television program on Peruvian historical traditions using works of art from the museum at Lima. The Indian affiliate published a small book commemorating the 100th anniversary of the birth of the poet and philosopher Rabindranath Tagore. The Colombian affiliate holds an annual prize contest for the best novel by a Colombian writer. The affiliate in Argentina sponsors musical performances by local artists. In both the Argentine and Chile, Jersey's affiliates have sponsored concerts and art exhibitions for musicians and artists to tour the United States. Film programs by affiliates are usual. These films, not necessarily on the oil industry, but often on the natural beauties of host countries, are made and shown. Others are made which show the cultural backgrounds of these lands. Local writers, painters, and designers are all used extensively in the writing and production of affiliates' publications. Every attempt is made to further the cultural life of the people in these countries.

This commitment to the nations in which Jersey is involved is easy to set as a policy. It is often difficult to carry out. A concerted effort by the affiliates is needed to carry it forward. Those on the spot are never allowed to forget that, while profit-making is the prime purpose of Jersey's overseas operations, it is not possible unless the local nationals believe that what Jersey is doing is good for the host country. Statesmanship of rare quality is often needed. If this is lacking, if the concept of good corporate citizenship and of public responsibility is not carried out, the whole profit-making structure is endangered. This, of course, is also true in the United States. But it is always more clearly evident abroad, where every action and gesture is carefully scrutinized by the local peoples, while watching over their shoulders are those opposed to any kind of foreign business, especially U.S. business.

In December, 1955, the National Planning Association published, as part of its series on United States business performance abroad, its case study of the Creole Petroleum Corporation in Venezuela. It was financed largely by funds granted by the Carnegie Corporation of New York and the John Hay Whitney Foundation. It was made by Wayne C. Taylor and John Lindeman with the collaboration of Victor Lopez R. of the Department of Sociology and Anthropology of the University of Caracas. It is the most complete study of how Jersey's affiliate in Venezuela accepts its responsibilities to the host nation.

In the chapter on "Creole as a Citizen," the authors have this to say:

> It is not difficult for Creole to identify its own interests with the interests of the Venezuelan economy, because these interests are in fact identical over a large range of subjects. Creole's fortunes rise and fall with the world market for Venezuelan oil. So, of course, do the fortunes of Venezuela. Similarly, Creole's long term prospects depend on proper development of Venezuelan oil resources so as to maximize their yield over a number of years. So do Venezuela's. Consequently, in some matters, such as the company's constant campaign to keep foreign trade channels open and foreign markets receptive to Venezuelan oil, it is not surprising that Creole and the Venezuelan government speak with what sometimes sounds like one voice.
>
> In fact, in establishing its over-all policies, Creole acts as though it intends to stay in Venezuela as a good citizen for the long pull, and not just for the life of its present concessions. This explains many of the company's actions and policies. If the company thought of itself as a temporary visitor, many things that are now given a lot of attention could be ignored, because they are of concern to Creole only in their long-range aspects. Among these things are the development of a skilled and literate

labor force not only for the oil industry, but throughout Venezuela; the diversification of the Venezuelan economy; and the gradual assumption by local communities of social responsibilities that now fall to the company.

However, in one important area Creole does not act like a citizen at all. This is in the field of Venezuelan politics, which Creole and its officials avoid completely. If anyone high in the Creole organization has an opinion about politics, he does not express it publicly. Political neutrality has long been recognized as the only sensible attitude for a United States company to have when it operates abroad, and especially in Latin America. On this point Creole bends over backwards to be sensible. Although it identifies its interests with those of Venezuela, it does not claim the right to advise Venezuelans about their form of government or about the men who are to run it. With this policy, Creole has managed to operate successfully under governments ranging from the personal and nonideological dictatorship of Gomez to the professedly leftist regime of Accion Democratica. For Creole, Venezuelan politics is like Venezuela's climate, terrain, and geography—something which the company must take as it finds it if it wants to produce oil successfully.

Of course the policy of political neutrality does not mean that Creole is indifferent to its relations with the Venezuelan government. On the contrary, it is a policy dictated by the company's desire to keep those relations as good as they are now. Today, both Creole and the government realize that the area of their common interests is very great indeed, and that their common interests are best pursued if they work together closely and constantly on matters that affect them both.

It is not in Venezuela alone that Jersey tries to adjust itself to the social environment. Its purpose is to act in this way in every country abroad where there is an affiliate. Nor does Jersey do this because its heart is tender and its eye moist. It does it simply because it must. It must because this is one of the means of assuring that it is accepted by the indigenous peoples and their leaders without whose good will the concessions to operate become mere pieces of paper.

Jersey's onus is exceptionally heavy. Its very size, and that of many of its affiliates, prevents it from living in obscurity. It can never hide from the general public, from politicians, from the intellectuals. It affects so many millions of individuals and so many governments around the world that what it does, or does not do, is of vast importance. It also has another obligation because of its leadership in the oil industry: whatever is thought of the oil business depends in large measure on what is thought of Jersey.

It has an obligation, too, to the very economic system in which it is such an important factor. Smaller companies may be able to avoid their duties to the public. They may even act in a manner that many may think is not in the public interest and not cause a wide reaction. Some oil companies may not do a single thing to influence public attitudes toward the acceptance of the U.S. economic system, and get away with their failures. But Jersey, by its performance and by continuous and effective communication of what it is doing, has to carry the heavy load of helping assure the system's survival in a world of bitterly competing ideologies. Much of the present satisfaction with the oil industry by large segments of the nation is due to the actions of Jersey. Its wiser managers are fully aware of this.

Being always alert to the wishes and needs of the general public cannot assure that a single failure will not bring on Jersey's head the kind of obloquy that can be frightening. But a misstep is forgiven by the public if the long record is good. This means that a company the size of Jersey can afford only to continue to act so that any reasonable person knows it is filling all its obligations to the nation. Jersey's reservoir of good will is reasonably full. To keep it so demands more than a good public relations department. It demands the kind of senior management that fully believes that its right to exist was given it by the public, the very same public that can also take it away.

THEY WORK AT IT

THE LEAN, HARD-JAWED, FORTY-ONE-YEAR-OLD CHAIRMAN OF THE
Senate's Special Committee Investigating the Munitions Industry was
fully prepared. By that time, late afternoon on September 12, 1934,
the big, high-ceilinged, white marble caucus room in the old Senate
Office Building was familiar fighting ground to Senator Gerald P.
Nye. In his eight years as the senator from North Dakota the wiry
Republican progressive-isolationist had already directed two Senate
investigations and this looked like his biggest. Electric Boat Company of Groton, Connecticut, submarine makers; Driggs Ordnance
and Engineering Company, manufacturers of anti-aircraft guns;
Curtiss-Wright Export Corporation, airplane makers—all had been
questioned. The next in line was E. I. du Pont de Nemours & Company, the largest and best-known munitions firm of the lot.

Piled two feet high on the long table in the hearing room were the
documents to be used in the investigation. During the entire previous
summer the committee's secretary and chief investigator, Stephen
Raushenbush, who had investigated and written on the "power trust,"
had directed a young and energetic staff—including Alger Hiss on a
short leave from the Agricultural Adjustment Administration—in the
search for evidence. All was in readiness, the material set out for the
senators to begin their questions.

Senator Nye was in full control. He had confidence in his staff,
and in the committee's advisory council, which consisted of Manley
O. Hudson of Harvard Law School, Harold G. Moulton of the Brook-

ings Institution, and John T. Flynn, the *New Republic* magazine writer. His fellow committee members, chosen by the Democratic-controlled Senate, were Arthur H. Vandenberg of Michigan and Warren Barbour of New Jersey, Republicans, and Homer T. Bone of Washington, Bennett Champ Clark of Missouri, James P. Pope of Idaho and Walter F. George of Georgia, Democrats. All had taken turns questioning the witnesses, as had Raushenbush and Hiss. And now, four members of the du Pont family—three brothers and a cousin—had been subpoenaed and were before the committee.

They came with seven lawyers headed by William J. (Wild Bill) Donovan, New York Republican candidate for Governor in 1932, and a retinue of clerks and secretaries. Distributed to the reporters covering the hearings were a forty-two page booklet and a thirteen page fact sheet about the company and its views on munitions. The spectators stirred as the four witnesses stood to be sworn together. Irénée, fifty-eight years old, had been president of the company from 1919 to 1926 and was now vice-chairman of the board; Pierre, sixty-four, had been president of the company from 1915 to 1919, and was now chairman of the board; Lammot, fifty-four years old, had been president since 1926, and cousin Felix, who was fifty-five years old, was general manager of the smokeless powder department of the company.

Nye had intended to question each of the du Ponts separately but a switch was made in the last moments before the swearing of the witnesses. Now the four were to be interrogated together so that all would be asked the same questions at the same time, on the theory that if one could not, another would probably be able to answer. For two solid hours the senators asked questions. They learned that the company's first war contracts negotiated in 1914 totalled $19,000,-000. In 1915 the value of the foreign contracts was $318,885,000; in 1916, $182,000,000; in 1917, $315,700,000; and in 1918, the final year of the war, the total was $410,000,000. When the war started, Pierre du Pont told the Senate committee, the company had very limited facilities and the huge increases in plant were charged against the nations for whom the munitions were made. This meant at the start the price was about one dollar a pound of explosive while in 1916 the price had been reduced by about half. Business in the war years represented a gain of 1,130 per cent over the years immediately preceding the outbreak in 1914. In all, war orders to the company totalled $1,245,000,000, and the total dividends paid in the years 1915 to 1918, inclusive, amounted to 458 per cent of the par value of the original stock, which was $100.

Questioned about the "enormous profits," the answer was that they were charged against the foreign governments, and not the United States.

"The profits accruing to us in the World War were not derived from the Federal Government or the American people," Pierre du Pont told the committee. The company's profits "climbed from a pre-war level of about $5,000,000 or $6,000,000 a year to an average of nearly $59,000,000 for the four years of the war." But the company also netted a larger annual return during the peace years 1927 to 1931 inclusive than it did during the war years 1915 to 1918 inclusive. Even during the bad depression year of 1933, which was also a year of general peace, the net income was more than six times what it had been in 1913. At the moment (in 1934), the munitions trade amounted to about one-half of one per cent of the company's total annual earnings.

The four du Ponts were, according to *The New York Times*, "confident, without being truculent, easy in their manner, ready to smile on occasion." To *Time* magazine, they were "very suave, very self-possessed but not very well dressed." It had been an in-depth examination on sales of munitions and profits. There was no case, no evidence, that the company had instigated, or tried to instigate, a war in order to sell its products. This was germane, for the argument against those who sold munitions was that they were the cause of wars.

Around the world the morning following the testimony of the four du Ponts, the headlines roared about "profits and blood." The witnesses were called evil men who cared not for human life; fomenters of war; men without conscience; bloodsuckers; peddlers of death. *The New York Times* ran a three-column picture of the du Ponts being sworn in the crowded hearing room with the caption: "Munitions makers called by Senate investigators." And the headline on the Washington-datelined story was "$1,245,000,000 Work To Du-Ponts In War"; below this was the drop headline: "Firm's swollen orders allowed 100% dividend in 1916, arms inquiry shows." The news magazines, the weekly opinion press, the radio commentators, the editorial writers and the columnists drew on their most violent adjectives to aid them in denunciation of the Du Pont Company. To a Congregational minister writing in the *Christian Century*, the four du Ponts looked like "men who could pass the plate at any church service without anyone looking at them twice," and went on to say, "It will do no good to think of these men as fiends who rejoice in dealing in blood and death, for they are not. They are average men who are using the business ethics and techniques of the average business man around the world . . . let us put the blame where it belongs, on the business techniques and ethics which go unchallenged among the leaders of our business life, and our willingness to allow private business to conduct an international trade in armaments."

The Nye investigation came at a moment in history when its purpose and its hearings had an immense impact and roused deep emotion. Americans were in a period of disillusionment. The League of Nations had failed to stop Japanese aggression. Mussolini was growing in power, boasting of the might of his arms, and threatening Ethiopia. The Nazi movement had begun to roll quickly in Germany. The depression had hit hard. The turmoil abroad had its effect at home and suddenly it seemed that there would be no end of foreign war. The best thing for the United States to do was to retreat within its own borders, let the foreigners stew in their own juices; they had caused enough trouble. Peace was the objective and that could only be reached by ending the causes of war, which were a combination of Wall-Street, the warmongers, and the corrupting munitions-makers who stimulated war so that they could make their blood-flecked profits grow greater and greater. Woodrow Wilson had been a simpleton, had brought America to ruin by entering a war whose causes had nothing to do with the Kaiser's Germany or the German U-boat attacks on American shipping. Wars only came because the munitions-makers wanted war, and if the profit were taken out of arms manufacture, the arms traffic would be stopped. And so the world could live in peace evermore.

The combination of forces was varied. The American Legion demanded that the profits be taken out of war by having the government take over the making of munitions from the private arms makers. The women's peace groups demonstrated against the manufacture of weapons of war. The *Nation* and the *New Republic* ran bitter attacks on all munitions manufacturers, accusing them of being the cause of war. Marxists and church leaders joined in the cause. There blossomed a whole literature in which the villain was visible and reason unnecessary. Issues were now simple; complexities were out. There was a "secret international" which fomented war, and in league with its members was big business, which was unconcerned about battle casualties. The Progressive-Populist movement was in full swing.

The Merchants of Death (New York: Dodd, Mead & Co.) published that year (1934), had a vast sale. Subtitled "A Study of the International Armament Industry," it was written by H. C. Engelbrecht, Ph.D., associate editor of *The World Tomorrow*, and F. C. Hanighen, with a foreword by Harry Elmer Barnes. It dealt almost entirely with the arms industry abroad, but touched on the Du Pont Company which it said owned "every daily in Delaware." (There were two.) The book was relatively friendly to the company, saying that "they have never sought prominence in national politics, though members of the family have—almost by accident—been United States senators. Their relationship with the government has always been very close, and that was due just as much to the government as it was to the du Ponts."

Fortune magazine, in March, 1934, ran a sensational article, "Arms and the Men, A Primer on Europe's Armament Makers." As a sort of afterthought, the editors decided to add an American angle to Krupp, Vickers-Armstrong, Schneider-Creusot, and Skoda, and named several American companies, including Du Pont. Then, drawing attention to *The Merchants of Death* for further information, it backed away from its own inclusion of American companies with this sentence: "Despite the size of our armament bill, our arms and munitions export to South and Central America and the Far East, we are essentially small fry in this game."

The article, appearing as it did in *Fortune*, had a startling effect. It seemed to put the support of Henry Luce's empire behind the violent cries of those retreating into isolationism. *Time* magazine, another of the Luce publications, referring to the *Fortune* article, said: "Editors found the peace-hungry public liked it and the headlines grew." Then it went on to say about the U.S. munitions industry: "Not only is it small fry compared to the European arms industries, but the men who run it are typical U.S. businessmen who abhor, in typical U.S. fashion, the idea of fomenting war for profit. The big arms makers of Europe may not be above such skullduggery, but up to last week Senator Nye's committee had produced no shred of evidence to prove that U.S. arms makers had stooped to such practices." *Time*'s assessment of *Fortune*'s fuel to the isolationist, anti-business fire appeared on December 24, 1934.

Academic involvement in the rewriting of the history of World War I was deep, and with it came the campus movement of Veterans of Future Wars, whose members demanded their bonuses and benefits before going to war, when they had a chance to spend them. Those who stood up against the tide were few. The State Department, despite its worry at the state of public opinion, which could tie its hands so seriously in foreign negotiations, announced, in keeping with the public's mood, its cooperation with the Nye committee. President Roosevelt, as James MacGregor Burns points out in *Roosevelt: The Lion and the Fox* (New York: Harcourt, Brace & World, 1956), "not only joined the chorus denouncing the arms trade but allowed Nye access to executive papers that were greatly to aid the Senator's efforts to dramatize the skullduggery of bankers and diplomats. Even more, he tolerated—and to some extent encouraged—the Nye committee in its ambition to use intensifying disgust with arms makers as an anvil on which to beat out a rigid policy of isolationism for the United States."

The entire movement, within which the Nye committee investigation was launched and flourished, had the support of the normally isolationist Midwest; those who were against capitalism; those who were simply for peace; and intellectuals who, in their emotional tantrum, were willing to rewrite American history. Of this revisionism, Dexter Perkins, in *The New Age of Franklin Roosevelt, 1932-45* (University of Chicago Press, 1957) says:

> The policies of the Woodrow Wilson administration were sharply criticized, and the thesis that American entry into the war was the work of wicked Wall Street bankers, aided and abetted by sinister arms barons, gained headway accordingly with American public opinion. The thesis, it is worthwhile to remark, was unsound. It was then, and is now, impossible to prove that these influences determined the course of President Wilson. Indeed, he was deeply reluctant to enter the war, and it is difficult to believe that, had the Germans not renewed the submarine campaign (temporarily suspended) in the winter of 1917, he could have been brought to such action. But in public affairs it is not the accuracy but the force of belief that counts, and there can be little doubt that the tide was running strongly toward revisionism in 1934 and 1935.

As for Nye himself, he had long been anti-business. According to Wayne S. Cole, in *Senator Gerald P. Nye and American Foreign Relations* (Minneapolis: University of Minnesota Press, 1962), "The Nye munitions investigation of 1934-36 was a logical extension in the realm of foreign affairs, of Nye's long crusade against big business, international bankers, and Wall Street. Initially, the munitions investigation was at least as anti-business as it was anti-war." And so strange were the times that the Nye committee itself came into being as a result of the lobbying of an energetic pacifist, Dorothy Detzer, national secretary of the Women's International League for Peace and Freedom. Allied with the National Council for the Prevention of War, the Fellowship of Reconciliation, the National Council of Women, and other like organizations, Miss Detzer's group persuaded many of the senators, including Senator Norris, to support an investigation. And Norris himself chose Nye as the one who should conduct the inquiry, out of which finally came the immobilizing Neutrality Act of 1935. In her book, *Appointment on the Hill* (New York: Henry Holt, 1948), Miss Detzer, described by *The New York Times* as "the most famous woman lobbyist," and who had worked in the relief services in Quaker Missions in Russia and Austria, tells how she chose Raushenbush and persuaded Nye to appoint him chief investigator of his committee, and how Raushenbush in turn picked Hiss for his staff. This unusual woman also was able to persuade the national board of the Women's International League for Peace and Freedom to support the American branch of the League Against War and Fascism. In this book she tells how she, with Roger Baldwin, director of the American Civil Liberties Union; Earl Browder, secretary of the Communist Party; and J. B. Matthews, who became an official of the party and, in a later turnabout, secretary of the Dies committee, signed the "call" for a meeting. She also reports her disillusionment; how, in 1937, three years after the first meeting, her organization withdrew from the League; and Norman Thomas' correct belief that the peace organization could never work with the Communists.

This then was the state of public opinion in which the Du Pont Company found itself. Throughout the world it was stuck with the label, "Merchants of Death." The nation's antipathy to war was in a large sense transferred to Du Pont. As the most important American company involved in the Nye hearings, as the company which in four years of World War I supplied the Allies with 1.5 billion pounds of explosives—including more than forty per cent of the smokeless powder fired by Allied guns—Du Pont was the only name remembered by large segments of the public. And worse, all the evils of all the arms industry throughout the world were attached, in the thinking of millions of Americans, to Du Pont. The problem facing the company was of vast proportions. Military explosives in 1916 accounted for eighty per cent of Du Pont's sales; in 1934 about one per cent of its total sales (and in 1966 it was less than one-tenth of one per cent). It was now a chemical company, which served civilian needs with vast research facilities that had developed innumerable products unrelated to war. Yet to millions the name Du Pont meant only one thing: munitions for human destruction. The company's contribution to Allied victory in World War I was, during the war years, highly valued. The fact that it made a profit was not, between 1914 and 1918, considered sinful, nor was it thought unusual. Yet, by a turn of public opinion, a corporation making profits in war material became an evil beyond compare, a horrendous thing.

Du Pont in 1934 had no public relations department. It did have a publicity bureau which knew little of the meaning of a corporation's relations to the general public or the groups which comprised it. Publicity for products—this the publicity people understood. But it was almost wholly unaware of the need for the adjustment of a corporation to public attitudes. Getting notices for Du Pont's products was something it performed reasonably well. But when it came to understanding public opinion, why it had suddenly turned on the company, and what could be done to point up the fact that Du Pont performed valuable peacetime services, the publicity bureau was beyond its depth. It was innocent of public relations, and Du Pont's management began to look elsewhere for guidance and help in explaining to the nation what the company was, what it did, and the contribution it made to the common good. It wanted the people to know Du Pont. It needed a program which would establish good relations between the company and the people at large, and Du Pont's publicity bureau was unequipped to advise or act in this field.

Before the Nye committee had begun its hearings, Roy S. Durstine of the advertising agency of Batten, Barton, Durstine & Osborn had conceived of a radio program which would tell the story of America's history and growth. In those days radio was at its best, with fine dramatic shows on networks, symphony orchestra broadcasts sponsored by corporations, and intelligent discussions of public issues. Its audience, wide though it was, included leaders of national opinion. Radio was able to provide entertainment and at the same time attract thoughtful people. Many of the country's most creative minds welcomed the opportunity to work in the medium, and this included most of the best writers of the period as well as leading performers. As the project turned over in Durstine's mind he called in members of the agency's creative department to help develop the concept. It was decided that this radio show would be called "Cavalcade of America," that it had to be of top quality, that episodes of American history should be dealt with in half-hour segments, and that it was best on a national network. It was also decided that since this was not an inexpensive program by the standards of radio of those days, it ought to have as its sponsor a large corporation whose history ran alongside the history of the country, and one which could afford such a program. At first Durstine thought it might be excellent for sponsorship of American Telephone and Telegraph. But then, it was thought—because of the Nye hearings, the problems the du Ponts had, the fact that E. I. du Pont de Nemours was founded in 1802—

that an approach might be made to the executive committee of the corporation to test its interest in "Cavalcade of America."

By 1935, Du Pont was ready to tell its story if it could find the proper way to do it. Its problem was reaching people and finding the vehicle that would have the kind of values to attract them. What it needed desperately was a public relations program, and it found a partial answer after Bruce Barton of BBDO responded to the advertising department's request for an educational program to be conducted in addition to product campaigns. Magazines were used first but it was radio that captured the imagination of Du Pont's management people. William A. Hart, Du Pont's advertising director, was a theatre buff; he had a taste for quality entertainment and immediately saw the advantages of "Cavalcade of America." Here was a chance to reach the ears and the minds of those very people to whom Du Pont had to explain itself. Hart supported Durstine's concept and Barton's salesmanship. The executive committee of Du Pont said yes. It turned out to be the exact program Du Pont's needs demanded. That it was under the advertising department was understandable; there was no public relations department.

The total budget for "Cavalcade of America," including a top fee of $5,000 a show for a name actor, was $10,000 a week. This was, of course, exclusive of radio time costs. But the budget was by far secondary to the concept of the show and the taste in its execution. The decision was made long before the show first went on the air at 8 P.M. on October 9, 1935, over WABC and a network of forty-three stations, that it would only be successful and serve its purposes if the best talent were used. Anything less would detract from the show, repel the kind of people it most wanted to attract, and so destroy the whole purpose of the program, for it was in no way intended to sell goods, but rather to serve a public relations purpose.

The commercials on the radio show were always designed to tell something of Du Pont and what it did. The theme of the commercials was: "Better Things For Better Living . . . Through Chemistry." It did not make any attempt, at any time, to answer the charges made by those who attacked the company because of the Nye hearings. In fact, four years of episodes of American history were broadcast before a shot was heard. Its commercials told of company products, the results of its research. None of the commercials was strident in tone or content. All commercials were factual and all ended with the company's theme: Better Things For Better Living . . . Through Chemistry.

The shows were done live from theatres, for the most part. Sometimes they originated in Du Pont's plants. They were taken on the road to various parts of the country. They became part of the weekly radio listening life of thousands of teachers, students, parents. In all, the radio shows ran for eighteen years, during which time seven hundred and eighty-one episodes were presented. Television presentation followed for another four years, and on June 4, 1957, "Cavalcade of America" finally went off the air. In these twenty-two years, during which two hundred and two television network shows were presented in addition to those on radio, sixty-three top broadcasting awards were won. From the George Foster Peabody award to that of the Institute for Education by Radio, from Billboard's Annual Radio Editors Poll to that of the Women's National Radio Committee and the United Parents Associations' Radio Committee, came acclaim for the shows and for the company presenting them. The radio shows went short-wave to Europe, the Middle East, Australia, New Zealand, and North Africa, as well as to the Armed Forces Radio Network. Five books of the show's scripts were published, and some of them were adopted by school boards for their students.

It is hard to find a good writer of drama at the time these radio shows were presented who was not asked to do a script for "Cavalcade of America." Arthur Miller did several. Norman Rosten, Robert Anderson, Morton Wishengrad, Robert E. Sherwood, Maxwell Anderson, Alexander Woollcott, Dudlay Nicholls, Norman Corwin, and Stephen Vincent Benét all wrote shows for Du Pont. And to assure historical accuracy of "Cavalcade of America," historians were retained, at between $100 and $150 a script, to make checks. These included Dixon Ryan Fox, the president of Union College in Schenectady; Julian Boyd of Princeton; James Truslow Adams of Yale; Frank Monaghan of Yale; and Arthur Schlesinger, Sr. of Harvard. For advice on the aesthetic qualities of the shows, John Anderson, the drama critic of the *New York Journal* and generally accepted as the leading drama critic in New York City, was retained. The directors were just as carefully chosen—such men as Arthur Pryor, Kenneth Webb, Homer Fickett, and Jack Zoller.

The first radio broadcast re-enacted two episodes in American history dealing with the men and women of Plymouth and the *Mayflower*, and the South Dakota grasshopper plague. Walter Hampden, who had last been seen on Broadway in 1930, and who on the night following the broadcast was to open in "Achilles Had a Heel," was the first stage star used. By design he also appeared on the final "Cavalcade" program. Naturally, the programs varied in interest, but one of the most unusual and most highly acclaimed was broadcast from Chicago in 1940 in honor of Lincoln's birthday. The script was written by Robert E. Sherwood, whose *Abe Lincoln in Illinois*, then being performed, won the Pulitzer Prize. The lead was Raymond Massey, then in the Sherwood play, and the "Cavalcade" show itself was an adaptation of Carl Sandburg's biography of Lincoln, *The War Years* (New York: Harcourt, Brace & World). By no means were all the shows of this quality but there was every attempt to meet the highest standards.

"Cavalcade" even had its own program folder. It looked like the *Playbill* used in New York theatres, was usually in four pages, and was distributed at the broadcasts to the audience present and sent to 8,000 company personnel and to special names outside the company who might have had an unusual interest in the show. The outside cover of the program was the usual *Playbill* design. The first inside page told the story of the show, page three ran the show's commercial, which was always a story on chemistry and Du Pont, and the back page carried the listings of the stations on which the show could be heard. The commercial broadcast from Louisville on May 16, 1950 over the NBC network is as good an example as any. Here is what the announcer read:

This evening's "Cavalcade" broadcast comes to you from the city of Louisville, Kentucky. In a plant just outside Louisville the Du Pont Company manufactures one of the most interesting, useful products of chemistry—Du Pont neoprene rubber.

Neoprene is a good example of an improvement on nature by chemical science. Until only a few years ago all the rubber you used came from nature. There was no other source for it. Then chemists asked the question which has so often meant progress—"Why don't we try to make it ourselves and make it better?" That is a question that costs a lot of work and a lot of money; for we don't succeed every time, you know. Actually in our experience, only about one research project in twenty does succeed. This one did, I am glad to say, and today we have a chemical rubber, a better kind of rubber in many ways than nature's own.

Neoprene is not a substitute for natural rubber. Not by any means! It does many things natural rubber cannot do. For example it resists oil, chemicals, sunlight, weather and heat. That is why you'll find in the new cars about thirty vital parts which give you improved performance because they are made of Du

Pont neoprene. That is why your crepe-soled shoes can hold their shape and last longer if the crepe is Du Pont neoprene, and why neoprene beach balls for the youngsters are not harmed by weathering.

Many of the 1,250 men and women from the Du Pont neoprene plant outside Louisville are in our studio audience here this evening. They may take a just pride in their work, and rightly so. In addition to making an improved material vitally important to the nation, they are contributing, these Du Ponters, to the success of dozens of American manufacturing companies now using neoprene. They are helping to supply you, the consumer, with products that serve you better.

Neoprene, an important development of modern research, is one of the Du Pont Company's BETTER THINGS FOR BETTER LIVING . . . THROUGH CHEMISTRY.

"Cavalcade of America" served many purposes. As a public relations program it told the country that the company's business was not munitions, but chemistry. It came to the people under the best of auspices, a fascinating string of historic and contemporary episodes of the country, which instructed as well as entertained. It established a rapport between the company and its listeners. And it was a factor in laying to rest the charges that Du Pont was a merchant of death. These were some of the answers to the problem of the company's relations to the American public after the Nye committee hearings. Something else followed. Du Pont's attitude in its work on the atomic bomb projects was done only on the condition, stipulated by the company, that its profit be $1 and that any patents growing out of Du Pont's efforts be the property of the United States Government.

It was not until 1937 that Du Pont decided to take a reading on what the public thought of it. The Psychological Corporation's first study in that year showed that forty-seven per cent of the people questioned had a favorable opinion of the company, thirty-seven per cent had no opinion, and sixteen per cent had an unfavorable opinion. That meant that even three years after the Nye hearings less than half of the American public thought well of Du Pont. These studies were made every year until November, 1958, when they were discontinued. At that point seventy-nine per cent of those questioned thought well of Du Pont, the "no opinion" had dropped to some eighteen per cent and the unfavorable to less than three per cent. And since the sample of opinion was based on questioning of 10,000 people representative of the population, experienced interpreters of polls were certain that they were an accurate reflection of the condition of public opinion.

As a company that for its first hundred years manufactured explosives exclusively, plant explosions and fires were a continuous hazard to Du Pont. Safety measures were slow in developing, and the company policy was that when there was an explosion, the best thing to do was to clamp down on information to the public. Immediately after an explosion, guards would surround the plants and keep the press away. No bulletins were issued. Du Pont had nothing to say to anyone outside the company on causes or damage. Nor would the death and injury toll be given. The Du Pont attitude, and that of other corporations in those days, was that it was none of the public's business what happened in the plants for the plants were, after all, private property. That it was a harmful policy, harmful to those who had a right to know and to the company itself, was not fully realized until the first month in 1916.

Beginning on January 9 in that year a series of explosions rocked Du Pont's plants. They ran for the entire month and ranged in intensity from five to 180,000 pounds of powder. Most of them were across the river from Wilmington in New Jersey, and they spread both desolation and panic. The newspapers, deprived of accurate information, picked up rumors, half-facts, wild guesses, and drew conclusions which had to be wrong because they were based on no solid information.

The files of three Philadelphia newspapers provide the best answers to Du Pont's secrecy policies. By the end of the month the explosions and fires had not only caused terror in the homes of hundreds, but the people besieged newspaper offices and officials for information. They pleaded for an explanation of some kind. Workmen in fear often refused to go to work.

Three Philadelphia newspapers for the month of January, 1916, *The North American*, *The Evening Bulletin*, and the *Public Ledger*, are revealing. They repeatedly mention "wild rumors" and these grew with each blast. Reporters quoted all kinds of sources, "bystanders," "workmen," "minor officials," "Du Pont secret service men," "local hotel owners." On occasion one of these "minor officials" would deny there was a "spy plot" or that there was "sabotage" and would say that the "evidence" the newspapers used and the "arrests" made were fictitious. In fact any statements issued by Du Pont were so limited that each reporter pieced together what he could from whatever sources available, and then wrote his story.

A *North American* reporter tried to compile a record of accidents for thirteen months prior to the issue in which his story ran, January 12, 1916, and he wrote that he got his information from the "hospitals and records at the coroner's office." Then the report went on:

> Despite their denials that the seventy-five explosions, fires and flare-ups in their plants during the last thirteen months have been caused by outside influences, officials at the Du Pont Powder Company . . . yesterday started their own secret service machinery. . . .
>
> While the workers appreciate that everything is being done to reduce the hazards to a minimum and that every device known to the powder-making industry that serves to reduce friction in the machinery has been installed, they have not shared the opinions expressed by officials of the company relative to the general suspicions of a plot.
>
> Several of the workers, including minor officials . . . asserted that the past thirteen months has produced a record of accidents that is without a parallel in war munitions plants.
>
> They also pointed out that many of the explosions were of a similar character and occurred when workers were not within the danger zones. . . . Naturally the officials of the company would not discuss them because to spread such information would serve the purpose of the plotters and create such a reign of terror among the workers that the plant would be depleted of men.

The January 10 *Evening Bulletin* story of the explosion described "wild rumors" and stated that "the number [of dead] was estimated as late as five o'clock, more than four hours after the building blew up, as forty-two." Other and later reports said there were three dead and one hurt; or six dead and seven hurt. On the same day *The Bulletin* reported, "Rumors were circulating . . . that two men had been arrested. . . . Coroner Ashcroft . . . was the only person so far as can be ascertained, except officials of the company from Wilmington, who was admitted to the plants. . . . 'We picked up an arm here, a leg there, and so on until we had assembled all,' he said."

The *Public Ledger* of January 11, 1916, carried this report:

> Officials of the company made practically the same explanation of all of the explosions which occurred today. All, they say, were due to accidents but the men employed in the plant stick to the story that before the big explosion here [Hagley] in which thirty

people lost their lives on November 30, notices were posted warning the men to quit work. Some declare that notices have been posted recently warning of dire things which were to happen between January 1 and 15. The officials declare that investigations have shown that the reports are without foundation, and none can be found to have seen one or who can find a reliable person who has seen one. . . . The fact remains however that today has seen more explosions than ever occurred in one day before in the history of the Du Pont Powder Company.

And on January 29 the *Public Ledger* reported that "Penns Grove was nearly crazed by the rumors that scores of men had been killed and hurt" while *The North American* on January 29 reported:

The fires caused terror in the homes of hundreds of powder-makers here and at Penns Grove, N. J. They besieged newspaper offices for information, and weeping women with babes in their arms ran all the way to the ferry slips at the Fourth Street wharf to await the launches bringing workmen from the Jersey mills. Officials of the company were, likewise, besieged for information, and the wives and children of some of the workmen ran to their homes and pleaded piteously for information. Others walked aimlessly about the streets and refused to enter their homes again until they had received information.

The newspaper stories and the distress among employees in the plants were bound to cause a change in Du Pont policy. It came about in this way: Pierre Samuel du Pont, president of the company since 1915 and the architect of the modern company, insisted on knowing the reasons for the inaccurate press reports. He asked R. R. M. Carpenter, who was director of the development department of the company, to investigate and recommend the means of improving the accuracy of the news stories. Carpenter telephoned Charles K. Weston, the city editor of the *Public Ledger*, with whom he was acquainted. He began by complaining about the handling of the stories, the gross inaccuracies, and the rumors carried. Weston told Carpenter that it was Du Pont's own fault; that the company made it impossible for reporters to get the facts; that the lid was tightly put on all relevant information the press had to know to write accurately about the explosions; and that this was probably going to continue as long as the company's policy remained in effect. No newspaper, Carpenter was told, and no reporter, could ignore an explosion, and the event was going to be covered, based on any obtainable information—whether it came from an employee, an employee's wife, a coroner, a fireman, a policeman, or simply an uninformed bystander whose accuracy in telling what he saw and heard was not very good. If Du Pont made it possible for the papers to get the facts they would be happy to use them. But as far as the present system was concerned, it was promoting exactly what the company did not like.

Carpenter reported to P. S. du Pont on his Weston conversation and his other inquiries. The result was a memorandum to the executive committee of the company from Carpenter, dated January 26, 1916. In it Carpenter said that he had

> recommended to Mr. P. S. du Pont, which recommendation he has approved, that the company establish immediately a Publicity Bureau along the lines established by other large corporations. . . . You are all familiar with the extremely damaging articles which have appeared for the last three or four months in the papers, giving erratic news in reference to explosions, attacks on plants, etc. . . . I have consulted with different people familiar with this subject and have found that other corporations who have experienced originally the same trouble entirely overcame it by the establishment of a Publicity Bureau where the newspapers could secure immediately, without asking for it, correct information on anything of interest to the public. I am informed by people familiar with this subject that the newspapers are anxious to secure correct information and that the reason there have been so many erratic articles in reference to our business is due to the extreme difficulty they have had in securing any authentic information. There are, of course, some cases with yellow journalism where they will still publish what they please, but after considerable study of the situation I am firmly convinced that the establishment of this Bureau will be one of the best investments the company can make at the present time.

Carpenter also recommended that an experienced man be hired for the job and suggested $20,000 to cover the expenses of the year, "although this amount may not be necessary." According to the minutes of the executive committee meeting of January 31, the Carpenter recommendation was accepted. On February 1 there was an "advice of action" setting up the publicity bureau with an appropriation of $20,000 for the year. On February 15, Irénée du Pont, vice-president of the company and the chairman of the executive committee, circularized all department heads, announcing the creation of the bureau.

In the same memorandum he asked the department heads to weigh their problems with a view to possible treatment of the bureau "without detriment to the company." Six days later the bureau's office was opened with two rooms in the Du Pont building. The director of the publicity bureau was Weston. The assistant director was Frank Byrne, who had been assistant city editor of the *Public Ledger*.

Weston and Byrne set out to do what they knew best: get information to the press. After a short period of getting to know something of the company, they moved to get more closely in touch with the newspapers, to try to get the Philadelphia and New York papers and the correspondents in Wilmington for outside newspapers to call the publicity bureau if any information on the company were needed. They also had to establish with the press that the information that the bureau did provide was accurate, that there was no attempt to "take" the press. It was not an easy job in the early days, for the press was unused to getting useful answers to their queries to the company. In fact, many of the newspapers had found the company such a bad source of news that they stopped trying.

At the end of six months of the operation of the new bureau Weston decided that monthly reports to Carpenter, his contact with management, would be useful. The first, dated August 12, covering the entire time of the bureau's operation, was addressed to Carpenter and forwarded by him to the executive committee with a covering letter. He was satisfied that "what they have been doing to date has well warranted the expense." He also called special attention to the work done by the bureau on the munitions tax, which Du Pont considered discriminatory, in these words:

If you will remember the Advertising Department recommended an expenditure of some $40,000 for placing an advertisement in a large number of papers, and after a discussion it was decided to see what could be done without the expenditure through the Publicity end, and as a result we secured large editorial comment and news items in numerous papers. In fact, we secured eighty columns of news together with editorial space on the subject without any cost.

Carpenter, if not the publicity bureau, found it hard to get away from the idea that publicity was a way of doing the job of the advertising department, but cheaper. As time went on, Carpenter learned, as do other business executives, that the functions of these two departments are not interchangeable and to try to make them so is fraught with all kinds of trouble for the corporation, not the press. In paid space, the corporation has full control over content; it can even, with limitations, decide on location of the ad in publications. When it comes to news, a publicity bureau which does not provide it soon becomes useless to the press. A management that believes that a publicity budget can take the place of an advertising budget is one that understands neither public relations nor publicity and certainly is innocent of what advertising can do.

Weston's first report showed that the bureau felt it had developed a standing so good that

> virtually all of the newspapers look upon this Bureau as a dispenser of news that can be depended upon, for quick action and reliability. Local correspondents for out-of-town papers have joined most heartily in an effort to secure accuracy and fair play in the handling of news. . . . In a very short time, we had convinced the correspondents that there was no concealment of facts, that mysteries were very rare, that sensationalism was akin to faking. . . . Almost every day the Bureau is called upon by newspapers for information as to fires, explosions, injuries and deaths in various plants. In a vast majority of these cases there is no foundation for the rumor, and the Bureau's report is accepted without question. On the other hand, when a news story is developed, it is given out for publication quickly and completely—the result being that newspapers are enabled to dispose of the stories in one issue instead of carrying them along for days continuously as heretofore.

Weston's report told the story of the Gibbstown explosion of May 15. It was a serious accident but through the cooperation of the high explosives department the bureau was able to get complete details to the press on the first day so that little was run the following days. The bureau, to provide quicker service for the press, was on call around the clock for inquiries. It certainly was a new kind of service, so different from the days before the establishment of the bureau. It also checked almost daily for inaccurate statements in newspapers about the company, "letting the newspapers know that the company would not tolerate inaccuracies and to offer facilities for the ascertainment of the truth."

The zeal of the convert is often overwhelming. In this report Weston, the new company man, tells how he got the Penns Grove correspondent of *The North American* in Philadelphia fired for "indulging in sensationalism" and how the paper since was "most friendly in its attitude, frequently printing pleasant notices about life at

Carney's." He also tells how *The Wall Street Journal* "acknowledged its error in several instances" and fired a reporter who "made himself obnoxious in Wilmington," and that the paper has since been "more accurate and more friendly." The report also outlines how the bureau, through private investigations, learned the source of unfriendly articles dealing with the company's affairs and closed several of the avenues through which these articles reached the public. Reported as well was the space it obtained for the annual report of the company in the newspapers and the space the bureau was able to get by the distribution of a copy of a letter from P. S. Du Pont to a congressman on the munitions tax. It also noted the space obtained by the releases of stories of what the company did to help during "the recent smallpox scare" and what Du Pont was doing to "help stamp out infantile paralysis."

A sign of real progress came in Weston's report of March 1, 1917. The chief aim during the whole first year of the bureau's operation, it said, was to get in closer touch with the newspapers in order to change their attitude of distrust and their sensational presentation of facts about the company.

> This effort has even been more successful than was hoped for. As far as the presentation of news is concerned the newspapers have reached the point where they depend almost entirely on the Bureau for their facts, and they depend very largely on the Bureau's judgment of the relative importance of these facts. . . . Many of the newspapers have changed their editorial attitude toward the Du Pont Company and do not seem to make opportunities to criticize it.

Weston ended his report by saying that the handling of the ordinary fires and accidents at the various plants had settled down into a matter of routine. A long way had been travelled in a short time.

As Du Pont grew and spread from a company mainly devoted to making commercial explosives to a producer of a broad chemical line including rayon, cellophane, synthetic ammonia, photographic film, seed disinfectants, fibers, and neoprene, the publicity bureau slowly grew. There were few changes of approach. The main accent was on product promotion. If anyone had suggested to Weston or his staff members that they might actually advise other groups in the company on actions which would attract public support or on public positions which would help explain the company, there probably would have been stares of disbelief. And as for management at that period, any such suggestion would have been considered the height of absurdity.

The publicity bureau's job was simply to publicize products. It had better stick to its last.

All was well with the world. World War I was over. The short post-war recession was past. Prosperity was growing. The public was satisfied that the highest wisdom was in the heads of the titans of industry. Woodrow Wilson with his fine-spun theories was gone. Warren Harding was followed by Calvin Coolidge and Herbert Hoover. By the time Hoover was inaugurated in January, 1929, it seemed that the upward spiral of jobs and profits would never stop, and with the growth of the economy grew the certainty of managers of large enterprises that they were experts in all things and that public opinion was of little influence.

The first crack came in the 1929 market crash. The bitter years of 1930, 1931, and 1932 shook the nation's respect for business, and suddenly capitalism could not perform wonders, let alone provide jobs for those who so desperately wanted work, any kind of work. Then came Roosevelt, who had the support of much of big business, including, in 1932, most of the members of the du Pont family. Roosevelt was the man who would put things to rights, cut spending, balance the budget, and provide the bright new face that would quiet the people. Business would go on as it had before the shocking days of the fall of 1929.

Du Pont's management began to worry about public attitudes. The ability of Roosevelt to capitalize on the public's disillusionment with big business, shown so quickly after his inauguration, brought problems to the fore that businessmen, including Du Pont's managers, had never had to cope with. What was happening? What would the future bring? Was the entire economic system about to go down the drain? Business was frightened, and Du Pont's executives were distressed at this strange turn of events. Something that they did not understand had happened to the nation's thinking. The publicity bureau was no help in explaining public attitudes and what they might mean to business. Du Pont began to want more than Weston and his staff could give them.

The Nye hearings in 1934, in which Du Pont took the hammer blows of public antagonism, convinced the company that it needed a better understanding of the changes that had taken place in the country. Although Weston and Byrne were at Washington for the hearings with the four du Ponts, their contribution was slight. They could still promote products and could answer questions that reporters asked about company details; but the problem of how the company had to adjust itself to the changed views of the nation was something on which management did not seek their help.

One sign of management's desire for more than the publicity bureau could give was shown in the change of name of the bureau in 1938 to that of public relations department and additions to the staff. Du Pont's managers now knew that its relations with the public were bad, wanted something done, and began to search for the men who could give them the answers. They wanted help in the battle of ideas that was being waged, and seemed unable to find it. Slowly the executive committee lost its respect for the men who had been running the old publicity bureau. Good men, men with ideas beyond the concept of newspaper space as the answer to all problems, were being hired. But there was still no direction or leadership.

At the beginning of 1939 Weston retired as head of the public relations department and was succeeded by Theodore G. Joslin, who had had a long newspaper background. He came to the job from the *Wilmington News-Journal* papers, owned by Christiana Securities, a holding company controlled by the members of the du Pont family. Joslin had been with the *Boston Transcript* before becoming President Hoover's press secretary. Of his job with Hoover, Elmer E. Cornwell, Jr., in *Presidential Leadership and Public Opinion* (Bloomington: Indiana University Press, 1965), says that he had "little capacity" and that before his appointment "had been among the least esteemed and admired of the Washington correspondents, and upon his elevation he grew pompous and unapproachable." When Hoover was defeated Joslin moved to the Babson financial service in Washington, and was with the organization from 1933 to 1936, when he was hired to run the Wilmington papers.

Joslin was not what Du Pont's management wanted either, as it turned out. He was poor at handling staff, did not get on very well with those who worked under him, and was short of ideas in the very area where Du Pont needed them. Instead of being an improvement over Weston, he was more of the same. He took his job with great seriousness and wanted the company to take it the same way, but put so much faith in newspaper space as the answer to all problems that he set quotas for his staff for the number of press releases to be written each week, regardless of the subject. Space and more space in the papers about the company was his goal. His reports to the executive committee were mainly concerned with the number of column inches published. What is worse, he evaluated them uncritically, not differentiating between a two-inch story on page one of the *The New York Times* and a three-column story on the inside pages of some obscure publication which remained unseen by those who helped form opinion in the country. The executive committee was distressed by this approach and wanted something a good deal better. The committee members did not believe the public relations department could justify its performance by adding up column inches in news media. They thought there ought to be a consultative relationship and a truly effective liaison between Du Pont and the press on the basis of mutual understanding and respect so that the company could get a fair hearing for its views in all media. And they knew this could not be measured with a steel ruler placed over clippings from newspapers.

Du Pont has been a successful company for long years, and one of the reasons is that its management has always been willing to look at a problem from a new angle. It is not hidebound, and, while it prefers to proceed in a conventional manner, it is prepared to depart from normal practices if this becomes necessary. And it became necessary to meet Du Pont's needs in the public relations department. The company did not, and still does not, like to go outside its organization for assistants to department heads. It prefers to have people join the company right out of college and then—as they learn the company and as management evaluates them—to move them up. The rule was broken in the case of Joslin, but thanks to his job at the Wilmington papers the managers were able to assess him. They were wrong, but since they were not prepared to fire Joslin they asked him to go outside the company to find a deputy who could take over when the time for change came, and who was at least a few years younger than the department head.

Joslin, since he had been a Washington correspondent, looked for an assistant director among the press corps in that city. He offered the job to Richard Wilson of the Cowles publications, who turned it down. His second choice was Paul Hodges of the *Cleveland Plain Dealer*, who accepted but could not pass the company's medical examination. Finally, in April, 1942, Joslin offered the job as his assistant to Harold Brayman, who was forty-two years old, had been in newspaper work for twenty years, fourteen of them as a Washington correspondent. Brayman was, in fact, the man Joslin had wanted in the beginning, but he had initially thought him too old.

Brayman's qualifications were impressive. A graduate of Cornell University, his entire experience before taking the job with Du Pont was in journalism. Politics was his specialty, and he had spent six years as a legislative correspondent in Albany, New York, before going to Washington in 1928 for the old New York *Evening Post*. After six years his paper was sold by the Cyrus H. K. Curtis interests in 1933, but Brayman stayed on with the Curtis organization as Washington correspondent for the Philadelphia *Evening Ledger* until 1940. He then moved over to Jesse H. Jones's *Houston Chronicle*. For three years, from 1937 to 1940, Brayman wrote a syndicated column, "The

Daily Mirror of Washington," and then, for two years, wrote another syndicated column called "Washington Preview." From 1928 through 1940 Brayman covered the national political conventions of both parties, crossed the country time and again on the campaign trains of Alfred E. Smith in 1928, Roosevelt in 1932, Landon in 1936, and Willkie in 1940. He also had another distinction: he was one of the few Washington correspondents to have been elected president of both the National Press Club and the Gridiron Club.

Brayman was on the job exactly two years when Joslin died suddenly. The executive committee immediately appointed Brayman as the director of public relations and so began the modern period of Du Pont's public relations. Management had finally found what it wanted, and from the beginning Brayman reoriented the direction taken by his predecessor. Publicity was put in its proper place as a valuable tool in some situations, but it was no longer the chief objective of the public relations department. The broader approach started.

Although Brayman had twenty-three members in his department, including some able public relations men, when he took over, he went outside for his assistant. Within six months, in October, 1944, he had hired Glen Perry, three years his junior, as his deputy. Perry, too, had a background of political reporting. The son of a newspaperman and a graduate of Princeton University, he started with the *New York Sun* in 1927 as a reporter in New York City. He covered political campaigns and City Hall; was sent to the *Sun*'s Washington bureau in 1937, moving up to assistant correspondent three years later, and stayed in that job until he went to Du Pont. In 1940 and 1944 Perry covered the political conventions of both parties and traveled some 20,000 miles with Willkie. Perry also collaborated with Roscoe Drummond, who at that time was head of the Washington bureau of the *Christian Science Monitor*, in articles for the *Saturday Evening Post* and *Look* magazine and wrote a book about the Coast Guard, *Watchmen of the Sea* (New York: Charles Scribner's Sons, 1938).

Rarely have two men been so close in their thinking of what public relations for a corporation should be. Together, Brayman in the lead, and Perry as a creative administrator, they built Du Pont's public relations department until—by the time of Brayman's retirement early in 1965 and Perry's succession—it had the reputation of being among the best in the country. Walter S. Carpenter, the president of Du Pont for eight years following Brayman's appointment in 1940, was delighted with him, as was the entire executive committee. It was during Carpenter's regime that the Brayman program got under way. In every step of the building process Carpenter, then Crawford H.

Greenewalt, president from 1948 to 1962, and now Lammot du Pont Copeland, have given the best kind of support to the public relations department. Without that understanding on the part of management, no one—not a Brayman or a Perry or any other combination—would have been able to succeed. Management wanted good relations with the public, was open to ideas, and was willing to do more than provide the budget. Management was fully aware that the only effective public relations in the long run must stem from corporate performance in the public interest. Du Pont's management worked at the job of developing and keeping good relations with the company's constituency; nor did it kid itself into thinking that by having an effective department of public relations responsible for the day-to-day operations nothing was left for the managers to do.

Since every major decision of the corporation has an effect, not on one, but many publics, what the executive committee and what the chief executive officers do are the keys to Du Pont's public relations. As Copeland told a group of bankers in New York City in October, 1965, "I have seen many definitions, long and short, of what constitutes public relations. The one which I prefer is perhaps an oversimplification: I would like to have other people believe that, in the Du Pont Company, we try to do what is right." On the same occasion, he went on to say that "our own specialists in this field frequently remind the rest of us that the primary responsibility for good public relations must lie with the line organization. . . . The staff function is to advise and assist."

On another occasion, three years before he became president of the company, Copeland outlined the role of the public relations director. He is the one, Copeland said, to whom the businessman looks for judgment and advice in matters involving public reaction. In today's era of widespread communication there are very few actions of importance which do not involve public reaction in some degree. The role of the public relations man, according to Copeland, was not that of an apologist or that of a "magician who distracts attention from undesirable or unpleasant things by creating diversions . . . not the role of the suave worker in words who seeks to avoid trouble by concealing or misrepresenting the truth." And while no one can overestimate the importance of maintaining communication with the public, the "*most* important activity in which public relations men and women engage is and will be that of counselling, of advising those charged with responsibility for the management of our varied institutions how their proposed words and deeds will affect the institution's public or publics."

To Copeland, the businessman needs around him men whose function is to concentrate; to look at problems in terms of their special point of view. He needs lawyers, research men, labor relations experts, financial experts, sales experts, trade analysis experts, and production experts. As he would need lawyers to advise him even if he were a lawyer himself, so he also needs public relations experts even though he may well be versed in public relations.

In Copeland's view, public relations men must subject all the organization's plans and activities to searching and continuing scrutiny from the single focus of probable public reaction. The businessman needs them to tell him their views, pro or con, with conviction and courage, and without shading for fear that what they say may not be well received. He needs to know that, when he asks, he will get recommendations based on thorough fact-finding, careful analysis, and thoughtful consideration. He needs to know he will not be given careless, hasty, ill-considered suggestions.

Copeland does not underestimate the power of public opinion. In his view, tenuous though the connection may seem to the average citizen, his opinions about the forces that mold our civilization are, in the final analysis, controlling. If he is in favor of them, they survive. If he is opposed to them, they die. If he is indifferent to them, then that, too, is a form of decision and results flow from it. In our society, the citizens control anything they really want to control. And when it comes to business, Copeland holds, if large numbers of citizens are convinced that business is evil and dangerous, it automatically follows that large numbers of legislators—senators, congressmen, members of state legislatures, and city councilmen—will try to derive political advantage from that emotion. Conversely, if the general public knows something about business and industry, and thinks well of them, then large numbers of politicians will feel the same way.

In decision making, Du Pont's policy has been not to attempt to maximize profits on a short-range basis even though it is difficult to find a company that is more profit-minded. This was especially clear in the fourteen-year period in which Greenewalt was president. And because he is such an articulate man, Greenewalt, now chairman of the board of the company, explained the relationship between profits and public support to the International Industrial Conference in San Francisco in September, 1965. He said:

Because business equates success or failure with profitability, the superficial conclusion is that profit is the sole objective. If this were true, the role of business leadership would be vastly simplified. All of us know, however, that profit is only one of the many factors influencing corporate decisions. Business leadership must of course be concerned with profit, but the difficult decisions, and those calling for the highest level of insight and judgment, are those involving the conditions under which profit may be realized.

Profit under what conditions? The grab for a quick killing is the mark of the worst kind of leadership, for it places immediate profit above the long-term interest of the organization and can lead ultimately only to disaster. The successful leader will define objectives within limits that his organization will find consistent with professional pride, personal satisfaction, and public esteem. He will take into account all parties at interest—employees, customers, shareholders, and his country, finding the way to an equitable distribution of the fruits of progress. The leader who established viable guide lines compatible with human values and public policy will insure to himself and his organization the essential backing and support of his associates, his subordinates, and his nation.

This is the kind of understanding of the public relations function by chief executives that makes it possible to do effective work in developing the corporation's relations with the public. Without it the job becomes almost impossible. However, the understanding must reach down to the lower echelons as well, and this demands a continuous educational operation. It is more so for a company the size of Du Pont, with its sales of more than $3 billion, its plants in eighty-four communities in twenty-nine states, and the necessity of communicating company policies to its 260,000 stockholders, 75,000 customers, and 30,000 suppliers, as well as its 175,000 employees, and a management organization structured to run the entire enterprise efficiently.

Du Pont's board of directors is in many ways unusual. Most of its members have worked for no other company. One group is made up of active managers, another of former managers now retired, and a third group is on the board because it has heavy stock-holdings. Sales, production, research, and finance are heavily represented. There is no member on the board who has not a deep interest, either through substantial stock ownership or actual employment in the company. The average director has been on the board for almost twenty years. If he is an employee or ex-employee, his length of service is more than thirty-five years. Here then is a board which is thoroughly versed in the company's history, its methods, its past mistakes. This intimacy with the company assures many things, one of which is that the policies involving its relations with the public are not hit and miss. There is a consistency here that helps build its barriers against repeated error.

The executive committee—which is made up of Du Pont's president, who is always the chief executive, and eight vice-presidents, and which is responsible to the board for the actual management—also has the long-view attitude which assures that the public interest in any decision making is to the forefront. It is this executive committee that guides policies, but having no responsibility in administering any one department, has a chance to take the whole view. This also has an immense advantage when it comes to making certain that the public relations aspects of operations are not overlooked.

Under this executive committee, the company's operations are carried on by twelve industrial or manufacturing departments, each of which is headed by a general manager. He in turn runs his department as if it were a separate company. He has both authority and responsibility and there is no attempt to dilute either under the board policies.

In support of the industrial departments are what the corporation's organization chart calls the auxiliary departments. There are thirteen of these and the public relations department is one. The others are advertising, central research, development, the economist's office, employee relations, engineering, general services, legal, purchasing, the corporate secretary, traffic, and treasury. Here are the specialists who do the bidding of management. In Du Pont's corporate structure this is the best place for public relations. And here it has no problem of knowing what the company's policies are or are in the process of being. The doors of management are always open to the public relations department.

There are three different ways in which the public relations department keeps in contact with the executive committee. The first consists of two regular appearances every year. One, on the third Wednesday in January, is when the department's budget and annual report are presented. It is at this time that the executive committee members review operations and discuss the public relations problems that lie in the future. The report presented is detailed. The other session with the executive committee is generally held in late spring or early summer. There is no formal agenda and the public relations department discusses general problems. This is also the time of personnel review with the committee. This meeting is always informal, and usually lasts from an hour to an hour and a half.

The second way in which the public relations department keeps in touch with the executive committee is when it is called. There is nothing regular about this, for the call comes when the committee is considering a subject in which its members see public relations aspects. Sometimes the department is called in conjunction with another department to give advice on specific problems.

The third method of appearing before the executive committee is through a request to be heard on some particular problem about which the public relations department is concerned, and which is of greater than usual importance to the company. This may be on the rare occasions when there is some disagreement between the public relations department and another department that can be reconciled only by the committee's decision. Both departments are then heard, the views thrashed out and usually the disagreement is resolved by discussion and the presentation of argument rather than by fiat. However, the committee dislikes the role of arbitrator and expects the various departments to reach agreement without appeal to it.

Once a year the public relations director or his assistant goes before the full board of directors to make a short report, usually no more than ten minutes, on some subject which he believes to be of special concern to the board, as distinct from the executive committee. These appearances are made by other departments as well as public relations. The public relations director, alternating with his assistant, attends the general manager's meeting, which comes on the third Monday of each month. This meeting is attended by all department heads or their assistants, all vice-presidents, and the president. Each general manager or his assistant makes a short report on what is happening in his operation department and there are often questions. The auxiliary departments, however, do not make regular reports but only are heard when there is something of special importance. In addition, the company's directors of sales meet at regular periods, and a public relations department representative involved in product information services attends.

Every Wednesday what is called the "Ex. Committee lunch" is held. At this meeting the entire top management group gets together. The public relations director and his assistant both attend and may bring one staff guest to the first luncheon of each month. Then, in addition to all this, the directors of the auxiliary departments lunch together monthly and discuss their problems. Here the public relations director and his assistant take turns in attending. Once a month the director and assistant director of public relations, with the member of the department who has a special responsibility with one of the operating departments have lunch with the general manager of that department and his assistant. This is done simply to discuss in a general way the problems that may arise, and to swap information.

Since Wilmington is a small city, the Du Pont executives, in addition to all these organized meetings, run into each other often. They not only work together, they play together; so the cohesiveness of the management group is continuously promoted. The men not only get to know each other well and assess each other, but the subject of business is never far below the surface. This may have defects, or may narrow the outlook of the company's executives in some ways. It does, however, make for continuous interchange of information, so it is rare for the public relations department's members not to know what is going on in the company and what management's problems are. In some companies it is difficult for the public relations people to get close to management. In Du Pont's case they are extremely close.

To keep the entire public relations department staff further in touch with the thinking of other auxiliary departments, the staff meeting device is used. Four times a year, on the first Monday of each quarter, the staff assembles in a meeting room. Each meeting has a speaker who is a specialist in some aspect of the company's operations. He usually speaks for some thirty or forty minutes, then answers questions for about an hour. These staff meetings have more than informational value. The public relations director can, for his staff's better understanding of some problem about an aspect of the company, lead the questioning so as to bring out the points he wants his people to be alert to.

The underlying theory on which the entire public relations operation is based is that no institution—whether it be a business, a foundation, a university, or a trade association—can endure or grow unless it has public support; and that the American people, if given the facts, will come to a sound judgment. To get public support, the business must so conduct itself that it deserves that support. This means that Du Pont, in every activity, must so act that those who have immediate contact with it respect it for its integrity, and for the quality of its goods and services. No pretense, no special publicity events, no legerdemain can bring public support to the company in the long run if its every action is not in the public interest. There is another responsibility for the company, as there is for any institution in our society, and that is to tell what it is and why it acts in the way it does. It is through the play of ideas and expressed views, in conflict with each other when need be, that the public can decide its preference or understand the organization.

As for its operational theory, the Du Pont public relations department decided in 1946, when it was still groping for a basic approach, that it would have to deal with those who had a special involvement with the company as a beginning. For lack of another name, and because both Brayman and Perry had spent so many years observing political organizations, it was called the precinct system. The thinking underlying this course was that of the entire population many never heard of Du Pont or never would, but there was an important audience that was concerned with the company and that would listen to what it had to say. This audience, or public, was itself divided into groups— employees of the company, suppliers, customers, stockholders, neighbors in the towns where it had plants, or was an economic factor for some other reason. This did not preclude some approach to the general public. It only assured that someone would be interested enough in what the company had to say, or was doing, to listen or pay attention. Also inherent in the precinct system concept was that if other companies did what Du Pont did, the cumulative effect would be such that ultimately a very large segment of the general public would be involved.

In developing this concept, Du Pont's public relations staff knew there were three factors. The first was that these special publics who were close to the company knew too much to be taken in with words that did not match deeds. This of course underlined the importance of living right before claiming to be living right. And while this was in accord with all sound public relations theory, it gave special emphasis to it so that there was no possibility of misunderstanding. The second factor was that the precinct system would only make an important contribution to long-range objectives of acceptance of the economic system, of all business, not just that of one company, if other major corporations followed Du Pont. This meant that Du Pont had to convince public relations directors and their managers in other corporations to follow the same line, and for many years this was one of the major efforts by Du Pont. The third factor in the development of the precinct system was that it set itself in opposition to the many organizations which had sprung up at the time to "sell" private enterprise. So much of this was so unrelated to reality that organized groups were soliciting funds in order to place advertisements advocating a belief in private enterprise in the *Wall Street Journal* and other publications devoted to business. There was at this period a good deal of this carrying of coals to Newcastle, and Du Pont's development of the precinct system was one means of putting this type of special pleader out of business—or at least blunting his activities.

The precinct system did not mean that Du Pont did not influence, from the very beginning, those outside the groups set out as targets of immediate concern. Speeches made by executives were reported in the press and otherwise widely distributed. Statements the company made and the actions of all who worked for Du Pont rippled out to a much wider audience. But it was felt that the ripple would spread most effectively if it started with those who had a particular reason for interest in the company.

Another theory on which the public relations department works is that Du Pont's relations with the public are not dependent only on the members of the department but on the activities of everyone in the company, from the chief executive to the secretary who answers the telephone, from the customer complaint department to the recruiter who goes to college campuses to hire researchers. No one believes or tries to give the impression that the public relations department is made up of miracle workers who can, by some secret incantation, change public attitudes.

But since the precinct system of operation delineated the groups with which it intended to work, new areas have been added. An effort had to be made to develop a rapport with the intellectual. This is one of the constituencies with which Du Pont is closely concerned. For the past fifteen years a strong effort has been made to cultivate an understanding of the company and the problems of business as a whole by the intellectual.

Another precinct has been added: government. There was a period when government was treated as an enemy to be avoided at all costs, for government was in continuous conflict with business. Today, Du Pont's public relations department considers government as a group to which it must be directly attuned.

In operations, Du Pont avoids becoming captive to one set of techniques. Often a public relations man will become enamoured of, say, films, as a means of reaching a particular group. He will get the budget for a film and then begin to search for something to say. Du Pont's approach is quite different. It begins with a theme, with some issue or problem it wishes to present to the public. Then, and only then, does it decide which technique is best for the purpose. It may be a film. It may be a series of speeches, or a widely distributed brochure, or a conference, or some other method. As Brayman has said, the company is "ends minded, not means minded."

When it comes to staffing the public relations department, great care is taken so that the right man, or woman, is chosen. Often it has taken as long as two years before the right person is found. If, after he is hired, he turns out to be right for the job, he can expect continuous employment. This is quite different from many companies, even large ones; there, when business falls off, or a recession sets in, one of the first actions of some managements is to fire members of the public relations staff regardless of talent or ability. Of course, when business improves, the search begins for new help. The result of all this lack of certainty of work by public relations people is a serious impairment of performance. Du Pont wants none of this. The result is that it has good quality performers who know the company, know their work, and are happy in it.

In all, Du Pont has seventy-five persons in its public relations department, exclusive of the secretarial and clerical help. They are paid well and are, on the whole, of a caliber which can stand up to management without backing away from hard decisions. This is not easy to do, for the man who says no has to be more than a technician. He has to have strength of character and the stature to present his case without fear. By the very nature of Du Pont and the variety of its operations, the public relations department must have a wide variety of people of both general and special backgrounds. Unlike any other Du Pont department, public relations can hire for senior positions from outside the company.

Of the seventy-five members of the staff three are former Washington correspondents. One is the former administrative assistant to a congressman; another a former legislative and research assistant to a United States senator. One was a special assistant to a former Secretary of Health, Education and Welfare—loaned to that newly created department by Du Pont to set up its public relations operation. There is also a one-time manager of a radio and television station, a former president of a small college, a war correspondent in World War II, a one-time executive director of a state manufacturers' association, a former *Saturday Evening Post* writer, a former managing editor of a newspaper. Sixty-one have college degrees running from law, journalism, English, and history, through political science, electrical engineering, government, education, music, business administration, home economics, and zoology. Twenty-eight came directly to Du Pont from a newspaper or a magazine, three from radio and television, thirty-two from other corporations, from other jobs in Du Pont and from public relations agencies, and twelve who had worked in various capacities in colleges. Almost all of them had extensive experience prior to their last posts before joining the company. The average age of these staff men is forty-seven.

As for the fifteen public relations people working abroad for Du Pont, all of them Europeans, eight have college degrees, including majors in languages, business administration, journalism, philosophy, and agriculture. Seven came from newspapers or magazines directly to the company, four from other public relations work, and three from other departments of the company.

It is safe to allow a wide degree of discretion and responsibility to men of this kind. This does make the staffers happy, but the reason was selfish on the part of the company. It wanted its public relations men to have the kind of judgment that can only come from good training, wide experience, and working for long periods in fields that provide them with both skills and an understanding of public attitudes. Du Pont has found it makes for greater stability in approach, and men of this kind are less likely to give managers unsound advice.

One aspect of Du Pont's public relations department is that it continuously looks at itself critically. It has never been satisfied to rest on its oars. That a policy has proved satisfactory, that a plan is working, or that an organizational set-up has been functioning reasonably well does not exempt it from questioning. In 1964, the public relations department undertook a complete reappraisal of what it was doing, where it was going, and the environment of public opinion. It was a four-month study to find answers to three basic questions: the problems with important public relations aspects confronting industry as a whole at that time and in the near future; those confronting Du Pont itself; how the company could best prepare for and handle those problems.

Three men—Perry, Thomas W. Stephenson, now the assistant director of public relations, and Charles M. Hackett, for many years one of the strong right arms of the department and at present vice-president and executive editor of the News-Journal Company of Wilmington—made the study under Brayman's direction. They interviewed thirty-seven executives of the company, including the president and chairman of the board; nine vice-presidents; the twelve general managers of the industrial departments; and the directors of the auxiliary departments. The executive assistants and the division managers of the public relations department submitted reports as well.

But to be worthwhile, the study had to include key figures outside the company: thirty-one were interviewed. They were men in government, politics, higher education, and journalism; corporate public relations directors; heads of public relations agencies; and management consultants. The final report, with recommendations for action, was then presented to Du Pont's executive committee. It is an interesting document, and deals with industrial problem areas, social problem areas, relations with governments, and the public relations area.

A listing of some of the fields gives an insight into the extent of the study: automation and employment; profits and competition; unions; business ethics; stockholder relations; foreign competition; personnel; pollution; integration; urban affairs; the corporation as a social support.

On the conclusions of this report, new directions were taken to steer clear of foreseeable shoals. But valuable as this study was, more important, in many ways, than its findings was the very fact that it was done. The inward look is taken in many corporations only under the pressure of crises, and then it is often done by firms called in from outside to do the job.

Another inward look was taken late in 1965, and completed in the spring of 1966, which resulted in structural changes in the department. Times had changed and attitudes both within the company and conditions outside called for a reorganization. This reorganization recognized changes in methods of work that had, in fact, already taken place. It provided better management for the job to be done by the public relations department to meet the coming changes in the public's thinking. It also provided greater flexibility and better planning to meet present and future conditions. As national opinion had slowly altered toward business, so it was necessary to change the internal mechanisms of the public relations department. It was a natural and wise step. It was not forced on the department. It was brought about by the solid concept that as issues vary and opinion undergoes change, so the means and the methods of dealing with them must be adjusted.

The present organization of the public relations department gives the director a minimum of administrative detail, keeping him as free as possible for consultation with top management and giving him time for broad policy thinking. It is to him that members of the executive committee of the company turn when they seek advice, and it is therefore essential to keep him clear of the minutiae of the department that so often bog down the public relations directors in companies. Essentially, Stephenson administers the department with two executive assistants and the heads of sections reporting directly. There is also a policy committee, made up of the director, the assistant director, the executive assistants and the three division heads, which meets informally every Monday morning to discuss problems. It is also occasionally called into special session. Because seven good heads are better than one when issues that may have many side effects are involved, no important decision by the department is made without being carefully discussed by the committee.

To carry out Du Pont's long-range program, the functions of the public relations department are clearly outlined in six areas: assistance to the industrial and auxiliary departments; assistance to management on the public relations implications of both internal and external developments; liaison with public media; production of communications materials; study and appraisal of public opinion; and special services, including planning for and counseling of trade associations in which the company has memberships.

The department is organized into three divisions: departmental services division, publications division, and personnel and control division. The last one handles personnel recruitment, training, evaluation, budget management, supervision of records, files, payrolls, and accounting for the whole department. The other two divisions have the responsibility of carrying out the public relations function for the company, and it is on the wisdom and competence of these that the operation stands or falls. The larger is the departmental services division comprising four groups, each headed by a public relations manager. These groups serve the industrial departments directly and some of the staff department, both in counseling and product-information services. To do these jobs effectively there must not only be the closest liaison between these four public relations managers and the industrial departments, but they must have intimate knowledge of those they serve and their public problems. Each one of the groups reports to the division manager. But these public relations managers are expected to stand on their own feet except when they need advice or help. A section in the personnel and central division—departmental services—provides the press and staff services to the groups and to the entire department. It also periodically analyzes what the press has to say about Du Pont—the favorable, the unfavorable, the neutral. Departmental services also provides information for editors, schools, home economists, and others who have an interest in the company.

Because Du Pont is so large, the four groups are allocated specific departments with which to work. One group works with employee relations, industrials and biochemicals, pigments, plastics and traffic. Another group has electrochemicals, film, legal, and photo products. The third group has elastomer chemicals, engineering, fabrics and finishes, and organic chemicals. The fourth has central research, development, explosives, and textile fibers. The heads of each of these groups, while advising the industrial or auxiliary department chiefs, have no authority to enforce their views. They have to persuade the various department heads that their views should be followed. It is the rapport they develop, the confidence they inspire, and the training they have had, that enables them to assure that their advice should be acted upon. In addition, the group heads in the departmental services division have to develop programs and provide the ideas that will enhance the reputation of the department and the company as a whole.

The product information services for the twelve operating departments are carried out by specialists in the departmental services division. Here is where there is a sharp departure from what is done by many other companies, for the specialists in this field are assigned to the various sales divisions, although they remain members of the public relations department's staff and are supervised by the public relations managers. This is done for the best of reasons: control. Without it, the product information men, under pressure from the sales divisions, might bow to their insistence and inundate editors with sales promotion materials—the last thing the editors need or want. Since they have the backing of the public relations department when they feel it unwise to issue releases that the sales people press them to, they are more likely to take the sound course. They know the problems of the editors, something the sales departments cannot be expected to appreciate.

When it comes to providing product information, the general principle the public relations department works on is to provide the trade magazine editors with material they would be willing to send one of their own reporters to get were it not supplied to them. As a result, this service to the trade press is not only appreciated, it is welcomed. Editors are certain, for they know it is policy strictly adhered to, that the product information staff will never try to pull the wool over an editor's eyes to grab space. This policy, which would be almost impossible to carry out if the product information members were not under the control of the public relations department, enhances the stature of the company with editors. It also assures fair coverage when the news is worth carrying.

The product information staff, however, does more than prepare articles and write releases. It runs meetings, arranges and conducts the press conferences, and helps on trade relations. There is an additional plus in having well-trained product information workers: they form an effective farm system out of which the public relations department can draw men for the more responsible work in counseling.

 The publications division is run by a manager and an assistant manager and uses publications to communicate with employees and other audiences important to Du Pont. *Better Living*, which is a bimonthly, twenty-four page magazine on glossy stock, is edited for all company employees. There is however a secondary distribution outside the company to special lists which the department considers valuable. The objectives of *Better Living* are to help employees develop an identification with the company and to get their support for an economic, social, and political climate in which large business can most effectively operate.

This Is Du Pont is a brochure issued twice a year on a subject the company believes important, and is distributed to the press, educators, general opinion leaders and special audiences that have a close interest in the subject. Each issue is an attempt to deal with a current and often controversial issue in some depth.

The *Management Newsletter*, a monthly bulletin, goes to all employees from foremen up, with company information and interpretation. Here management's point of view is stressed on current issues so that managers can both talk about the company with knowledge and can better interpret policies. The *Newsletter* runs four pages and is carefully read, particularly by foremen, who are the direct line from the executive committee to employees.

The plant publication service, which falls in the publications division, speaks to all local plant editors and through them to the employees in the plants. This service stresses to the plant editors the advantages of well-thought-out and well-edited papers. Cartoon features are provided for the employee publication editors, each designed to outline a specific policy or clarify an ideological point. This service and advice can mean an improvement in content and format of the papers to the forty-two plant publications editors. It helps keep policy lines clear in all company media that reach the employees. There is another function it performs: preparation of specialized publications for individual company departments. This service also helps recruit and train personnel for the plant papers.

In the entire publications division two basic questions are always uppermost: Who is the audience? What is the point to be communicated? Without the answers there is the ever-present danger that the content of all publications, because of the personal interests of the editors, may be diverted from the basic purpose of helping the company's managers reach their objectives of a healthy, profitable company.

A relatively new development in the public relations department is the establishment of a planning section, which is directly supervised by one of the executive assistants in the department. This group studies, evaluates, and may recommend changes in present departmental policies or the establishment of new ones or new programs. Planning also takes a hard look at the company's involvement in national economic, political, and social problems and issues. It also suggests new communications techniques. All the fields of the planning section's concern demand careful, objective and time-consuming research.

The overseas operations of the company are relatively new, but they are growing quickly, with $1 billion in sales expected by 1970. Here, the public relations department is responsible for providing public relations service and advice to the thirty foreign subsidiaries and affiliated companies. The first wholly owned subsidiary in Europe, Du Pont Company (United Kingdom) Ltd., was formed in 1956. Construction of a plant was started soon after to make neoprene synthetic rubber at Maydown, near Londonderry, in Northern Ireland. There are fifteen plants in operation in Europe and five more under construction. To meet the needs of these plants, public relations work was started with one man in 1959. There are now fifteen. Overseas public relations is centered in Geneva, where there are a manager and an assistant; the rest are located where they can function best. All are, of course, under the supervision of the public relations department in Wilmington.

Overseas public relations' approaches are generally so different from what they are in the United States that a broad policy decision had to be made before even a beginning was made. The issue was whether to take the general American approach or the approach that many U.S. companies abroad have taken historically. The treatment of the European press was an important part of this decision. It had been argued that company news would not be run in the papers in Europe. In some cases it was argued that the only news which would be run would be on a quid pro quo basis: that is, so much news space for so much advertising, or for outright payment. No other way was possible in many cases, ran the argument, and to attempt to get legitimate news stories in the press without backing them up with paid space would be an exercise in frustration. Experienced overseas hands advised against fighting local habits. But the decision was made in Wilmington that Du Pont would have none of the old methods, that the public relations function would be carried on in Europe as it had been in the United States. The short answer is that it worked. When it was made clear that there would be no special arrangements for the press, that if newspapers did not feel what Du Pont had to say was news worth running on its own merit there would be no change of policy, the troubles began to disappear.

There now is a direct contact between the European press and Du Pont's management abroad. Du Pont policies are being explained through publications, speeches, and press contacts. Every effort is made to see that Du Pont's installations do not cause dislocations in the community. Local residents are trained in Du Pont's public relations methods as well as in all the other management functions. Company purchasing of construction materials and raw materials, whenever possible, is done locally. And above all, the top managers of Du Pont in Europe are glad to meet the press and explain their positions clearly and frankly. What looked like an impossible chore for the public relations department—the use of the direct American approach to media—has vanished.

Another aspect of the public relations department's operations is worth looking at for its present approach to disasters in plants. It highlights the differences between today's practice and that of the old days. The risk of fire and explosion is present in almost all chemical plants, and is even greater in plants which make explosives. Despite the best possible safety precautions, explosions still do take place. They are handled today on a completely open policy of dealing with the press and informing the community. There is no attempt to hide behind a wire fence, a locked gate, and security guards. Just as soon as the accident area is safe, the plant manager takes the press into the plant for a briefing. Photographs are permitted. All questions are answered. That this disaster plan is welcomed by the press is underlined by an award to one of the explosives manufacturing plant managers by the Pennsylvania Press Photographers Association for his cooperation.

How strongly this policy of working with the press is embedded in plant managers is exemplified by what happened some years ago at Du Pont, Washington, where there is an explosives plant. A road construction program was under way, and every time there was a blast local residents would call the newspaper editor in the town and ask if the local Du Pont plant had blown up. The editor would call the manager to ask him if he had had an explosion.

Finally the plant manager said to the editor, "Look, you're wasting a lot of your time and mine, too. Let's make a deal. If and when we have a blow, I'll call you. You can depend upon it that if you do not hear from me, there's no need to call, for we will not have had an explosion."

The editor agreed. Every time thereafter, when there was a query from a subscriber about an explosion, the editor confidently denied there was an explosion at the plant. Then one day there was an explosion in the plant. Hardly had the echoes died away when the phone rang. It was the plant manager. "Well, we've had it," the editor was told. The manager then set out to give him all the facts, and answered the editor's additional questions.

It is almost impossible to pinpoint those responsible for modern public relations at Du Pont. But if one were compelled to do so, five names would be central: three of them chief managers of the company and the others public relations directors. Walter Carpenter, president from 1940 to 1948, not only wanted, but searched out, a new approach to the company's relations to the public. Greenewalt, president from 1948 to 1962, was one of the keys to the advancement of the company in this area. He is an unusual man, for he understood the necessity for public relations, was thoroughly sympathetic to it, and, while president, gave it his complete support. He was not only good in this field, he was also willing to do the things necessary as president to make it most effective. To achieve the results that were desired by the company, he was willing to make speeches, to write books, and to participate in conferences. He encouraged the public relations department in the new fields it was ploughing, and, because he was a highly articulate and impressive personality, his personal contribution was greater than was possible for some others. He did not always follow the advice of the public relations department, but he always listened to it and considered it carefully. When he did not agree he gave good reasons for not doing so. Copeland, an entirely different personality from Greenewalt, has been president since 1962 and is supporting the thrust of reorganization and adjustment to new conditions being made by the public relations department.

The two public relations men, of course, are Brayman and Perry. Brayman, the director for twenty-one years, had many strengths, one of which was his ability to choose good men. But there was a greater strength during his regime: he had the courage to back new ventures if he was convinced they were valuable to Du Pont. If he thought a new idea was a good one, he would not only encourage it at the beginning, but would put his own prestige on the line for it, knowing that if it turned out badly he would have to carry the blame. He did not hesitate to go to the executive committee of the company and fight for what he thought was the right course or for a departure from an old method. This may seem a normal thing to do for any man who is expected to head a department of importance. Actually, it is a rare public relations director who will stand up to management and battle it if he thinks it is wrong. Public relations directors are a long way from being the great leaders they give the impression of being when they are assembled for meetings. Then they are talking to their peers. When they have to stand up to their bosses they are not quite the bravest of lions. Perry—even though he was for twenty years Brayman's assistant director and has since early 1965 been the director—has remained his own man. He is creative, frank, and while his and Brayman's views in most cases are the same there is a difference in emphasis which made the men complementary in their work. Perry brought his own brand of innovation to the public relations department when he took over.

To Brayman, the whole philosophy of his work is based on the fact that we live in a country where the business climate is determined by the mass of the people themselves. Business freedom can be preserved only if it fulfills the aspirations of our society. To him, these aspirations, great as they have been in the past, are modest when contrasted with the insistent clamor of the demanding future. Nor can this be evaded, circumvented, by-passed, or ignored, for, as a result of the widespread growth of popular governments since both World Wars and the replacement of most of the colonial dependencies by independent governments, public opinion has become the dominant force. With vastly improved communications and a higher level of public education, the ordinary people in many parts of the world have discovered a new instrument of authority in their hands—control over government. So the problem of challenges to free enterprise becomes, according to Brayman, not a problem of government, of law, or of foreign ideology, but a problem of public opinion.

For these reasons, Brayman believes that businessmen must develop a more widespread understanding of how public opinion is made. He believes public opinion does not just develop amorphously, without order, but rather is made by people, by events, by development, and by those who interpret these. Part of this understanding demands a knowledge of communicators, that is, those who make their living out of conveying ideas or information to others. These fall loosely into three groups: newspaper, magazine and book writers; television and radio commentators and writers, and the scriptwriters of movies; and the academic group, for this one influences not only the classrooms, and therefore, future leaders, but also has a wide influence through research projects in the social science field and through its work as consultants with government departments.

Brayman feels that these three groups, plus the people in public life, constitute the real power in America today and until this is fully understood by business leaders, their lawyers, and others interested in private enterprise, little will be done to preserve it. He also is opposed to the old lobbying system with its hired professionals. He considers them passé, believes the system is distrusted by everyone and brings disrepute on those who continue it. To illustrate, Brayman tells this story:

"I remember a case a few years ago in a state legislature where a leading business in the state found itself faced with a proposed measure which would have been very costly to it. It poured on the heat through an intense lobbying campaign and managed to beat the bill, which never had any sound justification in the first place.

"The next year when the legislature met and its session continued for a month or so, there was a somewhat unhappy lobbyist, for he had only a modest retaining fee and no work to do. Much to his disappointment, no one had even introduced the controversial bill. But he was a resourceful lobbyist, and it didn't take him long to find a friendly legislator who could be persuaded to reintroduce the bill that year so he could again milk the big corporation to fight this pernicious idea."

Brayman is convinced that business must adjust to the world as it is so that the fight can be carried on effectively for the principles of private enterprise. This does not mean giving up ideas. Rather, they should be reconsidered carefully to make certain they are in line with the public interest, revised where revision is necessary, and then put to the public, which must be convinced they are sound.

Perry is under no illusions that public relations is controlled by his department, because the public's opinion of the company is, in the last analysis, based on thousands and ultimately millions of contacts—in writing, on the telephone, or in person—with those who, for one reason or another, have to be in touch with the company. Perry's department has a part in this, he says, but it is only a part. The public relations department can be helpful in maintaining relations with the press, for example, and the other media of information. Its members can also counsel and advise members of management how they should conduct themselves in order to win public understanding and support. But the main job has to be done by others not in the public relations department. This is a truth, says Perry, that many people in the management area of a great many companies do not appreciate at all, because it seems so easy to compartmentalize this thing in your mind and decide there is a public relations department to handle these matters. Obviously public relations is something you cannot delegate.

Perry thinks there is, unfortunately, a widespread lack of fundamental understanding that public relations is doing the right things for the right reasons. Perry's belief is intimately woven into the company's precinct system, the heart and soul of which is that those in the precinct are interested in you because they have a reason to be. They have contacts with you. They are employees and their families, stockholders, customers, or suppliers. They have a very real interest in what Du Pont says and does. It follows that they know what you are up to, and if what you say does not square with what they know to be your actions, then you would be a good deal better off if you had never said anything at all, because it is going to boomerang. This may be the hard way, but there is no easy way if you are going to have effective public relations.

Perry insists that the term "public relations" does a disservice to its purpose. If you call it "relations with the public" you immediately get a different context because then it becomes clear that anybody in your company who has relations with the public is to a degree responsible for your public relations. One of the functions of a public relations department, says Perry, is to establish such a relationship with top management and other departments that they will know when to call in the public relations director. This is important, he says, not because management does not desire to do the right thing, or because it does not know right from wrong, but because management is not expert in working with the public or in public relations. Nor should an executive be expected to be expert. That is not his job. He is a production man, or he is a salesman, or a research man, or he is a top management man where he has to combine all these. He needs somebody who has no other job but to be aware of the state of public opinion. It is in this area that the public relations department can make an enormously important contribution, provided its members have convinced management that the public relations staff is competent to practice.

Even if the chief executive of a company is a lawyer, he still needs a legal department to look over his shoulder. This is not because he intends to violate the law, but because the law is so complicated that many times the chief executive does not know whether he is operating in violation of the law or not. It is the same with public relations, says Perry, for public opinion is subject to so many changes and does change on issues, often with great speed. To watch these changes, or the events which may bring them about, needs men who spend all their time thinking of public opinion, and studying public attitudes and those events which have an impact on them.

Perry also thinks one of the great strengths of the Du Pont Company and its public relations department is that they are located away from New York City. Wilmington may bring a little insularity, but it has meant building a cohesive organization where people know one another well so that they can have a good estimate of the strengths and weaknesses of the people with whom they are dealing. It also makes it easier for the public relations department to establish a better rapport with management. They see each other on the job and off the job. They know each other and what each can do, so there is no managerial curtain that prevents the staffers of the public relations department getting managers on the telephone or discussing their problems frankly.

Du Pont has first class relations with the press, and this has not been done by the use of mirrors. It is, says Perry, because "we work very hard on our press relations. Our philosophy is that we will always give out information on request, unless there is a good reason not to, rather than not to give out anything unless there is a good reason to do so. We have never 'run one' on the press. We never go to them unless we are convinced that we are giving them genuine news of importance. Since the company's executive committee has directed that all Du Pont communication with editorial media shall channel through us, we control this situation for the whole company."

The press in turn knows that Du Pont's public relations department will quickly find answers if they do not have them on tap when a newsman or magazine writer needs the facts under the stress of a deadline. Indeed, many magazine articles have been written around Du Pont and its management for the very reason that when there are a number of alternatives, other things being roughly equal, editors, knowing they can get intelligent and quick-moving cooperation, will choose Du Pont instead of some other corporation.

How Du Pont's public relations department works in its advice to management and its preparation of printed materials is clearly seen in the case when a plant has to be closed because of the obsolescence of its products and manufacturing processes. No management can afford to keep such a plant going for long after it reaches an uneconomic level, for the corporation is in business to make a profit. Since the plant, therefore, has to be closed, the problem then becomes one of assuring that the employees are given an opportunity to get jobs in some other Du Pont plant, or are helped to find work with another company. At the same time, because the community in which the dying plant is located will feel the loss of the industry keenly, serious efforts must be made to lessen the impact of closing the plant. Badly handled, the closing could become a public fiasco. With proper planning, many of the worst employee and community relations strains can be eased.

The Arlington works, at Kearny, New Jersey, began as an independent enterprise in 1886 and was acquired by Du Pont in 1915. By 1950 it was manufacturing cellulosic plastics for which the market was diminishing. Its processes were outmoded by modern chemical technology and the location of the plant was such that large, continuous process chemical equipment could not be installed. It was bounded on the east by the New Jersey marshes and on the west by residential areas, and a main city street bisected the plant.

At the end of World War II the Arlington plant employed 3,100 people. By June 5, 1957, the date the company's plans for closing the plant were announced, the number of workers had dwindled to 757. Of these, 551 were wage-roll employees, seventy-seven non-exempt employees, and 129 exempt employees. More than ninety-seven per cent of the work force had been with Du Pont for fifteen years or more. One hundred of the employees were women, and the wage-roll workers were represented by an independent, non-affiliated union. There were also sales problems involved, for customers had to be notified well in advance that the company was getting out of certain lines.

The decision to close Arlington, of course, had not been made on the spur of the moment. There had been extensive engineering and market studies. Management was certain that the plant's processes and products, its lack of suitability as a site for modern chemical manufacturing, and its unprofitable position made it imperative that it be closed. So the problem became one of the company's human relations and of the specifics of how to arrange for the termination, transfer, or retirement of Arlington's employees. This is where the staff member of the company's public relations department, Harold G. Brown, Jr.—now one of the public relations managers in the departmental services division—assigned to this plant as part of his responsibility, played an important part.

Planning began late in 1954, almost three years before the date of the announcement of closing. Involved were the plant manager, the industrial department of which his plant was a part, the executive committee of the company, and the public relations department. The advantages of early planning, and of having the public relations representatives intimately involved early in the planning for closing the plant were clear to management. Here it needed a specialist, not for generalities or the restatement of principles, but for actual knowledge of the people in the plant, the plant itself, and its management and policies. Since Brown had been the consultant for the industrial department of which this plant was a part, he knew the plant, its people, and the community. His advice was valuable on policy, and in setting out the procedures and timetables so that all would go smoothly.

Plans for the announcement of the closing of Arlington were well on their way when the decision to shut down was postponed while a new approach to termination benefits was worked out. Because so many at Arlington were long-service employees, the old termination programs were not good enough. Management was willing to continue to run Arlington, even on a marginal basis, until the proper answer was found.

During the planning period another basic decision had to be made. How far ahead of the actual closing of the plant should the employees be told? The arguments were that the announcement should be made in stages. Brown argued that as much notice as possible be given to the employees, with a full and complete statement of intentions of management. This would be the only fair thing, he insisted, and the employees deserved maximum advance warning for their own preparations. Brown's judgment was accepted. It was decided that the announcement of closing would come two years before the actual closing.

Early in 1957, when the general economic outlook for the next few years was good, the decision on what to do had been taken. Now it was a question of what to say and how to say it. Brown continued to work closely with the plant and the industrial departmental management. He drafted the speech to be given the employees by the plant manager, the letters to community leaders, the letters to be sent to the employees' homes, and a press release. He visited the plant several times during this period and, on June 5, the day of the announcement of the plant's closing, was in Arlington with his own special duties carefully outlined.

Prior to the announcement day, the schedule was carefully worked out. On Monday, June 3, at a luncheon held for all other North Jersey plant managers, Arlington's plant manager told them what was being done and gave them all the details. On the afternoon of Tuesday, June 4, the program to be announced the following day was reviewed with all the Arlington plant superintendents. Management representatives explained the reasons for the closedown to the president of the trade union, and visited the Mayor of Kearny and told him the plans. Salesmen saw key customers and told them of the closing.

On June 5, the announcement day, the timetable was as follows:

8:15 A.M. Management met with union officers and delegates. Department heads notified all exempt personnel.

8:30 A.M. Mail announcements, using the news release as a basis, were sent to five groups: independent laminators; area opinion leaders; key suppliers; block method customers; key industrial leaders.

9:00 A.M.   Department heads notified employees, with union delegates in attendance.

Supervisors notified their shift people by telephone. At the end of the employee meetings, each employee received a letter from the plant manager about the closedown, including a copy of the news release.

The New York sales office was notified by the sales department.

10:00 A.M. All plants and sales offices were notified by teletype from Wilmington.

The plant manager visited the Kearny Chamber of Commerce office and told the president and secretary.

11:00 A.M. News releases were hand-delivered to the *Kearny Observer*, the *Newark Evening News* and the *Newark Star-Ledger*.

12 NOON   Local Kiwanis Club and Rotary Club were notified at their luncheon meetings.

On Thursday, June 6, letters were mailed to all Arlington plant pensioners with the announcement of the plant closing.

On Monday, June 10, letters were sent to all North Jersey personnel groups, which included most major plants in the area, reporting the closing and the kind of personnel which would be available for hire.

The press reaction to the announcement was low key and informed. Here is an extract from Brown's report:

It had been decided to release the story to *Kearny Observer*, local weekly, and to Newark papers about 10:00 A.M. after the bulk of the employees had been notified. The plant manager called on *Newark News* and *Newark Star-Ledger*. Few questions were asked, and stories received only passing attention on business pages of both papers. Next day *Newark News* suburban section carried somewhat long article developed by reporter assigned to cover Arlington. *New York Times* picked this up and carried brief report based on this article. *Observer* carried a longer, but entirely objective story. The plant manager cooperated fully with newspapermen who called him.

Because the Arlington plant was unionized, careful, full, and frank discussion with the union officers was a critical part of the program, for it must be remembered that the intention was to close the plant two years after the announcement, and an unhappy or distressed union leadership could have made the following two-year period exceedingly difficult. How the union felt can be gauged from this excerpt from the employee relations superintendent's report:

> The union president summed up the feelings of the employees when he pledged to the plant manager that the union would continue the same cooperation and friendliness that have always marked the union-management relationship at Arlington. I'd like to elaborate a little on this. I am quite sure that all of you appreciate the fact that the union officers and delegates carry weight with the employees. How they immediately react to a proposition is extremely important. We wanted to get their support. Studying their faces as Hunter Lewis, plant manager, briefed them, you could see each was thinking of his own personal situation. This briefing was done with the utmost sincerity and solemnity. When Lewis completed it, [Norman] Doyle, the union president, took over.
>
> He went back to Mr. Diver, former manager, who established the foundation of good employee relations at Arlington which had been maintained to the present day by successive managers. He then instructed the delegates that there would be no change in management-union relations because of the closedown. The benefits, he pointed out, were generous and far better than in any plant he knew of. Everyone was to do his best to maintain the same relationship as in the past and do whatever he could to maintain morale. The delegates echoed his sentiments. Doyle, in his review of the closedown, showed his clear understanding of management's position. We cannot overestimate the effect his position has had on the present favorable employee relations situation.
>
> To sum it up, when good employee relations exist, they need not break down when adversity strikes. This is true so long as employees are treated as mature individuals and that their treatment in general is commensurate with that accorded them formerly. The sincerity with which management made its announcement was recognized.

As might be expected, even though fully briefed, the town was deeply distressed. The loss of the Du Pont plant was a serious blow to a city trying to provide a favorable climate for industry. The Mayor of Kearny appointed a committee to call on the plant manager to find out if the plant's closing could be avoided by some form of city aid. The manager and the committee toured the plant, talked for several hours, and the mayor's delegation was finally convinced that every factor had been considered by Du Pont before the decision to close was made and that no other course was possible.

Two years after the announcement of the closing of the plant, when the last Du Pont employees had left Arlington and the property had been sold to another industrial firm, the operating department's final report said that

> The mutual respect on the part of management and employees did not suffer or fail in this period of adversity. . . . the Du Pont Company withdrew from the community of Kearny enjoying the same respect and good will accorded it through many years of residency as a first-class corporate citizen . . . the employees were mature people who were relieved that the company had confirmed what they had long expected. They appreciated the fact that they had up to two years' notice to make their plans. . . . Next to the liberality of the benefits program, this act impressed them the most.

Severance pay; insurance adjustments for employees with fifteen years' seniority; the immediate setting up of an employment office which for more than two years worked closely with other firms in the area to find jobs for the Du Pont employees; the explanation of what the company was doing and why; all were an important part in closing the Arlington plant with the least injury to the community and the employees. Of the 757 employees at the time of the announcement of the closing, more than a hundred were transferred to other Du Pont plants; almost two hundred were pensioned; eighty were found jobs in other plants after taking their severance pay; others found jobs for themselves during the two-year period; none was left in need.

But this could not have happened had there not been long planning during which management had confidence in the advice of its public relations advisors, who in turn had the competence to do the job in a situation as delicate for the corporation as the closing of a plant. Du Pont's management, because of the ability shown by members of its public relations department in this instance and others, now call in their experts in this field early.

November 2, 1948, was a shock to more than newspaper editors and political commentators who were so certain that Thomas E. Dewey would be the new President. President Truman's re-election threw some managers of big business enterprises into a funk, for much of the Truman "give 'em hell" campaigning was directed against large corporations, and he fought the National Association of Manufacturers as much as he fought Dewey. In the Truman campaign oratory, bigness and badness were synonymous. Managers of large corporations had hoped that a Dewey victory would end their companies being made the whipping boys for all the world's ills. Du Pont's management was no exception.

Early in 1949 the executive committee asked the public relations department for recommendations to improve the company's public reputation. It was the first time the department had been asked to develop programs. In the past, ideas and suggestions had come up from the department to the executive committee. They had always been carefully considered. Some had been accepted, others rejected. But now, since the request had come from the top, Brayman and his department set out to develop a program to meet a problem which had concerned them for some time.

The lack of a rapport between business and the academicians had always been worrisome. The department's own feeling, confirmed by research, was that the general relationship between educators and businessmen was one of mutual distrust interlaced with active antagonism. Much of the academic community looked on big business as anti-social, predatory, and not in the least interested in the common good. In turn, managers of big business often thought of college teachers as wild-eyed theoreticians with no sense of balance, who, if they were not determined to destroy the economic system themselves, were sympathetic to those who were organized to do so.

To Du Pont's public relations department, what university teachers thought about business had a special meaning, far beyond the number of professors involved or any immediate effect they had. It was the long term that was important, because the public relations heads at Du Pont knew that what the intellectual thought today the general public would think tomorrow. Perry put it this way, in the Spring, 1962, issue of *The Business History Review*, published by Harvard University Graduate School of Business Administration:

> I want to emphasize that we are perfectly convinced in our own minds of the validity of our thesis about what the intellectuals think today being what the public thinks tomorrow. We make no special pretensions to erudition, yet our reading of history seems to us to make crystal clear that all of the great revolutionary movements have had their origins in the thinking of the intellectuals. They have not sprung into being through a sort of

parthenogenesis, feeding on public discontent until they have
burst into flame. Always behind them has been the force of
ideas, and the ideas have been formulated by the intellectuals,
the scholars.

This was so basic to the belief of the public relations department
that it felt that if industry could not solve the problem of antagonism
between business and the intellectual, in the long run it would not
matter very much whether the other problems were solved. Accordingly, it began an extensive program of discussions and interviews
before working out a program to meet the problem. In the course of
the study, it was found that the least favorable view of business was
held by the "younger instructors on the one hand, and by those whose
information had the largest content of theory and the smallest content
of actual practice on the other." The least favorable view of educators,
according to the study, was held generally by the "older executives
on the one hand, and by those whose information had the largest
content of actual practice and the smallest content of theory on the
other."

Du Pont also found that in the physical sciences relationships were
much closer with business than where the social disciplines were
involved. The reason for this, according to Perry, was that industry
often could see the advantages of consultation with the chemists,
physicists, agronomists, and metallurgists of the academic world, and
it "is a rather unusual physical scientist who doesn't have some sort
of consulting relationship with some company or some industry. There
is real understanding and mutual respect."

One of the conclusions of the Du Pont study was that while it was
by no means the whole story, one basic reason for the lack of understanding between business and the social scientist was a lack of
knowledge each had of the other and an almost total lack of communication between the two. It was essential, then, that a plan be
developed so that there could at least be some kind of dialogue which,
if it did nothing else, would get the two groups to know each other,
what they were like, and why they acted as they did.

It was out of this request by the company's executive committee
for the development of better relations with the public that the Du
Pont Educators Conference was conceived. It did much to develop
a better understanding between business and the universities, and
has had long-lasting benefits for the company itself, big business as
a whole, and the academicians. The manner in which Du Pont went
ahead to develop the Educators Conference, the ground rules for it,

and its content show the emphasis the company put on better relationships with those it thought crucial to the long-term functioning
of the economic system.

The first conference of educators and Du Pont's top management
was approved by the executive committee for the spring of 1950.
The ground rules, fundamental to the success of the whole project,
were drawn on this basis: if the academicians came to know the
management people, if they were given the freedom to probe into
the company's affairs to find out what it did, why it did it and who
benefited from the actions, the result could not help but be favorable.
The public relations department's view was that the company's story
was good enough to be questioned critically, and that if it were understood it would be believed. As for the management group, if it came
to know the educators through association, through answering questions, through argument, it would end up by respecting them. Accordingly, six ground rules were drawn for the conference.

The first was that there would be no fewer than forty nor more
than forty-four educators invited. These would represent institutions
of higher education from all sections of the country and of different
sizes. The thought here was that the group would be small enough
so that free discussion would not be inhibited and large enough for
top management to give the group a great deal of its time.

The second rule was that the educators would not be invited directly to come to the conference at Wilmington but the invitations
would go to the presidents of the colleges and universities who in
turn would decide who would attend. The reason for this method was
simply that Du Pont felt it lacked the criteria by which to make an
intelligent decision on those who should come.

The third rule was that the educators would be brought into close
contact with all the top management group of the company, not just
a few of them or those who were free at the time of the conference.
Included were all nine members of the executive committee and all
twenty-four department heads. No attempt was to be made to have
only the freshly scrubbed and more articulate "smoothies" of management. All top managers, the progressive as well as the conservative, would be present, so that there could not be the slightest hint
that skeletons were being kept in the closet.

The fourth rule was that all questions would be answered except
those involving competitive or product secrets. This was vital to prove
that there was no issue or company policy that would not bear examination. It was one of the most vital rules for the success of the
conference.

The fifth rule was closely interwoven with the others. Under no condition was the management group or anyone else on its behalf to do anything more than make the facts available to the educators. They could make up their minds on the merits of corporate actions. The public relations department was certain that any attempt to block embarrassing questions or refuse to answer them or to divert them would frustrate the whole purpose of the conference. And for the same reasons there could be no "selling" job done.

The last rule was that there would be no stipend to the guests. All expenses were paid, but nothing more. The reasoning here was that there be not the slightest cloud of hint that in any way would make these men feel that they would be beholden to the company, or that anyone observing the conference be given a reason for thinking that this was an attempt to "buy" the good will of those who came.

The conferences covered nine working days, beginning the third Monday in June and ending the second Thursday thereafter. At the formal sessions, a leading executive in the company would be the discussion leader with a panel of three or four or even five members of management. They ranged from the president of Du Pont, or a vice-president, to men well down the management ladder. They were chosen because of their specialized knowledge of the field under discussion. The subjects of the conferences included management function, sales, employee relations, production, research, finance, international trade, and the problems of bigness. When the Educators Conferences began, the chairman of the board of directors was Walter Carpenter. During his period in that office he always discussed the management function. Crawford Greenewalt as the Du Pont president always took the session on the problem of bigness by himself without the help of a panel. Copeland had a key role. The higher the rank of the managers, the greater was their responsibility in discussion with the educators. Two plants were visited, a modern textile fibers plant, such as the one at Seaford, Delaware, to study community relations, and one of the older plants, the Chamber Works in New Jersey, to watch employee relations in action. There was social activity to enable the two sides to get to know each other, ask questions, and get answers that are often franker in a completely informal atmosphere.

The program for the 1963 conference is typical of what went on at all of them. It ran from June 17 to June 27 inclusive. The program notes that "most sessions will consist of a brief talk by the discussion leader, followed by a question and answer period of about an hour and a half. The intention is to bring before the group, for each subject at hand, the best qualified company people."

After the Monday morning registration at the Du Pont Hotel in Wilmington, a talk on the development and structure of the company and lunch, Greenewalt, who was then chairman of the board of the company and chairman of the finance committee, led the discussion on "Management of a Modern Corporation." His talk dealt with the managerial function with particular emphasis on the principles that guide and motivate Du Pont. Company panelists were Pierre S. du Pont, vice-president; Henry E. Ford, secretary of the company and director of the secretary's department; William C. Kay, general manager, organic chemicals department; and Charles A. Rittenhouse, III, director, legal department. The educators asked questions for an hour and a half. After dinner on the first day, James Q. du Pont spoke on "History of the Du Pont Company with a Personal Slant."

On Tuesday morning, the theme was employee relations, with special emphasis on wage roll, bargaining practices, and union relationships. A vice-president, Charles B. McCoy, was the discussion leader, and his panel was made up of Russell C. Weigel, general manager, textile fibers department; Frederic A. C. Wardenburg, director, employee relations department; Philip J. Wingate, assistant general manager, elastomer chemicals department; and G. Gordon Mitchell, manager, industrial relations division, employee relations department. That afternoon, personnel was the subject, with special references to salaried personnel, general relationships, and planning. A vice-president, George E. Holbrook, was the discussion leader. The company's participants were: Walter H. Salzenberg, general manager, plastics department; Walter O. Simon, general manager, film department; Gordon O. Andrews, assistant director, employee relations department; and R. Carter Wellford, manager, organization planning division, employee relations department. After dinner the group left Wilmington for an overnight train ride to Danville, Virginia, to visit the Martinsville nylon plant. The subject at that plant on Wednesday morning was community relations, an examination of the impact of a major industrial unit on a typical American community. Here the discussion leader was W. Donald Hartford, the plant manager, with a panel of members of the plant staff. There was a tour of the plant, further discussion, a reception attended by the plant staff and community leaders, dinner, and then the return to Wilmington.

On Thursday morning the educators were taken to the Experimental Station, for a visit to the company's largest research facility and a discussion of Du Pont's research activities. The discussion leader was Paul L. Salzberg, director, central research department. Panelists were: vice-president, Robert L. Hershey; Winfield W. Heckert, assistant general director of technical divisions, textile fibers department; and Julian W. Hill, executive secretary of the committee on educational aid. There was a visit to laboratories in small groups, lunch, and then back to the hotel in Wilmington for a discussion of production. This was an outline of the company as a producing organization, including the development of its technology, tools, equipment, operating personnel. A vice-president, Samuel Lenher, led the discussion. The company participants were: John M. Clark, general manager, electrochemicals department; Bill H. Mackey, general manager, explosives department; William F. McGown, general director, manufacturing divisions, textile fibers department; and Frank H. Beadles, director of production, fabrics and finishes department. That evening the educators were guests for dinner at the Wilmington Club with the company's president, Lammot du Pont Copeland, as host.

On Friday, finance was the morning subject. The company's policies and practices in the fields of financial controls and procedures were discussed with two leaders: R. Russell Pippin, treasurer of the company, and H. Wallace Evans, first assistant treasurer. The panel was made up of Greenewalt, Crawley Davis, a vice-president and member of the company's finance committee, and Ira T. Ellis, the company's economist. That afternoon the theme was "Problems of Bigness," bigness in business and problems relating to the scale of a modern industrial enterprise. The discussion leader, who handled the entire session without a panel, was Copeland.

Saturday and Sunday were taken up with social activities including a trip to The Henry Francis du Pont Winterthur Museum and the Longwood Gardens, as well as a trip to Eleutherian Mills-Hagley Foundation which is devoted to the industrial history of Brandywine Valley and the Middle Atlantic states area.

The following week's program was structured in generally the same way, with the themes being sales; the company's policies in distributing its products; the company's international operations; employee relations, which included a visit to Du Pont's largest plant, the Chamber Works at Deepwater Point, New Jersey, to observe employee relations practices at first hand; and economic problems in the sixties. There was also an afternoon set aside for individual group sessions, which were arranged for small groups of educators with appropriate departmental staff on topics in which the guests might have a special interest.

The conference wound up with a general session led by Copeland, in which the educators were free to ask any questions that had not been dealt with.

These conferences ran for fourteen years, through 1963. They were worth while only if the quality of the educators who came to the conferences was high; if they asked questions which bothered them; and if the discussion leaders and the panelists were clear in their statements and frank in their answers. There was no lack of questioning. The questions were answered, not by attempting to convince the educators that the Du Pont way was the only way, but rather by stating the reasons for the company's policies, why they were taken, the context in which the corporate decisions were made, and the rationale behind the company actions. Du Pont's managers hoped that the educators would understand why they acted as they did, but at no time was the conference turned into a popularity contest with management's views and reasoning shaded to make the visitors happy. The best that could be expected by Du Pont was that there would be some two-way communication and that there would be a clear explanation of the thinking behind the courses taken by the company.

The results were better than the company had expected. From the first conference, and this happened at all fourteen, it did not take long for Du Pont's executives and the educators to establish contact. There was a perceptible difference in attitude, according to Perry, on the part of the educators between when they arrived and when they left, and it was found that the educators proved to have, in many cases, a knowledge of business that was almost wholly theoretical. It was also found that there were "surprising cases of misinformation or lack of information as to how a company really operates. The opportunity to observe an industrial corporation at work has been helpful and enlightening to quite a few of these people. We know because they've told us so."

There was, of course, no full success. By the very nature of the conferences there could not have been, and some of those who went to the conferences must have left with the feeling that their worst fears about big business were confirmed—but there were signs of few of these. In addition, it was very seldom that the universities sent faculty members for any purpose except to benefit from these sessions. Management itself found that in preparing for and answering the questions asked, their own views broadened, particularly when those who had little use for the college professors found they had no horns.

Since ten institutions were invited every year, forty-four institutions every other year (that is, twenty-two a year), and eight institutions every three or four years, there was a good cross-section during the conferences. In all, 590 educators from 143 colleges and universities, including some from France, Britain, and Mexico took part. They were largely from the social sciences. There were administrators, deans or department heads, full professors, associate professors, and, in some thirty cases, lecturers and instructors. None came for fun and games. Management treated the conferences as serious business. They were.

The colleges and universities from which the educators came ranged from the University of Alaska to Yale. The 1963 conference, for instance, included the University of Arizona, University of Arkansas, Boston University, Bowdoin College, the University of California at Los Angeles, Columbia, Cornell, Dartmouth, University of Detroit, University of Illinois, Indiana University, State University of Iowa, University of Kansas, Kenyon College, Massachusetts Institute of Technology, Michigan State University, Mount Holyoke College, New York University, University of Nebraska, Ohio State University, the University of Oklahoma, Nuffield College, Oxford, Princeton, Smith College, University of Rochester, University of Southern California, Southern Methodist University, Stanford, Tufts, and Wellesley. No area was missed. The big state universities and the Ivy League colleges were always well represented.

Paul A. Samuelson of MIT was there. So was Karl Kaysen of Harvard, who is now director of the Institute for Advanced Study at Princeton. George Stocking of Vanderbilt University and Walter Adams of Michigan State University also attended, in addition to men like Allan Nevins and Oskar Morgenstern. There were also many less well known to the general public but highly regarded by their peers. There was no attempt to work the star system. The small and the large, the rich and the poor, the women's colleges, and the church-directed; all were chosen so that the dialogue between Du Pont and the academic world had both meaning and effect.

The out-of-pocket expenses to Du Pont were slight, running about $25,000 a year for the conferences including travel expenses for the educators. No cost accountants were put to work to figure the cost to the company in time of its leading managers.

It was early in 1964 that the executive committee of Du Pont decided to end the Educators Conferences. The reasons were varied. They had been successful in the eyes of management. They had served more than a useful purpose. But the nation's thinking about big business had changed in those years. The attacks on business were fewer. Polls had shown that the public believed that industry was important to its welfare. Both the economic climate and the company's operations had changed. After fourteen years of what were essentially the same programs, there was some boredom. It was not on the part of the educators, for the same men did not return. The executive committee wanted a new approach. It still wanted to maintain contact with the academicians. Good relations with the colleges and universities were still essential for the same reasons that the conferences were started. But it was a time for change. This was in part due to some of the educators themselves, who believed that it was about time that they told a few things to management who would in turn ask questions.

A reassessment began by the public relations department. In 1964, no conference was held, but plans for a new type of idea exchange were being developed. In 1965 the old Educators Conferences changed into something quite different. Instead of one type of meeting it became three: lectures, seminars, and conferences. And as the years go by these, too, may well change. At present they are run very much along the lines of what was done in 1965.

In May of that year Samuelson of MIT lectured to 250 of the leading executives of the company on "Major Factors Affecting the Economy During the Next Five Years." In November, Dean William Haber of the University of Michigan spoke on "Developing Trends in Labor Relations." These were more than formal lectures with a question period following each. Each man was in Wilmington for a day and a half, meeting with small groups or in conference. He had lunch with the general managers of the twelve operating companies, and dinner with the executive committee, the chairman, and the honorary chairman of the board. At dinner, Samuelson and Haber were questioned on their opinions given during their lectures.

The seminar was held in October. Twelve academicians met with ten members of Du Pont's management for two and a half days of discussions. The theme was: "The Individual's Identity and Fulfillment in a Society of Large, Complex, Fast-Changing Institutions and Organizations." To encourage the freest possible discussion there was no audience. The visiting participants were: Frederick H. Harbison, Director, Industrial Relations Section, Princeton University; Charles V. Kidd, Federal Council for Science and Technology, Executive Office of the President; Avery Leiserson, Chairman, Department of Political Science, Vanderbilt University; Seymour M. Lipset, Center for International Affairs, Harvard University; Emmanuel G. Mesthene, Executive Director, Harvard University, Program on Technology and Society; James G. Miller, Director, Mental Health Research Institute, University of Michigan; David G. Moore, Dean, New York State School of Industrial and Labor Relations, Cornell University; Wilbert E. Moore, Russell Sage Foundation, Visiting Lecturer at Princeton University; Charles A. Myers, Professor of Economics and Management, Massachusetts Institute of Technology; Herbert R. Northrup, Professor and Chairman, Department of Industry, Wharton School, University of Pennsylvania; Arthur M. Ross, Commissioner of Labor Statistics, Department of Labor; and George P. Shultz, Dean, Graduate School of Business, University of Chicago.

The participants from Du Pont were: Clarence D. Bell, director, commercial resins division, plastics department; Norman A. Copeland, assistant chief engineer, engineering department; Edwin A. Gee, director, development department; Harlan L. Graham, general manager, photo products department; Robert L. Hershey, vice-president; George E. Holbrook, vice-president; William F. McGown, general director, manufacturing divisions, textile fibers department; G. Gordon Mitchell, director, employee relations department; Edward L. Rodowskas, manager, Newport plant, pigments department; and Herman E. Schroeder, director, research and development, elastomer chemicals department.

Under the general theme, subjects discussed were the effect of social changes on attitudes toward work; the average college graduate in the large organization; the top management reservoir—keeping it filled; and top talent—attracting, exciting, and rewarding it. In all these there was full and open argument between the twelve academicians and the ten Du Pont managers trying to get to the heart of the problems being examined. The participants rated these sessions highly with satisfaction on both sides. The academicians said that they found the meetings stimulating and would like to see them repeated.

The third part of the 1965 plan for relations with educators was an attempt to telescope the old Educators Conference into a single day at a single plant location. The conference was held in October at the Washington Works at Parkersburg, West Virginia. Key faculty members and administrators from four degree-granting institutions in the general area, Marietta College, Ohio University, Ohio Valley College, and the Parkersburg Branch of the University of West Virginia, were invited. The leading officials of the plant were the hosts and the discussions covered economic and other problems of running a plant in the region. Every attempt was made to make it a two-way, frank meeting. The educators did get a quick plant tour but this was done only to give the conferees one more basis of discussion. This third part was experimental and if others, which will be held at other locations in later years, prove as satisfactory to both sides, other plants will run these one-day sessions.

The academicians who gave the lectures and the social scientists who participated in the seminar were paid a fee in addition to their expenses. The faculty members who took part in the one-day session at the Parkersburg plant were only given their expenses, for the same reasons that those who attended the original Educators Conferences were not paid. Since the preparations for the lectures and seminars took the educators into a teaching or lecturing area, the public relations department recommended payments, which were negotiated with each educator.

The long, slow process of developing an understanding between Du Pont and educators at colleges and universities makes it clear that there is no such thing as a quick change of public opinion by the use of gimmicks or some kind of sleight of hand. Public opinion can on occasion be changed by events, like a war, the rise of fascism or communism, or a major depression. But to bring any change of a nation's thinking by use of some magic wand is utterly impossible, and the only ones who say it can be done are charlatans who trick management that is foolish in the ways of public attitudes. Good performance, intelligently explained with frankness and honesty, are what makes good relations with the public. This holds as true for truck drivers or elevator operators or hired hands on the farm or kindergarten teachers as it does for university professors or housewives. No one knows this better than the serious worker in the field of public relations.

 In the early days of the Du Pont empire there was no problem of stockholder relations, for the family was the company and the company was the family. Even as late as 1910 it was easy for the company to keep a close personal tie to its owners, for there were only 2,200 stockholders most of them directly involved with Du Pont. But as time went on, the number of stockholders grew until there are now some 260,000, all but 24,000 being individual holders. Among group stockholders are all kinds of organizations: churches, colleges, trusts and estates, investment funds, hospitals, banks, insurance companies. For this company with sales of more than $3 billion, the holders of common stocks have steadily increased while the number of preferred stockholders have decreased. Of the individual stockholders, men number slightly more than 100,000, women slightly less than that figure, while some 25,000 are joint accounts. Of 175,000 employees, 52,000 are stockholders. Stockholders live in sixty-nine countries, every state of the Union, and the District of Columbia.

Keeping relations good between the company and its stockholders is the direct responsibility of the secretary's department, although the treasurer's department and public relations are closely involved. It is the treasurer's department which prepares the single most important document, the annual report. Public relations works closely with the treasurer in this, with a public relations manager in the departmental services division, Tremain F. Robinson, as the contact between the treasurer's department and the public relations department. Public relations is also consulted by the secretary on general and specific questions that have public relations aspects. Answers to letters from stockholders (there are about 1,000 of them a week, every one of which, except those from cranks, is promptly answered) that demand more than ordinary treatment are often drafted by the public relations department, usually by Stephenson or Perry. The broad policy questions of communication with stockholders intimately involves public relations.

In addition to the annual report and quarterly statements the new stockholder gets a letter of welcome from Copeland and a copy of a basic booklet, *This Is Du Pont*, which outlines the history, structure, and operations of the company and is a sort of primer on Du Pont. Usually, once a year, the secretary will enclose with the quarterly report a reply card offering one of the publications that explains some aspect of the company's views of a public problem or describes a new product. These cards usually get responses from some 35,000 to 40,000 stockholders.

More than ninety per cent of Du Pont's production does not go to the ultimate consumer under the Du Pont name or in recognizable form. Nylon, for instance, is lost in the garment and Freon (fluorocarbon products) is lost in the refrigerator. So the stockholder as consumer is secondary to the stockholder as an owner. Therefore the publications sent to those who hold stock in the company are not sales tools.

The annual report is a good example of this. It is aimed at doing a specific job with a particular audience and so does not need a four-color brochure with pictures of products and plants. The target is the financial experts: bankers, brokers, securities analysts, market followers, businessmen generally. There is no intention to entertain or amuse, only to inform those who want to know for themselves the financial position of the company and the comparisons of performance with previous years. Perhaps seventy-five per cent, or even more, of the stockholders are interested only in dividends, stock splits, and growth possibilities. The others are laymen to whom the company is a good investment and these bother little with the figures that have special meaning to the expert.

The report itself is an odd size for an annual report, different from so many of those issued by other companies. It fits into a man's coat pocket without folding. The cover has remained unchanged over the years although the insides have been brightened with improved charts, clearer writing, a wider range of subjects, and better typography. The cover, as one man wrote to the company, "looks as if you could tear it off, take it to a bank, and cash it." The annual report is by no means a modern example of art or typography. Nor is it easy to file with other reports of other corporations, but the financial analysts generally like it, and so do the other professionals who have to seek information on which to base their investing judgment. It is hard information they want and the report gives it to them in the way they want it, with a minimum of nonsense thrown in. The annual report is very much like the company: practical, hard-headed, pragmatic, with little room for excitement or color. Profit is the purpose of this business and profit the annual report shows.

It may be that some time in the future the executive committee of the company will use the annual report and other mailings to the stockholders to reach the twenty-five per cent of those investors who know little of the economic system, how it works, and the issues which are vital to the survival of the company as a profit maker. Other companies try to develop the stockholder as a political force in the community but Du Pont has resisted using the annual report as a propaganda vehicle for the company's views. Management prefers to have it tell only the financial story of operations, with the theory that the best job it can do for the stockholder is to assure him that Du Pont is managed so that sales and profits continue to go ever higher. That alone is the justification for investing in the company and is the best advertisement for the economic system.

The concept of corporate philanthropy is relatively new. The idea that a corporation had any civic responsibility beyond that of running a profitable business was foreign to the early entrepreneurs in the United States and Europe. The industrial revolution, even though it brought with it all kinds of new problems, did not compel the business owners or managers to have any concern for their employees or their environment. Charitable contributions were entirely dependent on the good will of the individual industry owners. Du Pont was no exception, although from the time of his founding of the gunpowder business, Eleuthére Irénée du Pont was concerned with the well-being of his employees and their families. He did much more than was normally expected in providing for the better health, safety, comfort, and general welfare of those who worked for him. This philosophy carried through the years with those managers and partners who worked with and followed him. Their personal gifts would be considered charitable by present standards. Charity was believed to be a personal, not corporate, responsibility. In the case of the Du Pont Company, family-owned and -run as it was for so long, when it came to giving away money for good causes, the family members made their personal contributions.

Urbanization, industrialization, and population growth brought new sociological obligations. As the communities in which the employees worked and lived grew, so concern for employee welfare increased. The improvement of the total environment rather than the immediate surroundings became more and more a private and corporate responsibility and not alone that of the government or the worker. Slowly, financial help in meeting this problem began to be recognized as a responsibility of business and became a cost of doing business.

There was little development in corporate philanthropy until after World War I, and even then it came slowly. In the case of the Du Pont Company there was little in the way of corporate contributions, and, in 1929, contributions by the company totalled some $147,000. That dropped during the depression years as business slowed. In 1939 the total given by the company was only $189,000. But with the Red Cross drive and the old United War Fund leading the way during the war years, the company began to increase its contributions, and from 1943 the advance became substantial, until in 1945 it reached $1,500,000. It tapered off until the Korean war and since 1954 there has been a steady rise. It is now about $4 million annually.

Du Pont does not contribute through a company-sponsored foundation. Its gifts are not significantly related to the profits of the company year by year. At present about fifty per cent of the corporate gifts go to educational aid; about twenty per cent to hospitals, health and welfare; thirteen per cent to united and community funds; and the rest to other causes. None of this is haphazard. All the giving is organized with carefully developed procedures. There is no contribution to any causes on whim or because of pressure of friends of the directors or executive committee members. Personal desires to aid particular good causes are left to personal contributors.

It is essential that there be some organized system for corporate gifts, because the company has plants in more than one hundred communities and thousands of requests for money are received each year. Some two thousand organizations are helped every year, and memberships are paid for in more than five hundred organizations. Land is given for a park; laboratory equipment is given to schools and colleges; x-ray film is given to hospital ships on medical missionary service; health and welfare groups are aided, as are some 125 community funds and a score of hospitals each year. No sectarian organizations are helped; no gifts are given to national health bodies such as the American Cancer Society, the Heart Fund or March of Dimes or others in this general field. Always in mind is the fact that this is stockholders' money and despite the Smith Manufacturing case which permitted corporate funds to be given to education without restriction as to use, Du Pont operates as if the case had never been decided and all aid is directly related to the corporation's operations.

Generally, Du Pont's contributions fall into two categories, educational and non-educational, and each has its own committee. The Committee on Contributions and Memberships has four members plus a full-time secretary. These are: the assistant to the president of the company, William G. Weisbrod, who is chairman; the corporate secretary, Henry T. Bush; the director of employee relations, G. Gordon Mitchell; and the assistant director of public relations, Stephenson. The Committee on Educational Aid consists of the director of central research, Paul Salzburg, chairman; the assistant director of employee relations, Irénée du Pont, Jr.; and the technical director for the engineering department, Vincent W. Nacdrich. The assistant to the president of the company and a member of the public relations department sit with this committee in liaison or advisory capacities. This committee has a full-time executive secretary and a staff of one assistant and a secretary.

The contributions, other than those in the educational field, are decentralized, with a delegation of authority similar to operations in other areas. In general each of the twelve operating departments functions independently of the others and the general managers have a good deal of freedom of decision as to how much and to whom they may give, within limits as to amounts, and with the interests of the community and over-all public relations considerations. Of course, when giving involves the broad interests of the company it goes to the Committee on Contributions and Memberships. This committee makes no contributions itself but recommends action to the president if the amount is less than $20,000 and to the executive committee if it is more than $20,000. If it goes over $50,000 the finance committee must approve it as well.

The program of annual gifts to educational institutions goes back to 1918. In these cases, the Committee on Educational Aid, working largely on the college/university level, recommends to top management its annual support program. These programs are publicly announced each year. As good an example as any was the announcement in 1966 of grants totaling nearly $2,200,000 to 213 colleges and universities. The major part of this was for strengthening the teaching of science and engineering, particularly at the undergraduate level. The grants for teaching came to $887,000 and were in the form of grants to colleges and universities for the improvement of undergraduate teaching; postgraduate teaching assistantships to encourage the best qualified graduate students to teach undergraduates; and summer scholarships for prospective high school teachers of science and mathematics. An additional $167,200 went for younger staff teachers at universities to develop their own scholarly development during the summer months.

Grants totaling $505,000 went to forty-four universities for fundamental research in science and engineering. Here the purpose was to improve the training of graduate students, and to build up scientific knowledge by helping the institutions strengthen their basic research. In addition, capital grants of $500,000 went to twenty-two privately directed institutions to help finance new buildings, equip new space, or renovate existing facilities for teaching and research in science and engineering.

A new development in Du Pont's aid to education came in 1966 in fellowships for business schools. These, amounting to $4,000 each, are given to Master of Business Administration candidates whose majors in their undergraduate work were in physical science or engineering. This new program highlights the entire thinking of Du Pont in its aid to education, since the grants go to develop technically trained students who have graduate training in business, now in short supply, and cover eight universities: Columbia, Cornell, Harvard, Chicago, Delaware, the University of Michigan, the University of Pennsylvania, and the University of Virginia. The same holds true of the 1966 capital grants. Twenty-two institutions received grants, which ranged from $15,000 to $50,000, for buildings for physics, chemistry, science, and engineering education, the fields of Du Pont's direct involvement as a company. Not a single capital grant went for buildings used for the humanities. In all its history

Du Pont management has never taken its eyes off its main target of acting always in the direct interest of the company's field of operation.

Du Pont's annual report to stockholders for 1965 carried a short item announcing that the final distribution of about twenty-three million shares of General Motors common stock to Du Pont common stockholders had completed the divestiture of the investment in compliance with the final judgment in the Du Pont-General Motors antitrust case. Three distributions had been made in all, in which sixty-three million shares of General Motors common stock with an aggregate value of $4.5 billion had been disposed of.

Behind that notice in the annual report was a history of thirteen years of litigation; special relief legislation by Congress; and a public relations program designed to create understanding of the Du Pont Company in the country at large. Without such a program the company might have suffered tremendous losses that could have inflicted a wound of major proportions. The whole series of events began during the Truman administration, went through the eight Eisenhower years, involved President Kennedy, and was only concluded in the third year of the Johnson administration. They strongly influenced everything that was done by the public relations department and deeply colored the thinking of the entire corporation.

Du Pont's interest in General Motors began after World War I. Three factors impelled Du Pont into automotive manufacturing: the need to invest the heavy profits the company had made during the war; the abundance of first-rate managers who were surplus since the demand for explosives had dropped to almost zero; the acute business sense of John J. Raskob, who had started as Pierre du Pont's secretary and by this time had risen to be a vice-president of the company. It was Raskob who persuaded Pierre, Lammot, and Irénée du Pont that it would be a sound investment for the company to buy into General Motors. It was an excellent decision made, however, at a time when many wise bankers believed that the automotive business, if not a fly-by-night business, was a wild and woolly one. Financiers had little respect for it since it was shot through with promoters whose business sense and organizing talent were far less than their ability to turn a fast corner. On December 21, 1917, Du Pont's executive and finance committees authorized the company's first investment in General Motors. By the fall of 1919 Du Pont had bought shares of General Motors and Chevrolet, later exchanged for General Motors shares, equivalent to about twenty-nine per cent of General Motors' stock outstanding at a cost of approximately $49,000,-

000. In 1920, Du Pont bought some more stock from William C. Durant, the founder and chief stockholder of General Motors, bringing Du Pont's holdings to the equivalent of about 7,500,000 shares.

In 1923, Du Pont sold the equivalent of about 2,250,000 shares of General Motors stock to Managers Securities, the corporation organized by General Motors to provide additional incentive to the principal executives of General Motors. This was just about the amount bought in 1920 from Durant. It brought Du Pont's holdings to the equivalent of about 5,250,000 shares. In 1924 these shares were exchanged at the rate of four for one of new stock in General Motors. The total held by Du Pont at the end of the year was about 1,330,800 shares.

A fifty per cent stock dividend in 1926, an exchange of two new shares for each old share in 1927, and an exchange of two and a half new shares for each old share in 1929, brought Du Pont's total holdings to about 9,981,200 shares. In 1931, Du Pont bought 300,-000 shares of General Motors for cash. In 1933, it sold 81,200 shares. In 1935, Du Pont bought 950 shares for cash and distributed 200,950 shares as a dividend to Du Pont stockholders. This left Du Pont with a total of 10,000,000 shares, or about twenty-three per cent of the outstanding common stock of General Motors.

In 1950, there was a two-for-one stock split, which brought the total to 20,000,000 shares. In 1955 Du Pont exercised options offered to all shareholders of General Motors to purchase new stock, buying one million new shares. A three-for-one stock split in the same year brought Du Pont's total holdings to 63,000,000 shares, still equivalent to about twenty-three per cent of the outstanding common stock.

In 1927 the Federal Trade Commission and the Department of Justice made studies of Du Pont's investment in General Motors but no action was taken. It was not until June 30, 1949 that a complaint was filed by the Antitrust Division of the U.S. Department of Justice. It was a civil action, brought under sections 1 and 2 of the Sherman Act and section 7 of the Clayton Act. The complaint named as defendants and conspirators the Du Pont Company, General Motors Corporation, United States Rubber Company, Christiana Securities Company, Delaware Realty and Investment Company and 184 individual "members of the Du Pont family," including minor children ranging in age down to eight months. The complaint described "members of the Du Pont family" as being the lineal descendants of the original Pierre Samuel du Pont de Nemours, and the wives and husbands of these descendants. The complaint charged that stock ownership had been used to obtain and perpetuate common control of Du Pont, General Motors, and U.S. Rubber, with the effect of dividing fields of activity among the companies and requiring the companies to buy goods from one another.

Naturally, since the Antitrust Division of the Justice Department had done a great deal of probing, the filing of the suit was no surprise to Du Pont. It was clear to the public relations department, as it became clear to the management of the company, that because of the magnitude of the suit the case had to be won in two places: in the law courts and in the court of public opinion. It was obvious to the company that if the case were lost with the public it would be that much more difficult to win it in the courts. The internal lawyers and outside counsel representing Du Pont agreed with the public relations department.

The Justice Department's five-page press release announcing the filing of the suit in the Federal Court at Chicago stated that the relief sought included the sale by Du Pont of all its stock in General Motors. The press release also carried the following paragraph: "In commenting on the suit the Attorney General said: 'This case is directed to the breaking up of the largest single concentration of industrial power in the United States.'" To Du Pont, that looked like an admission by the government that the suit was filed because of bigness rather than because of any actions in violation of the law. It was on this ground that the public relations department decided to take its stand with the public. In little more than an hour after Attorney General Clark's statement, Du Pont took issue. The company's answer was phoned to all the principal news bureaus in Washington that might be writing the story, and was carried in the same stories that announced the filing of the suit. Du Pont's preparation enabled the papers to carry the defense at the same time as the charge.

It was no time for silence by Du Pont. On July 11, 1949, Greenewalt sent a letter to his stockholders stating the company's position. This served a double purpose: it gave management's story to the stockholders and at the same time it was the basis for the story carried by the newspapers, and so informed the public. In November of the same year Greenewalt was invited to testify before the Special Committee of the House Judiciary Committee on the Study of Monopoly Power. Long and careful preparation was made before Greenewalt's appearance and he handled himself well both in the original testimony and the long questioning. The committee, which might well have been hostile, was favorably impressed. The public relations department then circulated the Greenewalt testimony widely, sending out some 3,000 copies, mimeographed, to all important newspapers and editorial writers across the country. The result was many friendly editorials.

The next important development was with *Fortune* magazine. The magazine, which in the pre-World War II years had taken hard pokes at the company, asked for cooperation in doing a major study of Du Pont. *Fortune* had been flatly turned down in 1947 when it asked to do a definitive study of the company. The first reaction of management this time, as in 1947 because of the earlier *Fortune* articles, was to say no. But the public relations department's views were accepted. Not only would there be cooperation, but everything would be thrown open to *Fortune*'s investigation. An office was set aside at Du Pont for the *Fortune* researchers and writers, and all managers were instructed to answer fully all queries. *Fortune*'s team, which varied in size from two to eleven people who worked for a period of six months, was welcomed. When the story was published in October, 1950, most of the issue was devoted to Du Pont. It was highly favorable, with six major articles, under the general heading of "The World of Du Pont." They were Prologue; The Top Level; Markets: How They Are Opened; The Look of Du Pont; Orlon: Case History of a New Fiber; How to Win at Research. The *Fortune* issue carried the first pictures ever taken of Du Pont's board in session; gave details of the men who ran the company; and was heavy with color photographs. In all, the story treatment was laudatory and in the Lawrence P. Lessing introduction to the portfolio of articles this appeared:

> One of the great phenomena of the American industrial revolution, even to those most distrustful of or mystified by its power, is E. I. du Pont de Nemours & Co., founded in 1802. In present size and power, indeed, it is a new phenomenon, not yet clearly defined or accounted for by the old or new economics. Du Pont is Big Business. It is one of that handful of great corporate growths—neither monopoly nor the pure competitive ideal of nineteenth century liberalism—that find themselves in uneasy conflict with the cross currents of the age. Since Du Pont is also the leading company in the premier industry of the mid-twentieth century—the chemical industry—its bigness takes on symbolic proportions.
>
> That such bigness meets some vital need of the people and the times is bluntly and brutally proved in war. If such great aggregations as Du Pont did not exist, it is not too much of an

exaggeration to say that the military would have had to invent them as prime contractors in the country's defense. And maybe the improvisations would have been too clumsy and too late. When the huge, complex Hanford plutonium works had to be created in a hurry for the last war's atomic-bomb program, only a company of the size and skill of Du Pont could have rushed it through from design to production. When the stepped-up program for the new hydrogen bomb called for another tremendous plant last July, it was again Du Pont that was called in. Yet it is typical of the disjointedness of the times that even while Du Pont was being enlisted in that greatest of all projects to prevent the next war, or failing that, to win it, Du Pont was in the midst of a heavy antitrust attack from another branch of government seeking to penalize it for bigness.

Neither Du Pont nor any other intelligent Big Business, however, can pin its justification on war. Those companies that are opportunistically attempting to do so are tragically mistaken. Du Pont's contributions to peace have been more considerable than any of its contributions to war, and its bigness resides inherently in the greatness of the country and the technology it serves. It took on the H-bomb assignment with much the same provisos it exercised on the Hanford project: that it receive a fee of $1, the government paying all costs; that all the patents from its work become the property of the U.S.; and that it be permitted to withdraw at the end of the emergency, as it did from Hanford. Du Pont feels that its proper sphere is chemistry, not physics, and its greatest growth and earnings have come and will continue to come from peacetime sources.

The *Fortune* issue was important to the company, for here was *Fortune* praising Du Pont, not Du Pont patting itself on the back. The public relations department bought 1,500 copies of the issue and circulated them to newspaper and magazine editors. This one article probably did the company more good with the media of communication, and accordingly the public, than any other single development.

Before the opening of the trial not much took place that had a dramatic impact. But following the *Fortune* study of the company, other magazines and newspapers asked for information from the public relations department, and in every case fullest help was given. *Newsweek* had already done a cover story with Greenewalt's picture on the cover and the theme "Is It Bad To Be Big?" on May 2, 1949.

On April 16, 1951, *Time* carried a cover story, also with Greenewalt the focus, which stressed Du Pont's public service.

While these publications had a general public impact, Du Pont's public relations department used the period before the trial to recommend to its top management that a few speeches be made, and that the spots where they be made be carefully chosen to have the greatest effect on opinion formers. One of these came as a result of an invitation to Greenewalt from the National Press Club for September 29, 1949. Often at periods of this kind management will shy away from public speeches and the company lawyers are usually the first to shout No! Instead, the invitation was quickly taken up, and this helped a great deal in establishing the Du Pont case to a very important sector of Washington correspondents. This, to Brayman and his staff, was of greater importance than the space in the newspapers and the time on radio news broadcasts given to what the president of the company said. Another speech, this one made by Harold Haskell, who was general counsel of the company, shows the public relations department's thinking on speech making.

The Haskell speech was made in his home town of Rockland, Maine. He was one of the town's most distinguished sons. The forum was the Rotary Club with fifty members. It was made during Haskell's vacation time, in August, 1949. It was a careful statement of the Du Pont case. The spot treatment of the speech by the news media and the fact that the audience was small did not bother Brayman and his men. What was important was that the location was right. The speech was then distributed to every newspaper editor in the country in its entirety, for news reports always tend to be sketchy. Here was the whole story delivered to those who help form public opinion. The reading of the speech in editorial offices and the effect it had on the editors' thinking was by far more important than the news stories which came on the delivery of the speech, or the size of the immediate audience. It turned out to be one of the more successful speeches made before the trial began.

Another speech of importance at the time was made by Copeland, then secretary of the company. It was on the relations between big and small business and it was made because there was a government attempt at the time to stir up the small businessman against the big companies. It too was distributed to the opinion formers who then commented on it, from the text, rather than from the spot news reports.

When the Department of Justice filed the suit on June 30, 1949, the complaint included as class defendants "wives, husbands, children, grandchildren, of the individual defendants Pierre, Lammot and Irénée."

Reading this, Perry turned to his boss, and said: "Harold, if we could only figure out a way to get a picture of a baby into the papers as a defendant, we'd really have some fun."

It took a while, but the break came on March 5, 1952, when the government, in an amended complaint, specifically named 183 members of the Du Pont family, in addition to the three brothers, as class defendants. The public relations department was asked to prepare a brief comment on the government's action, for immediate release. Perry turned to his typewriter and quickly wrote two short paragraphs.

"Think we can get somebody to stand for this?" he asked.

Brayman read it, grinned, answered, "We'll sure try." He began the clearing process. And so it was that, for the afternoon papers of the same day, Lammot du Pont, speaking for the family, issued a statement to the press in which he pointed out that of those named ninety-six were minors, about two-thirds of them fourteen or younger and that the youngest of them was "a hardened conspirator of eight months, she having been born last July, two years after the suit was filed."

Brayman and Perry knew what would happen now. They didn't have to wait long. Hardly had the wire services cleared the statement when telephones began to ring in the public relations department, demanding a picture and identification of the "hardened conspirator." The news services, newspapers, news magazines, *Life*, all began to clamor for the picture. There was of course a problem. The family tradition, as it is with all families of immense and old wealth, was to protect the children from publicity of any kind, with the danger of kidnapping as an important factor in these decisions. But the needs of the issue were greater than family fear and reluctance. The public relations department won its point and photographs of Alletta du Pont Bredin, in her playpen, accused of conspiracy to violate the antitrust laws since 1915, were spread over the nation's papers. Hardly a daily newspaper in the country failed to carry the picture, almost always on page one. Some were published in three, four and five columns. The press analysis submitted to management, made by the public relations department and dated April 14, 1952, told the story:

> Newspapers in every state of the Union and in practically every American city used a picture of Alletta du Pont Bredin, "the hardened conspirator of eight months." They used it with

captions that caused readers to wonder what the Department of Justice, already under fire, was up to now. Clippings are still arriving at a heavy rate, and at the time this analysis went to press, 376 had been received. The ultimate number will be larger, and since it is estimated that clipping bureaus catch only one-third of any given story or photograph, it seems reasonable to say that the picture appeared in more than 1,200 American newspapers.

This was the highlight of the large press play touched off when the Antitrust Division attempted to add 183 members of the du Pont family to the three members already being sued in the General Motors case. With only two exceptions, all of it was critical of the Department of Justice and favorable to Du Pont. Some was in humorous vein and some was serious, but there was little comfort for the government in either category. What is more to the point is that the absurdity of the government suing a child of eight months as an antitrust violator has been impressed upon the American people. And it will influence their reaction toward this case as long as it lasts.

To Brayman, "an impression was created in the minds of millions of people which won the case for us with the public—if we could keep it won when the case came to trial."

The case came to trial November 18, 1952, in Chicago in the District Court of the United States for the Northern District of Illinois, Eastern Division. It was before Judge Walter J. LaBuy sitting without a jury. During the trial the government dropped the charges against all individual defendants except seven who were charged with participation in the alleged unlawful conspiracy and twenty-six others who were retained as "beneficiary defendants" because of their interest in the United States Rubber stock. Presentation of evidence was completed on June 29, 1953, after ninety-one court days, and the final briefs were filed on February 26, 1954. Du Pont's defense was that each of the three manufacturing corporations purchased from the others only such products, and in only such quantities, as each considered appropriate to the efficient conduct of its own business; that the full history of dealings among the three corporations showed neither restraint of trade nor monopolization, but free and open competition. No witness was produced by the government to testify that he had been excluded from General Motors' markets or that he had been injured in any way by Du Pont's investment in General Motors.

Long before the case came to trial the public relations department recognized that this would be probably the most extensively covered non-murder trial of the period. Since the press coverage was vital to the public's attitude toward Du Pont, it was decided that a staff member would be placed in charge in Chicago and that it would be his full-time job for the trial's duration. The choice was Robert E. Curtin, Jr., an executive assistant who knew the company thoroughly and who had proved himself first rate in working with the press. A University of Delaware graduate, he was on the editorial staff of the *Wilmington Morning News* for ten years and had acted as Delaware correspondent for *The New York Times*, the *Cincinnati Enquirer*, and *Variety*. In 1940, he was hired as a member of Du Pont's public relations department, and four years later was appointed manager of the information division. He became executive assistant in October, 1949. He was forty-two when he was assigned to work with the press in Chicago.

Six months before the trial started he moved to Chicago from Wilmington. He set out from the start to know the media men in Chicago, the correspondents for out-of-Chicago newspapers, the wire service reporters and writers and the locally based magazine men. His job had two aspects: to serve the newspapermen covering the trial by providing them with documents, and access to company executives, the company's counsel, and the witnesses; and to advise the lawyers on the problems in which public reaction was involved.

Brayman or Perry, and often both of them, were present a great deal of the time at the trial. Irénée and Pierre du Pont, Greenewalt, and Walter Carpenter, as well as other important witnesses, were persuaded to be present constantly during the early days of the trial even though they would not be called to the witness stand until months later in some cases. They were readily accessible to newspapermen covering the trial, from a dozen to twenty of whom were in the courtroom throughout the entire period. The result was a great deal of good copy. The presence of Pierre and Irénée du Pont for interviews and pictures was particularly important, for they had rarely been available earlier. Almost without exception, the stories, pictures, and comments depicted the company's top executives as very human people and helped win public support.

During the whole trial, all briefs and statements were made quickly available to the working press and Curtin made himself so genuinely useful and helpful to them that a great many of them developed a high respect for Du Pont. Nor was Curtin only willing to assist the press with Du Pont material. He even provided, for those who needed them, copies of the government complaints and briefs when these could not be readily obtained directly.

On December 3, 1954, Judge LaBuy ruled that the government complaint should be dismissed. In the course of his judgment he said:

> When read as a whole the record supports a finding, and the Court so finds, that there has not been, nor is there at present, a conspiracy to restrain or to monopolize trade and no limitation or restraint upon General Motors' freedom to deal freely and fully with competitors of Du Pont and United States Rubber, no limitation or restraint upon the freedom of General Motors to deal with its chemical discoveries, no restraint or monopolization of the trade and commerce between Du Pont and United States Rubber.
>
> It may be that a violation of the Clayton Act can be made out in the absence of an actual restraint of trade where it is established that there is a reasonable probability that a condemned restraint will result from acquisition of stock. The acquisition challenged by the Government—Du Pont's investment in General Motors—took place over thirty years ago. In those many intervening years the record discloses that no restraint of trade has resulted. Accordingly, the Court is of the opinion that there is not, nor has there been, any basis for a finding that there is or has been any reasonable probability of such a restraint within the meaning of the Clayton Act.
>
> The Government has failed to prove conspiracy, monopolization, a restraint of trade, or any reasonable probability of a restraint, and for those reasons the Amended Complaint should be dismissed.

Brayman *et al.* were ready for the decision. Elaborate preparations had been made to make it available to all the media. Arrangements were made with the clerk of the court to have several hundred additional copies printed at Du Pont's expense and delivered to the Du Pont public relations representatives simultaneously with Judge La-Buy's delivery of copies of his decision to the newsmen in Chicago. These texts were distributed widely to newspapers as quickly as it was physically possible. Members of the public relations department carried them by hand to New York, Philadelphia, and Washington to provide speedy service. An objective summary of the opinion was also sent to all newspapers that had shown any interest in the case. This summary went to both news editors and editorial writers. All possible requests for texts from media were supplied.

Also remembered were the employees of Du Pont. Greenewalt's statement went to all of them, emphasizing Judge LaBuy's findings.

Newspaper editorial approbation was widespread for the LaBuy decision.

On February 4, 1955, the Justice Department filed notice of appeal to the Supreme Court of the United States. In its appeal, the Justice Department abandoned all parts of the case except that which applied to the relationships between Du Pont and General Motors, accepting the District Court's dismissal as it applied to all individuals and relationships with United States Rubber.

The appeal was argued before the Supreme Court on November 15, 1956. The government did not challenge the District Court's findings that there had been no conspiracy or agreement between Du Pont and General Motors relating to trade between the two companies. It contended, rather, that Du Pont's stock relationships with General Motors constituted a "combination" which exerted an influence whereby some purchases by General Motors were channeled to Du Pont.

Du Pont contended that the record amply supported the District Court's findings that Du Pont did not control General Motors; that General Motors made its own purchasing decisions and bought from Du Pont and others on the basis of quality, service, and price; and that the General Motors divisions did not buy from Du Pont when they did not want to and had good business reasons for buying when they did.

On June 3, 1957, the Supreme Court, by a vote of four to two, reversed the District Court's dismissal of the complaint, and remanded the case to the District Court "for a determination after further hearing of the equitable relief necessary and appropriate in the public interest."

The Supreme Court found that "all concerned in high executive posts in both companies acted honorably and fairly, each in the honest convictions that his actions were in the best interests of his own company and without any design to overreach anyone, including Du Pont's competitors." Nevertheless, the court, bypassing the Sherman Act question, ruled that Section 7 of the Clayton Act had been violated because Du Pont's acquisition and ownership of twenty-three per cent of the outstanding common stock of General Motors was sufficient to create a "reasonable probability" that Du Pont would receive a preference in supplying General Motors' requirements for automotive fabrics and finishes.

Justice Burton, in his dissent, pointed out that, to reach its decision, the four-judge majority "disregards the language and purpose of the statute, forty years of administrative practice, and all the precedents except one District Court decision" and that "to make its case the Court requires no showing of any misuse of a stock interest—either at the time of acquisition or subsequently—to gain preferential treatment from the acquired corporation."

The majority opinion was read by Justice Brennan, with Chief Justice Warren and Justices Black and Douglas concurring. Justice Frankfurter joined in Justice Burton's dissent. Justices Clark, Harlan and Whittaker took no part in the decision. Justice Clark had been Attorney General at the time the suit was filed, Justice Harlan had been chief defense attorney for Du Pont in the original trial suit in Chicago and Justice Whittaker was not appointed to the Court until after the appeal had been argued.

On October 25, 1957, the Department of Justice filed with the District Court its proposed final judgment which would require divestiture of Du Pont's General Motors stock by sale or distribution to stockholders.

On November 21, 1957, Judge LaBuy directed the parties to obtain a ruling from the Commissioner of Internal Revenue as to tax consequences of the Department of Justice proposal.

On May 9, 1958, the Commissioner of Internal Revenue ruled that distributions of stock under the government proposal would be taxable to recipients as ordinary income. On February 16, 1959, hearings began before Judge LaBuy on the question of appropriate relief and went on until April 9. On October 2, 1959, Judge LaBuy handed down his opinion that stock divestiture would be "unnecessarily harsh and punitive," and on November 17 he entered his final judgment. Then the Supreme Court of the United States heard the arguments on appeal on February 20 and 21, 1961. On May 22, 1961, by a vote of four to three, it ruled that there must be complete divestiture of Du Pont's 63,000,000 shares of General Motors stock.

It was here that Du Pont decided it was necessary to seek legislation permitting distribution of these shares without the heavy tax burden on its individual shareholders that would have been applied under the existing tax law, which was that the distribution would be treated as a dividend to the full market value of the General Motors shares and so would be taxable to all recipients as current income on top of the regular income tax rates. The relief Du Pont sought was to have the market value of the General Motors shares treated as a return of capital to individual stockholders.

Then came the problems of working with Congress. A new team operation was set up. Greenewalt was to lead and with him was the head of the legal department of the company, two of his associates, and four members of the public relations department. The job of getting a relief bill through Congress was staggering.

There was first of all the problem of inertia—535 members of two houses of Congress had to be persuaded that the bill was necessary, was fair, that it was not a special privilege for somebody that would boomerang against the legislators in the next election campaign, and that they ought to get busy and put it ahead of other things and pass it.

Secondly, the bill was bound to be known as the "Du Pont bill" although in the first instance Du Pont tried to make it general legislation applicable to all cases. Nevertheless, it was the only one pending and it was a spectacular one.

Thirdly, in spite of everything Du Pont could do, it might even be known as the "Du Pont tax relief bill." The effect of this kind of description of a bill on the average voter and the average congressman was bound to be: "Tax relief for the du Ponts? We need it more than they do."

The fourth problem was the competition of other, and what was considered by many more urgent, legislation.

Having made the big decision to ask Congress for tax relief, other decisions had to be made. The major one was that Du Pont executives would do the job of talking to legislators themselves. This meant that Greenewalt would have to carry the big burden and that he would have to talk to all the key people in Congress. He did.

He talked first with all the top leaders of both parties in both houses, with practically every member of the Ways and Means Committee of the House, with every member of the Senate Finance Committee, and a large number of other key people. Some he saw two, three, and even four times.

Greenewalt was welcomed. His personal discussions with them were a basic factor in the success of the legislation. In all he saw some eighty legislators in their offices, telling Du Pont's story and making its case. This was unusual, for the heads of large corporations generally hire expensive Washington lawyers as lobbyists and never go near a legislator themselves.

How effective this direct, personal approach by Greenewalt was is made clear by the story the present Speaker of the House of Representatives, John McCormack, told a friend of his at the United States Chamber of Commerce. Here is what he said: "You know, I had an interesting thing happen to me today. The president of the Du Pont Company called on me. I don't remember his name. Greenewalt? Yes, that's right. Anyhow he sat down with me and told me his

story. And he convinced me that the Du Pont Company is entitled
to relief. I'm on my way right now to tell Wilbur Mills of Ways
and Means that he and his committee have got to do something for
Du Pont.

"You know, in all my time here in Washington, this is the *first
time* the head of a big company came down here personally to talk
to me about his problem. Mostly they send lobbyists or lawyers."

When Greenewalt was told this story early in the campaign to get
the bill through Congress, any lingering doubts that he had taken
the right course were completely wiped out. This chief executive-to-
legislator approach with all members of the Ways and Means Committee occurred prior to the hearings, so when the hearings did start
the members were familiar with the legislation.

The big push for the legislation came in the 87th Congress, which
met in January, 1961, and continued through its two sessions until
its adjournment in 1962. The first problem here was a major one. It
was simply to get the attention of the Ways and Means Committee
focused on this legislation. By the time the committee began to consider its order of procedure on legislation, there were 108 tax bills
pending before it, including the Du Pont bill. Most of them had
backers pushing for prompt action and several of them were important administration bills with the power of the White House and
the newly elected President Kennedy behind them. But as it turned
out, the Du Pont bill was the first of the 108 reported by the committee.

Here again, preparation, planning, and more preparation was the
order. Du Pont did not wait for hearings to be scheduled and a date
to be set to begin preparations for them. Testimony was carefully
planned and fully documented; and when the committee was ready
for hearings, Du Pont was ready for the committee. A good case
was made.

Unexpected help came when Senator Harrison Williams, a Democrat from New Jersey, turned up at the hearings to testify on Du
Pont's behalf without the company's prior knowledge. There were
35,000 Du Pont stockholders in New Jersey. Senator Williams had
heard from a lot of them and had been impressed.

After the hearings the legislation was reported out on September
9, 1961, by a vote of 21 to 3. House action followed with a brief
debate and without a recorded vote, on September 19.

The Senate Finance Committee reported favorably on September
21, and the debate in the Senate began in January, 1962. It lasted
some two weeks, primarily because Senator Gore conducted a filibuster

THEY WORK AT IT

against the bill's passage. On January 23, 1962, the Senate final vote on two key motions was 67 to 25 and 72 to 18. And on February 2, President Kennedy signed HR 8847 into law as Public Law 87-403.

In all this there were several basic factors, and if any one of them had been missing no legislation would have been possible.

At the top of the list was the fact that Du Pont's reputation was good right across the country. This was the result of years of hard work. If this legislation had been sought at the time of the Nye investigation and the cry of "Merchants of Death," it would have been hooted out of Washington. Even in the 1940's it could not have been done, because to much of the public, and therefore to many politicians, Du Pont was not very far from being Public Enemy No. 1 because of the Liberty League and President Roosevelt's attacks on the du Ponts. The climate of public opinion had to be right, and by 1961 it was.

The second basic factor was the careful preparation and documentation of the case before the general public. This was started long before there was any thought of legislation but was done because the public relations department realized from the beginning that the General Motors case was so newsworthy and was going to be so big on the news budget that it had to be won before the bar of the entire nation as well as in the court. The careful documentation of Du Pont's case was continued throughout the entire litigation.

Greenewalt never forgot to provide written data and information to individual members of Congress. Whenever new developments occurred in the case, background memoranda were sent out to newspapers and all interested media of communication as well as to congressmen. Just as important were the letters by Greenewalt to stockholders. But in none of his letters were the stockholders directly asked to write to senators or House members. The farthest he went was to suggest the idea. The language used, for example in the letter dated July 27, 1960, was: "It would seem to me that every stockholder should consider carefully whether, in his own interest, he should tell his Senators how he feels." The stockholders took the hint in great volume and the letters that poured in to all members of the Senate and the House were a factor in persuading the senators and representatives, both on the committee and off, to vote for the legislation. The mail ran in very heavy volume in support of the legislation. The mail against was almost negligible.

The effect of all the preparation and documentation was pronounced across the country. Brayman had always been a strong believer in newspaper editorials as a measure of public opinion—not because the editorials influence public opinion so much, but because, if a given set of facts is available to the editorial writer and his reaction to them is favorable or unfavorable, the chances are strong that the reaction of the general public to the same set of facts will be similar.

Of all the commercial newspapers there were only four in the country which opposed the legislation. The largest of these was *The Nashville Tennessean*, a supporter of Senator Gore, and a leading opponent of the legislation. The other three were all small—the *Auburn* (N.Y.) *Citizen-Advertiser*, the *York* (Penna.) *Gazette and Daily*, and the *Madison* (Wisc.) *Capital Times*. Even such ardent supporters of the Antitrust Division of the Justice Department as the *St. Louis Post-Dispatch* and the *Washington Post* gave strong editorial support to the legislation. In all, more than five hundred newspapers supported the Du Pont legislation in their editorials. It was this public support, in Brayman's view, that made it possible for the members of Congress to vote for a bill that was so often labeled the "Du Pont tax relief bill" without jeopardizing their political future.

The third basic factor was the decision of Du Pont to go it alone when it came to explaining the legislation to Congress. Brayman feels that "we never would have succeeded" if the company had relied on outsiders to talk to the members of Congress. It was luck, too, for Du Pont that it had Greenewalt as its chief executive, for the contribution he made by his knowledge, his sophistication, his personal charm, and his analytical ability was tremendous. Above all he reversed the usual corporate method by personally going to members of Congress.

Du Pont did have registered lobbyists in Washington during the progress of the legislation. Both of them were lawyers and they worked primarily with the staffs of the Ways and Means Committee and the Finance Committee on language, draft, and technical problems. They served a useful purpose but they did not carry the argument with the members of Congress themselves. They were vital, but they really served as technical assistants to the committees. They were not, in the usual sense of the word, lobbyists. They did not attempt to persuade the legislators.

The fourth factor was the strong feeling of the stockholders of General Motors as well as those of Du Pont. Large numbers of these stockholders who wrote to representatives and senators were answered; the answers or copies were sent to Du Pont's management. These answering letters were helpful to Du Pont, for they gave the company a line on the reaction of Senate and House members. They let Du Pont know the doubtful members so that additional efforts could be made in these cases. By the time the final vote was near in the Senate, Du Pont had a count on the senators that proved to be accurate except for two, including one who would have voted for the relief legislation if his vote had been necessary.

There was a fifth factor: Du Pont kept in touch throughout the entire controversy with able Washington lawyers who knew the political field, and did not ignore their advice. Many corporations that would not dream of getting into an engineering or financial problem without the best advice obtainable figure that somehow they can get into a political situation without any competent advice. Du Pont is not one of them, or at least was not in its efforts to get the relief legislation passed.

Just as Du Pont did not neglect the press during the long litigation, so it was not forgotten during the period of the passing of the legislation. Prior to the hearings before the Ways and Means Committee and the Senate Finance Committee and before the final debate in the Senate, all newsmen who were covering the events were fully briefed by the public relations department. So, when it came to reporting the hearings and the debates, the news reports showed a better awareness of the issues than if there had been no press briefings.

Again, at the suggestion of the public relations department, Greenewalt was never attended by a retinue. There were of course other Du Pont men in the hearing room and available if needed. But neither during the hearing before the House committee nor the Senate committee did Greenewalt need to call on any help, so thoroughly did he know his case in all details. During the debate in the Senate, all the Du Pont representatives stayed away from Capitol Hill with the exception of one man. He sat in the galleries to watch the debate and to keep the public relations department men in Washington informed. The rest of those on duty in Washington stayed at their hotel, ready to provide information or documentation to senators on any details they might want. The Du Pont supporters knew where the Du Pont staff members could be reached. The absence of buttonholing around the Hill during the debate made a very favorable impression.

For the obvious reason that its role, though important, was secondary, no one in Du Pont's public relations department has ever attempted to try to take the credit for the successful conclusion of the Du Pont-General Motors case. Brayman, Perry, and the senior staff members are too understanding of the facts and the events to make any such claims. It was successful because management, particularly Greenewalt, understood that while the finest legal counsel was essential, without a solid case nothing could have been accomplished, and that public opinion was of first importance. The public relations department was, without the slightest doubt, of invaluable help. It not only provided first-rate judgment on the public's mood, it also understood the techniques, and knew how to develop those techniques that would be used properly, in good taste, and with the long run view in mind. It is unlikely while any of Du Pont's managers who were closely involved in the case remain active in the company, that the key role a public relations department can play in the company's success will be forgotten. There were no slick tricks used by the public relations department. Its members are the first to admit freely that had the company not acted in the public's interest for years before the case was judged and the legislation acted upon, had the public not been certain that its interest was being protected, the case could never have come to a conclusion satisfactory to Du Pont.

From the very beginning of the Du Pont Company, good government relations have been important. It was Thomas Jefferson who helped put Eleuthére Irénée du Pont in business. Jefferson had known his father, Pierre S. du Pont, the economist-philosopher, in France, and the memoranda and advice he wrote on all manner of subjects to Jefferson, their close relationship over many years, paid off when the gunpowder business was set up on the shores of the Brandywine River outside of Wilmington. Du Pont's first order from the United States Army for gunpowder came from President Jefferson. Relations with governments since have continued as vital, even though the payment for work done, or goods sold to the government since the end of World War I have been only a tiny part of the Du Pont business. Today it is not government orders for goods, but government actions on business regulation that are of greatest importance.

Traditionally, since the first favors by Jefferson, the du Ponts had been Democrats. The large family, with few exceptions, were a strong influence in the Democratic party, supported it continuously, and backed Franklin D. Roosevelt when he ran for President in 1932. The close relationship between the company, the family, and the Democratic party was shown when Raskob, a vice-president of Du Pont, was national chairman of the Democratic party from 1928 until 1932. It was only after Roosevelt began to act on his New Deal measures that the du Ponts took fright, and when managers of large corporations are scared and bewildered, anything can happen. It did in the incorporation of the American Liberty League on August 15, 1934.

The changes FDR had made in his first year of office, the general instability of the period, the clear attitude of the President that the status quo was not good enough, worried business leaders. Not understanding the political facts of life and fretful because taxes would go higher and because Roosevelt's pre-election promise of a balanced budget was illusory, they turned inward. They began to listen to those who would preserve the old system exactly as it was, and to others who had an axe to grind. There was no hope for the Republican party, which had been badly shattered in November, 1932—so badly that some thought it was done for good. How then could one save the kind of freedom that businessmen understood, the freedom to operate their business with the minimum of governmental interference? Dexter Perkins, in *The New Age of Franklin Roosevelt, 1932-45* (University of Chicago Press, 1957), on the early New Deal, states:

> Roosevelt was more and more led to antagonism toward those who wished to stand pat; in so doing, he cut himself more and more from the fortunate classes; and in so doing, he aroused an intense resentment among those classes, which was to last for a long time. More than once he was to disclaim any hostility to wealth as such; more than once he was to stress his desire to preserve and not to destroy the capitalist system. The measures that he advocated or approved, however, involved heavier taxation on the well-to-do, greater governmental expenditures, restrictions on the freedom of the business class, and further legislation in the interest of agriculture and labor. It is not strange that they provoked a movement on the right, of which the not very effective prototype was the Liberty League, founded in the fall of 1934 with the object of arresting what its members deemed the alarming drift toward governmental extravagances and the extension of governmental power.

The du Ponts were no exception to those business leaders who were angry and then despairing of stopping the trends under Roosevelt. Nor were those who worked for the du Ponts. R. R. M. Carpenter, who had married a du Pont and was a Du Pont vice-president, wrote to Raskob, still a vice-president of the company, complaining that "Five negroes on my place in South Carolina refused to work this spring . . . stating they had easy jobs with the government. A cook on my houseboat at Fort Myers quit because the government was paying him a dollar an hour." What Carpenter wanted to know from Raskob was if the President really knew what was going on in the country, and if anything could be done about it.

Raskob wrote back with the suggestion that "I know no one that could better take the lead in trying to induce the Du Pont and General Motors groups, followed by other big industries, to definitely organize to protect society from the sufferings which it is bound to endure if we allow communistic elements to lead the people to believe that all businessmen were crooks." Raskob then suggested that there was a need "for some very definite organization that would come out openly with some plan for educating the people to the value of encouraging people to work; encouraging people to get rich." Raskob felt that Carpenter and his friends Pierre and Irénée du Pont were the right men to take on the job since they were "in a position to talk directly with a group that controls a larger share of industry . . . than any other group in the United States."

Another man also felt the need for a definite organization. He was Jouett Shouse, a former chairman of the Democratic party's executive committee who had headed the campaign to end prohibition with the American Association Against the Prohibition Amendment. Shouse, since the repeal of the Eighteenth Amendment, was looking for a job. He had the experience of organizing a national group which had supporters in both parties, knew Pierre S. du Pont, a backer of his repeal committee, and was right ready for another big post. He became president of the American Liberty League at a salary of $36,000 a year with $18,000 for expenses.

The Liberty League's announced purposes were simple enough: "to teach the necessity for respect for the rights of persons and property" and also "the duty of the government to encourage and protect individual and group initiative and enterprise, to foster the right to work, earn, save and acquire property, and to preserve the ownership and lawful use of property when acquired."

In addition to stopping Roosevelt from continuing his activities that were so burdensome to business, there was also the hope, and in some even the expectation, that an organization so strong could be built that it could be a major factor in the defeat of the President. Most of the leading officers and backers of the League were Democrats. Many were independents or Republicans. Included in the powerful supporters were Irénée, Pierre, and Lammot du Pont; Ernest T. Weir, the steel man; Will L. Clayton, the Texas cotton broker; Alfred P. Sloan, Jr., of General Motors; Edward F. Hutton, chairman of the board of General Foods; J. Howard Pew, president of Sun Oil; William S. Knudson, of General Motors; Joseph E. Widener, the Philadelphia transit man; Sewell L. Avery of Montgomery Ward; George H. Houston, president of Baldwin Locomotive; John W.

Davis, the Democrats' candidate for President in 1924; Alfred E. Smith, the Democrats' presidential candidate in 1928; Bainbridge Colby, Woodrow Wilson's Secretary of State; as well as many academicians who were strong believers that if the government would take its hands off the economy, prosperity would return by itself. The biggest contributors were the du Ponts, who were so enthusiastic that at one meeting at which Al Smith spoke twelve of them turned out to applaud.

The League asked Herbert Hoover to join it. His answer, according to his memoirs covering the years 1929 to 1941, was that this was the group that "financed the Democratic smearing campaign" and were "hardly the type of men to lead the cause of liberty"; he had "no more confidence in the Wall Street model of human liberty, which this group so well represents, than I have in the Pennsylvania Avenue model upon which this country now rides."

The whole plan was bound to fail. No group, no matter how eminent, can ever take the place of a political party. It was out of tune with the times; it failed to take into consideration the needs of those who were in serious distress and willing to follow a leader who promised to alleviate their distress. The Liberty League provided just the target that Roosevelt needed. The Roosevelt followers in and out of Congress bracketed the Liberty League and the du Ponts in their attacks. They were the almost-perfect targets for a hard-hitting politician in times of economic depression. Roosevelt, as well as Charles Michelson, the Democratic National Committee's publicity chief, knew how to set up sitting ducks and shoot them down.

Alfred Landon, the 1936 Republican candidate for President, never had a chance. It seemed that the only ones who did not know this were the Liberty League supporters. After his defeat, the League petered out. It failed because it had to fail, not because the virtues supported by the League were untenable, but because the kind of freedom and liberty stressed and campaigned for by the League had no relevance to the man who needed a job badly, could not get one, and was bitter with frustration.

The League also failed, according to Frederick Rudolph, writing about it in the October, 1950, issue of the *American Historical Review*, because of the "absence of any concern for the social and economic dislocations of the 1930's which documented the League's great skill at self-delusion. It sincerely thought it had something vital to sell, but it miserably misjudged the consumers whom it hoped to win. Frantically, it tried to save a people who would not be saved."

Free enterprise, states' rights, the open shop, and the end of the

New Deal were not what the nation wanted. When businessmen enter politics outside the political parties, when they are the men who make the judgments instead of the politicians, they are bound to lose. The Liberty League was no exception to the rule. Businessmen can no more run political campaigns than politicians can organize and run big businesses.

For the first time in their history, thanks to the American Liberty League, the du Ponts were projected into the limelight. They were so little in the public's general notice in the past, so remote was their work from the public, that when the Government sued Du Pont as a monopoly on August 7, 1907, and it was broken up into three parts on June 13, 1912, it brought so little notice that Mark Sullivan does not even mention the event in his *Our Times*, the most carefully wrought book on the first quarter of this century. When the organization of the League came right before the *Merchants of Death* charges against Du Pont and the investigation by Senator Nye's committee less than a month later, the du Ponts and the Du Pont Company were fully in the public eye. To this day, many of the Du Pont executives and leading members of the public relations department are certain that both events were part of the same operation by Roosevelt.

Until the Liberty League and the Nye Committee hearings, Du Pont had never been called unfavorably to the attention of an administration. Never before had Du Pont been the target of invective and scorn by a President. Never before had Du Pont had to withstand the onslaughts of a major political party, which knew how to use a target that was so juicily set up for attack.

It took a great deal of care, hard work, and public-spirited actions by Du Pont to overcome the bad relations the du Pont family and the company had with the public. Government relations can never be divorced from a company's relations with the public, for there is no value in a politician attacking a company if the people as a whole believe the company is a good company and that its activities are in their interest. Politicians' attacks are only effective against a corporation if the climate is right, which means that there are large numbers of voters who are prepared to believe what the politicians are saying.

Today, the way Du Pont conducts its relations with the government at the national level is not typical of industry as a whole. It has no Washington representation, and no lobbyists, registered or otherwise. This is not an accident; it is company policy, decided by the executive committee on the recommendation of the public relations department. The public relations department's view, and the executive committee decision made on this basis, was that it makes a company vulnerable to attack to have Washington lobbyists. This applies especially to a company as large and well-known as Du Pont. The argument runs that if you put a man in Washington the first thing you know he is a member of the Carlton Club, the lobbyists' meeting place. Pretty soon the lobbyist is scratching another lobbyist's back so that the other will scratch his when the need arises. He is a natural target for politicians looking for money, perhaps in the form of a couple of tables for $100-a-plate dinners, perhaps in the form of some concealed contribution. It is almost impossible for a man in this position, the public relations department believes, not to get involved. If he did not, the chances are his ability to do the job would be seriously weakened or perhaps eliminated. Yet when he does play the game, he lessens the respect in which he is held and which his company is held, and may even be the agency through which his company can be subjected to really scarifying attacks by a congressional committee, or by some government agency like the Department of Justice or the Federal Trade Commission.

In addition, the argument runs, such a man is not likely to be able to do the job that has to be done. He is known as a messenger, not the sender of the message; as the underling, not the boss. When he calls on a member of Congress or an important official of a government department, it is not a meeting of peers, but a call by a man with his hat in his hand on a man who regards himself as superior—and who tends to dislike the company for not respecting him enough to send someone of equivalent rank to see him. This is true even though the messenger may bear some honorific title.

This does not mean that the public relations department does not believe that Du Pont has not the right, or even the duty, to present its case in Washington when the need arises. On the contrary, the strong belief is that if the representation were not made it would mean letting the company down, and the executives of the company would be derelict in their duty as citizens. Du Pont takes this position seriously. When Du Pont has something to say to Washington, or something to ask from Washington, the responsible man in charge goes there and says it, or asks for it, face to face with the responsible man or men in government. The resulting talk is informative and authoritative. And it gets results.

The tax legislation which provided the relief in the case of Du Pont's divestiture of General Motors stock is the prime example of this. At the time Greenewalt made his rounds in Washington, there were quite a number of knowledgeable people who said that this method would not work. The answer is that it did. Out of this experience has come the fixed company policy now in effect. Further, the company also has a policy of making people available before congressional committees when their testimony can be helpful or informative. It has also made employees available for government service for periods of up to several years.

The company also recognizes that it has to do business no matter what kind of administration is in power. It would be happiest to be in a situation in which its management could be indifferent to whether the Republicans or Democrats were calling the shots. For this reason one of the long-range aims of the public relations department's program is to increase popular understanding of the operations of industry generally, as well as of Du Pont, so that there will be a climate of public opinion that will be conducive to this condition. The way to do it, the public relations people at Du Pont feel, is to so act that the public will support business.

The public relations department also thinks that, no matter what a politician may believe, he cannot be expected to hold on to his belief if it looks as if it might cost him his election or re-election. Occasionally a politician may hold onto his beliefs but he is an exception. On the state and local levels the feeling is no different about government relations than it is at the federal level. Du Pont believes here too in direct contact. This of course involves people at a different level most of the time. At the local level, the plant manager does the talking for Du Pont, since he is "Mr. Du Pont" in his area. If the public relations professional appears at all, it is to advise the plant manager, not to be his front.

Du Pont wants its personnel at various levels of management to take an intelligent interest in politics, and the number of those who do so is growing. These people are encouraged to be active in partisan politics, although the company itself keeps apart from this as a matter of firm policy. These activists in politics are on their own, not as Du Pont employees.

It is not uncommon for Du Pont employees to be mayors in their local communities, or even members of state legislatures. When they are elected to offices that mean long absences from their jobs, special rulings are made. The decisions on which the rules are based are made by the company's Civic Affairs Committee, headed by a vice-president of the company and consisting of the directors of the employee relations, legal, and public relations departments, with the assistant directors of each as alternates. This committee, which meets on the call of the chairman, considers the various aspects of questions like this: an employee is considering running for Congress. What shall the company tell him, how shall it treat him? Can he receive a salary or wages while campaigning? Can he be given a leave of absence, with or without pay? If he is elected, can he be given leave without pay during his term, or must he resign?

The company has also been sponsoring a new approach by industry to government. The campaign for this was started by Brayman on November 18, 1963, in a speech at the San Francisco convention of the Public Relations Society of America. In it he told other public relations practitioners that better government relations depended on a better understanding of the problems of politicians. He said that, to be effective, businessmen "can no longer hire other people to do their job of communication with government for them. This they must do themselves. They will need advisers, and there is no reason why they should not have them in this field any more than in the field of law, labor relations, or any other field."

It was Copeland, before the New York Chamber of Commerce in New York City on February 10, 1964, who urged other companies to do what his was doing. What he asked for was "a conscious, determined effort on both sides to improve the relationship between business and government." It was in this address that Copeland told his audience of the work of his predecessor, Greenewalt, when the company sought the tax legislation that would permit an orderly divestiture of its General Motors stock; how it took months of pacing corridors, knocking on doors, calling personally to explain the facts to virtually every member of the House and Senate committees involved, to key people in interested government agencies, and to leaders of both parties in Congress.

"I don't think we shall ever forget the lesson we learned at that time," Copeland said. "In relationships with government, it is not enough for businessmen to be convinced that what they advocate is fair and right. We must also win the understanding of the appropriate people in government that it is fair and right. They will listen if we approach them with honesty and integrity, and I think you will find that, regardless of political affiliation or ideology, it is the exception who has a completely closed mind."

Then Copeland said what few businessmen had said publicly before, that "it would be in the national interest as well as our own interest, to put an end to what, at times, has seemed like a cold war between government and business."

That is a long, long way from the American Liberty League.

But so is it a long time from 1934 to Copeland's announcement of new policy in 1964.

There are a number of reasons why the public relations department is thought of by management as an important part of the Du Pont organization. The company found that the department was of help to the managers in advising them how to adjust their views in the conduct of operations so as to keep out of trouble; what to do when decisions got them into trouble; how to carry through the objectives of policy in which relations with the public are involved. So management increasingly used the department. And when, in addition, the public relations executives were not intent on getting credit for themselves but were primarily motivated to do the best job for the company, greater confidence and cooperation was given the director and his department.

There is an overriding reason why Du Pont is willing to think and perform so that the company will be able to get the approval of the public: it is managed to succeed in the long run. Du Pont's heads are interested in the company's staying in business long after they are dead, for it is in many ways family run. At one time it was wholly owned by members of the du Pont family. Often, many managers get their companies into trouble because they refuse to think of the success of the company into the next generation. As a result, short-term decisions are made that may pass unnoticed in the immediate years ahead. But the du Ponts appreciate that a quick profit—letting the public's desires and the public interest go by the board—is not a proper course of action if the future is to be safe. Too many company managers, hired to get a fast profit and unworried as to what the reaction will be when they are no longer with the company, can bring serious damage. But the du Ponts have been running the business since it was founded in 1802 and in this context are fully prepared to build for the future.

E. I. du Pont ran the company from its beginning until 1834. Alfred Victor du Pont headed it from 1834 to 1850. Henry du Pont was the top executive from 1850 to 1859 while Eugene du Pont took over on that date and headed the business until 1902. Then came T. Coleman du Pont, president from 1902 to 1915 with Pierre S. du Pont taking over until 1919. Irénée du Pont, who established the committee system still being used, was president from 1919 to 1926, with Lammot du Pont the chief executive from 1926 to 1940. Walter Carpenter, Jr. ran it from 1940 to 1948 with Crawford H. Greenewalt as president from 1948 to 1962. Today Lammot du Pont

Copeland is the boss. In all, there have only been eleven chief executives of Du Pont. All have been du Ponts with the exception of Greenewalt and Carpenter. Greenewalt married a du Pont. So did Carpenter's brother.

Today's philosophy of the du Ponts was put this way by Copeland, a great-great-grandson of the founder, when outlining the public relations objectives of the company:

> We would like to stay ahead of public opinion. We would like the public to regard the Du Pont Company as an institution operating in the social and economic interest of the people of the United States; holding to the highest standards of employee, customer and stockholder relations; reflecting the highest skill in management; contributing broadly useful products and services; and leading in technical accomplishments. Whatever can be done to build those components of our reputation will, I believe, ultimately enhance our business. We work at it.

As long as all Du Pont's managers work at it on this base, so long will E. I du Pont de Nemours & Company continue to be accepted by the public.

UNDER THE SAME UMBRELLA

CHICAGO POLICE PICKED UP A PROSTITUTE IN A BAR FOR SOLIC-
iting. She had been handing out cards with her name, phone number
and address. Below her name were printed two words: PUBLIC RE-
LATIONS.

A minor Tammany Hall clubhouse politician in New York, with
ties to a former local political leader, acted as the go-between in shady
operations. On the door of his office appeared these words: PUBLIC
RELATIONS.

In Washington, a former administrative assistant to a congressman
entertained politicians and tried to influence their views on pending
legislation without registering as a lobbyist. His letterhead carried
the words: PUBLIC RELATIONS.

A former newspaperman in Los Angeles was the liaison between
the head of a corporation and politicians in the California Legislature,
arriving with his little black bag at the right moment before campaigns. He listed himself as a public relations counsel.

There is no restriction on the use of the words "public relations."
Anyone can use them. And all sorts of characters do, without performing any of the functions normally associated with the practice
of public relations. They are usually the fringe people who, for the
lack of another title for their work, are happy to use "public relations."

But those on the narrow edge of legitimate society are not the only
ones who work close to the line. Others who run public relations
agencies and who do, in some cases, a great deal of the proper work

of public relations, operate in a fashion to bring contempt on a legitimate, essential business.

Not long ago the public relations man for a major corporation was charged with conspiracy to libel a United States senator.

In the same year the partner in a public relations firm, with a number of highly regarded private business and government clients, pleaded guilty to ten counts of perjury and was sentenced to a year in jail and fined $50,000. He had told his clients that the money he requested from them was necessary to pay off a politician.

Also in the same year another public relations man, who had the year before been sentenced to two years in prison for conspiring to bribe a liquor authority official, was named as a co-conspirator in a case after the grand jury charged that he was used as a "conduit."

In still another case, a widely read chit-chat columnist in a respected daily newspaper, who owned a public relations firm as well, had been found guilty of acting as a lobbyist for a foreign country without registering. He lost his newspaper job and his public relations firm was dissolved.

Professor Scott M. Cutlip, of the University of Wisconsin School of Journalism, author of *Fund Raising in the United States: Its Role in America's Philanthropy* (Rutgers University Press, 1965), is one of the historians of public relations. In a speech in New York before the Public Relations Institute, which is sponsored by the Public Relations Council of Health and Welfare Services, on June 8, 1964, he said—after pointing out that thousands of health and welfare agencies in the United States and Canada are served by a like number of "dedicated, devoted practitioners"—that there are many instances of malpractice in this field. He mentioned a few and said that other examples could be cited. The few he named were:

> Public relations practitioners were deeply involved in the scandalous National Kids Day Foundation which raised nearly four million dollars in five years and then spent more than three million of this amount in administrative costs in a highly questionable enterprise. To say the least!
>
> A public relations practitioner was one of the main looters of the Sister Kenny Foundation in Minnesota. This PR man took out nearly one and one-half million dollars for public relations expenses in a nine-year period—all paid with dollars given by a public in good faith to fight polio. He was also involved in payoffs and kickbacks.
>
> Finally, you may recall that the principal beneficiary of the

ill-fated Federal Epilepsy Association was the public relations firm serving it, not the victims of epilepsy.

Crooks are to be found in almost every business and profession. The percentage of them in public relations is probably no higher than in any other field where competition is intense and clear proof of effective performance is difficult to measure. But it is not only this outright dishonesty that plagues public relations. There is also a certain charlatanism that has been the deep concern of those thousands of practitioners who do a thoroughly ethical job day in and day out and whose clients, corporations and institutions, would be horrified at any other kind of practice.

Charlatanism, in fact, is far too widespread in the public relations business. And here the agencies are the greater offenders, although again the preponderance of those who run agencies and are employed by them are hard-working, as honest as the next man in any other business. They are offended and deeply concerned with those who make public relations a business to be snorted at by those who assume that the antics of the small minority are the norm. This is most certainly one of the reasons why public relations men are so status conscious, so sensitive in their reaction to even the mildest criticism. They know that they perform a needed function and do so within the bounds of decency. But all too often they are so jumpy that they refuse to face the problems of the field in which they earn their living. Until they do so, realistically, they will fail to find answers to the ills that afflict the business as a whole, whether they work for a trade union, a university, a trade association, a corporation, a health and welfare agency or a government body.

There is a dangerous idea, too often promoted by public relations practitioners themselves, that, by some magic trick, public consent can be engineered so that—presto!—a corporation can suddenly achieve a favorable public reputation. That this is utter nonsense is understood by sophisticated management and underlined by the best public relations directors of large corporations. But not all corporate managers understand this simple fact. Instead they prefer to believe that all their ills will end if only they can find and hire the right public relations counsel to tell them how they can immediately end their trouble, be it with the general public, a union, their employees, the local community, or the government.

As long as managers think this way there will be firms and individuals who will agree with them, for some accounts are highly profitable. So when a public relations agency makes a presentation in the hope of being chosen to represent a firm, all kinds of promises are made which can never be fulfilled. One agency even used to promise vanity-puffed potential clients that they could be made into national figures, if not overnight, at least during the life of the contract. Another made a habit of promising the businessman, usually from a smaller community, that with the proper fee the agency could get his picture on the cover of *Time*. Or if not *Time*, then *Newsweek*. And as for *Business Week* or *Forbes*, why that is a sure thing, and please read the contract quickly and sign here.

The founder of a successful agency told a friend not so long ago that he had two basic approaches, and they always worked. One was never to give the client an answer to a problem at once. His method, he explained, was to wait and be sure, no matter how long it took, what the client himself wanted to do. Then the successful way was to give the client the answer he wanted. The theory was that the client wanted confirmation of his own view, not a new one, and the last thing he welcomed was having someone say no to him.

The second approach to keeping a client was never to take him out of hot water completely. The agency head tries to take him out, barely, and then drops the client back in again. The theory, and it has worked with him for a long time and at high fees, is that just as soon as the client is fully out of trouble he will end his relationship with the firm. Ethical? To the successful head of the public relations agency that was not the question. The simple question was: Could he keep the client or lose him? Of such material are some owners of firms made. Others, who are quite willing to say that their purpose is to stay in business, admit that if they say no to a client they may lose him. Since they are hired in the first place only because a client has troubles, he will usually depart as soon as the troubles are over. Yet they are prepared to lose clients and gain new business because they have done a good job and helped put out the fire. Until clients are sensible enough to understand that it is cheaper for them to keep out of trouble than try to get out of it after they have been burned, this kind of practice will continue.

Another owner of a public relations firm, who likes to speak of high ethical standards when he talks to college groups, has a different method of operation. It involves over-promising. It works this way: After he is retained and makes a short study of the client's problems, he draws up an extensive media program. Here are excerpts from what he promised a foreign government: Under four separate sections —economics and trade, politics, cultural, science and technology—he had six columns. The first column was headed "Working Title."

Under this went the subject of the magazine article, or news feature, or television plan. Under the second heading, "Medium," was the name of the magazine, or newspaper, or television program. Under the third heading, "Contact," was the name or names of those on his staff who supposedly were in contact with the medium. The fourth heading was "Research, Writing." Under this was the name of the person who was doing the research and the writing in the field. The fifth heading was "By-Line." This section listed the name of the person who would sign the article. The sixth heading was "Status." And here would go numbers: (1) in planning, (2) medium contacted, (3) outline prepared, (4) outline discussed with medium, (5) outline revised, (6) outline accepted, (7) story scheduled, (8) story published. Here are some of the media listed: *The New York Times Magazine; Business Week; Forbes, Magazine of Wall Street; Consumer Reports;* Hall Syndicate; *Harper's* magazine; *Nation's Business; Wall Street Journal; Time; U.S. News & World Report; Saturday Evening Post; The New York Times; Christian Science Monitor; The Reporter; Dun's Review; Journal of Commerce; Current* magazine; *American Legion* magazine; *Commercial and Financial Chronicle; International Trade Review; Foreign Affairs; Life;* CBS-TV; *Saturday Review; Editor & Publisher; Parade;* NEA Syndicate; *The Atlantic; Reader's Digest; Architectural Forum; Pageant; Family Circle; Look; McCall's; Ladies' Home Journal;* King Features; *Seventeen; Holiday; American Scholar; New York Post; Catholic Digest;* AP; McNaught Syndicate; *American Girl; Washington Post; St. Louis Post-Dispatch;* Religious News Service.

If a member of the public relations firm knew someone in the medium, that person was named. If there was no contact at the publication the magazine editor's name was put in the proper column. For instance, Edward Weeks was listed for *The Atlantic.* DeWitt Wallace was down for *Reader's Digest.* In some cases the contact on the magazine listed had long ago left the magazine. When it came to by-line, in one case a member of the United States Senate was listed. He had never been contacted, nor had any member of his staff.

Obviously it was impossible to complete this kind of program within the duration of the contract, or even with many years of extension. The status column could be dragged out, from (1) to (8) over an indefinite time. The media program was written in two evenings by two members of the public relations firm with a media list, some imagination and an overabundance of guile and gall. Of course the time came when the client finally asked, "Where are the stories?" Then came a new approach. After some fast talking and a tiny measure of print exposure, a new tack was taken with the client. The range of the promises was narrower. And the new over-promising started once more.

In their drive for publicity, public relations men have developed techniques which are far ranging. But one of the most frequently used, which almost invariably brings media space and time, is the press junket—a trip, lavish and expensive, to which newsmen are invited, all expenses paid. The purpose, no matter how stated or rationalized, is to obtain free time on radio and television and space in newspapers and magazines, which otherwise would not be obtainable. The most expensive are the junkets organized by the movie industry, long expert at promotion that will draw patrons to the box office.

The most lavish was the one arranged by producer-director Stanley Kramer for the exploitation of the film *It's a Mad, Mad, Mad, Mad World*. The junket cost $250,000. Two hundred and fifty reporters were brought to Hollywood from twenty-six countries and fifty-three cities in the United States, for a four-day visit. The writers were brought by chartered planes. They were lodged without charge at one of the best hotels in Hollywood. Their food and liquor bills were paid. A press room at the hotel was set up with its own switchboard and provided twenty-four-hour service. One night the reporters were guests of Kramer at a lawn party at his home. Another night they were taken to a nightclub. A trip was arranged for them to Disneyland, and they were given a tour of the Universal Studios. All cable tolls were paid by the producer and all telephone calls to their newspaper offices were free for the reporters. Only five newspapers paid their representatives' expenses. All the rest, surely with the knowledge of the newspaper publishers, the magazine editors, and the radio and television station managers, had everything on the cuff. The build-up was for the showing of the film on the final night of the excursion.

The New York Times, in a story from Hollywood dated November 7, 1963, quoted Kramer as saying that "during this junket we received an enormous amount of space in the newspapers and there is much more to come in the papers and on television. These stories and the interviews will build up audience anticipation so that it hits a peak as our movie opens in major cities." He is also reported to have said that the vast majority of the reporters turned in at least one story a day, and "if the stories were all like those that many newspaper reporters showed to me, then they were very favorable." The stories, again according to Kramer, created "an aura that the movie is all-out entertainment." And while this created a favorable climate for the film, none of this, according to Kramer, could be construed as a form of payola. "My own frankness would negate any payola of this kind. I placed no limits on questions. Nobody held back. The stars of the picture were available for unhampered questioning."

Did this expenditure of a quarter of a million dollars justify itself to Kramer? He said he could not tell, but the advance sales of tickets had jumped since the reporters had arrived in Hollywood and had started writing their stories. In New York City alone, he said, the advance sale had quadrupled since the junket began. "By and large," Kramer told the reporter, "I look at this in an emotional way. I feel we have stirred up a great deal of attention to the movie. That is the most you can expect at this time."

Obviously news of the film and its preview would not have received the same media exposure without the junket. Just how newsworthy was this event? Obviously, not important enough to be paid for by the magazines, the newspapers, the radio stations, the television stations—except for the five papers which paid their own way. What are the ethics of this? In return for the free trips for their reporters and writers, the media gave free space. And the reading public, the television viewers, and the radio listeners—have they a right to expect that they are reading and listening to and seeing what the news media believed was newsworthy? Just how unpolluted was media by this junket and just how much space was devoted to the film, and not marked "in return for favors received" because of the money spent on the free ride, the free drinks, the free entertainment, the free hotel? And could all this have happened if the media were not willing, and in a great many cases only too happy, to play the film producer's game?

On July 25, 1967, *The Wall Street Journal* ran one of its long, carefully researched news roundups under the heading Ethics and the Press in which it dealt with the conflicts of interest that distort the news coverage by some newspapers. Although it noted that "in recent years, a growing number of papers have taken steps to end or restrict junketing, questionable outside work, the acceptance of gifts and other practices that might compromise objectivity," it found these evils far too prevalent. Here is what the article had to say on junketing:

Junketing also is widely viewed as a threat to objectivity, but is widely practiced nonetheless. Junkets are trips by reporters whose travel and other expenses are paid by the news source, not the newspaper. The source often stages some "event" or shows off some facility of marginal interest to give the reporters some excuse for going, but the real intent in many cases is to maintain good relations with the press as well as to garner some publicity in the process.

These junkets sometimes are little more than bacchanals for attending newsmen. Reporters still recall with relish a Caribbean trip staged by one big company a few years ago; the firm bankrolled everything, including the services of a bevy of prostitutes. On one stopover during the return trip, some of the more rambunctious journalists were jailed by the police, and company attorneys used their good offices to get them sprung ("These are very important editors from New York . . .").

The "news" stories that emerge from such affairs are almost always complimentary, if not gushing, and almost always have little or no intrinsic worth. Some editors frankly admit this, and say they use junkets mainly as a way to give deserving staffers expense-paid vacations.

Travel, hunting, and fishing have become big business, particularly with the increasing affluence of Americans. They have money to spend, and there is intense competition to have them spend it on travel at home and abroad, at one hotel instead of another, on one airline instead of another. The same holds true in the attraction of hunters and fishermen to a stream in one state or a fishing paradise in another and to better game shooting in one locality instead of another. Elaborate means have been developed to propagandize the attractions of fishing and hunting lodges and of open spaces. All means of reaching the public to tell of the advantages of sports and entertainment and unusual areas to visit have expanded with the growth of the amount of leisure time the nation has. Here then is a legitimate place for the public relations man, and particularly the publicity expert. With their growing number have come other results. Travel writers write books and magazine articles after free trips on planes, with free hotel lodgings and meals, with free fishing trips at the opening of the season or hunting when the law says the time is ripe. Here is the book on travel which does not tell that the writer has seen and heard and eaten and slept and traveled as the guest of the town or the hotel or the airline. Here is the magazine story which tells that the writer of the article has done his on-the-spot viewing at the expense of the subject he writes about. The more frequent the free trips, the more frequent are the plugs given to the airline or the hotel or the lodge or the nations visited. The public relations men for the countries or airlines or vacation spots or hotels arrange for all-expense-paid trips for the writer in these fields, and large numbers of magazines and newspapers and television and radio stations are willing to return space or time. Where does the blame lie here? With the public relations men, who could not otherwise get these writers to visit the spots they are paid to publicize, or with the owners of the media for permitting this conflict of interest?

There is another type of magazine or newspaper writer with whom the public relations man must deal. He is the two-hatter: the man who writes about travel, motor cars, or other fields, and whose job it also is to solicit advertising for his publication. Clearly, in most cases where this happens, the amount of editorial space given is related, and often very closely, to the amount of advertising received. Should the public relations man ignore the two-hatters and thus see his organization lose space? Or does the fault here lie with the media, the publishers who not only support this but appoint the two-hatters?

Newsweek in its issue of August 31, 1964, ran an article on two-hatters, specifically those who write about the motor car industry. The story dealt with the introduction of new model cars by Chrysler Corporation in New York City. Of the three hundred newsmen who came to the event, *Newsweek* said,

> They were bedded down at the Waldorf-Astoria, fed and watered grandly, and of course given a long peek at the firm's 1965 cars and trucks. The tab for all this chromium treatment—$400,000 —was picked up by Chrysler. Most reporters were on hand to do just one job—report what they saw. But not the so-called "two-hatters," who both sell automobile advertising and cover the news beat for their papers. Among the two dozen major newspapers that permit such double duty are the *New York Post, The New York Journal-American, The Boston Herald, The Boston Globe, The Boston Traveler, The Boston Record-American, The San Francisco Chronicle,* the *San Francisco Examiner, The San Francisco News-Call Bulletin,* the *Los Angeles Herald-Examiner, The Cincinnati Post & Times Star* and the *Cincinnati Enquirer.*

Newsweek reported the Detroit bureau chief for the *Wall Street Journal* since 1959, "a solid one-hatter," as saying: "When I came to this beat I was aghast at the number of newspapers that use two-hatters. These guys are much like those South American or French reporters who will write a favorable piece if the price is right." And as *Newsweek* commented, "the price, of course, is advertising."

The magazine went on to say that the director of corporate identity and advertising, who plays no favorites, and other advertising officials were so assiduously courted that even one two-hatter was embarrassed. But few others, said the magazine, are "guilt-ridden," and the legitimate reporters on the beat place the blame squarely on the publishers who are too often, quoting one of the reporters, "newsprint salesmen and little else."

The public relations men for the motor car manufacturers deal regularly with these two-hatters, for they are the ones who are responsible for the automotive news appearing in their papers. Is this an ethical problem, which is easily solved by the public relations men, or is the onus entirely on the newspaper publishers? In this hard world, the public relations man, no matter how he may detest the system, has little choice but to go along.

News Front, in the November, 1965, issue made its own study of "what comes of feeding martinis and roast beef to the press, plying editors with scotch on Christmas or junketing them to Puerto Rico for a long week end." Under the heading of "The Way to an Editor's Heart," and the subhead, "Press parties, junkets, and gifts to hard-working editors do pay off; at its best, the p.r. man's originality earns valuable editorial space that money alone can't buy," the magazine had its own tales to tell. One of them is the following:

> Last spring, for example, The Clairol Co., manufacturers of hair coloring, preceded the introduction of a new product called "Nice and Easy" with an ingenious tie-in gift for editors. Described as an "*at home* press party" the handsome package contained all the ingredients for taking it nice and easy—at home. In the kit were a quart of champagne, a generous jar of imported caviar and a recording of Frank Sinatra crooning the song of the same name. In cities other than New York, the gifts were delivered in person, which gave the local p.r. man a chance to get his foot in the door—and thus that much closer to the editor's ear.

Another tale in the same *News Front* article is about the large-scale expedition to London of the Group W, Westinghouse Broadcasting Company, to explain the switch to all-news format by its radio stations, WINS in New York and KYW in Philadelphia. The trip cost an estimated $100,000. A plane load of advertising agency executives as well as advertising and broadcasting reporters were taken on a four-day news seminar in London.

According to the magazine the guest list was drawn up with a double purpose:

The agency men were invited for what was reported to be a completely subtle soft-sell, and the press was asked along in order to publicize the trip to the folks back home.

In addition to the good will the trip created among agency guests, which appeared to be substantial, the pickup in the press was enormous. All the most important advertising and broadcasting reporters in New York and Philadelphia filed long stories about the trip. The value of such top drawer coverage is obvious.

The magazine also tells of the opening of Hilton Hotels' new hotel in Tel Aviv; how it flew 150 guests, seventy-five of whom were press and the rest business associates and executives, to Israel for five days. The junket was reported by *News Front* this way:

Dancing girls and government officials greeted the guests, who were kept on a round of gala balls, parties and sightseeing. The opening of one more hotel, regardless of how exotic the location, wouldn't normally create much of a ripple anymore. This kind of joy ride makes for contented guests—and good reading.

The magazine ends its article with this conclusion: In order to get space for his client the public relations man has to

pique the curiosity, stimulate the interest, satisfy the intelligence and soothe the ego of the working press. The parties and junkets are only his mechanical aids—his bait. After all roast beef and plane tickets are not such potent—or secret weapons. The real secret weapon is the p.r. man's creativity and ingenuity which he quietly draws on as a matter of course day after day as part of his job.

But the problem still remains: Are these events, involving gifts to editors and long, free trips, worth the space they get on their merits? If so, should the publishers not pay for the trips? If they did, the chances of conflict of interest would be fewer. And if they are not worth the cost to the publisher, or the gifts have nothing to do with getting space, would the media give them space? Should the public relations men stop handing out presents to editors and providing free trips if this is the only way they can attract attention and space in the papers?

On April 3, 1963, Chapter IX (C) of the Report of the Special Study of Securities Markets was issued by the Securities and Exchange Commission (SEC). It was prepared as part of a wide-ranging investigation and is titled "Corporate Publicity and Public Relations."

It distressed responsible public relations practitioners not so much because of its recommendations but for what it revealed of the practices of fringe operators in public relations, and particularly those in the specialized area of financial public relations. The report is written in calm fashion, without any attempt to stand the reader's hair on end. It draws a picture of some aspects of financial public relations that are shocking. The practices described were not completely unknown, but because they are documented in the report there can be no doubt that they existed and in some form probably still do.

Financial public relations practice has been in existence for many years, but in more recent years the specialists have had a phenomenal growth. These figures quoted in the SEC report tell the story: According to the *Financial Public Relations Directory* of 1962, a useful yardstick of the growth of financial public relations, there were some six hundred firms in this field, an increase of twenty-three per cent over 1961. With this growth came practices that resulted in the distribution of false and misleading information, stock-pushing, and conflict of interest that make a shambles of any semblance of ethical practice.

While these antics were the work of relatively few in the business, the report felt it important enough, on the basis of its study, to say that though it is difficult to estimate how widespread were the questionable practices uncovered, "there is evidence that a substantial number of issuers and financial publicists have engaged in them, and that they pose serious problems." The report was also meticulous in saying that while what the study reveals should not be regarded as an exhaustive description of financial public relations activities by U.S. corporations, and the more questionable activities should not be regarded as typical, "even though to the extent that they do exist, they are far from being inconsequential."

The report also points out that it is "desirable for issuers to disseminate publicity through the channels of news distribution as well as by other means" and is quick to underline the SEC policy of encouraging publicly held corporations "to employ publicity and public relations for these purposes." In fact, it draws attention to the Securities Act of 1933 Release No. 3844, dated October 8, 1957, which announced that the practice of giving publicity concerning corporate affairs through many media "reflects a commendable and growing recognition on the part of industry and the investment community of the importance of informing security holders and the public generally with respect to important business and financial developments. This trend should be encouraged . . ."

The SEC report does not hesitate to document abuses. Some public relations firms have received all or part of their compensation in options to buy the stock of their clients. This practice is criticized because it gives the publicist "an incentive to try to increase the price of the client's stock rather than to disseminate unbiased corporate information."

Some financial public relations firms, says the report, have informal arrangements in which the underwriter recommends the public relations firm to issuers and the public relations firm reciprocates by bringing the underwriter together with those of his clients who are looking for new financing.

It is hardly open to question, says the report, that "corporate publicity can have a powerful effect on the prices of securities." By virtue of his access to the financial press and investment advisors, the financial public relations man often has the ability to increase, or decrease for that matter, the market prices of securities issued by his clients.

Despite their denials, in the selling literature of the public relations firms aimed at prospective clients, financial public relations men emphasize that one effect of a financial public relations program

> will be to increase the price of a company's common stock. They point out that the communication of a company's "story" to its stockholders and the investing public will result in "full capitalization," "equitable evaluation," or "more realistic market appraisal" of the company's securities; and they state that companies that are well known to the financial community generally have a higher price-earnings ratio than obscure companies of the same worth. Whatever words were used, little doubt remains that their purpose is to increase stock prices. Indeed some financial public relations men concede that they are salesmen of their client's stock.

There are many ways in which public relations men can so publicize the common stock of a company that its price is raised, for a quick profit to the client and to the public relations man himself, if he buys stock or gets an option to buy from the company that retains him. But if the mass media are to be used—or the financial publications or the security analysts—then it must take more than a public relations man to get results. It needs a willing magazine editor, or a willing security analyst, or a willing financial reporter. Often the editor or analyst or reporter is taken for a ride, or is "had." In these cases the first time is the last time, for the men of integrity will either refuse to deal with the public relations man again or will scrutinize with exceptional care any material he presents.

The SEC report says that "the business editor of a national publication for several years made a practice of purchasing the stock of small companies which the publication was about to write up, and selling his holdings shortly after the article appeared, usually at a considerable profit." The case the SEC had in mind is by no means the only one. It happens all too often. But what is the responsibility of the publisher or owner of the magazine to be ever alert to this kind of practice, to supervise his staff? This is not only an evil in itself but of great harm to the magazine's reputation for integrity. In these cases the magazine's owners or the newspaper publishers have been unaware of these activities of their editors and reporters.

A case to which the report devotes a great deal of space is one involving Joseph Purtell, the senior editor in charge of the business news section of *Time* magazine. At the time the report was released Purtell was no longer with *Time*. When he testified to the Special Study, Purtell said he knew of no policy at *Time* which prohibited him from purchasing securities of companies about to become the subject of articles in *Time*. But according to the editor-in-chief of *Time*, such a policy had existed since the magazine was first published, and any detected violation would have meant summary dismissal. What is more, the editor-in-chief further stated that Purtell's violations were not detected. In fact, a written statement reflecting such a policy was distributed to *Time* employees on June 6, 1961. In part, under the heading, "Profiting from Special Information," it said the following:

> It has been a long-standing point of policy that no employee of Time, Inc. should try to profit (by buying or selling securities or otherwise) from special information that one of our magazines plans to carry a story or picture on a company. In the very unusual case of a staff member who holds a significant interest in a company and who might be assigned to work on a story about that company, his personal interest should be referred to the managing editor or his supervisor in advance.

There is no doubt that this is the policy of *Time* and has been from the beginning for it is in *Time*'s own interest. There is not the slightest reason to think that *Time* knew of the Purtell activities which the SEC report deals with in detail.

The best way to tell the story of Purtell is to quote verbatim what the report has to say. It begins in early April, 1961 when Purtell telephoned Technical Animations, Inc.

> [He] expressed an interest in it as a possible subject for an article in *Time*. According to Purtell's testimony, he had first

heard about the company from his broker, Benjamin Weiss, a partner in the New York Stock Exchange member firm of Wineman, Weiss & Co., who had suggested that Technical Animations might be an interesting company to look into. Purtell subsequently had an interview with Harold Wolff, the company's public relations man, who demonstrated the company's process to him. On April 13 and 14, Purtell purchased 2,500 shares of Technical Animations' B stock at prices of 6⅛ to 6¾ through Wineman, Weiss & Co. On April 18 Purtell assigned a *Time* writer and a researcher to prepare an article on the company. Between April 13 and 21, Weiss purchased 1,500 shares for his own account and an additional 4,500 shares for four of his regular customers at prices of 6⅛ to 7¾. By this time, word had leaked out in financial circles that Technical Animations was expected to be written up by *Time*, and on the basis of these rumors registered representatives of at least two brokerage houses were recommending the stock to their clients. The full extent of the circulation of the rumors is unknown.

Apparently, as a result of these rumors and the consequent increase in the volume of trading, the price of the stock, which had been at 6¾ on April 19, rose to 7½ on April 21, and 9¼ on April 24. The article appeared in the business-news section of the April 28, 1961 issue of *Time*, which became available on the nation's newsstands late in the day on April 24 and on April 25. The stock continued to rise, reaching 10⅛ on April 25, 12 on April 26, and 13½ on April 27. On that day, Technical Animations shares were purchased by members of the public for as much as 15⅛. During the first three days after the article appeared, Weiss and his four customers sold 4,700 shares, officers of the corporation sold 2,400 shares, and its public relations man sold 1,300 shares (acquired through the exercise of options), at prices from 9¾ to 13¼. The public relations man sold an additional 400 shares on May 3 at prices from 10⅝ to 11. On the following day Purtell sold 1,000 shares at a price of 11⅝. By May 31 the stock was down to 8¾. Purtell sold his remaining 1,500 shares on October 26, 1961, over six months after purchase, at a price of 5¼. On December 31, 1962, Technical Animations Class B stock was priced at 1¾.

It is clear that the *Time* article was the principal cause for the rise in the price of the stock. Questionnaires were sent to approximately 300 customers who purchased the stock in April and May 1961, in order to determine their motives for investing. The article was the determining factor for 101 customers out of a total of 160 who returned questionnaires and who made purchases after its publication. It is likely that many of the other 59 who stated that the stock was recommended to them by friends, acquaintances, or brokers were indirectly affected by the article in *Time*.

There were a number of reasons for the impact of the article. First, the article was unduly favorable, stating that the company's "sales have risen in five years from $7,000 to $600,000 this year," and that it "went into the black" in 1961. Sales for the year ending October 31, 1961 totalled approximately $450,-000 and, although the company had earnings in one quarter of 1961, it had a small net loss for the year. Secondly, the volatility of the stock was undoubtedly increased by the fact that the country was in the midst of a speculative bull market; also, stocks of companies in the photographic and related fields were particularly popular with the investing public at the time. A third reason for the dramatic price rise was the smallness of the floating supply of the stock. The purchase before the publication of the article by persons who knew of the impending article contributed to the demand for the stock which helped to push the price up. Their sale of these shares shortly after the publication of the article no doubt contributed to and hastened the stock's rapid descent.

Technical Animations was not the only company in whose stock Purtell, Weiss, and Weiss's four customers had transactions of this nature. Between August 1957 and April 1961, Purtell had transactions in the securities of 64 companies, of which 27 were written up in the business-news section of *Time*. In each of the 27 cases he purchased the stock a few days or a few weeks before the date of the publication of the article concerning the particular company and he usually sold the stock within a few days following the date of publication. A substantial number of these companies were small and little known. In general, Purtell held the shares of the companies not written up in *Time* for a longer period. He made a considerable profit from trading in stocks of companies that were written up in *Time*, since in most cases the price of the stock rose sharply upon the publication of the article or shortly before. Purtell's average purchase was about 1,000 shares, but in some cases he purchased considerably more, the largest purchase being 2,500 shares. His investment in each security was usually about $20,000 and on a few occasions it exceeded twice this amount. During this entire period Purtell was the business editor of *Time*. These transactions, which constituted a substantial part of Purtell's total trading, ceased abruptly at the end of April 1961, when Purtell's employment at *Time* terminated.

Purtell did all of his trading through Wineman, Weiss & Co. In the case of 16 of the 27 transactions, Weiss also purchased stock immediately before the article appeared and sold soon afterward. Purtell testified that prior to a number of these transactions, he may have discussed with Weiss the possibility that *Time* would publish an article about the company. Weiss' four customers made similar transactions on several of these occasions.

The SEC report also deals with public relations men, their relationships with the security analysts, and how junkets and entertainment have their effect on the advice given by the men who are supposed to be objective in what they report.

The Florida land development corporations have the advantage, the SEC report underlines, of being able to offer analysts and financial writers sunshine as well as a resort. It tells of the 1961 junket organized by General Development Corporation for twenty-one analysts to visit its Florida properties in two groups. Each of these trips lasted four days and included tours of the company's principal real estate developments as well as interviews with officials of the company. The trips also included a day at a country club owned by the company, where there were facilities for golf, swimming, and other forms of relaxation. The analysts who participated were advised to bring their golf shoes—the company promised to supply the other equipment. Of the eighteen brokerage houses represented on these junkets, five issued market letters favorable to the company within three months of the visits, and six others indicated approval in internal communications. In addition, an investment advisory service recommended the stock, and a large foundation which was represented on the trip bought a large block of convertible debentures.

The SEC report comments that

> security analysts and members of the financial press who have participated in such junkets almost invariably say that they could not possibly be "bought" for a free meal or a night's lodgings. Nevertheless, it cannot be denied that "entertainment," especially in its more lavish aspects, constitutes a problem. To give a group of analysts a free vacation, complete with country clubs and parties but with little business activity, would seem to cross the

line of propriety. The need is clear for more rigorous supervision by employers of the analysts and writers, and for a keener awareness of the inherent ethical problems on the part of the issuers and also of the firms and publications furnishing the purportedly objective financial analysis and news upon which members of the public may base their investment decisions.

In the section of the report dealing with the "Content of Corporate Publicity" this comment appears: "The corporate publicity examined in the course of this study ran the gamut from straightforward reporting of corporate affairs to what can only be described as deliberate attempts to falsify a company's financial condition or prospects."

On page 78 of the section devoted to "Summary, Conclusions and Recommendations" this bald statement is made:

The financial press too often permits propaganda to pass as news. Financial analysts too often depend upon public relations material rather than official disclosures or independent research as the basis for the investment advice which they give the public. Not only may these practices and others described in this report seriously mislead stockholders and potential investors; they also tend to corrupt the media of communication upon which the investing public must rely for its information.

This country is not alone in having sharpies among its public relations practitioners. The British newspapers have often exposed them. The *Sunday Times*, after its own investigation in June of 1965, published the story of a front operation, citing chapter and verse leading to questions in the House of Commons for which two members of the Institute of Public Relations were suspended in March, 1966, for a year. The case was a clear one.

London Rubber Industries Ltd., the biggest manufacturer of toy balloons and conventional contraceptives, had been upset by what it felt was the one-sided publicity in favor of oral contraceptives. Two public relations men, financed by the company, set up the Genetic Study Unit. On the surface it was to conduct a disinterested compaign against the misuse of drugs. In fact it propagandized against use of the "pill."

Suspicions were first aroused late in 1964, according to *The New York Times*' report from London dated March 4, 1966, when the first of two bulletins by the Genetic Study Unit was published and distributed. The bulletin said it sought to "protect women of the world from a mass conversion to faith in oral contraceptives." Statements were culled from speeches of doctors, frequently out of context, to support the position of the front organization. There was no public identification of this supposedly impartial scientific body with London Rubber Industries. The company did not announce its backing until the *Sunday Times* expose. The company's excuse, as given to the *Sunday Times*, was that the front was set up to counterbalance what it called the "one-sided publicity in favor of oral contraceptives."

As long as the source of information is clearly labeled, special pleading is no great danger to our society, for there are counterforces. It is when groups such as the Genetic Study Unit are set up with no way for the public or media to know its backers or its true purposes, that all sorts of evils can arise. Special pleading is not wrong in itself. Presidents, prime ministers, clergymen, university presidents, editors, union executives, lawyers—all these plead for the cause they support. But it is clear to the public who is pleading for what, even though why is not always as manifest. As long as that condition continues, no one is hurt, nor are the channels of communication seriously misused. Public relations men are special pleaders, and since they are clearly so, it is fully acceptable to have men who are specialists retained to support or advocate a cause. Newspapers, television stations, radio stations, and magazine editors know the source and the client or the corporation that the public relations men represent. In this way, media men can assess the objectivity with which the information is presented. As long as that continues and as long as the media are alert to distortion, untruthfulness, or deception by omission, so long can the public have a measure of protection.

Thoughtful public relations practitioners have long been disturbed by the general attacks on their business. Much of the criticism has been deserved, but so many of the public relations workers show such a misunderstanding of the nature and function of their field that little has been done to answer charges hurled at them. Others feel that little can be done to curb the operators who work on the fringes of the business, and that these can be ignored. Others believe that in the long term good practice will drive out bad, and that time and events will clear out the dishonest. In total effect, little is done to flush the stables.

The difficulties are many, since there is nothing to prevent anyone from using the title of public relations. There is nothing to prevent a corporation, college, trade association, government, or any other organization or individual from hiring someone who they want to perform what they think is the public relations function, no matter how ineffectual he may be. In many of these cases they hire incompetents, not cheats, and wonder why they receive such bad advice or are unable to get any kind of performance to equal the money spent. Too often, since the field is so new, management thinks that anyone who "likes people" can be an effective public relations man. That is why in some organizations the boss's nephew who is not capable of doing any other job is given the post of public relations director. Or, in other cases, it may be an out-of-work old college buddy of the chief executive who is provided with a safe position in public relations.

There are many examples of corporate chiefs, their recruiting officers, or executive search firms looking for a public relations department head without knowing what his qualifications should be. Here we can have the case of a blind executive recruiter leading a blind corporation. In one case, a medium-sized corporation, together with the executive recruiting firm, drew a profile for a public relations director who had to have these qualifications: He had to be between thirty-eight and forty-two years old; tall, preferably over six feet; well-built, with a good over-all appearance; a graduate of an Eastern college, preferably Ivy League; soft-spoken; with a liking for people and a willingness to re-locate.

The qualifications here listed for their man had nothing to do with how he might perform his job. A good public relations director can no more be measured by age, college, height, size of smile, timbre of voice, and fondness for people than a good history professor can be chosen by the number of hairs on his head.

Actually no one can specify the "right" background for a good public relations man. Good ones have come from a wide variety of work. They have been high school teachers, newspaper reporters, magazine writers, sales promotion men, opinion pollsters, radio and television broadcasters, and fund raisers. Some have gone directly from college into corporations and learned the techniques of the trade by watching, listening, and above all by doing. Some have been men with advanced degrees; others have not finished high school. There is then no special background from which to choose a potentially good public relations man.

In the stated case of the corporation-executive recruiter, the search was not to discover potential, but to find a relatively mature man to head a department; and in seeking such a man consideration must be given, over everything else, to his general competence. This is more difficult to measure in public relations than in many other fields, but it can be done. There are, in addition to experience in the techniques of the business, such general qualifications as knowledge of how people react under special conditions, an understanding of business and our economic system and, highly important, a knowledge of the means of communication through which the public can be reached.

It is certainly pleasant to have a public relations man "like people."

In fact it is pleasant to have anyone like people. But liking people has little more to do with performance in public relations than liking mashed potatoes. A public relations man deals only with a tiny part of the public in person. A man may love people to death and still not understand what motivates them or how they will respond to certain actions at various times.

In addition, a public relations director must not only meet these qualifications, but his approach must suit the company. The kind of company, its problems, its size and objectives, its position in the industry, its area of operation, and the general attitude of the public toward it and the industry—these, too, are related to the kind of man needed for a particular corporation.

Those in public relations who have themselves had extensive experience are able to make an assessment of qualifications and ability of others. Just as an expert craftsman knows shoddy work when he sees it, so an experienced public relations man can best judge a good man. He will not make the mistake of looking for a super glad-hander, a stereotype that has gained too much currency. Knowledgeable managers never try to hire a public relations director as if they were movie directors casting a character for a grade-B film.

Public relations practitioners have an organization of their own— the Public Relations Society of America. It was founded in 1948 as the result of the merger of the American Council on Public Relations and the National Association of Public Relations Counsel. On July 1, 1961, the American Public Relations Association merged with the PRSA so that today the Society is the only major national organization in the general field of public relations.

It now has a membership of almost 6,000, active and associate, from business and industry, public relations firms, trade and professional groups, all branches of government, and education, health and welfare organizations. There are some sixty chapters, each with proportional representation in the governing body of the society, the Assembly of Delegates; also represented are members who do not live in any of the organized chapter areas. The society is run by a nine-member board of directors.

PRSA states its major goal as "the advancement of the public relations profession." It serves its members through regional conferences and local seminars; an information center and library; an annual conference; a public relations institute at which public problems are discussed, mostly by outsiders; and an annual awards competition. It supports a Foundation for Public Relations Research and Education, a new accreditation program, and a code of ethics and an enforcement program.

There are no accurate figures on how many persons in the country are in this field. *Public Relations News*, the oldest newsletter serving the field, published weekly, estimates the number at 100,000 men and women. *PR Reporter*, another weekly trade newsletter, makes an estimate of 50,000. So there is no doubt that the PRSA has in its membership only a small proportion of those in the business. Many of the leading counselling firms have members in PRSA, as do some of the largest corporations. But by no means are all the leading practitioners in the Society, and many of the most competent are not active participants in its affairs even though they are members. The job of policing the public relations field, even under the best of conditions, cannot be fully effective. It is a long way from a membership of 6,000 to a total number in the field, be it 50,000 or 100,000.

The code of ethics, or, as the PRSA calls it, the "Code of Professional Standards for the Practice of Public Relations," adopted in November, 1959, was amended in 1963 and replaced a similar code put in force in 1954. The seventeen articles of the code include the banning of front organizations and poaching on a member's clients by another member; the derogation of another member, or his client or employer; the insistence on identification to the public of any communication for which the member is responsible; the prohibition of intentional dissemination of false or misleading information; the opposition to acceptance of contingent fees; and other laudable principles.

Three of the articles have a special interest to the general public. The first one is that "a member shall conduct his professional life in accord with the public welfare." The second is that "a member has the affirmative duty of adhering to generally accepted standards of accuracy, truth, and good taste." A third is that "a member shall not engage in any practice which tends to corrupt the integrity of the channels of public communication."

But, like all codes of ethical practice, they are basically no better than their enforcement. On March 17, 1964 for the first time a member was suspended from PRSA for unethical practice. Previously three members had been expelled from the Society after conviction for a felony or misdemeanor. But here the courts acted first. There have been three censures of members in PRSA's history, all involving either attempts to lure clients away from other members or criticism by one public relations man of another's handling of an account. In none of these three cases was an offense against the general public involved—only offenses by one public relations man against another.

The first suspension was noteworthy for it was a precedent, even though the evidence against the member of the Society was developed in an investigation by the Senate Foreign Relations Committee and made generally known through public hearings of the committee chaired by Senator Fulbright. The committee, during its study of influence on American policy of registered foreign agents, dealt with the activity of public relations firms and individuals and how free vacation trips were given to influential persons in the communications field from whom firms had sought favorable treatment in the press.

The PRSA, in response to the SEC report on Corporate Publicity and Public Relations, also drew up an official interpretation of its code of professional standards for the practice of public relations "as it applies to financial public relations," which sought to meet the demands of the SEC. How good it will be in fact, not on paper alone, only the years will tell. The chiefs of two different organizations that have a regulatory responsibility in the field show a marked divergence in their reaction to the values of the code.

William L. Cary, chairman of the Securities and Exchange Commission, wrote to the PRSA's president, Ward Stevenson, on December 13, 1963 saying that

> by adopting this Code, the Society—like a number of other unofficial self-regulatory groups in other areas—has expressed recognition of its responsibilities to the public. I am sure that the Society understands, however, that the new Code is merely the foundation for a program of self-regulation and not in itself a complete program. In the last analysis, the Code will have to be evaluated in the light of the level of conduct which it inspires or commands. I trust the Society will build on this necessary foundation and enhance its efforts to achieve a level of practice in financial public relations consonant with the needs of investor protection.

Cary was saying: Show me.

G. Keith Funston, then president of the New York Stock Exchange, wrote to the PRSA on January 3, 1964, saying that the code covering the practice of financial public relations

> represents a significant step forward in a field of great importance to shareowners. The Society is to be congratulated for the leadership it is displaying in this area. . . . The efforts the Society is making in this direction will further strengthen the self-regulatory system under which the securities industry functions . . .

So far the self-regulation has been little more than "merely a foundation."

The Society is at present also struggling with an Accreditation Program through which its members may become PRSA-Accredited by passing a written examination supervised by a professional testing of examiners "drawn from a panel all of whom are accredited." All of the applicants for this status must have a college degree or ten years of public relations experience; must have "a reputation for high standards of personal and professional conduct"; and must have been active members of the Society for at least two years.

This program originated as a competitive tool of some established public relations firms against newer ones. The older firms felt it would be to their advantage to be accredited, and the proposal, in its beginnings, had no intention of including any but counsellors. But at an annual meeting of PRSA dealing with the subject, men working for corporations said they too wanted to be accredited for prestige with their management. Thus the plan was extended. Even then it would never have got off the ground had it not been for the "grandfather clause," which admitted to accredited status old-timers in PRSA without examination of any kind. So far, the bulk of those accredited have reached this stage through this route. Had it not been for this clause, where the insiders went "in" the easy way, it is doubtful if this program would ever have been accepted by the Society. The value of this accreditation program to cleaner, more ethical practice of public relations has of course not been visible so far. To many members of the Society, the problems confronting the business are largely ethical, and they claim the accreditation program tries to deal with ethical matters through a form of examination under which the charlatans have no trouble being admitted to the inner circle. There was never any doubt in their minds that the sharp operators had skill and ability. What they lacked was character. Whether the accreditation program can solve this problem remains a moot point. But whatever the results in this area, there is no doubt that the force of public attacks on public relations is forcing some beginning steps by the Public Relations Society of America.

One of the areas of great trouble involves the article in PRSA's code of ethics which says that "a member shall not engage in any practice which tends to corrupt the integrity of channels of public communication." Press junkets, expensive Christmas gifts to newspapermen, tips on the stock market—all are part of a practice which "tends to corrupt the integrity of channels of public communication." But while the onus here is on public relations practitioners, it cannot be theirs alone. It takes two to make the deal, and often the newspaperman with his hand out is the governing factor. The writer or broadcaster who is known as being clean is not likely to be approached with shady deals.

This is, of course, known and fully understood by the best publications. They forbid their staff members to take expensive gifts from those who have an interest in getting notices in the press. They insist on paying for the trips to cover news. If all the newspaper and magazine publishers insisted on doing the same, the malevolent influence of corrupting public relations men would be sharply curtailed. It will not happen, however, until all publishers meet this threat to the integrity of their editorial columns and insist on policing their staffs.

Volume 23 of *Editorially Speaking*, the 1965 edition (issued by the Gannett Group of Newspapers, with shop talk about its editors and executives), carries an article, "A Focus on Junkets," by Mason C. Taylor, the executive editor of the *Utica Observer-Dispatch* and the *Utica Daily Press*. In it he discusses what has been a recurring topic at editors' meetings: the acceptance or rejection of courtesies and luxuries from news-seeking organizations.

As an introduction to the Taylor piece, Clifford E. Carpenter, editor of the *Rochester Democrat and Chronicle*, another Gannett paper, puts the issue this way:

Is it proper and moral for a newspaper to write purple exposures and scathing editorials about a junketing congressman who takes his secretary along to a flea-bitten hotel in Panama, while the editor, the sports editor and the food editor are making supreme sacrifices to protect the people's right to know about California wines and Florida baseball and popularly-branded foods? Actually the morality of the issue may become more oppressive. There is nothing a knee-jerk liberal or an automatic reflex conservative likes more than to pin a junketing tag on a newspaperman. So we should examine this practice and find where we stand; which junkets are permissible if any, which are not, if any. And it seems to me we ought to have more justification than one member of another newspaper organization who—when asked how he squared an all-expense trip to South Africa with his conscience—replied that he first investigated the situation and determined that South Africa had neither received nor wanted American foreign aid.

Taylor, in his discussion, tells of the decisions he has to make in his work in one short period: Metro-Goldwyn-Mayer wanted to fly the paper's Sunday features editor to the west coast to visit the studios and see what was in the works for the coming winter; a cement association had invited a reporter on a two-day trip to compare the merits of cement and "bituminous material" in connection with the New York State Thruway Authority's tentative plans to blacktop the Thomas E. Dewey Thruway; a fashion designers' organization invited the women's editor to a party in New York City with first-class air fare and a stay in the Hotel Pierre for a week.

Taylor's answers to such invitations usually is a polite No.

Nobody is providing expensive junkets or expensive invitations unless they expect to get some of their money back in the form of space in your newspaper. . . . If we were a big newspaper, I think we should always say "no" and if we send someone, we should pay our own way. But on the other hand, if someone offers some kind of a trip or whatever that has genuine news value, if you honestly believe that you are giving something to your readers more valuable than what you otherwise would put in that space, and you can print whatever you print honestly and objectively, without any feeling of indebtedness to whoever picked up the check, I don't see anything wrong with it. But making decisions like that are more in Solomon's line, than an editor's. We find it much easier to say "no."

Taylor also reports how he turned down Mohawk Airlines and its offer to fly a reporter and photographer to England to see their new Rolls-Royce-powered jets on the production line so they could come back and write glowing articles that Mohawk "could reprint in its publicity material"; how he declines invitations from car manufacturers to visit Detroit and "see what marvels they are creating"; how he turned down an offer of a loan of a new car for a vacation; how he rejected free admissions, with free drinks, at the Vernon Downs race track Key Club for his staff; how the Ringling advance man was bewildered when he found he did not have to hand out any free tickets for the circus.

The Associated Press policy is clear on its staff accepting gifts, free trips, and the other favors that so many publishers still permit. A memorandum dated November 13, 1959, from Frank J. Starzel, then general manager, to bureau chiefs, correspondents (domestic and foreign), and chiefs of departments, re-stated AP's policy that it "would be wholly improper for a member of our staff to accept money, valuable gifts, expense-paid trips or other favors from news sources."

In his policy memo, the general manager wrote that further steps had to be taken to see that the policy is adhered to rigidly. Money and gifts were clear enough, the general manager wrote, but invitations to junkets needed further clarification and he set it out in these words:

1. The AP will participate in organized trips only if they are sufficiently newsworthy to be worth a man's time *and* his expenses. Thus, junkets—in the sense of free, expenses-paid trips—are OUT.

2. NO individual AP staffer is to accept any offer of such a trip, whether on his own time (days off or vacation) or on AP time. His bureau chief or department head will decide whether the proposed trip is newsworthy, consulting with this office if in doubt.

There may be questions sometimes as to whether a trip is newsworthy. There can be NO question about a man going on a junket on his own time, however. If the AP considered it newsworthy it would send him or somebody else on assignment and pay his way. If it is NOT newsworthy, no AP man is to go. It is impossible to separate a junket invitation from an individual's employment. Junket invitations are invariably extended on the basis of the recipient's occupation. The Associated Press cannot be a vehicle for a junket's payoff, *nor give the appearance that it will be.*

The question undoubtedly will be raised: What about a trip on which it is impossible to pay? In the first place, it is extremely unlikely that payment will actually be impossible except on government-arranged trips such as a submarine cruise or something similar. In the second place, we will make a real effort to pay our way *everywhere.* Finally, we will examine all such invitations especially carefully to be sure they are newsworthy. So the exceptions should be exceedingly rare.

This has been spelled out not because we have any doubts about the personal integrity of the AP staff or because we feel that there has been any misuse of the AP news report. But we just cannot accept favors and maintain the public posture which is expected of The Associated Press. It is essential for all of us to have this clear policy to guide us. And it must be adhered to.

AP's policy is strictly interpreted and carefully carried out. It is also well known among public relations men, so fewer attempts are made "to corrupt the integrity" of this channel of public communication. But AP cannot do the job of individual newspapers, which certainly need such a policy of their own if the tango danced by a public relations operator and a newspaperman is to be stopped or to have less chance of success.

The New York Times, as the newspaper of record, takes its own precautions to keep its news columns clean. Its rules are not as carefully delineated as are AP's but the policing is continuous, and the policy clear. Clifton Daniel, the *Times'* managing editor, put his paper's policy in these terms:

> As a general rule, we do not allow editors and reporters to go on junkets. I use the term "general rule" because there are some occasions when making use of the facilities of a junket is the only way to get at a story. For example, visits to military installations can often be made only on conducted tours. Whenever we join up with a junket, we make it a practice to offer to pay our own way. This is sometimes not feasible, and we don't make an undue fuss about it, but we do try to keep our integrity intact in all circumstances.

The *Times* is not so naive, Daniel says, that it believes that gifts are refused by all its staff members. But when one is found who has violated the paper's policy he is "asked to turn in his uniform." This is an old policy of the *Times* but the staff is reminded of it every Christmas, the time when news sources, including public relations men, are wont to show their appreciation, or influence their future dealings with the *Times* by providing substantial gifts or other favors.

Early in November, Ivan Veit, a *Times* vice-president, sends a memorandum to all department heads of the newspaper notifying them that letters are being written to all the paper's suppliers, and business and news contacts to remind them that the *Times* "has asked its staff not to accept Christmas gifts." Attached to the Veit memo is a list of those who are to get the letter and a request for additions or changes by November 10.

By November 17, Harding P. Bancroft, the *Times'* executive vice-president, writes to all names on the Viet list that

> . . . as the holiday season approaches, may we again remind our friends that, as a matter of policy, *The New York Times* has asked members of its staff not to accept gifts from individuals, groups or organizations which are sources of news or who do business with the *Times*.

> We appreciate the friendly sentiment that usually accompanies business gifts given during the holiday season. Nevertheless, after

careful consideration of the whole problem, we have requested staff members not to accept gifts of any kind.

The *Times* also has a form letter which can be used by those who receive gifts, despite the letters. It reads: "I appreciate and reciprocate your friendly holiday greetings. However, I am returning this gift with thanks. The enclosed letter explains *The New York Times* policy in these matters." Enclosed with this form letter is a copy of the Bancroft letter on gifts.

The New York Times does not oppose dealing with public relations men. It finds them very useful. But the lines between the two functions—representing the news source and representing the newspaper—are kept clear. This is sharply seen in the financial pages of the *Times*. There are no pages of the newspaper in which space is more eagerly sought by public relations men. It is a fact of life to business and financial public relations men, particularly in the East, that reports in the *Times* of annual meetings, executive changes, new products, and other corporate events are greatly valued.

Thomas E. Mullaney, the financial-business news editor of the *Times* understands the value of public relations men as sources of news, but he does not take what is provided in their handouts as gospel. He never ceases urging his staff of more than sixty to get behind the news release, to get the facts, to get at the basic sources of the story. He even speaks before such groups as the Public Relations Society of America, the Institute of Life Insurance, the Banking Executives in Chicago, the Institute of Financial Executives, the New York Chapter of Certified Public Accountants, the Corporate Treasurers Society of New York, and the American Management Association's Presidents Association. In all these he hits the central theme that the public has a right to know, whether it is news of national policy, international developments, civic activities, or business, and it is the responsibility of the press to serve that right. In the case of business, Mullaney, who has been with the *Times* since 1942 (except for three years in the Navy) and was appointed to run the financial-business news pages in August of 1963, insists this right to know means a steady flow of accurate, trustworthy corporate news that truly tells the story the paper's editors believe the public should know. Mullaney does not deny that there has been managed business news and that it is dangerous to the investing public. To Mullaney, "the modern public relations man must not simply be the fellow with great ability to pipe out the canned corporate line and utter inability to answer any other questions. He must have a vast store of knowledge about his company or clients and a more sophisticated understanding of the industry involved, so that he can propose meaningful stories to the press and not simply self-serving ones, and can meet the probing queries" of the careful, accurate, thorough financial and business reporter.

In far too many cases, Mullaney finds, the public relations men block the financial or business reporters from getting through to the company official, controller, financial vice-president, or president to get correct and accurate answers to queries. Since Mullaney feels his job is to make certain that his staff gets "all the unvarnished facts so that the reader can make his own proper decisions about the story the *Times* prints," he objects strongly to the public relations man acting as a buffer instead of a channel of accurate information.

To newspapermen, says Mullaney, there are probably more pluses than minuses in what most public relations men do in servicing newspapers with news of their clients. Good newspapermen realize they can be served properly by good public relations men and must often rely on the public relations men for information. Still, the relationship is best served if it is an arm's-length one. So junkets are strongly discouraged—as are gift giving, unnecessary press luncheons and socializing—for the newspaperman must be under no obligation to news sources. The newsman must also, says Mullaney, resist overtures to invest in a company's new stock issue, and he urges his reporters to be "extremely circumspect in their investment activities, avoiding stocks of companies they cover and speculative trading."

Since we are entering a more complex age, says Mullaney, it becomes even more important for public relations men to become more expert in their fields—be it steel, banking, computers, and others— for, if the public relations man cannot explain adequately the activities of his client or his corporation, it is that much more difficult for the newspaperman to get the facts.

The *Milwaukee Journal* is another daily that has no written policy on junkets but whose practices are clear. Arville Schaleben, the *Journal's* associate editor, puts his paper's position this way:

> As a matter of fact, our practice is markedly rigid against free rides offered by companies or individuals or agencies other than governments. We are neither prudish nor priggish and we are not unappreciative of the courtesies offered us. But we do insist on paying our way to automotive and other previews, do not go free to hotel openings and movie extravaganzas, and the like, pay for our travel editors' travels, buy a drink back when we accept a drink, buy a meal back when we accept a meal. Our

general practice is to judge every junket from the standpoint of news value—does the proposal promise enough genuine news to justify paying our own way to it?

We do accept some government junkets, the test being whether the junket has genuine news value. I equate government transportation with, for example, rent free space in Congress or City Hall. Mass communicators have a responsibility to represent the public in countless circumstances and there is a recognition of that responsibility in government practices toward the press. Government spending of money for junkets is dependent upon funds voted by legislative bodies and legislators are answerable to people for how the money is spent. When we travel at government expense, we say so in the story.

One might say at first glance that our rejecting private junkets and accepting public ones permits clean and definitive judgments. However, the question of public funds is often cloudy. An example is the opening of an air route by a government-owned foreign air line in the private or public area.

Sometimes organizations, a transport company for example, join with state organizations to promote some tourist attraction through inviting travel writers on a junket. Untangling the per participant cost sometimes becomes next to impossible. The possible situations are so endless and involved, we pretty much decide what to do one at a time—except that we know our intent always is to keep ourselves and our people as far removed as possible from influences created for private purposes. This by no means is intended as an affront to promotion enterprises. We think they usually are justified and deserve publicity support, but we also don't feel a company should have to wine and dine us to insure attention from us.

We best serve public and private interests, we feel, by thinking always to retain confidence in our news columns.

The public relations practitioner, in his capacity as a publicity man, has a heavy burden of responsibility in making certain that false information is not distributed. But in many ways the burden lies even more heavily on the media if they carry distortions and promotional material instead of news. Newspaper publishers, magazine owners, and television and radio station managers get the kind of reporting they want. As long as they, to make it easy and cheap for themselves, allow their staff to be put in a position where they become indebted to public relations men for fancy gifts, free trips, or expense-paid vacations, then the public will be fed pap instead of facts and distortions instead of accurate information.

Many publishers, knowing this, and having a respect for themselves and their publications, are serious in cutting off what can only be called "payola." These generally, and naturally, are the better newspapers. However, there are still far too many publishers who, to save expenses, will permit the junket, the big Christmas gift, or the moonlighting that is in outright and clear conflict. They do it not out of ignorance but out of cupidity. It is they who give media a bad reputation. A public relations man can corrupt only those media that either knowingly permit it or are lax in the policing of their staffs.

Many of the troubles that plague the public relations business stem from its relative newness. It is an unstable business for the men who work in it. This is particularly true of the agencies, most of which will fire a staff man when an account is lost. There is too often a premium on the man with a little larceny in his heart and the one who thinks nothing of the long-run effect of his actions. With most of the firms, and in the overwhelming number of corporations, the public relations function is simply getting publicity. Management is here at fault, for it generally gets, except by accident, what it wants.

Managers, thinking in terms of their relations with the public and seeking outside counsel, rarely know how to go about picking a public relations firm. They often shy away from all public relations activities after having had the bitter experience of being taken. When the glibness of some practitioners is added to the lack of sophistication of some corporate managers, it is small wonder the public relations contract often comes to an unhappy ending. In too many cases the clients feel they have been cheated. Sad to say, they are often right.

But can the client, in a field where it is difficult to measure results exactly, protect himself from the faker? How can the honest, hardworking agency people, who are the overwhelming majority in the business, safeguard their own reputations? How can they prevent the potential client from being bamboozled with promises that can never be fulfilled or with tales of "contacts" that do not exist?

The growth of the number of public relations agencies and public relations counsellors does not make it easier for the would-be client to pick the man or the firm best suited to his needs. A study of the yellow pages of the telephone books in New York, Chicago, and Los Angeles shows the extent of the problem faced by the businessman seeking public relations advice or service.

First, in New York: In the early telephone directories there were no firms offering public relations help. From 1906 through 1910 there is no listing of any type of public relations or publicity practitioner.

The 1928 yellow pages list ninety-two publicity service bureaus; in 1935 there were twenty-nine public relations counsellors listed; in 1940, 177 were listed; in 1950, 368; in 1960, 735; in 1964, 753.

In Chicago this is the story: There were no listings in the yellow pages from 1906 through 1910. In 1928, six public relations counsellors were listed; in 1935, eighteen; in 1940, twenty-six; in 1950, 115; in 1960, 144; in 1964, 291.

The Los Angeles yellow pages list no publicity bureaus or public relations counsellors through 1910. In 1928, twenty-six were listed as publicity agents. In 1935, twenty-seven were listed as publicity agents and one as in public relations. In 1950, 116 were listed under public relations service; in 1960, 244 were listed; and in the 1965 directory, 304 were listed.

With this vast number of firms, which vary from very large organizations with as many as two hundred employees to counsellors who operate alone, how is the corporate head to choose? There is no easy answer. Careful investigation is necessary by the businessman who needs public relations help. First he must define his own problem in general terms: That is, what is his basic trouble? Is it a governmental problem? Is he or his industry about to be investigated by a Congressional committee? Does he want his firm to be better known to the financial community? Does he want his business to be better known generally? Has he a community relations problem? Is his firm launching a new product that must have national publicity? Has he an employee relations problem? Or has he suddenly become aware of the importance of public opinion as a whole to the successful conduct of his business?

Having defined his needs, the businessman must, before hiring a public relations counsel, do his homework, as he would for any other specialist. Inquiries to his business friends can be a start. Having narrowed the list to a reasonable length, with ethical practitioners as a prime consideration, he will, if he is not to be burned, find out what the specialties of the firms are. Even among the honest, hardworking, competent firms, some are better at one type of practice than another.

Here is where the focus of the businessman's needs comes into play. For his purpose, bigness does not necessarily mean goodness. His account may be small. Then, a second line of firms might be the ones from which to make the selection. He should study the clients they have; how long the agencies have been in business; the duration of service given the client by the firm; what the present clients think of the agency; and, above all, the competence of the person who will work on the account and his judgment in a crisis. A good rule for the would-be client is to remember that to develop maturity and wisdom in the public relations business demands long experience. No matter how attractive the firm's sales pitch or brochure may be, there is nothing to take the place of good judgment. Mistakes in judgment can be costly, as many corporate presidents have found, not only in the money spent, but for the trouble the company can get into by following bad advice.

Fees for the services of public relations firms are important, of course. If the firm is too high-priced for him, and if it is a reputable one, the businessman will be so told. If he asks for a less expensive firm he will be given honest direction. But if one firm's fee is, say, $100,000 a year for a particular service and another offers to do the same for half the price, a good rule of thumb for the businessman is to turn down the cut-rate agency. Personnel costs money, and no one has yet found a way of giving $100,000 worth of service for half the amount. In public relations, as in any other field, the businessman will generally get what he pays for. There is no easy way for him to find the firm best suited to his needs. There are, however, some sure signs which should warn him against an agency. When he is told that public opinion can be changed overnight by some trick; that difficult problems are easy to solve; that he can be guaranteed maximum results at the drop of a fat check—then he had better save his stockholders' money and leave the slick operator's office before he loses his wallet. Public relations is a difficult business. There are no pat answers to hard questions. The more quickly the businessman learns these facts the more readily will he be able to protect himself and help the honest practitioner drive out the sleazy operator.

If evidence were needed that the public relations agency business is not yet solidly established, one could find it in the survival rate of firms. Few of them survive the death of their founders. The relationship between the head of the agency and its clients is so personal that, in most cases, the firm loses its meaning to the client if he can no longer do business with the one man in whom he has confidence. The ten or fifteen years to come may show that agencies can survive the death of the firms' builders, but a study of the business to date makes it clear that it is the rare firm which can continue very long after the disappearance of the man who started it and who, in most cases, was the business-getter. The history of the business shows too that the man who builds the firm can be as important to its success as the service rendered. How many of the present firms will be in business five years after the death of those who started them? On the basis of past performance, precious few.

The two most dramatic examples of large agencies that went under shortly after the death of the men who started them were both in New York. In 1936, Bernard Lichtenberg founded what became probably the largest firm in the country. The accounts were highly diversified and included trade associations and corporations of varying size. Some first-rate men worked for the firm. Yet, when Lichtenberg died in September, 1944, his firm almost immediately began to break up. In a short time there was no trace of it. Of the 125 executives with the firm, an exceptionally large number even by today's standards, there was not one who could hold it together.

The other important firm that just could not carry on after the death of its founder was Steve Hannagan Associates. Hannagan started his firm under his own name in 1935. By that time he had already done publicity for the City of Miami, Jack Dempsey, Gene Tunney, and Gar Wood, and had been for two years vice-president of the advertising agency of Lord & Thomas. When he died in February, 1953, at the age of fifty-three, he had forty-two executives on his staff. The firm's clients included Sun Valley, Idaho; Coca-Cola Company; Union Pacific Railroad; Owens-Illinois Glass; Olin Industries; and Admiral Corporation. After several changes of name, and new leadership when it became William E. Robinson Associates, then Robinson-Hannagan Associates, it was bought by Hill and Knowlton. That was in August, 1955.

There are today only five good-sized firms whose founders are dead. T. J. Ross and Associates dates back to 1905 when it was Lee & Parker, the Lee being Ivy Lee, one of the true pioneers in the public relations business. The firm was dissolved in 1908 when Lee went to work for the Pennsylvania Railroad. In 1916 Lee revived his firm and Thomas J. Ross joined him in 1919 when he got out of the army. Ivy Lee died in 1934, and the present firm is not only the end product of Lee's work but it is prospering with a solid base of many of the clients that began with the founder.

The Hamilton Wright Organization is now run by the third generation of the family. The firm was founded by Hamilton M. Wright in California in 1908. It moved east and went into the field of international public relations with offices in New York. In 1954, the firm's founder died and his eldest son, Hamilton Wright, Jr. became president and chairman of the board. The third Hamilton M. Wright, grandson of the founder, is now executive vice-president of the firm. This is a remarkable record of longevity.

Carl Byoir and Associates is the largest firm that has continued in business after death of the man who started it. In 1930, when Carl

Byoir founded his firm, he had already been a Hearst magazine editor and circulation manager, associate chairman of the U.S. Government's Committee on Public Information—or the Creel Committee as it was generally known—and had run two English-language newspapers in Cuba. His firm then—as today—was known for having probably the highest fees in the business. In February, 1957, Byoir died, but the plans to carry on had been completed a year earlier. As a result, there was no panic, no loss of clients, but a shift, which had been carefully worked out, of the top management of the firm. Today Byoir is one of the largest agencies in the country, vying with Hill and Knowlton for the top spot.

Harshe-Rotman & Druck had its origins in Chicago when William E. Harshe started Harshe Associates in 1931. In 1946, the firm was joined by Morris B. Rotman, who had been with the Community and War Fund of Metropolitan Chicago. It was incorporated in 1948 with a survivor's agreement in the employment contract. In January 1950, Rotman bought all Harshe's stock from the founder's widow. It was not until a year and a half later that the firm's name was changed to Harshe-Rotman. Kalman Druck joined it in July, 1960. This is another case where planning made it easier for the firm to continue.

The fifth firm of importance to survive its founder is different from the others. Newmyer Associates is unusual in that it operates as the counsel, eyes and ears, for corporations interested in government relations. The firm does no lobbying, and has offices only in Washington. It serves many of the top corporations in the country and is respected by government officials, politicians, and other agencies that do business in Washington. It was in 1943 that the firm was founded by Arthur G. Newmyer, a former newspaper publisher in Washington. It still does what it set out to do at the beginning, and it does it well. In October, 1955, Newmyer died. The business was carried on by his two sons with no change in client relationships. Arthur G. Newmyer, Jr. and his brother James M. Newmyer have increased their business still further.

Today there are many well established firms whose founders are near retirement. Doubtless some of them will continue to be successful. But, if the past is any measuring rod, most of them will go not long after the men who started them die.

It is difficult for managers to pick a corporate public relations director who can do both parts of his job: interpreting his company to the public and interpreting public opinion to management. It is in the latter area that public relations men as a whole, with a few honorable exceptions, have shown their greatest weakness. In these days of rapid social change it is essential that the man advising top management be courageous enough, and frank enough, to warn of the effect these changes may have on business. When the public relations director fails to do this part of his job he loses much of his value. Managers will begin to look elsewhere for the understanding and integrity they have a right to expect. They may even have to look outside the entire public relations field.

The outstanding example of public relations practitioners' failure to alert management to important shifts in public attitudes is in the Negro rebellion. The Supreme Court decision on desegregation of the schools came in 1954. Yet only in rare cases did the public relations directors, and those in counselling firms as well, warn management that this would affect the conduct of business. They either failed to grasp the implications of events, which were clear to political observers, or they did the ostrich act because they were fearful of disturbing management by warning of a potentially explosive problem. It was not until impending changes culminated in new and massive civil rights legislation, boycotts, and riots that they acted. In too many cases, calling the police or hiring a pretty Negro secretary as a receptionist was what they recommended as answers.

The fault, however, does not lie solely with public relations directors; far too many chief executives act only when their feet are put to the fire. Also, too many managers believe that public relations is a function which builds a false front so that the corporation can operate as it deems easiest behind it. Some managers even consider the public relations director disloyal if he warns that a certain course of action may bring unfavorable results or may be construed as not being in the public interest. The devil's advocate is considered by blind organization men as a troublemaker who does not quite belong on the team.

Public relations directors with major corporations are likely to be in their fifties or sixties. They often have stock options. Getting a new job at their age is not easy. They may have children at college and expensive living habits. Above all, they may have chief executives who believe that the only interpreting that should be done by a public relations department is the communication to the public of the wisdom of the corporation and the brilliance of top management.

The result is that, in many cases, the public relations director, as a defense mechanism, begins to parrot management's prejudices. He berates any critical or even objective discussion of business practices, or of anything he thinks may upset the applecart. So he devotes himself to special efforts in the choice of colors for a glossy brochure, or making a new and expensive film no one will look at outside the executive offices, and begins to convince himself he is doing the whole job. That he should be tempted to work this way is understandable. That he do so is unforgivable if he has any real respect for his work or himself. The fact that he will bring further contempt to his field in the long run is pushed to the back of his mind, or forgotten altogether.

There are, however, managers who do not want their public relations directors to be anticipatory yes men. They understand how essential public acceptance is to their corporation and the domestic turmoil has set them to thinking along new lines. Not many of them make public speeches about this but one, the chairman of the board of directors of The Bank of America, Louis B. Lundborg, did. He felt so strongly about his views that he gave them before the Public Relations Society of America Conference in Denver on August 9, 1965, under the title "Management Looks at Public Relations."

He said, "It's possible that the average public relations practitioner of today might be headed straight toward the junk heap of obsolescence unless he develops some new and creative ideas about his place in our society." He went on to tell his listeners that public relations people had to be "tough minded," have a "healthy cynicism," have "guts," "speak out persuasively, honestly, critically," be "profit oriented," and "recognize and predict social change for if we do not plan for and manage change we will be in an endless series of profitless, unplanned, and haphazard rear guard actions with debilitating consequences for our institutions." To cap it all, Lundborg told the assembly that "no public relations man is worth his salt if he isn't willing to put his job on the line every day of his life."

Those who have watched publicity men attempt to brainwash the public have often seen dangers in the skills and techniques that are used to get an idea or a product across. Is it possible to "sell" the public an idea inimical to the national good? Is it possible for shrewd and amoral public relations men working for an unconscionable client to change the course of the nation's thinking? Is it possible to convince the general public that the shoddy has merit and that evil is good? The answer is: Certainly not in the long run. It is doubtful that it can even be successful in the short run. It is true that the public reputation of a large corporation can differ from reality, but that can only be temporary. Too many people have personal relationships with a large company. They may be stockholders, customers, employees, suppliers, government officials, or politicians. Not for long can the true nature of the corporation be glossed over by smooth publicity. For no matter what the media say about a company, those who are in frequent and direct contact with it learn what is really happening, and whether the company is truly acting in the public interest. When it comes to ideas, "selling" is even more difficult. Public relations men and advertising agencies have had extensive experience selling products, but they have not yet been able to market an idea as well as they do goods or services.

Even when it comes to selling goods, the public will not accept what it does not want. Successful campaigns have convinced people that an electric toothbrush is better than any other kind. Or color television better than black and white. Or an electric carving knife better than the old type. But no amount of advertising, packaging, publicity, and good location on the supermarket shelves will make the housewife buy a can of peas a second time if she does not like what is inside the can after she has tasted its contents.

Marketing experts know this, and the number of new products that fail is far greater than the number that succeed in any given year, despite the push of million-dollar budgets behind them. Even in the case of such widely used products as soap, toothpaste, or detergents the most successful companies, like Procter & Gamble, or Lever, or Colgate-Palmolive, have had their failures. The classic case, of course, was Edsel. No motor car was ever given a greater build up. There was hardly a magazine, from the slicks to the qualities, that did not run stories—and favorable ones at that—about the car. It was a brilliant exercise in the kind of publicity that is usually only dreamed of, with a first-rate advertising agency handling the account. When the car was in the showrooms the public swarmed to see it. The end result was a mammoth flop. Buyers did not want the car. Persuasion could not make them buy it.

Fairfax Cone, a respected advertising man, speaking to the Regents Advertising Club in London in April, 1961, told how fallacious it was to think that the public could be sold something it did not want, or that it was soft-headed, weak-willed, and congenitally unsuspicious. He said, in part:

> Five years and the equivalent of $350 million were put into the development of the Edsel and the channels for its distribution.
>
> The Ford Motor Company engaged a group of the best-known professional researchers in the United States to study car owners' wants and wishes all over the country. Then the Edsel was designed and built to the pattern of what the researchers found out.
>
> An enormous barrage of publicity was begun while the car was still in the clay-model stage, and several million pounds

worth of paid advertising, helped to attract 2,500,000 men and women into almost four thousand dealers' showrooms on a weekend in September, 1957, when the car was formally introduced.

Nevertheless the result was calamity. The public that had been expected to gobble up Edsels at a starting rate of more than 200,000 cars per year, took a fast look and saw only disappointment.

The Edsel, despite all the probing, was something the public didn't want on sight and couldn't be coaxed, through any amount of advertising, to buy. In the twenty-six months of the Edsel's struggle, before Ford threw in the sponge in December 1959, only 109,466 people had succumbed to any kind of blandishment on its behalf.

Robert F. Carney, chairman of the board of Foote, Cone & Belding, Inc., the advertising agency that was responsible for the Edsel advertising, in a speech before the New York Society of Security Analysts on December 30, 1963, made this comment on the views Cone had expressed to the Regent Advertising Club:

> The plain fact of the matter is that advertising is totally incapable of exercising the Svengali-like control over the buying habits of the public that the propounders of the subliminal-influence concept claim in our behalf. The public cannot be cajoled, mesmerized or driven into buying a product it doesn't want nor will there ever be a repeat sale if the product does not live up to the claims made for it.

If this cannot be done for a motor car with the massive professional advice, help, and skill of one of the country's best advertising agencies, in addition to the Ford publicity department, the chances of convincing people to accept an idea or concept they do not want are even more remote. Herein lies one of the strengths of the public in a society as open as ours. The counterforces to any idea are so great, the conflicts among competing ideologies so strong, that in the long run the people, in their own common interest, make correct decisions.

Every institution or organization, be it the AFL-CIO or Harvard University, must concern itself with the views of the different groups with which it has some relationship and with the general public, even as a corporation must. Trade unions, colleges, and universities must all have public acceptance if they are to continue their work. Although there are many unions that do not have an organized public relations department and program, there is no college or university of importance that does not have a public relations department and a public relations director, regardless of the titles used. Some colleges avoid the words "public relations" but others are happy to use them. Still others call the public relations director "director of university relations," "information director," "assistant to the president," "news director," or "development director." As colleges differ so does the manner of carrying out the public relations function. Even though Harvard University is not typical of other universities in the performance of the public relations function, it is worth looking at for it, like all the others, is deeply affected by public opinion.

Harvard's president, Nathan M. Pusey, has seven "staff" officers who are all involved in public relations, although those words are never used in connection with any of them. Each one of these men is responsible to Pusey and reports directly to him. Each has responsibility for large and important publics. In addition, many aspects of Harvard's relations with these publics are directed by the deans of the faculties. The deans all have active relations with their own alumni, private donors, foundations, federal agencies, the community, other institutions, the press, and the general public. Thus the public relations function continues with sharper focus in each dean's office. Of course, public relations policy is set for the university by Pusey. Within each faculty the dean sets policy. Conflict is avoided, both in policy and tactics, by the university's staff officers' close contact with the faculty office staffs. The functions of each of Pusey's assistants are also worth examining. The secretary of the governing boards has charge of the private and public use of buildings, and is Harvard's representative for television, radio, and for the Lowell Institute Cooperative Broadcasting Council. He handles all official correspondence and in many other ways affects the impression that Harvard makes on the alumni and the public.

The assistant to the president, or personal assistant, keeps Pusey's office running. He is a short cut for communications, assists with the correspondence of the university, helps with research and editorial work, serves on the board of the *Harvard Alumni Bulletin*, and is editor of the semiannual publication *Harvard Today*. He is directly responsible for the publications office, the alumni office, and the class report office.

The assistant to the president for development has the general responsibility of the development office, which receives and acknowledges gifts to Harvard. He handles both the general donor relationships and the continuing search for gift sources, whether they be individuals, foundations, or corporations, and he publishes a biannual magazine for all Harvard alumni. The development assistant also acts as part of a clearing house for information that prevents the too frequent solicitation of the same potential source of funds. While his job is in large measure a fund-raising one, he is not in charge of all fund raising at the university. Each of the principal graduate schools has staff members primarily concerned with fund raising.

The assistant to the president for civic affairs is almost the full-time ambassador to Cambridge and Boston. (In a business he would be in charge of community relations in a corporate public relations department.) As a communications link between Harvard and the two communities with which it is most closely involved, he is active in fourteen local organizations. The university marshal also has his public relations work; each year he arranges special programs for about 1,000 individual official visitors, mostly from foreign institutions, sets up tours of the campus for special groups, and arranges Harvard commencement and other university ceremonies. The general secretary of the alumni is the key man in charge of keeping in touch with the university's alumni. His general responsibility includes co-ordination of the organizations that keep the lines open between the university and the individual schools, which, except for Harvard College, have their own alumni associations. These associations cover the three major areas of alumni operations: reunion and class activities, fund raising, and bulletins. In addition, there are some 130 active Harvard Clubs in the United States and abroad serviced by the alumni office.

The news officer of the university handles all queries from newspapers, radio and television newsmen, magazine writers, wire services, news magazines, and the Boston and New York dailies. He also helps foreign journalists and visiting reporters. The news officer searches for and reports developments within the university that might interest the public. When he finds what he wants he puts out a press release but he does no "placement," that is, he does not push for stories. He has a staff of three trained newsmen, a general assistant, a science writer, and a photographic editor. An editorial assistant directs part-time student workers in distributing news about individual students to their home newspapers.

Three other full-time news centers function within the university: the office of the director of medical information, the Radcliffe College news office, and the office of director of sports information. There are also the liaison officers in the graduate schools and other centers who work closely with the News Office in answering queries. All these efforts devoted to public relations for Harvard are carried on for the same reasons a corporation employs them: to get public understanding as a step to public acceptance. As Pusey's personal assistant, who, as he says, "represents the president's deep concern in the general tone and expression of the university's voice to the public, the alumni, and the university community," told an Alumni Association group, "President Pusey devotes a major part of his life to the question of Harvard's public image . . ."

Since Harvard, whose objective is learning, must make a direct effort to explain itself to the public, how much more necessary is it for a corporation, whose purpose is profit, to make such an effort? Since a university, which is generally believed to be set up to serve the public interest, must convince the public that this belief is warranted, so must the corporation convince the nation that it in fact does serve the public interest.

To Georges Clemenceau, war was too serious to be left to the military. Similarly, it may be said that the public relations of major corporations is too serious to be left to the public relations practitioners. For no matter how competent the public relations director may be, no matter how skilled his staff, the corporate manager dares not divorce himself from a constant consciousness of public attitudes if he hopes to avoid disaster.

It is sad to say that in far too many cases the chief executive of a corporation, having found an able man to head the public relations department, and having given him adequate support, has gone on his way with little thought of his own responsibility in the area of public opinion. To other managers, the public relations department is a bulwark or a papier-mâché front, or both. But to the wise executive, public relations is an essential part of his job; unless he fully appreciates what is going on in the country, the context within which his company operates, and the public effect of his decisions, he is letting himself in for serious trouble.

Today, even more than in the recent past, it is vital for business managers to understand, or try to understand, what is bothering the country. Why, for instance, is there so much unrest in the colleges? What happened to so stir the students that authority seems to mean little to many bright young people? Not since the depression has there been so much ferment at the universities, yet on the whole the country has never been more prosperous. What was the meaning of Selma, Alabama? Of Watts? Of Newark? Of Detroit? What do marching and picketing nuns mean? What is the effect on national opinion of the ecumenical movement? Why the violence of the academic debate over the U.S. position in Vietnam? What does the emergence of the

New Left portend? What effect is the civil rights movement, including the Voting Rights Act, having on our society and therefore on business? What shifts of balance will take place as a result of the Supreme Court's decision that there must be reapportionment so that one qualified voter is equal to any other? What will this do to the power balance within states and in Congress? What does greater urban representation really involve?

It is as important for business managers to see where their business fits into this changing pattern as it is for them to try to understand what is happening in the trade union movement. It is obvious that the "labor bosses" cannot boss their own members. What caused the revolt of the rank and file of the International Union of Electrical Workers when they rose against the hierarchy and threw James Carey out of the presidency of the union after nearly two decades? And why could I. W. Abel beat David J. McDonald for the presidency of the United Steelworkers after McDonald had dominated it for so many years?

Is the turmoil in the colleges, the unions, in the Southern states, and in the Negro community all part of a greater upheaval? Whether it is or not, what is happening in these areas and the sharp conflict among intellectuals have a direct bearing on business, for business must adjust itself to the climate of national opinion.

To some business leaders, all this will sound like so much "garbage," the new word for anything one doesn't understand or takes one's time away from "running" the business. Yet this garbage is directly related to the profits of a corporation. The business executive with a long-range view understands this clearly and acts accordingly. For those businessmen who think they have no time to worry about public opinion and to whom public relations means only product publicity, there is extensive testimony to the contrary from others who have a deep concern for public opinion and are profit-oriented managers of highly successful companies. To intelligent business leadership, good relations with the public involve continuing concern by all who have an interest in the corporation's success. It is the road to public consent.

INDEX

the Munitions Industry,
235
See also Congress
Senator Gerald P. Nye and American Foreign Relations
(Cole), 240
Sherman Anti-Trust Act, 41, 301
Sherwood, Robert E., 245
Shouse, Jouett, 319
Simon, Walter O., 288
Since Yesterday (Allen), 137
Sinclair, Upton, 30
Sloan, Alfred P., Jr., 180, 319
    directive on public relations by,
    103
    as president of General Motors,
    95–110
    public relations and, 95–97, 100,
    102–4, 109
    report to stockholders, 96, 104–5
    unions and, 135–36, 137
Smith, A. P., Manufacturing Company, 170–71
Smith, Alfred E., 320
Society of Automotive Engineers,
123
Sonotone Corporation, 174
Sorensen, Theodore C.
    antitrust case and, 154
    on steel-price increase, 9–11
Spang, Joseph P., Jr., 8, 9
Special Committee Investigating
    the Munitions Industry,
    Senate, 235
Standard Oil (original company),
168, 211
"Standard Oil: Axis Ally"
(Straight), 164
Standard Oil Company incorporated in New Jersey, 23, 30,
162–233
    affiliates of, 182, 187, 198–200,
    204, 209, 211, 226, 228,
    231, 232

education and
    aid, 178–80
    Council for Financial Aid to
    Education, 180
    educators, 213–16
    ESSO Educational Foundation, 180
    Roundtable, 214–16
government and
    disloyalty charge, 163–65
    foreign investments, 186
    host countries, 188, 225–32
    political problems, 163–66,
    188, 216–17
    responsibility to capitalism,
    233
Government Relations Department at, 218–221
    functions of, 219–20
    host countries and, 219
    lobbying done by, 220
management of, 187
profile of, 186–87
public relations at, 167–233
    artists hired by, 204–13
    audience reached by, 203–4
    beginnings of, 170–75
    characteristics of, 185–88
    cost of educational television
    to, 213
    disregard of public opinion,
    167–69
    management and, 184–91
    objectives, 189–90
    operation, 191–94
    overseas, 196–99
    patron of the arts, 194, 204–13
    press, 194–96
    publications of, 191–92
    shareholders' division in, 223–25
    staff, 200–2
Starzel, Frank, on public relations
    ethics, 352–53